MW00774421

Hairs vs. Squares

HAIRS VS. SQUARES

The Mustache Gang, the Big Red Machine,
and the Tumultuous Summer of '72

Ed Gruver

UNIVERSITY OF NEBRASKA PRESS

Lincoln and London

All photographs in the gallery are used by
permission of Ron Riesterer/Photoshelter.

Library of Congress Cataloging-in-Publication Data
Gruver, Ed, 1960–
Hairs vs. squares: the mustache gang,
the big red machine, and the tumultuous
summer of '72 / Ed Gruver.
pages   cm
Includes bibliographical references.
ISBN 978-0-8032-8558-3 (cloth: alk. paper)
ISBN 978-0-8032-8817-1 (epub)
ISBN 978-0-8032-8818-8 (mobi)
ISBN 978-0-8032-8819-5 (pdf)
1. Baseball—United States—History—
20th century. I. Title.
GV863.A1G78 2016
796.357′6409047—dc23
2015031805

Set in Cambria by L. Auten.
Designed by Rachel Gould.

Hairs vs. Squares

PROLOGUE

This book is three decades in the writing.

It was written in phone interviews through the years with Vida Blue, Gene Tenace, Don Gullett, Al Oliver, Bruce Kison, Harmon Killebrew, and Tony Oliva, among others. It was written in a card show interview with the late Jim "Catfish" Hunter, who graciously invited me to pull up a chair and talk awhile; in on-field interviews with Reggie Jackson and Jim Palmer; in a meeting with Mickey Mantle, who along with teammate Whitey Ford named a certain young Cincinnati Reds player "Charlie Hustle"; and in an interview with Alvin Dark, who recalled his memories of managing the A's in the mid-1970s.

There was a dugout chat with Don Zimmer, who in '72 was San Diego's rookie skipper; a memorable BP session in which an aging but still effective Pete Rose lined frozen ropes at Veterans Stadium and an interview with Rose years later; and a 2014 interview with Mike Schmidt, considered by most the greatest third baseman ever and a Phillies rookie in 1972. And finally this book was written with the help of former media and front-office people—the late and legendary Hall of Fame sportscaster Curt Gowdy, A's announcer Monte Moore and his Reds counterpart Tom Hedrick, general manager Buzzie Bavasi, Phillies longtime public relations director Larry Shenk, and *Philadelphia Inquirer* sports columnist Bill Lyon.

The telling of this story begins on July 15, 1972. I was twelve years old and going to the original Yankee Stadium for the first time. I had been to big league games before. In 1969 I sat in Shea Stadium and watched Tom Seaver fire fastballs for the Miracle Mets. I had only seen Yankee Stadium—"the Stadium," as it was known to fans—on the black-and-white screen of the

Zenith TV in our living room. In Kearny, New Jersey, where I grew up, my father John, older brother Mike, and I watched the Mets on WOR Channel 9 and the Yankees on New York's WPIX Channel 11. The latter was famous for its reruns of Jackie Gleason's *The Honeymooners* and rebroadcasts of Laurel and Hardy's *March of the Wooden Soldiers* on Thanksgiving Day and the Yule Log every Christmas Eve.

Walking inside Yankee Stadium, seeing for the first time its famed interior—the emerald green expanse of Death Valley in left field, the monuments in deepest center field, the trademark façade—was unforgettable. Framed by a bright blue sky that day, Yankee Stadium was truly a green cathedral. Seemingly coming down from the heavens were the resonant tones of public address announcer Bob Sheppard, a man said to have the "voice of God." The afternoon air was thick with the scent of cigars, and to this day that smell is enough to transport me in memory back to that summer day at the Stadium.

The A's were attired in green, gold, and white uniforms; white cleats; and turn-of-the-century mustaches that were revolutionary in the clean-cut, conservative world of Major League Baseball. The Yankees wore traditional pinstripes that perfectly reflected their big-city background. Oakland won as Ken Holtzman beat fellow lefty Fritz Peterson. Bobby Murcer homered for New York, and Jackson and Sal Bando launched countering shots for Oakland. Reliever Rollie Fingers wrapped things up for the A's in the ninth, as he would so many times that season.

The soon-to-be-famous Mustache Gang went on to claim the first of its three straight world championships with a wild seven-game victory over the Big Red Machine in the most competitive Fall Classic in history. Four of the seven games have been ranked by baseball historians to be among the greatest ever in the World Series.

"Our 1972 World Series was more than amazing," remembers Nancy Finley, the daughter of Carl Finley who served as maverick Oakland owner Charles O. Finley's right-hand man during the A's glory years. "I'm still searching for the word to describe this feeling."

The Swingin' A's, as they were known, were a team of character and characters—Reggie, Rollie, Catfish, Campy (Bert Campaneris), Sal, Vida Blue, Dick Green, Joe Rudi, et al. I have covered the World Series, playoffs, and All-Star Games, and one thing I have come to realize is that baseball is built in part on personalities. In the early 1970s, an era in which one's personal appearance was often a political statement, the free-spirited, long-haired, and mustachioed A's represented the California youth movement, campus protests at UCLA, and the counterculture.

"All the people in this modern generation identified with the Athletics," Charlie Finley told *The Sporting News* after being named "Man of the Year" in 1972. "They saw us as their mod team. We were their symbol."

Conservatives considered the A's hippies and Yippies, clothed in Technicolor uniforms and conjuring up images of acid Westerns. Even their surnames and nicknames—Green, Blue, Blue Moon—were as colorful as a painter's palette. Like the swashbuckling outlaws of the popular Western movie of that era—*Butch Cassidy and the Sundance Kid*—sports fans looked at the A's and wondered, "Who are those guys?"

The A's may have had more costume changes than Elton John, but they played a game that was fundamentally sound. NBC-TV *Game of the Week* color analyst and former Yankees shortstop Tony Kubek stated that the A's biggest asset was the fundamentals insisted upon by manager Dick Williams. They excelled at sacrificing runners into scoring position; they could hit the cutoff man. In short, they executed.

The Mustache Gang protested the stereotypes stuck on them because of their appearance: "They called us renegades, a bunch of hippies from California," recalls A's catcher and first baseman Gene Tenace, who earned the 1972 World Series MVP award. "But it doesn't matter what you look like. Can you play? And they found out we could play."

Motown furnished the sound of young America in the early '70s; the Swingin' A's, the look of young America. Oakland's opponents in the 1972 World Series, the Cincinnati Reds, were seen as defenders of the traditional values. Their general manager, Bob Howsam, believed white cleats like those worn by the A's made players look like clowns, and he thought their outlandish uniforms resembled a Sunday school softball team.

The A's were acrimonious and contentious. Alvin Dark, who took over as Oakland's manager in 1974 and helped lead the team to a third straight World Series title, remembered the Mustache Gang as a talented team that battled the baseball world and itself. Team captain Sal Bando likened the club to an encounter group. Their emotions and passions were raw and on display. When an A's player struck out, he would often fling his bat to the ground in disgust or slam his batting helmet on the dugout bench.

The Reds, by contrast, had team rules against helmet tossing. When a player reached base, he did not throw his helmet toward the first-base coach. Instead he waited for the coach to come to him and then politely handed him the helmet.

Typical team flights for Oakland's wild bunch saw players barely settled into their seats before half a dozen portable stereos emitted a loud mix of rock music. Beer was in abundance, as were advances toward stewardesses. On one flight an inebriated A's player threw punches at teammates blocking his path to the bar.

Reds' road trips saw players wearing ties to restaurants. Dress codes were enforced on plane trips as well, and alcohol was not served. Stewardesses often complimented Cincinnati players for being the nicest team they dealt with.

In appearance and style of play, the A's were throwbacks to the rowdy, raucous St. Louis Cardinals "Gashouse Gang" of the Depression-era 1930s. The Reds, in contrast, invited comparisons to the businesslike Yankee clubs of the early '60s. Just as the Bronx Bombers were built to take advantage of the unique dimensions of Yankee Stadium, the Big Red Machine was constructed to take advantage of its home—spacious, carpeted Riverfront Stadium.

Among those fascinated by the Reds' style were a young Greg Maddux and his older brother Mike. In wiffle ball games in the family's backyard, Greg, who turned six the day before Opening Day in 1972, would imitate his favorite player, Pete Rose. While Mike went into his windup, Greg would crouch like Rose in an imaginary batter's box and announce the play like broadcasters: "Here's Pete Rose, looking for the first hit of the game. Here's the pitch. . . ."

Some saw the two championship clubs in the simplest terms possible. The Reds represented Middle America; big, broad-shouldered, and uncomplicated, they were John Wayne in cleats. The A's were more malleable: Marlon Brando method actors in a complex modern world.

With the game's biggest stage serving as a backdrop, the 1972 Fall Classic was billed as a collision between the Hairs and the Squares. "Pete Rose, Johnny Bench, Joe Morgan, and the rest of the Reds were clean-cut and conservative; they looked like businessmen," Tenace recalls. "We had long hair, mustaches, and colorful uniforms. We looked like bikers on a month-long bender."

This wasn't a World Series, Reds star Johnny Bench recalled in his autobiography. It was a war between the Old and New Orders, with the players in between. This mash-up of the Mustache Gang and Big Red Machine, the Hairs and the Squares, the avant-garde and the conservative mainstream, struck some as surreal. The collision of cultures symbolized the '70s. To paraphrase outlaw journalist Hunter S. Thompson, who was on the presidential campaign trail in '72, there was fear and loathing at the Fall Classic.

Yet amid the chaos the teams developed respect for one another. Speaking of Rose in a 1990s interview, Hunter said, "Pete Rose was the kind of player you hated to play against but would have loved to have had on your team."

The passions and personalities on vivid display in '72 were not confined to baseball. There were Nixon and Mao in China; Brando and Pacino in *The Godfather*; American Bandstand and Soul Train.

It was a time of Woody versus Bo; Nicklaus versus Trevino; Fischer versus Spassky. There was John Wooden and the Walton Gang; Franco Harris and the Immaculate Reception; Team Canada, the Soviets, and the Summit Series; Wilt, West, and the Lakers; Mark Spitz at the Summer Olympics.

Jane Fonda was exalted in Hanoi, and Governor George Wallace was gunned down in Maryland. George McGovern was at the Democratic National

Convention and the Gainesville Eight at the Republican National Convention. There was Black September and "Bloody Sunday."

Hurricane Agnes hammered the United States, Nixon landed back in the White House, and Apollo 17 landed on the moon.

"There were a lot of things going on," remembers Dave Cash, a young and socially aware second baseman for the defending World Series champion Pittsburgh Pirates in 1972. "Civil Rights, people coming back from Vietnam after fighting for their country and facing discrimination. It was a trying time for minorities. I grew up in upstate New York and wasn't used to racial discrimination. We rallied around each other just like we did on our baseball team."

Life in the early '70s was a ball of confusion. The Temptations had it right when they sang, "Round 'n' round 'n' round we go, where the world's headed nobody knows." Art imitated society so that just as in the 1972 blockbuster disaster film *The Poseidon Adventure*, up was down and down was up.

The times they were a-changin', as Bob Dylan said. Yankees left-handers Mike Kekich and Fritz Peterson not only swapped wives, but they traded their families and pets as well. America no longer spent Sunday evenings with Ed Sullivan; *Life* magazine would publish its final weekly issue on December 29, 1972. It seemed as if America's cultural icons were crashing down all around us. Even John Wayne took a fall. In the January 1972 release of Wayne's film *The Cowboys*, the man whom Elizabeth Taylor once said "gave the whole world the image of what an American should be" was shot in the back and killed on screen by a rogue outlaw played by Bruce Dern. "America will hate you for this," Wayne warned Dern. The young actor's response was a sign of the times: "Yeah, but they'll love me in Berkeley."

Boyhood memories of this era bring back a time of baseball cards, blue jeans, and comic books. It was summer days playing stickball in the deserted A&P parking lot in Kearny and sitting on the porch foraging through Topps cards and the stale but sugary bubble gum stick that came in every pack. It was summer nights under the street lights playing boxball—a form of stickball played with the same pink Spalding high-bounce ball but without the broom handle for a bat; you used your fist instead. Nearly every yard had a PIC Mosquito Repellant Coil, a spiral-shaped coil that burned from the outer end toward the center and produced an incense to ward off mosquitos. It's a world gone away, as Chicago later sang, but memories make it seem like yesterday.

A gallon of gas was fifty-five cents, and the average cost of a new home, $27,550. Afros and sideburns were in style, as were polyester jackets and bell-bottom jeans. The annual Sears Wish Book was both a holiday tradition and mirror of its times. Highly anticipated each fall, the six-hundred-plus page catalog of Christmas toys and gifts arrived in the mail just after the World Series and just before Halloween.

Sears once described its Christmas catalog as a time capsule, "recording for future historians today's desires, habits, customs, and mode of living." The same can be said for the '72 major league season. The tumultuous and unforgettable campaign marked a historical intersection between the game's past and future. It was Alpha and Omega, the beginning of one era and the ending of another.

Irrevocable alterations were under way. The American League would introduce the designated hitter in 1973, making life both easier and at the same time more difficult for AL hurlers. Hunter opined that the DH took 3–5 years off his career.

St. Louis Cardinals star outfielder Curt Flood had challenged baseball's reserve clause in 1969 and helped open the Flood-gates to free agency. In April the first players' strike in major league history occurred on, of all days, April Fool's Day, and wiped out the first 6–9 games of the regular season. The only strike called on the scheduled Opening Day of April 6 came from the players, not the umpires. Major North American sports were suffering their first labor pains, and for fans of the national pastime, Day One of the strike was, to borrow from Don McLean's hit song of that era, the day their music died.

The strike set a destructive precedent for further stoppages and lockouts, not only in Major League Baseball, but also in the NFL, NBA, and NHL.

Between 1972 and 1994 there were seven work stoppages in MLB, ultimately culminating in the 1994 strike that canceled the World Series.

Until the spring of '72, the owners had wielded the power. "We operated under the Golden Rule," Buzzie Bavasi, one of the game's great front-office executives, said. "Whoever has the gold, rules."

The '72 strike led to an uneven number of games that season. Some teams played 156 games, others 153. Rather than play an entire 162 games and thus push the World Series deeper into October, the owners opted not to play makeup games. The unbalanced schedule proved disastrous for the Boston Red Sox, who played one less game than the Detroit Tigers and finished one half game behind them in the Eastern Division.

Baseball's past and future collided in '72. The old brick ballparks in Cincinnati, Philadelphia, and Pittsburgh, whose designs would ironically become the rage for the retro fields of the future, were replaced by multi-colored, multi-purpose steel-and-concrete stadiums. They were hailed by sportscasters as pleasure palaces but were utterly devoid of the personality of their predecessors. The city skylines and quirky features that marked Crosley Field, Shibe Park, and Forbes Field were replaced by superstructures that blotted out their surroundings and brought a sanitized feel to the game.

Still a dynamic group of stars became identifiable within the carpeted confines of these new stadiums. You can't think of Mike Schmidt and Greg Luzinski without thinking of Veterans Stadium. The same goes for the Big Red Machine and Riverfront Stadium, the Battling Bucs and Three Rivers Stadium, and the Glasshouse Gang and Houston Astrodome.

"Veterans Stadium was a jewel when they built it," said Larry Shenk, the Phillies' public relations director in 1972 and a member of the club's front office for more than five decades. "We were so glad to get out of Connie Mack Stadium, it was unbelievable. It was small, dirty, and smelly. There was very limited [fan] parking, the food was pretty much hot dogs and hamburgers, and the offices were antiquated and spread out. We needed a change, and when we got to the Vet, it was awesome."

The 1970s saw an outbreak of synthetic surfaces and cookie-cutter stadiums. "Artificial turf changed the game, made teams play differently," says Cash. "The game became very fast."

Several ballparks maintained their iconic identities. In the east there was Yankee Stadium and Fenway Park. The big ballpark in the Bronx was still "the House That Ruth Built." Known for its history—Lou Gehrig's "Luckiest Man Alive" speech, Roger Maris's record-setting sixty-first home run in 1961, etc.—Yankee Stadium was also known for its deep dimensions (463 feet to center field) and iconic features (the three stately monuments in center field, the dignified copper façade on the third deck).

While Yankee Stadium was majestic in size and grandeur, Fenway Park is often referred to as a large minor league stadium. Its seating capacity in 1972 was 33,379, but one of Fenway's charms has always been its coziness. There's the Green Monster in left, Pesky Pole in right, and in deep center the "Triangle," an area where an outfielder must be part pinball wizard to play the many ways the ball bounces off the walls.

In the Midwest there stood the hallowed grounds of Tiger Stadium and Wrigley Field. Tiger Stadium was Ty Cobb, a trademark overhanging upper deck that turned deep fly balls into round-trippers, and Ernie Harwell; Wrigley was Ernie Banks, ivy-covered brick walls, and, later, Harry Caray. Both parks had an early twentieth-century America feel few other venues could match. In the golden west the Oakland Coliseum and San Francisco's Candlestick Park were awash in sun and scented with a salty sea air.

Pull up to the stadium and you could park your car for twenty-five cents and buy a seat in the bleachers for fifty cents. Inside the ballpark you could get a hot dog and cold drink for ninety-five cents, a large soft drink and popcorn for sixty cents.

The game was changing, but some constants remained. Curt Gowdy, Tony Kubek, and Jim Simpson were fixtures on NBC-TV's Saturday afternoon *Game of the Week* and provided a soundtrack for summer. Doubleheaders ruled the day. The A's played sixteen twin bills in '72, and there was an East Coast swing in late July that led to Oakland's playing thirteen road games, including four doubleheaders, in ten days. In New York the annual Mayor's Trophy Game between the Yankees and Mets presaged interleague contests.

In this era games were played faster. An MLB game in the 1970s averaged two and a half hours, as opposed to three-plus hours in 2014. Pitchers worked quickly—it was a point of pride for starting pitchers to go the distance—and hitters tended to stay in the batter's box for the entire at-bat. They didn't engage in rabbit's foot rituals, tightening and retightening their batting gloves between each pitch while the minutes piled up like student loans.

Players also choked up on the bat far more frequently. It was as common for the powerful Bando, whom Gowdy described as being built like a blocking back, to choke up on the bat and shorten his swing to protect the plate as it was for light-hitting infielders like Felix Millan, Gene Michael, Eddie Brinkman, Bud Harrelson, and Larry Bowa. Millan may have choked up on the bat higher than it was thought humanly possible, but Brinkman was close. He had a wide-handled bat that had a knob on it to remind him not to place his hands any lower.

It was also common to see a pitcher reach base and button up a nylon jacket even on the most sweltering summer afternoons. Hitters often followed their at-bats by removing their batting helmets and pulling out their cloth caps from their back pockets. Some wore their caps beneath their batting helmets. "A player like me can appreciate the differences in those kinds of little things in the years I played and before I played and today's game," says Mike Schmidt, who made his major league debut in 1972. "[The players are] bigger, stronger, physical specimens. Hitting technique is probably better across the board. But the little baseball skill things have gone the other way."

Depending on where you lived in '72, you could tune your transistor radio or local TV channel to Vin Scully and Jerry Doggett, Ernie Harwell, Harry Caray, Chuck Thompson, Bob Prince and Nellie King, or Ken Coleman and Johnny Pesky. Philadelphia fans could listen to Byrum Saam, Harry Kalas, and Richie "Whitey" Ashburn. In the New York–New Jersey metro area we had Phil "Scooter" Rizzuto, Frank Messer, and Bill White broadcasting Yankee games; Ralph Kiner, Lindsey Nelson, and Bob Murphy were on the Mets' network.

Sportscasters in the 1960s and '70 were extensions of the team itself. In Chicago Harry Caray became as identifiable with the White Sox as Lloyd Pettit was with the Blackhawks of Tony Esposito and Bobby Hull and the excitable Jack Brickhouse was with the Ernie Banks–Billy Williams Cubs and the Dick Butkus-led Bears. The same could be said for Los Angeles, which featured Scully with the Dodgers, Chick Hearn with the Lakers, and Dick Enberg with UCLA basketball; and Detroit, where Harwell broadcast the Tigers and Van Patrick, the "Ol' Announcer," the Lions.

New Yorkers were similarly blessed with iconic sportscasters. Along with Scooter Rizzuto and Kiner's Korner, there was Marty Glickman calling Giants games, Merle Harmon the Joe Namath-led Jets, and Marv Albert the Knicks ("Frazier cuts to his left, stops and jumps. . . . Yes!") and Rangers ("Giacomin kick save and a beauty!"). The Red Sox's Ned Martin's elegant erudition and signature phrase ("Mercy!") made him as beloved an orator in Back Bay as the Celtics' gritty, gravelly voiced Johnny Most ("Havlicek stole the ball!").

These men were masters of their craft, many of them having grown up listening to sportscasting giants Red Barber and Mel Allen, who were in turn following in the footsteps of baseball broadcast pioneers like Graham McNamee, a man blessed with a rich baritone and the first "star" sportscaster. They knew how to let a broadcast breathe. Their commentaries and observations were tempered; their quiet pauses allowed listeners to soak in the sounds of the stadium. Longtime listeners of the leathery-voiced Kalas learned to lean in a bit toward the radio during dead air to hear their beloved Harry clicking his cigarette lighter to light up a Parliament. They could hear the soft scraping of his metal lighter on the microphone, a small nuance fans loved.

The glory years of these great voices coincided with the rise in popularity of transistor radios. They were the iPods of their era, pocket-sized devices propelling a change in popular culture. The hand-held radio was perfect for a post–World War II public with disposable income. This period of prosperity changed people's habits. They could listen to a ballgame anywhere, and children fell asleep on summer nights to the muffled voices of favorite announcers beneath their pillows. The voices were distinctive, and we formed a connection to Lindsey Nelson's elegant Tennessee tones and the excited cries of Scooter Rizzuto, his signature "Holy cow!" and "What a huckleberry!" dripping with his native Brooklyn. These storytellers made us feel like part of the game, and our younger days remain forever linked to the sounds of their voices.

We read the newspapers every day—my boyhood days usually began by reading the *Newark Star-Ledger* or New York *Daily News*—and listened to live broadcasts with a transistor radio pressed to our ears. Every October in the late '60s and early '70s we hid a radio in our pockets and snaked the cord under our shirts and up to our ears as we sat in grade school listening to that afternoon's World Series game.

It's difficult to explain to younger fans since the last time a Series game saw the sun was 1984, but Fall Classic contests in the daytime led to a holiday-like mood as you looked forward to that early-afternoon opening pitch. As kids we ran home from grade school in October 1970 to catch NBC's broadcast of the Orioles' domination of the Reds on Channel 4 from New York. One October later I was with my parents, John and Roberta, in Jersey City listening on the car radio to the Pirates-Orioles Series.

The friendly and familiar voices of your favorite broadcasters accompanied you to the ballparks, where their calls mingled with the voices of the public address announcers. In classic venues like Yankee Stadium, Fenway Park, and Wrigley Field it meant Bob Sheppard, Sherm Feller and Pat Pieper respectively. In newer stadiums like the Vet it meant Dan Baker, who in 1972 was in the first year of his more than five decades with the Phillies. Unlike today, when trips to a major league game mean a three-hour audio assault, in the early 1970s the PA announcer and stadium organists like Eddie Layton and then Toby Wright in Yankee Stadium, Jane Jarvis in Shea, and Helen Dell in Dodger Stadium worked in low-key concert with one another.

There were other sights and sounds to capture our attention: the rumble of the elevated IRT trains outside Yankee Stadium, the deafening roar at Shea Stadium by the procession of planes from nearby LaGuardia, the scenic stroll into Three Rivers Stadium across bridges spanning the sparkling waters of the Monongahela.

It was an era of revered umpires: skillful arbiters Augie Donatelli, Shag Crawford, and Nestor Chylak; showboats in blue like Ron Luciano and Emmett Ashford; and umps who earned national notoriety for being pitchmen—Bill Haller hawking El Producto cigars and Jim Honochick on Miller Lite Beer commercials with a famous Baltimore slugger ("Hey, you're Boog Powell!").

The umpires themselves were at the center of a seemingly annual debate every October about the differences between the leagues. American League umps had the reputation of giving pitchers the high strike—good news in the early '70s for hurlers like Oakland's Vida Blue, who had a rising fastball. AL and NL umps also positioned themselves differently behind home plate. In the American League the plate umpire worked directly behind the catcher; National League umpires worked inside the hitter. For a right-handed batter NL umps were positioned behind the catcher's left shoulder; for a left-handed hitter, the ump would be just off the catcher's right shoulder. One other difference was that American League umps wore outside chest protectors, and even a devoted Mets' fan like New York City poet Joel Oppenheimer thought there was something wonderful about the sight of an umpire shifting his chest protector around, a sight that was sadly lacking in National League games.

One other difference between the leagues was also sartorial. In the National League it was common to see hitters reach base and discard their batting helmets in favor of their caps. Their American League counterparts had no such option; they were required by rule to wear their batting helmets on the base paths. Certain hitters did, however, have the option of wearing batting helmets or cloth caps at home plate. The rule requiring the wearing of batting helmets was passed in December 1970, but veteran hitters were grandfathered in, giving them an option. Some chose not to wear helmets or wore them only in certain situations. Detroit left-handed hitter Norm Cash wore a batting helmet when facing southpaws but a cloth cap when facing right-handers.

The '72 season was the first for the fledgling Texas Rangers, formerly the Washington Senators. The franchise went from the AL East to West, while Milwaukee moved West to East. The season also marked the final summer the Kansas City Royals would spend in Municipal Stadium. The following spring they would take up residence in the sparkling new Truman Sports Complex in suburban Kansas City.

The overlapping of eras was exemplified in various and vivid ways—Reggie Jackson digging in against Bob Gibson in the 1972 All-Star Game; aging legends Willie Mays and Juan Marichal sharing the same fields with young stars Carlton Fisk and Cesar Cedeno. There were familiar faces in unfamiliar places: Mays, Rusty Staub, and Jim Fregosi in New York; Nolan Ryan in California; Dick Allen in Chicago; Frank Robinson in Los Angeles; Denny McLain in Oakland; Sam McDowell in San Francisco; Gaylord Perry and Alex Johnson in Cleveland; Lee May in Houston; Joe Morgan in Cincinnati.

New, form-fitting double-knit uniforms were in style, having been inaugurated by the Pirates in 1970. In the blue and white of the Atlanta Braves, Hank Aaron continued his relentless pursuit of Babe Ruth's career home run record.

Still some reassuring constants remained—Brooks Robinson and his magic mitt were in Baltimore, and in Pittsburgh Roberto Clemente was still lord of the flies in right field.

There are other vignettes from the unforgettable summer of '72:

> Clemente, swinging as usual off his front foot, strokes a double off Mets lefty Jon Matlack for his three thousandth hit. The historic hit comes in Clemente's final regular-season game. Two months later on New Year's Eve Clemente boarded a DC-7 for a humanitarian mission bringing supplies to stricken earthquake victims in Managua, Nicaragua. The plane crashed a mile off the coast of Puerto Rico and within sight of several of his Pirate teammates at a party. There were no survivors of the crash, and Clemente's body was never found. "Dock Ellis and I cried when we heard the news. We broke," Pirates slugger Al Oliver remembers;

Dick Allen, waving what appeared to be a tree trunk at home plate, having an MVP summer for a White Sox squad revered for saving Chicago's South Side franchise;

Steve Carlton, so twitchy on the mound he could make coffee nervous, staring in for the sign and then snapping off his sharp-breaking slider. He wins 27 games in '72 for a Phillies squad that claims just 59 victories;

Sparky Lyle stepping from the pinstripe-painted Datsun as Wright pounds out "Pomp and Circumstance" on the Yankee Stadium organ and the crowd chants, "Dee-fense!" Chomping down on a wad of Red Man tobacco, Lyle retires hitters with his wicked slider;

Willie Mays, traded by San Francisco back to New York, where the Say Hey Kid's career started in 1951, makes a triumphant return to Gotham and thrills a Shea Stadium crowd with a game-winning homer against his former mates;

Joe Morgan furiously pumping his left elbow while he awaits a pitch;

Willie Stargell windmilling his bat as the hurler goes into his windup;

Bob Gibson's fallaway delivery;

The NBC peacock ("The following is brought to you—IN LIVING COLOR—on NBC!") and the network's familiar theme music that heralded its *Game of the Week*.

The summer of '72 saw the birth of the brilliant Dodger infield of Steve Garvey, Davey Lopes, Bill Russell, and Ron Cey, and their union would last longer than many marriages; on the opposite coast was the equally iconic twisting, twirling windup of Luis Tiant, a.k.a. El Tiante. Other ornaments included the clipped, burnt-orange bill of Brooks Robinson's batting helmet and the matte finish on Manny Sanguillen's; Horace Clarke wearing his helmet in the field; the smear of dirt on the right leg of Tom Seaver's uniform pants, courtesy of a delivery that has his knee scraping the mound.

Teams had style and personality—the Mustache Gang, Big Red Machine, Glasshouse Gang, A-Mays-in' Mets, Battling Bucs, Bronx Bombers, Sesame Street Gang, and South Siders. Powerhouse clubs of the past were driven by a sense of the years descending—the Baltimore Orioles, fronted by the elegant pitching corps of Palmer, Dave McNally, and Mike Cuellar; the Tigers of Cash, Al Kaline, and Mickey Lolich; the Cardinals of Bob Gibson and Lou Brock.

The '72 season saw much needed attention brought to former Negro League players. In February Commissioner Bowie Kuhn announced that Josh Gibson and Buck Leonard would be inducted into the Baseball Hall of Fame. At the World Series, Jackie Robinson, who had broken the major league color barrier in 1947, threw out the ceremonial first ball prior to Game Two.

Worn down in part by the strain of being the first black ballplayer in the major leagues, Robinson's eyesight was failing and his health deteriorating due to diabetes. He thanked baseball for the "tremendous opportunity" presented to him twenty-five years earlier. He was pleased and proud, he told the sun-streaked crowd, and said he would be "tremendously more pleased and more proud when I look at that third-base coaching line one day and see a black face managing in baseball." He didn't live to see the day. Three weeks later, Jackie Roosevelt Robinson died at age fifty-three on October 24. It was seventeen years and a day after Branch Rickey had announced Robinson's historic signing with the Brooklyn Dodgers.

Along with Robinson and Clemente, a third giant of the game passed away. Gil Hodges, Robinson's teammate on Brooklyn's "Boys of Summer" squads and the man who guided the Mets to their 1969 world title, died April 2 of a sudden heart attack following a round of golf at a West Palm Beach course. Hodges's untimely death—he was two days shy of his forty-eighth birthday—and the Mets' December 1971 trade of Ryan to the Angels for Fregosi haunted the franchise.

Dickens wrote in *The Battle of Life* that there were victories gained every day in struggling hearts to which "fields of battle were as nothing." In the summer of '72 such victories were won in the hearts of Bench, Tiant, and Bobby Tolan, among others. Such a victory was also won in the heart of Tigers hurler John Hiller, who on July 8, 1972, took the mound for the first time since suffering three heart attacks on January 11, 1971, at the age of twenty-seven. Having undergone the experimental procedure of intestinal bypass surgery to lose weight, Hiller shed the pounds that had pushed his weight from 185 in 1968 to 220 in January 1971.

On his comeback afternoon Hiller worked the middle three innings against the White Sox. He went on to make 24 appearances and post a 2.03 ERA for playoff-bound Detroit. Over the next two seasons he would win a combined 27 games in relief, and in 1973 he led the league with 38 saves, a major league record until 1983. He was named Comeback Player of the Year and Fireman of the Year. Along with contemporaries like Lyle, Fingers, Cincinnati's Clay Carroll and the Mets' Tug McGraw, Hiller helped define the role of the modern reliever.

A campaign of captivating races—nine teams were still in the hunt in September for a division title—culminated in a postseason marked by bruising intensity. For the first time, both league Championship Series required the full five games to determine a winner. The heightened drama got the better of at least one participant—veteran Oakland shortstop Bert Campaneris. Campy was one of the few players in major league history to play all nine positions in a single game. He once pitched both right-handed *and* left-handed in a minor league game.

But in October 1972 Campaneris made headlines for a much different reason—throwing his bat at Detroit pitcher Lerrin LaGrow in Game Two of the American League Championship Series (ALCS). The fleet-footed Campy terrorized the Tigers with his dash and daring. He opened Game Two with a single and then stole second *and* third en route to scoring the game's first run. He got two more hits and scored another run before facing LaGrow in the seventh inning. LaGrow's first pitch was a low, inside fastball that flew in the direction of Campy's feet. Campaneris tried to jump out of the way, but the ball struck him on the ankle. The shortstop snapped. He flung the bat toward LaGrow, the Louisville Slugger spinning and whirling toward the pitcher like a helicopter blade.

The intense play continued in a World Series that saw a showdown of two of the most vivid and contrasting dynasties in baseball history. Between them, Oakland and Cincinnati qualified for the postseason a combined ten times between 1970 and 1976. They were the dominant teams of their era, winning five straight World Series in those years.

The collision of these dynasties resulted in six of the seven games being decided by a single run—still a record. Game Seven went down to the final at-bat in the final inning with two of the game's all-time greats going mano a mano in a hitter-hurler showdown for the ages. Played out before sold-out crowds in Oakland and Cincinnati and to millions more watching on TV and listening on radio, the '72 Series was the first seven-game Fall Classic in which all seven games were sold out in advance.

The ultimate Octoberfest came down to Game Seven in Riverfront Stadium, to Rose, the future all-time hits leader, in a one-on-one duel with Fingers, a future Hall of Famer. His team trailing 3–2, Rose strode to the plate in the bottom of the ninth with two outs and the tying run on base.

In rare moments in World Series history the drama of an entire summer narrows to a very small focus—the final play of the final game. With the hopes of the largest crowd to that point in the history of Cincinnati baseball living and dying on every pitch, Rose assumed his exaggerated crouch and glared out from behind his upraised right shoulder at Fingers and his Salvador Dali–style 'stache.

Jim Simpson made the call on NBC Radio: "This Series isn't over yet. Rose steps in. He is 2-for-4 today and has made great contact all four times. The other two were driven deep to the centerfield wall."

Fingers wound and delivered. Uncoiling from his crouch, Rose redirected the ball toward left-center field.

Framed by the leaden sky of late autumn, the ball flew in a white blur toward the gap. Many believed Rose's liner might fall in, thus tying the game and extending the season until, as William Leggett of *Sports Illustrated* wrote, "half-past Halloween."

Some observers felt time was freezing into a series of tableaux: Charlie Hustle churning up the first-base line; Darrel Chaney, the runner on first who represented the tying run, sprinting around second; Rudi, the A's left fielder, running—"very carefully," A's writer Ron Bergman noted—on Riverfront's slick surface.

Rudi had saved Hunter's Game Two victory with a marvelous catch against the left-field wall in the ninth inning. Gowdy recalled Rudi's wall-climbing web gem as "absolutely fantastic," a play fans would be talking about for years to come.

Indeed. More than forty years later fans still talk of Rudi's literally rising to the occasion with his levitating leap in left field. But there was one more to play to make, and as Rudi dashed to his left, his white cleats flashing over the bright green Astroturf, he was running toward the outfield wall.

He was also running out of room.

Simpson: "Fly ball to left field. Rudi goes back. . . . Near the warning track."

Rose's drive was carrying. And carrying.

CHAPTER ONE

Reginald Martinez Jackson loved to hit a baseball. In the spring of 1972 the star right fielder for the reigning American League Western Division champion Oakland Athletics *lived* to hit. He was twenty-five years old, stood six feet tall, and weighed 204 pounds. Heavily muscled—he had been a running back at Arizona State—he boasted seventeen-inch biceps and twenty-seven-inch thighs.

There was no one in baseball, Jackson believed, who could do as many things as well as he could. He had only a fair batting average, but he hit with great power and ran with surprising speed for a big man. *Baseball Digest* would feature Reggie on the cover of its June issue, along with Pete Rose and Willie Mays, and declare the '72 season to be the start of baseball's Jacksonian Era. "This Will Be *His* Year!" the magazine proclaimed.

Prior to a 2009 World Series game against the Philadelphia Phillies in Yankee Stadium, Reggie held court on the field with a group of writers. He talked about hitting, about hitting in the clutch, about how he had loved to hit the ball—"that little white sum-bitch," he used to call it. In July 1971 Jackson smashed one of the longest home runs in history when he connected with a pitch thrown by Pittsburgh's Dock Ellis in the All-Star Game. The ball was still rising when it struck one of the light standards on the roof of Tiger Stadium, 520 feet from home plate.

NBC Radio color commentator Sandy Koufax was impressed by what he had witnessed: "It looked like Dock got the breaking ball up just a little bit to Reggie Jackson and, I mean, he hit it hard. I don't know when I've seen a ball hit as hard as that one. That would have gone out at the airport."

In his first weekend in the majors late in 1967, Jackson blasted five balls into a forty-foot-high screen in Kansas City's Municipal Stadium. They went for doubles and triples but would have been homers in almost any other ballpark. Two summers later, in just his second full season in The Show, Reggie hammered 47 homers and drove in 118 runs. Several of his drives went five hundred feet or more. By the end of July he had belted 39 homers and was being called the next Babe Ruth. At the time Ted Williams called Reggie the "most natural hitter I've ever seen." A's teammate Sal Bando believed Jackson had more ability than anyone in the game.

By the spring of '72 Jackson had established himself as one of the game's most feared hitters. He exuded power, charisma, and confidence, but he was also a complicated man. He was intelligent and sensitive, given to fair amounts of introspection. He was dogged by mood swings and depression. In 1973 he began seeing a therapist to deal with the demands of stardom and the end of his marriage to college sweetheart Jennie Campos. It was his interracial marriage, Jackson thought, that caused the Mets to pass him over in the amateur draft and allowed him to be signed by the Athletics.

When the A's 1971 season ended abruptly with a three-game sweep by defending World Series champion Baltimore in the American League Championship Series, cameras caught Jackson slumped on the dugout steps, his head bowed. He had hit two home runs off Orioles ace Jim Palmer in Game Three and batted .333, but Reggie was inconsolable in defeat. After six long months Oakland's season was suddenly over. The A's star slugger couldn't believe it. It took half an hour for Jackson to finally make his way to the somber locker room. When he arrived, Reggie's eyes were red and swollen.

In time Jackson was able to put the playoff loss in perspective. Oakland's division title in 1971 was its first; the A's weren't prepared to go any further, he reasoned. Just winning the division had been enough for them. Jackson thought they had acted afraid of Baltimore, a veteran squad with marquee names—Palmer, Brooks and Frank Robinson, Boog Powell, Dave McNally, Mike Cuellar. The Orioles were a group of established stars whose experience in October baseball extended back to 1966.

Six months later, as he stepped into the batter's box beneath a bright

Arizona sun at the A's spring training headquarters, Jackson was a hard man playing a hard game. He prided himself on having a working man's hands and body; he beamed with pride when one of the younger A's referred to Reggie as "one big callus."

He wanted to be the leader of the A's, the man the other guys looked up to. "Just call me Mr. B & B, Mr. Bread-and-Butter," he would say. "That's me, the guy who does it, the guy who puts it on the table so everyone can eat."

Not all of the A's appreciated Reggie's bombast. Mike Epstein, a slugging first baseman obtained in a trade the previous May from the Washington Senators, represented the other half of Oakland's power from the port side. Epstein's resentment eventually resulted in a shouting match between him and Jackson over Epstein's use of *free* game tickets.

Catfish Hunter took Jackson's outsized personality in stride. Reggie, Hunter said, was the kind of guy who would give you the shirt off his back. "Of course," the Cat added, "he would call a press conference to announce it."

A's catcher Dave Duncan knew that while Jackson was an outspoken person who would stir things up, Reggie also meant a great deal to a team and a city. A guy like Reggie could mean as much as two hundred thousand more fans in a season. Duncan also knew Jackson had a lot of natural leadership.

Oakland manager Dick Williams considered Reggie one of three leaders in the A's rollicking clubhouse. The other two were Hunter and Bando. Bando was the captain, the quiet leader, the guy who led by example. Hunter led through practical jokes that kept the clubhouse loose, and the Cat never let teammates take themselves too seriously.

Williams considered Jackson the guy "with the lungs, the vocal one." As far as Williams was concerned, Jackson's constant chatter gave his teammates something to both laugh at and rally behind. The best thing about it, Williams wrote in his autobiography, was that it was all an act. Cut through all of Reggie's B.S., Williams said, and he was a guy who would play his heart out for his team.

There was a time when Jackson didn't want the responsibility of leadership, when he didn't want to stand out. But he found he could handle pressure. He would bend, but he wouldn't break. He had grown up. He was a mature man. He didn't fear anyone or anything on the baseball field.

Jackson may not have feared any situation or any man, but at the plate he could present a frightening picture to pitchers. With his feet spread wide as he settled into his stance, he glared out at the mound from beneath the bill of his two-toned batting helmet. He wore Oakland's brand new green and gold pullover jersey with alternating piping on the sleeves, a large "A's" on the left breast, and number 9 on his back. His baseball pants—called Sans-a-Belts because they had an elasticized waistband that eliminated the need for a belt—were white with green-and-gold trim on the outside of each leg. Green stirrups, gold socks, and white cleats completed the A's new look.

The A's, who had as many uniform combinations under Finley as Elton John had stage outfits, began wearing alternating jerseys in 1966. While it's become common for teams to have numerous uniform combinations to increase revenue, the A's were a team ahead of their time when it came to alternating jerseys and pants.

Oakland's pullover tops were a double-knit made of synthetic material popularized by the Pittsburgh Pirates in 1970 and by the St. Louis Cardinals and Houston Astros in 1971. Oakland and others followed suit in '72, and by 1975 two-thirds of major league clubs had adopted the new look.

Straddling home plate from the left side, Jackson's right hand, covered by a white batting glove, gripped his thirty-six-ounce bat near its handle. Whipping his bat through the strike zone, the man known to teammates as "Buck" blasted balls to the outer reaches of the sun-drenched diamond. He knew his main asset as a hitter was his strength, so he concentrated on putting every ounce of himself into each swing. Strong as he was, he could have used a heavier bat; Babe Ruth had toted a fifty-four-ounce tree trunk. Jackson, however, preferred a lighter stick, one he could swing with more bat speed.

Putting on a hitting clinic, Reggie would rip at each pitch, scraping the skies with prodigious drives and lashing liners that crashed into outfield fences with frightening force. Onlookers were impressed; Jackson, however, was not. Some hitters could catch hold of a pitch and feel satisfied. Reggie was never satisfied. One great hit only served to make him want another.

Contrary to league practice, he had grown a mustache for the new season. He would become the first major league player since Wally Schang in 1914 to have facial hair in a regular-season game. In time eighteen of Jackson's teammates and even his manager followed his lead, growing long hair and mustaches that gave the Mustache Gang an *esprit de corps*.

Oakland owner Charlie O. Finley grew to like his team's unshorn appearance and offered each man $300 cash to grow a mustache for a Father's Day promotion. Relief specialist Rollie Fingers opted for a waxed mustache; Epstein favored a Franz Josef look.

Finley's promotional ideas flowed throughout the organization and the sport. He gave his players headline-grabbing nicknames—"Catfish" Hunter, "Blue Moon" Odom—and tried to convince southpaw ace Vida Blue to legally change his name to "True." Blue declined, angrily suggesting the owner change *his* name to True Finley.

Finley built a team of colorful characters: Dagoberto "Campy" Campaneris; Fiore Gino Tennaci, a.k.a. Gene Tenace; Salvatore "Sal" Bando; Vida Blue, John "Blue Moon" Odom, and Dick Green; Reggie, Rollie, and Joe Rudi; Catfish, Kenny Holtzman, and Mateo "Matty" Alou.

Throughout his tenure as A's boss, Charlie O. livened up game days by using a yellow cab to drive pitchers in from the bullpen, installing a mechanical rabbit named Harvey that popped up behind home plate with new baseballs for the umpire to the tune of "Here Comes Peter Cottontail," and hiring Miss USA as a bat girl.

Bored with baseball's conventional ways, he dressed the A's in gaudy uniforms at a time when every other team wore home whites and road grays. He pushed for the adoption of a permanent pinch hitter for pitchers. Charlie O. and his Mustache Gang would prove to be trendsetters. The designated hitter rule would be adopted by the American League in 1973. By the midpoint of the decade, big league players were expressing their individuality through flamboyant coiffures, mustaches, and beards.

Emboldened by their maverick owner, members of the Mustache Gang would look the way they wanted to look and act the way they wanted to act. Outfitted in eye-popping colors and wearing hair that hung in thick clumps, they would shoot from the lip, speak their minds, and punch each other out when tempers flared. They got away with all of it. No longer were the A's the team that in Jackson's estimation had acted afraid of the Orioles the previous October. They had been toughened by tough times.

Bando believed the organization had developed a nucleus of players who loved a challenge. In time the A's would develop into a fearsome squad that didn't know how to lose. Come game time, Hunter said, no matter how mad the A's were at one another, when they stepped on the field, they played as a team.

That's the way it is with the Mustache Gang, Jackson said at the time. The A's say what they have to say and do what they have to do. They would fight and fuss among themselves, but they were together when it came time to take on another team. It was a matter of attitude, and the A's were at their best when they had attitude.

Like the St. Louis Cardinals' "Gashouse Gang" who preceded them and the Philadelphia Phillies' "Macho Row" who followed, the Swingin' A's of the seventies swaggered through life. They were rebels but with a cause. They wanted to leave their mark on the game.

The Mustache Gang was badass, and Reggie was the biggest badass of them all. He was one tough cut of hardtack. Frank Robinson, one of the game's great sluggers and the only man to win Most Valuable Player awards in both leagues, was a contemporary of Jackson who served multiple roles in the young superstar's life: friend, confidant, mentor, manager. Robinson said Reggie had so much strength and ability, nothing Jackson did on the field surprised him.

Jackson credited Robinson with influencing him when he was at the crossroads of his young career in 1971. At the height of his great season in 1969 Reggie began feeling the pressure of the chase of Ruth's hallowed home run mark of 60, set in 1927. It was the same pressure that caused Yankees slugger Roger Maris's hair to fall out in '61. In Jackson's case it was hives on his body, and he was hospitalized for nervous exhaustion. Without their slugger the A's faltered in a Western Division race won by Minnesota.

Jackson never really thought about breaking any records, but he did want to hit 50 homers in '69. Because he went yard just once in his last thirty-five games, Jackson finished with 47 homers. It was the closest he would ever come to his goal of 50 homers in a season. Reggie took the blame for the A's collapse and put pressure on himself to carry the team in 1970. But his disappointment was mixed with defiance.

Jackson rebelled the next season, and his contract holdout in spring training set the tone for a personally traumatic season. The tortured young slugger struggled with slumps, benchings, and ultimately with a threatened demotion to Des Moines.

He never expected to be an overnight sensation, an anguished Jackson told the media in the middle of his nightmare season. He just wanted to progress steadily until he reached his full potential. Now he was on the bench part of the time, and there was talk of sending him to the minors.

Monte Moore, the A's longtime broadcaster, recalls thinking that baseball humbled Jackson. Reggie had been through the mill, Moore said. He'd had his ups and downs and knew the game wasn't easy. Jackson, Moore thought, had expected too much too soon.

Moore remembered that when Jackson had first arrived in the majors, he had loved to show off the strength and accuracy of his throwing arm. There was one occasion when Reggie made a magnificent throw from deepest right-center field in Yankee Stadium. The ball zipped to third base on the fly, causing everyone on the A's to talk about it for a long time. The problem was, Moore said, Jackson kept trying to top it. As a consequence, Reggie would make a great throw one day and then fire the ball over the fielder's head the next.

Jackson was having problems at the plate as well. He had a big swing and struck out a lot, and the more Reggie struck out, the more he sulked. Moore recalled seeing Jackson brood and fret over his mounting whiffs. The result was that one strikeout would lead to another and perhaps still another, all in the same game. Suddenly the biggest talent in the A's starting lineup was facing a fragile future.

The career-saving changes came when Jackson played winter ball in Puerto Rico in 1971. His manager was Frank Robinson, and it was Robby who gave Reggie renewed confidence in his ability. After Frank told Jackson to just go out and play the game and allow his ability to take care of the rest, Reggie believed Robinson all but guaranteed he'd have a good season. Jackson also credited Gary Walker, his friend and partner in the land business, with giving him direction.

Moore, among others, saw the positive changes in Jackson starting with the '71 season. Moore said Reggie stopped worrying about his strikeouts. Jackson realized he had a big swing and was going to fan a certain amount of times. When he did, he forgot about it and concentrated on getting a hit the next time. Jackson batted a respectable .277 in '71, with 32 homers and 80 RBIs. His base running improved, and in the field he worked hard on throwing to the right base, hitting the cutoff man, and using his arm to the A's advantage. He also became a leader in the outfield, moving fielders into the proper position for different hitters. Moore thought Jackson had a great baseball mind and knew the abilities of every hitter in the American League.

As Jackson found consistency in his play, he became more of a morale booster. Moore thought Reggie never failed to take a rookie under his wing, take the kid out to dinner, talk to him, coach him, and encourage him. Moore had seen Jackson give clothes to a young player who didn't have much. Reggie was also fluent in Spanish, and this allowed him to have an influence on Latin players.

Maturity had come late to the tailor's son, but by the spring of '72 it was obvious to Moore and others that Jackson had found himself. The man who had once displayed as many moods as there are days in the week told reporters at the time, "My attitude is better now. Sure I get down when I'm not hitting but I've convinced myself to battle back."

Jackson's personal growth and huge potential promised big things for the A's. Moore said everyone connected with the club in '72 figured Reggie was ready to have two or three seasons where he hit 40–50 homers every year. He had the mental part licked, Moore said, and since Jackson was sport's equivalent to a Mach 1 muscle car—powerful and quick—the A's boasted a man many considered baseball's best young star.

"I don't think there's been a player since Mickey Mantle that has all the skills Reggie Jackson has," Moore said at the time. "He's ready to break out."

While Reggie was the most visible member of the Mustache Gang, Mickey Lolich was, by his own admission, the Invisible Man of the Detroit Tigers. "Half the time," Lolich said then, "nobody knows I'm around."

NBC sportscaster Curt Gowdy said Lolich had "always been in the shadows." He was overshadowed by teammate Denny McLain in 1968 and by Oakland phenom Vida Blue in '71. In 1968 McLain became a household name with his 31 wins and larger-than-life, Dizzy Dean–style personality. Lolich? He was a guy who hung around; "my sway-backed left-hander," then manager Mayo Smith called him. But it was Mickey whose three wins in the World Series, including a Game Seven victory over McLain conqueror Bob Gibson, delivered a championship to Detroit.

In 1971 Blue won 24 games and the American League Cy Young Award. Lolich won 25 games, led the majors in strikeouts with 308, and pitched more innings (376) than any American Leaguer since 1912, when Big Ed Walsh hurled 393.

It was Lolich who kept the Tigers in contention in 1971, their 91 wins the most of any team that finished second in the majors that season. Early that summer Tigers manager Billy Martin told reporters that his thin pitching rotation would consist of Lolich and whomever and two days of rain. Billy the Kid's quip was a takeoff on *Boston Post* sports editor Gerald Hern's famous poem, "Spahn and Sain and Pray for Rain," written during the 1948 Boston Braves' pennant drive.

Right-hander Joe Coleman joined Lolich as a 20-game winner for Detroit in '71, and by late September Martin was so impressed with Lolich's efforts that he allowed him to bat for himself in the eighth inning of a game the Tigers were losing 3–2 to the Yankees. The standard move is to pinch-hit for the pitcher in such circumstances, but Martin was giving Lolich every opportunity to earn the highest number of wins for a Detroit lefty since Hal Newhouser's 26 in 1946.

That Lolich suffered from invisibility was surprising—not only because of his success on the mound, but also because as writer Ray Robinson noted in 1972, Mickey was one of the most unusual looking athletes in America at that time. The thirty-one-year-old native of Portland, Oregon, carried a paunch that caused *New Yorker* baseball writer Roger Angell to compare him to an aging Irish middleweight and Robinson to state that Lolich appeared to have done his training in a barroom or a brewery.

The likable Lolich agreed. Noting his portly physique during his playing days, he described himself as the "beer-drinker's idol." All the fat guys watched him, he told reporters, and told their wives, "See, there's a fat guy doing okay. Bring me another beer."

Robinson noted that Lolich's stomach rolled out like a niagara over his belt, his pants drooped continuously as if the Tigers couldn't find a tailor in town, and his uniform number 29 was drenched in sweat before the fourth inning was over. Robinson thought Lolich's face had softness about it, but if it did, it belied the fighting spirit Martin and others were well aware of.

Martin thought Lolich "a battler," a guy he could give the ball to every four days and get a top performance just about every time. Lolich, in whom the fires of competition were well banked, returned the praise to his fists-first skipper. "I'd do anything that guy wants," he told a reporter while nodding in Martin's direction.

Lolich's relationship with McLain was another matter. There was talk that Mickey was critical of McLain's attitude, and it was noted by sportswriters at the time that McLain, who was flying his own plane at the time, didn't give Lolich a lift back to Detroit following the 1969 All-Star Game. Lolich was quoted as calling it "a crummy trick" and was reported to say that McLain "just doesn't ever think of his friends or teammates." Lolich denied saying anything as harsh as that about McLain and stated he and Denny would always be friends.

When the former mound mates met in the opening game of a May doubleheader in '71—McLain having been dealt to Washington—their duel in Detroit was advertised as a mutual vendetta. With a crowd of fifty-two thousand crammed into Tiger Stadium that Sunday, Lolich four-hit the Senators and won 5–0.

On August 21 Lolich beat Milwaukee 7–2 to win 20 games for the first time in his career. Afterward a congratulatory note was wired to Lolich. It was sent by Denny McLain.

Lolich grew tired of the comparisons to McLain and Blue. He was his own man, a guy who loved motorcycles, collected pistols, and enjoyed archery and slot-car racing. Though many athletes prefer to be apolitical, Lolich openly favored Hubert Humphrey over Richard Nixon in the 1968 presidential race.

In baseball's conformist circles Lolich was considered by some a "flake"— not surprising since in baseball many southpaws are considered crafty and crazy, wily and wild. Except Lolich was not a left-hander early on. As a toddler he favored his right arm, but when he was two years old, he rode his tricycle up the back of a parked motorcycle. The motorcycle fell on him, breaking his collarbone and causing damage to his right arm. Doctors ordered exercise and therapy for the injured wing, thus marking Mickey's transition to southpaw. He would still do many things right-handed, including batting and writing.

Despite excessive use, Lolich's left arm never suffered disrepair. His 29 complete games in '71 topped the American League, and his innings pitched dwarfed that of famed contemporary and National League iron arm Ferguson Jenkins. Lolich would say his arm felt tired at times but never sore.

The Tiger ace earned his stripes over the course of thirteen summers in Detroit. He did, in fact, seem destined to play for the Tigers. Michael Stephen Lolich was born September 12, 1940, the same day Schoolboy Rowe kept the Tigers in first place in the AL pennant race by beating the Yankees. Mickey's father was a parks director, and his job kept his kids outside and close to playgrounds and athletic and exercise equipment.

Lolich developed a strong arm as a boy by throwing rocks and grew up idolizing another southpaw, Yankee great Whitey Ford. Yet it was another future Yankees left-hander, Al Downing, who proved instrumental in Lolich's signing with Detroit. Mickey starred for Babe Ruth and American Legion teams and dueled Downing in amateur games. Both Lolich and Downing were being scouted by major league teams, and when Downing signed with the Yanks, Lolich figured that rather than battle Al through the minors for a spot on the Bombers, he would sign with the Tigers.

Lolich reported to the minors weighing all of 160 pounds. By his own recollection he was "skin and bones" but determined to succeed. Called up to the Tigers in May 1963, he made complete games one of his trademarks. One of his more memorable outings came on September 9, 1964, when he beat his idol, Ford, and the Yankees 4–0 at Tiger Stadium.

Aided by Tigers manager Charlie Dressen, who noted that Lolich was tipping his pitches—he raised his arms higher in his windup when he threw a fastball and lowered them when he delivered a breaking pitch—Mickey won 18 games in '64 and 15 more in '65. By 1967 White Sox manager Eddie Stanky was comparing Lolich to legendary Lefty Grove—enormous praise since Stanky had previously labeled Lolich a "second-line pitcher."

Flourishing under the tutelage of Tigers pitching coach Johnny Sain, whose laid-back approach appealed to Mickey, Lolich went 9-1 in his final eleven starts of the season, helping bring the Tigers to the brink of a league championship. The "Impossible Dream" Red Sox eventually edged out the Tigers, Twins, and White Sox in one of the great pennant races in history, but the Tigers roared back to win it all in '68, Lolich beating Gibson in Game Seven.

The Invisible Man had become a World Series hero, the twelfth pitcher in major league history to win three games in a single Fall Classic. He is still the last to win three straight complete games in one Series.

Lolich built on his great October by winning 19 games in '69 and twice striking out 16 in a game. To that point he was a two-pitch pitcher—fastballs and curves. Tigers catcher Tom Haller noted that Lolich at times relied on his rising fastball the first half of a game before switching to off-speed pitches the second half.

Lolich's strategy was straightforward: he would try and throw strikes on two of his first three pitches, basically telling the hitter, "Here, hit it." He would try to get ahead of the hitter in the count, then let the batter get himself out. Martin called him "a thinking guy who knows how to get out of trouble."

Art Fowler, Detroit's pitching coach at the time, cited Lolich's determination, and rookie right-hander Phil Meeler, whose locker was next to Mickey's in the clubhouse, was impressed by another Lolich attribute: "His guts," Meeler said.

In '71 Lolich added a cut fastball to his repertoire. It was a pitch Sain had been working with him on for years, but it wasn't until spring training in '71 that Lolich began noticing his pitches were dipping and had a new and unusual movement in the strike zone. Some mistakenly believed Lolich's new pitch was a slider because it broke down and away from hitters.

Baltimore third baseman Brooks Robinson thought Lolich "just plain tough." Teammate Boog Powell agreed. He could think of more pleasant things to do, Powell said, than head to home plate to face Mickey Lolich.

Lolich owned a unique delivery. He would raise both arms high above his head at the height of his windup and then finish his picturesque delivery with an exaggerated low leg drive. The latter earned him the nickname "Lo-Lo."

Mickey Mantle thought Lolich "threw easy," without great strain and with a smooth motion. But Lolich often surprised hitters, especially National League batters in World Series and All-Star Games, with his sharp breaking stuff and hard four-seam fastballs.

In the '71 Midsummer Classic Lolich got the call to relieve in the eighth inning. It came from Baltimore's Earl Weaver, who was managing the AL stars. Pitching to battery mate Thurman Munson of the Yankees, Lolich protected a late lead. He struck out Bobby Bonds, surrendered a home run to Roberto Clemente, then retired Lee May and Ron Santo on groundouts back to the box. In the ninth Lolich got former World Series foe Lou Brock on a grounder bunted back to the mound. He eventually induced Johnny Bench to pop out to Brooks Robinson for the game's final out. Lolich got the save as the AL snapped an eight-game losing streak.

"He knows the kind of pitches you have to make here," Weaver said of Lolich pitching in Tiger Stadium, a renowned hitter's park.

Armed with his new cut fastball and what he called a "God-given arm," Lolich racked up innings and strikeouts in equal abundance. Perhaps to bring a little more color to his performances, he began wearing a blue baseball glove in 1972.

Unlike many pitchers, he never iced his arm after games. He would instead stand in the shower and soak his arm under hot water for up to thirty minutes. The water was hot enough to turn his arm bright red, but within a couple of days he would be throwing on the sidelines in preparation for his next start. NBC color analyst Tony Kubek, who had hit against Lolich in the sixties, noted the lefty's "live arm" and said his fastball often had more movement as the game wore on. It's not unusual for pitchers to throw harder as the game progresses. Nolan Ryan, a Lolich contemporary, often had his fastball timed at 92–94 m.p.h. in the early innings and 96–98 m.p.h. in the latter.

By the start of spring training in '72, the man who had entered the minors as "skin and bones" had matured physically and as a professional. Lolich's expanding repertoire on the mound was matched by his expanding waistline. He filled out a Tigers uniform that was classic in its simplicity— white with black trim and an old English "D."

Lolich was part of a long line of hefty lefties, portly southpaws like contemporary Wilbur Wood and later incarnations like Sid Fernandez, Terry Forster, (whom David Letterman famously called a "fat tub of goo"), David "Jumbo" Wells, and C. C. Sabathia.

Gowdy said on a *Game of the Week* telecast in July 1972 that Mickey "might not be as good a pitcher if he was trim and lean." Kubek said Lolich told him he felt stronger when he had "a little weight" around his middle. Lolich said when he was throwing well, no one mentioned his belly. It was only when he lost a few games that some would say he was out of shape.

Regardless of what the critics thought of his shape, Lolich and the Tigers were planning on shaping their destiny in '72. They were determined to be invisible men no more.

CHAPTER TWO

As Reggie Jackson and the shaggy young A's reveled in their renegade ways, Johnny Bench and the Cincinnati Reds arrived at their spring camp as clean-cut and close shaven as Kiwanis Club members.

Unlike Oakland owner Charlie Finley, Reds general manager Bob Howsam strictly enforced the three S's among his players—clean shaves, high socks, and shiny black cleats. Howsam even trimmed the mustache from the Reds' traditional team logo. For decades the franchise logo had honored baseball's first professional team—the 1869 Cincinnati Red Stockings. It featured an old-time player sporting a black handlebar mustache. Howsam, however, felt that the image, no matter how time honored, was no longer representative of *his* Reds. In 1968 the player in the Reds' logo was shorn, and a clean-shaven image was presented to the public.

If the A's green-and-gold uniforms and white shoes struck some as garish—"Wednesday Night Bowling Club uniforms," according to *Sports Illustrated*—Cincinnati's white-and-red accoutrements were so conventional that they might have been worn by 1930s Reds' southpaw Johnny Vander Meer. The Reds' hierarchy insisted upon the concept of "team" regarding the appearance and conduct of every one of its players.

When Howsam's lieutenant and chief enforcer, Dick Wagner, noticed during a televised game in Atlanta that Rose had scrawled his uniform number 14 on the back of his batting helmet in black ink to distinguish it from others in the Reds' helmet rack, he dialed long-distance to Atlanta and got word to Rose to remove the numerals so that his helmet conformed to those worn by his teammates.

Cincinnati skipper George "Sparky" Anderson was smart enough to know that hair length didn't make a man play better or worse. But he did believe that when men operated as a team, there had to be behavior guidelines. Anderson felt that if the Reds' organization didn't have discipline on dress and manners and cleanliness, it didn't have anything.

Still it wasn't their all-American boy appearance that made the Reds contenders in the National League. It was a ferocious offense—fronted by Hall of Fame caliber stars in Bench, Rose, and Tony Perez. Together they formed the heart and soul of the Big Red Machine, a moniker said to be the creation of one of three people—Rose, Cincinnati *Enquirer* sportswriter Bob Hertzel, or Los Angeles *Herald-Examiner* baseball writer Bob Hunter.

Team historians John Erardi and Greg Rhodes trace the nickname to a July 4, 1969, article written by Hertzel. Hunter says he gave the Reds the name after hearing that Cincinnati had outslugged Philadelphia 19–17. Hunter thought of the Reds' uniform colors, and in previewing a series with the Dodgers, made mention of the invasion of the "Big Red Machine." Rose claims he hung the tag on the Reds at a time when Pete was driving a red 1934 Ford. That car was his little red machine, Rose said, and the team he played on was the Big Red Machine.

Regardless of its origin, the nickname became immensely popular, and the organization trademarked it. In 1970 the Big Red Machine's wrecking ball attack wreaked havoc on the National League. Cincinnati stormed to 102 victories, a franchise record at the time. The Reds won the Western Division by 14½ games and swept Pittsburgh in the National League Championship Series (NLCS) but was beaten by Baltimore in the World Series.

The wheels came off the Big Red Machine in '71. Problems began that January, when center fielder Bobby Tolan tore his Achilles tendon playing for the Reds' basketball team. Tolan missed spring training but still made an unusually quick recovery. By May he was able to begin working out. While running in the outfield at Dodger Stadium, Tolan broke down again. The man who had teamed with Rose at the top of the batting order in 1970, batted .316 and stolen a league-leading 57 bases, scored 112 runs, and legged out 56 extra-base hits was out for the season without having played a single game.

When Tolan went down with an injury, he took Cincinnati's speed with him. Reds second baseman Tommy Helms thought losing Tolan upset the balance of the team. The Reds were never out of a game with Tolan in the lineup, Helms said, because Bobby would get on base and the bombers—Bench, May, and Perez—would bring him home.

Tolan's injury was just the start of the Reds' troubles. Strange things were happening in Cincinnati's spring training in '71. Amid talk of a new National League dynasty, southpaw Jim Merritt, a 20-game winner in 1970, struggled with a sore left arm. May, who had launched 34 homers the season before and driven in 94 runs, collided with the Mets' Tim Foli at first base in an exhibition game in St. Petersburg, Florida, banged up his knee, and was lost for three weeks. Perez hurt his hand sliding into third and wouldn't be right physically the entire season. Shortstop Dave Concepcion tore ligaments in his right thumb and missed a month. By the time the Reds were ready to head north for their season opener, they did so minus Merritt and right-handed complement Wayne Simpson, who had been 14-3 the summer before and had led the league with an .824 winning percentage.

Injuries helped drop the defending league champions to a fourth-place finish behind front-running San Francisco. The Big Red Machine was in serious need of recharging, and Howsam responded. He had a history of building championship clubs, having arrived in St. Louis in August 1964 with the Cardinals nine games back in the pennant race and putting together deals that eventually delivered a World Series title. The Cardinals claimed another Series title in 1967 and repeated as league champions in '68.

Howsam was a Branch Rickey disciple. As owner and operator of the Class AAA Denver Bears, a club that had a working relationship with Rickey's Pittsburgh Pirates, Howsam had known the Mahatma since the 1950s. He had overcome a potentially disastrous flippant first encounter with Rickey and his son Branch Jr.

Upon their initial encounter Howsam rather loosely greeted the man known mainly as "Mr. Rickey" with an informal, "Hi, Branch!"

He then turned to Branch Jr.

"Hi, Twig!"

Howsam survived and went on to become a Rickey protégé. When the Mahatma was winding up his days as a Cardinals consultant in 1964, he advised team owner Gussie Busch to name Howsam the club's new GM. Howsam oversaw the Cardinals' rise to the top of baseball in the mid-1960s, with some help from his future Reds manager.

In 1965, when Howsam was GM in St. Louis, Anderson was hired to skipper the Cardinals' Rock Hill farm club in the Western Carolina League. Anderson didn't really know Howsam at the time. Sparky's immediate superior was Sheldon "Chief" Bender, a World War II veteran and Purple Heart recipient who spent sixty-four years in baseball as a player, manager, scout, scouting director, and farm system director.

Anderson soon discovered how Howsam operated when the GM called a meeting during spring training in '65 in St. Petersburg. The night before the meeting Anderson dined with Bender, Cardinals superscout Mo Mozzali, and coach George Kissell. Talk soon turned to Julian Javier, who had played second base for St. Louis since 1960. Known as "Hoolie" by some and "the Phantom" by Cardinals catcher Tim McCarver for his ability to avoid runners sliding into second, Javier was also considered one of the fastest men in baseball. He led the team in stolen bases every season from 1960 through 1963 and teamed with first baseman Bill White, shortstop Dick Groat, and third baseman Ken Boyer to form an all-Cardinal infield in the 1963 All-Star Game.

Still Mozzali, Kissell, and Bender spoke of the possibility of dealing Javier before the season started. Despite having been with the Cardinal organization just three weeks to that point, Anderson felt compelled to speak.

"Does he have good range?" he asked.

Yes, he was told. Javier had arguably the best range in the National League.

"Does he make the double play?"

Hoolie was the best, Anderson was told.

"Then why the hell," Sparky asked, "are you talking about trading him?"

In the clubhouse the next day, Bender, Mozzali, Kissell, big league boss Red Schoendienst, Anderson, and three other minor league managers met with Howsam. After Schoendienst talked about the team, Howsam turned to Mozzali, who brought up the possibility of a trade involving Javier.

"Mr. Howsam," Mozzali began, "we were talking at dinner last night, and Sparky here had some opinions that I think you might want him to bring out to all of us."

"Yes," Howsam replied. "I'd like to hear his opinion."

In his autobiography Anderson recalled being petrified. Three weeks with the organization and he's supposed to tell the brass what to do?

Anderson apologized for speaking out at dinner, but when Howsam repeated that he wanted his views, Sparky said it didn't seem logical to deal the league's number one man at his position for someone else's number two, three or four guy.

Howsam thanked Anderson for his views. Javier stayed with St. Louis and anchored the infield for the great St. Louis squads of the sixties. Anderson never took credit for the non-trade. What was more important to him was that he learned what kind of man his boss was. Howsam was a listener; he would hear any man's opinion. And he never considered himself above taking the counsel of even the newest and lowest-ranking man in his operation.

After three years in St. Louis, Howsam moved from the Gateway City to the Queen City. Employing Rickey's principles, he transformed the Reds from a shoestring operation to one of the sport's most sophisticated franchises.

Howsam fit perfectly in the conservative burg. He wasn't big-city slick or articulate, but as Sandy Hadden, the commissioner's aide, once said, Howsam was well respected and had a lot of friends who were influenced by what he thought.

With help from Wagner, his number two man, Howsam instituted a marketing strategy so refined that it rivaled what the Dodgers were doing in the foothills of Hollywood. For the first time in their long history the Reds aggressively sold season tickets. They expanded their base from twelve hundred to seventeen thousand and through in-stadium questionnaires and phone calls built a list of eighty thousand fans on computer.

After drawing as many as one million fans in a season just four times prior to Howsam's arrival, the Reds became the first team aside from the Dodgers to draw at least two million in back-to-back seasons. It helped that the Reds moved on June 30, 1970, from tiny Crosley Field, with its 29,600 seating capacity, to Riverfront Stadium, which at 53,000 could accommodate almost twice as many paying customers. In 1972 local brewers produced a print ad highlighting the fact that Riverfront was the lone stadium in the world located within one mile of four major breweries.

Cincinnati was a beer-driven culture and economy, and its brewers had been major sponsors of the Reds for decades. When the team played in Crosley Field, buildings beyond the outfield wall were plastered and painted with beer ads, and additional signs were posted on the foul poles inside the park. Beginning in 1942 the Burger Beer Broadcasting Network and later Wiedemann sponsored the Reds on radio. In 1956 Hudepohl sponsored the team on TV, an association that would last through the Reds' championship years of 1975–76.

By 1970 Howsam not only had a new state-of-the-art stadium, but he had also succeeded in rebuilding the Reds into a state-of-the-art team. It was a juggernaut that in 1970 rumbled to the franchise's first postseason appearance since 1961, and Howsam was its architect.

But as the Big Red Machine prepared to rev up for the 1972 season, its power gear had become a question mark.

Johnny Lee Bench was named the National League's Most Valuable Player in 1970 after hammering 45 homers, plating 145 runs, and batting .293—all of this at the tender age of twenty-two. A native of Oklahoma City, one-eighth Choctaw Indian on his father's side, Bench was already drawing comparisons to the great catchers of the past: Mickey Cochrane, Gabby Hartnett, Bill Dickey, Josh Gibson, Roy Campanella, and Yogi Berra.

Walter Alston, who skippered the Dodgers in Brooklyn and Los Angeles, said at the time that Bench would be the National League's catcher in the All-Star Game "for the next 10 years." From the day in 1967 day when he completed his minor league apprenticeship with the Buffalo Bisons, where he crushed 23 home runs—one of his every four hits was a homer—and was tabbed Minor League Player of the Year, the career arc for Bench was progressively upward.

His future manager knew it. Anderson never forgot the first time he saw Bench play. It was the fall of 1965, and Anderson traveled along with the Cardinals' other minor league managers to the Florida Instructional League to check out the organization's prospects. Sparky was coaching third for St. Louis's Instructional League team in a game against a combined Cincinnati-Houston squad. From his vantage point in the coaching box, Anderson began studying the opposing catcher. Watching him work, Anderson thought, "This boy's a good-looking catcher. He must've played for awhile."

Between innings Anderson asked players on his team about the opposing catcher. It was the first time he would hear the name "Johnny Bench." Anderson was told that Bench was still a baby—only seventeen and just out of high school in Oklahoma. He'd only been playing professionally for one season, at Tampa.

It was hard for Anderson to believe that Bench was so skilled at such a young age. Two years passed before Anderson saw Bench again, this time in a night game in Tampa between the Reds' Buffalo farm team and a club comprised of their other minor league teams. Bench was catching for Buffalo, and Anderson noted that the kid's body had filled out and his actions behind the plate were more polished.

Berra noted the same thing. The former backstop for fourteen Yankees' World Series teams, Berra had seen Bench play in the minors. "He can do it all *now*," Berra said then. Ted Williams signed a baseball for Bench at the time, the inscription reading, "A Hall of Famer for sure!"

Bench joined the big club in August 1967 and in '68 spent his first full season in the majors. His impact was immediate. Collecting 15 homers, 82 RBIs, and a .275 batting average, Bench was named NL Rookie of the Year, the first time a catcher had earned the award. He claimed the first of his ten consecutive Gold Glove awards, the first rookie to win the honor. He made an appearance in that summer's All-Star Game in the Houston

Astrodome. It was the first of ten straight Midsummer Classics for Bench, who was named to the NL team fourteen times.

In '68 Bench had been named an alternate behind Jerry Grote of the Mets. But in an NL locker room before the game, Giants great Willie Mays approached the Oklahoma kid.

"You," Mays told Bench, "should've been the starting catcher."

Bench was the NL's starting catcher the following season, when he improved his season totals to 26 HRs, 90 RBIs, and a .293 batting average. The 1970 season was Bench's best, and the stories spread about him sounded like urban legends:

He could hold seven baseballs in one of his huge hands, and his big paws allowed him to adopt the hinged glove and one-handed catching style popularized in the mid-1960s by Randy Hundley of the Chicago Cubs. "They're the biggest mauleys I've ever seen," Cubs skipper Leo Durocher said;

He once caught a pitch from Reds fastballer Jim Maloney *bare-handed*;

Trained by his father, Ted, to throw 254 feet from a crouch—more than twice the distance from home plate to second base—Bench's beeline bullet throws to the bag amazed even his own pitchers, who wished *they* could throw like Bench.

Bench was confident in his abilities; he predicted he would win the NL's Rookie of the Year honors and was once quoted as saying, "I can throw out any man alive." But he was also humble. When Anderson said Bench would do more for baseball than Babe Ruth, Bench asked that he not be spoken of in such glowing terms.

Bench had difficulty comprehending that kids were idolizing him the same way he had idolized fellow Oklahoman Mickey Mantle. Part of the reason was that it had been such a short time since he had been on the other end of the hero worship.

Following the breakout season in 1970, Bench was ready for another big year in '71. Usually a slow starter, Bench instead got off to the best start he'd had in baseball. Injuries, however, helped bring down the Big

Red Machine, and the incredible 70-30 start they had enjoyed in 1970 was nowhere in evidence in '71. The Reds couldn't put their "real" club on the field, Anderson said. They started poorly and their situation did not improve.

Bench believed the Reds had resigned themselves to the belief that this wasn't going to be their season. Realizing their chase of the Giants and Dodgers was futile, the Reds went into a slide. By August 1 they were a season-high eighteen games behind in the standings.

Bench played much of the summer in a funk. What Sparky saw was a guy trying to carry the load and thus pressing too much. His batting average dipped from .293 to .238, his home runs from 45 to 27, his RBIs from 148 to 61.

Reds fans resented watching their star catcher/slugger struggle. Bench knew Cincinnati was a very conservative town. Its German-Bohemian traditions were centered on hard work and production. The Cincinnati citizenry watched as Bench appeared on *Mission Impossible* and drew a smoldering glance from Lesley Ann Warren. He joined actress Ursula Andress, dancer Lola Falana, singer Gloria Loring, and the Gold Diggers dancers in entertaining U.S. troops at Christmas on Bob Hope's USO Tour. He played golf with Arnold Palmer and was introduced to Frank Sinatra and Spiro Agnew.

All of the above might have gone over in New York, Los Angeles, or Chicago, but Cincinnati was another story. The negative response from fans bothered him and he withdrew. In his mind, he had gone from MVP to MDP—Most Disappointing Player. He was jeered by Reds fans as he walked to the plate in Riverfront Stadium and, following an out, was booed even more loudly as he headed back to the dugout.

Bench took the booing personally and felt the fans showed a lack of memory and lack of appreciation. Chicago Cubs star third baseman Ron Santo thought the same. "How quickly they forget," he told Bench during a Cubs-Reds game.

As the second baseman for the Houston Astros in 1971, Joe Morgan watched the Bench saga unfold from the outside. In his autobiography Morgan theorized that Bench's problem in 1971 was that he realized he might never have another year like 1970 again. The Reds catcher was a mature guy on the outside, Morgan thought, but there was no way he could be that mature on the inside at such a young age.

Morgan knew it was hard in a young player's mind to keep boos from affecting him. When you're twenty-three or twenty-four, you want cheers all the time. Morgan believed it difficult to say to a man like Bench that he had to accept the bad with the good. Johnny had only had the good. Now he was getting the bad.

The slump and the booing were just part of Bench's bad times. As his income had begun to rise, Bench began looking for good investments. By his own admission, he was a frugal guy—mainly, he thought, because he had been raised pulling cotton for two cents a pound and delivering newspapers. However, many of his investments went bad.

Bench and Rose, the two most visible stars of the Big Red Machine, went into a number of businesses together. In early 1970 they opened the Rose-Bench Lincoln-Mercury dealership in Dayton with a wheeler-dealer named Hy Ullner. Ullner was a self-made millionaire who operated Rink's Bargain City. He went on TV as the "Bargain City Kid," complete with a holster and six-shooters, and shot the TV screen full of bargains.

Despite Ullner's salesmanship, the Rose-Bench dealership failed, largely due to the fact that Dayton at the time was second in the nation in unemployment and was lurching through one labor strike after another. Most people in town weren't in the mood to buy cars, and it wasn't long before Rose and Bench had to close their dealership.

Bench lost $27,000 in the venture, about one-third of his savings at the time. Bench and Rose went in on another venture, but that didn't work out either. Rumors circulated in and around Cincinnati of differences between the two Reds stars. But the business problems Bench and Rose experienced didn't affect their relationship in the locker room. Rose, the Cincinnati Kid, had taken Bench under his wing when Johnny had first come up to the majors. And even though Bench believed his breakout 1970 season had been a challenge for Pete—who was no longer the only star in town—Bench knew that more than anything else, Rose wanted to win.

What did affect their relationship was a fan newsletter called *Pete Rose's Reds Alert*. Rose put his name on it, but the newsletter was written by Bill Matthews, a guy Bench believed showed up at the ballpark only once or twice during the season. Bench thought Matthews issued some "cheap shots" about some of the Reds' players. Some of the players had hard feelings, particularly since Pete's name was on the newsletter.

Bench went to the front office and stated that while freedom of the press was fine, the newsletter bearing Rose's name was hurting the team. Bench took his case to Rose, confronting him before a game about having a newsletter that was being used to cut on his teammates. Management sided with Bench. Rose, who was being paid to have his name on *Reds Alert*, was furious.

Bench noticed Pete's "square jaw" thrust out farther than ever. The two stars went a long time without saying a word to one another. A season-long slump, nagging injuries, cascades of boos on his home turf, bad business deals, and now a fractured relationship with Rose had all been heaped on Bench in the space of a season.

But what lay ahead was far worse. In September 1972, as the rejuvenated Reds were rolling toward the Western Division title and Bench had bounced back from his problems and was en route to a second NL MVP award, he was rocked to his heels.

Following what was supposed to be routine physical examinations the Reds receive every September, Bench was given shocking news by one of the doctors: "We've found a spot on your lung."

A million thoughts raced through the reeling mind of the Reds' catcher. Why? How? I'm strong as a bull, Bench thought. I've never smoked.

Finally, he was left with just one thought: "What now?"

It was a question Bench would carry with him as the Big Red Machine made a push to take care of unfinished business.

Bench's and the Reds' biggest challenges to National League supremacy, Roberto Clemente and the Pittsburgh Pirates, had taken care of business the previous October, beating Baltimore in a classic seven-game World

Series. After the Bucs won Game Seven in Baltimore, Orioles owner Jerry Hoffberger entered the lathery Pittsburgh locker room, sought out Clemente, and told the Pirates right fielder, "You're the best of all."

Hoffberger's words carried weight with a man who felt he had been denied the acclaim given to other great outfielders of his era—Mantle, Mays, Aaron, Frank Robinson.

Pirates teammate Bill Mazeroski called Clemente "the total ballplayer." Maz thought some players were considered superstars when they were really just super hitters. In Maz's mind there were only three true superstar outfielders in the National League in Clemente's era—Mays, Aaron, and Roberto. While people talked about the homers Mays and Aaron slugged, they forgot that for most of his career Clemente played home games in Pittsburgh's Forbes Field, where center field was the deepest of any park in the league.

Despite their many years of playing in the same league at the same time, Clemente, Mays, and Aaron had combined to form a dream outfield on just three occasions, three magical midsummer days—the 1965, '66, and '67 All-Star Games. Together the three legends would patrol the same expanse a total of twenty-three innings. Clemente and Mays, however, did play in the same outfield in 1954 in the Puerto Rican Winter League for the Santurce Cangrejeros.

In 1954 Mays was a twenty-three-year-old sensation with the world champion New York Giants and was only recently removed from his stunning over-the-shoulder catch of Vic Wertz's deep drive to center field in Game One of the World Series in the Polo Grounds. Clemente was fresh off his rookie season with the Montreal Royals, the Brooklyn Dodgers' top farm team. It had been a frustrating campaign for Clemente, whose playing time was limited by a Dodger organization trying to hide their prospect from opposing scouts.

A rule at the time (Rule V) stated that any player who received a bonus of at least $4,000 had to be placed on the major league roster within a year or he could be drafted for $4,000. Thus though Clemente batted just 148 times for the Royals and hit only .257 with 2 home runs and 12 RBIs, he was chosen by the Pirates with the first pick of the Rule V draft the following winter.

Had he not given his word years before to Dodgers scout Al Campanis to sign with Brooklyn, Clemente might instead have been a member of the Milwaukee Braves, who had offered him a $30,000 bonus, three times what the Dodgers offered. Clemente and Aaron had come that close to sharing the same outfield for the Braves.

In their brief time on the same Winter League team, Clemente and Mays contributed to a lineup nicknamed El Escaudron del Panico (the Panic Squad) and, together with a young shortstop and eventual Most Valuable Player named Don Zimmer, helped Santurce go 5-0 to win the round-robin tournament.

Six years later, in the Pirates' 1960 World Series season, Clemente, short-stop Dick Groat, and third baseman Don Hoak were the three players who contributed most to Pittsburgh's pennant. Clemente was a five-tool player whose career path had been guided in part by Mays's advice: "Listen, Rob-bie, don't let the pitchers show you up. Get mean when you go to bat. If they try to knock you down, act like it doesn't bother you. Get up and hit the ball. Show 'em."

Clemente showed them, and in the summer of '60 he, Groat, and Hoak were MVP candidates. Groat won the award, and Hoak finished second. Clemente finished *eighth*. Maz thought the snub affected Clemente on a personal level and made him bitter.

Some believe it took Clemente several years to get over it. The reality was that Roberto never got over it. He refused to wear his 1960 World Series ring, preferring instead his All-Star ring from the same season. It wasn't that Clemente felt he should have won and didn't that bothered him. It was that he couldn't see how he had finished eighth in the voting.

While Clemente rarely set goals, the snub made him set one in 1961. "I made up my mind," he said later, "to win the batting title in 1961."

Opposing pitchers paid the price for the MVP slight. Clemente raked enemy hurlers, leading the league in '61 with a .351 batting average while banging 23 homers, driving in 89 runs, and scoring 100. Writer Larry

Bortstein thought it a violent reprisal from Roberto. Clemente, perhaps still leaning on the advice from Mays, did not disagree. "I play better," he stated then, "when I am mad."

He led NL outfielders with 27 assists and gained a Gold Glove award for his fielding excellence. He would win a Gold Glove every year for the remainder of his career.

Clemente's outfield play was almost without peer. His cannon-like throws—he squeezed a rubber ball to strengthen his throwing arm—terrorized base runners. Fans around the league loved it when a ball was launched deep to right field and would lean forward in anticipation as Clemente, sometimes out of sight of viewers if he was chasing a drive deep into the corner, would retrieve the ball, whirl, and unleash a laser-like throw from the deepest recesses of the outfield. Still the proud Clemente took it as a slight when people said he had "one of the best arms" in the game. "If you can find one better," he would say, "let me know where."

Like teammate Manny Sanguillen, Clemente was an exceptional bad-ball hitter. Roberto lashed at pitches outside the strike zone but made contact while doing so. Beginning in 1961 he had started using a heavier bat to slow down his swing. He often hit off his front foot, and replays show Clemente's back foot completely off the ground.

When Clemente crushed a drive to deep right-center off Detroit's Mickey Lolich in the 1971 All-Star Game, NBC color analyst Tony Kubek broke down the mechanics of Clemente's swing: *"Here's that Clemente swing once again. . . . Look at that bat stay back, cocked. . . . Now a trademark: hitting off the front foot. Look at that right foot, the rear foot, a foot off the ground, something that is not advisable as a hitter. But don't tell that to Clemente or Hank Aaron."*

Teammates and opponents knew Clemente could hit and knew also that he didn't need a strike to swing the bat. He was rambunctious at the plate, in the field, and on the bases. Jack Hernon of *The Sporting News* noted fans in ballparks "oohing" and "aahing" as Roberto raced around the base paths in his signature style.

"Robbie was something special," teammate and second baseman Dave Cash recalls. "In the outfield he was exceptional; there wasn't anything he couldn't do. He was great in the locker room as well, especially with Latin players like Jackie Hernandez."

For all his daring play, Clemente was considered by some a hypochondriac. It was a charge he hotly disputed. He insisted he was a great player because he could perform despite the assorted aches that afflicted him over the course of his career: a severed ligament in his thigh, fever, left shoulder injury, intestinal virus, strained tendons in both heels, and in particular a lower back pain due at least in part to having had his car rammed at sixty miles per hour by a drunken driver.

Clemente would roll his neck and stretch his chronically bad back before taking his place deep in the batter's box. Bobby Bragan, who played for the Phillies and then the Dodgers, said once that the case history on Clemente was that the worse Roberto felt, the better he played.

Entering the 1972 season, Clemente was closing in on the club record for games played set by Honus Wagner, the Flying Dutchman. Wagner led at the time 2,432–2,331. Roberto noted that it had taken Wagner eighteen years to reach his number while Clemente was just beginning his seventeenth season. It should be noted that in the Flying Dutchmen's era full major league seasons ranged from 139 to 154 games while Clemente's campaigns were 154 to 162 games.

Hypochondria was one complaint critics leveled at Clemente. He knew there were others, knew people said he complained and that he was moody and selfish and didn't get along with teammates. But he played the game the way it is supposed to be played. He wanted to be remembered, he said, for the kind of player he was. "I give everything I have," he told reporters, "according to my ability."

And yet that wasn't enough to silence the critics of a man who would win four batting titles; compile non-league-leading averages of .320, .317, .345, .352, and .342; and carry a .318 lifetime average into the '72 season. Still the snubs continued. Clemente recalled a 1965 All-Star publication that carried a feature on the fading Mantle and omitted Clemente: "I hit

.329 that year and Mickey Mantle hit .255 and they put Mickey Mantle in right field just to get him on the team," Clemente said then. "Why wasn't I put on the team in right field?"

Clemente knew the answers. He played in Pittsburgh, not in New York or Los Angeles. Sportswriters and fans failed to appreciate the nuances of his game. He was a Latino who spoke broken English, and he was a Puerto Rican in a city in which just a small part of the population could identify with him. "I have to come to New York for the fans to give me a night," he said in September 1971, when the Puerto Rican community honored him with a night at Shea Stadium.

The native of Puerto Rico was a proud and dignified man, handsome with noble features that appeared to be carved from marble. Then baseball commissioner Bowie Kuhn said Clemente had about him a "touch of royalty." He was the Great One, "El Magnifico" to his Latino fans, and a man of fierce ethnic pride. Clemente was of mixed descent. Both black and Latino, he saw himself as a representative of Latin America.

As a Spanish-speaking man of color, Clemente encountered racial discrimination throughout his life and career. Just as Jackie Robinson had opened the door for African American athletes by breaking the color barrier in 1947, Clemente believed the way he played baseball helped make the lives of Latin Americans, and in particular underprivileged Puerto Ricans, better.

"Always, they said Babe Ruth was the best there was," he said after edging Dodgers great Sandy Koufax for the NL's MVP award in 1966. "They said you'd really have to be something to be like Babe Ruth. But Babe Ruth was an American player. What we needed was a Puerto Rican player they could say that about, someone to look up to and try to equal."

In 1970 Clemente and the Bucs led baseball into the modern era from a sartorial standpoint. Their two-tone caps—mustard gold with a black bill—set the standard for the seventies and beyond. The new uniforms earned national attention as Pittsburgh broke a ten-year drought by winning the East and advancing to the postseason for the first time since 1960. In 2013 the Pirates channeled their predecessors and unveiled alternate uniforms that would be worn for Sunday games and were a throwback to the 1970–75 teams. Once again the uniforms helped usher in a change in the franchise's fortunes. Just as Clemente, Stargell, Sanguillen, and company had done decades before, Andrew McCutchen, Francisco Liriano, Pedro Alvarez, and the 2013 Bucs broke extended droughts by earning the Pirates' first postseason appearance since 1992 and snapping the longest stretch of consecutive losing seasons—twenty—in the history of North American professional sports.

Clemente's second world championship came in October 1971 and was the product of his MVP performance. Against a reigning world champion Orioles squad that flashed four 20-game winners that season, Clemente batted .414, hit two homers, and sent Baltimore base runners scurrying back to their bases with his rocket-like pegs from right field.

The triumph over the Orioles came before a massive television audience and, together with a victory over Mays and the San Francisco Gants in the NLCS, finally earned for Clemente the national recognition he deserved. *The Sporting News* previewed the 1972 major league season with cover art of Clemente alongside the title "Pirates' Mister Big."

Bruce Kison was a teammate of Roberto's in 1971–72. "Besides being a hell of a ballplayer, he was an interesting character," says Kison. "He was a leader, a showman the way he performed."

Clemente believed he had been born to play baseball and that God had given him the talent to play the game at its highest level. But baseball did not define him. When Dr. Martin Luther King was assassinated on April 4, 1968, Clemente was distraught. To honor the slain civil rights leader, Clemente convinced teammates to stand with him and not play the scheduled season opener against Houston on April 8—the day before Dr. King's burial. Due to Clemente's extraordinary stand, the Pirates and Astros agreed to postpone their opener to April 10 in observance of Dr. King's memorial service.

Like Dr. King, Clemente championed racial equality and social justice. Roberto was angered when his friend Vic Power, "El Gran Señor" and the first black Puerto Rican to play in the American League, was dragged off the team bus by local authorities for buying a Coke at a whites-only service station. Clemente himself was the subject of racial slurs and taunts, some by his own teammates. Sportswriters watched his basket catches and referred to him in print as the "Puerto Rican hot dog." At times they exaggerated his accent when quoting him.

Some writers who covered him considered Clemente to be anything but perfect. To them Clemente was vain, occasionally arrogant, and often intolerant and unforgiving, and there were moments when they thought for certain Clemente had cornered the market on self-pity. Critics believed the Bucs' star acted as if the world had declared all-out war on Clemente, when in fact Roberto was lavished with affection.

At the same time no one would deny that through all of Clemente's battles there was about him an undeniable charisma. Perhaps that was Roberto's true essence. Pirates writer Phil Musick thought Clemente won so much of people's attention and affection that they demanded of him what no man can give: perfection.

Clemente knew the world was far from perfect, but the racial barbs and insults confused a man who insisted he didn't see color. "I see people," Clemente said then. "I always respect everyone and thanks to God, my mother and father taught me never to hate, never to dislike someone based on their color."

As the Pirates prepared to defend their World Series title, Clemente commented that a goal of his was to get his three thousandth career hit. But he had a larger destiny in mind. He wanted to help build a utopian sports city for the children of Puerto Rico. "If I get the money to start this, if they tell me they'll give us the money and I have to be there to get it started," he said then, "I'll quit right now."

He was one of the game's greatest players, but more important, he was a great humanitarian. If you have the chance to make things better for people and you don't, he would say, you are wasting your time on earth.

Clemente was speaking of issues bigger than baseball. But the Bucs' clubhouse leader was about to strike a blow for solidarity in the players' union and make things better for generations of players who followed.

CHAPTER THREE

The first strike in Major League Baseball history didn't last long—thirteen days, to be exact, from April 1 to 13, 1972. Eighty-six games were canceled, never to be made up. Most clubs lost six to eight games; San Diego and Houston had nine games erased, the highest number in the National League.

While the strike wasn't long-lasting, its impact was. It set the stage for future labor disputes in each of America's four major sports.

What took place in those thirteen days was as intriguing as much of what would happen on the field in the 1972 season. The principals on the front lines of the strike—Marvin Miller and Dick Moss; John Gaherin and the hard-line owners—waged a war as engrossing as the pulse-quickening confrontations that would take place in October when Roberto Clemente dug in against Don Gullett and Vida Blue fired fastballs to Al Kaline.

Miller, the executive director of the Major League Baseball Players Association (MLBPA) from 1966 to 1982, had grown up in Depression-era Brooklyn. His father Alexander was a garment salesman; his mother Gertrude, a schoolteacher. Miller rooted for the Dodgers as he worked his way through school. He graduated from high school by age fifteen; by nineteen he owned a BA degree in economics from New York University. Newly married, he took a job with the New York City Welfare Department. It was with that department that he joined his first union—the State, County and Municipal Workers of America. Disqualified from serving in the military in World War II due to a shoulder damaged at birth, Miller joined the National War Labor Relations Board. The federal agency had been created to settle labor disputes and ensure that there would be no strikes or lockouts to slow FDR's "Arsenal of Democracy."

Miller later worked for the International Association of Machinists and United Auto Workers. In 1950 he joined the staff of the United Steelworkers, becoming its principal economic adviser and assistant to its president. In time he became the United Steelworkers chief economist and negotiator. He was appointed to labor-management panels by President John Kennedy and his successor, Lyndon Johnson.

A man who could smile from beneath his slicked-back hair and matinee-idol mustache even while losing an argument, Miller was quiet and urbane. But he loved baseball and loved a good fight. To him baseball players were among the most exploited workers in America.

In 1966 Miller visited major league spring training camps in a campaign to be elected executive director of the Major League Baseball Players Association. Miller was voted in, but his hiring sent shock waves along the corridors of power. Owners well aware of Miller's background in labor warned against his getting the job, but the players, by now less naïve and increasingly restless over their small union gains, sensed the owners' fear and gave Miller the job.

Being head of the MLBPA seemed a thankless task. There was a war chest of just $5,400 and no staff. Over the next seventeen years Miller would forge one of the most unlikely yet strongest unions in the nation, all the while battling the entrenched power of the owners.

In 1968 Miller negotiated the MLBPA's first collective bargaining agreement. Players were given a nearly 43 percent increase in minimum salary, from $7,000 to $10,000. The deal brought structure to relations between players and owners, but that foundation was tested in 1969, when St. Louis Cardinals All-Star outfielder Curt Flood feuded with management over his salary and protested what he viewed as a "get-even" trade to Philadelphia.

Flood informed Commissioner Bowie Kuhn that he would entertain offers for his playing services from all clubs. Flood sued MLB and Kuhn. The commissioner cited the reserve clause, which stated that a player must sit out a season before he could negotiate with other teams. The celebrated case made its way to the Supreme Court in March 1972 and was settled that June, the court siding with the owners in a 5–3–1 vote.

Flood's loss was ultimately his fellow players' gain. In 1974 A's 25-game winner and Cy Young recipient Catfish Hunter challenged the reserve clause and was declared a free agent. One year later, the reserve clause was abolished, and the era of free agency began.

The floodgates had opened, and Miller was at the forefront of MLB's economic revolution. Kuhn's initial impression of the union boss, formed at their first meeting in 1966, was favorable. To the commissioner, Miller was all low-key charm. Miller offered no threats or demands; Kuhn saw him as neither "pussycat nor radical." What he was, in the eyes of Kuhn, was pedantic, a man who fussed over details and was unwilling to deal straightforwardly with the issues.

Miller, meanwhile, had at first thought the 6-foot-5 Kuhn an imposing figure. Yet Miller later recalled realizing one didn't have to deal with Kuhn for very long to become unimpressed with his physical stature. In time Miller considered Kuhn the single most important contributor to the success of the MLBPA. The union boss believed the commissioner's moves constantly backfired and his attempts at leadership created division. Paraphrasing Voltaire on the Almighty, Miller insisted that if Bowie Kuhn had never existed, the MLBPA would have had to invent him.

Moss was a bright young Harvard Law graduate who was believed by many to be the sharpest arbitration lawyer in the Steelworkers' legal department. He battled often, and with success, with the likes of American Can and Bethlehem Steel. A devoted baseball fan, he had moved to New York from Beaver Falls, Pennsylvania, to combine his love of the game with his love for law. Though he worked well with Miller, the two men were vastly different. Older by fifteen years, Miller, hardened as he was by the Great Depression, saw labor relations as life-and-death issues. To Moss they were a game. Be it chess or baseball, Moss loved games. And he *had* to win.

In his autobiography Kuhn regarded Moss as a counterbalance to Miller. To the commissioner, Moss was a real fan, a man who liked to talk about the game and cared about it. Moss was a dedicated fan of the Pittsburgh Pirates. Opening Day left him giddy. His Steelworkers boss, Ben Fisher, said once that if there was a conflict between watching a ball game and negotiating a contract, one never knew what Moss would do.

Kuhn thought Moss neither the philosopher nor the zealot, as he saw Miller. Moss was irreverent to the point of sassy, but practical; he knew the realities of the marketplace. He was also a personality with a human touch. In a 1968 meeting one of Moss's wisecracks had left Kuhn demonstrably angered. Moss reacted by reaching out. "I don't know why you got so mad but maybe I was wrong," he told Kuhn. "Can we forget it?"

Under no circumstances could Kuhn imagine Miller saying anything like that. Miller, Kuhn thought, *never* admitted he was wrong. Where Miller was seen as ultra serious, Moss was lighthearted, with a ready wit and a sense of fun. Miller's adversaries mocked what they considered to be his deep, wrenching sighs and funereal visage; Moss, by contrast, once wheeled into San Diego Padres president Buzzie Bavasi's reserved parking space just for kicks.

Confronting Miller and Moss was Gaherin, a street-smart New Yorker who was the director of the Player Relations Committee. Hired by the owners in 1967, Gaherin was a veteran negotiator who knew firsthand what life was like in the trenches of a labor war. He had been on the front lines of such battles involving the airline and newspaper industries. Regarding the latter, Gaherin, as president of the Publishers Association of New York, had been through the brutal union battles of the 1960s. His resume included his having been vice president for labor at American Airlines; labor chief for various northeastern railroads, and head of the Eastern Conference of Carriers, a joint bargaining association of railroads.

Gaherin's feel for gritty, labor-relation trench warfare went well beyond plush corporate boardrooms. And while his public persona was tight-lipped—Miller thought of him as the "very professional John Gaherin"—the man was a character. His Irish wisdom and jokes had been handed down to him by his father, and Kuhn found that tense moments in backroom meetings were often defused by Gaherin's snappingly effective comments on the game's characters and colorful stories of past labor negotiations.

One such story harkened back to Gaherin's days as chairman of the

New York Harbor Negotiating Committee. In the midst of a strike, Gaherin obtained a back-to-work order that he presented to the union chief. The man was unimpressed. "Well, now, that's a pretty piece of paper," the union chief said. "Will that thing steer a tugboat?"

Kuhn thought Gaherin an excellent student of human nature, as any successful negotiator needs to be, and quickly and accurately figured out the good guys from the bad. Sizing up the two sides as they prepared for battle in the spring of '72, Kuhn saw a potential problem for owners, and it lay in public relations. Of all Miller's talents his greatest may have been his ability to cultivate the press. He was a superb communicator, as effective with the press as anyone Kuhn had ever seen in the sports field. And that superiority with the media, Kuhn knew, was going to be a major problem for Gaherin. John's backroom humor didn't translate publicly, and while he worked at courting the media, he was never able to do it with the success Miller enjoyed. Still Kuhn held out hope. Gaherin, the commissioner thought, was a "skilled professional."

The focus of the disagreements between labor and management was binding arbitration and player pensions. The end result was that MLB owners agreed to an increase of $500,000 in pension fund payments. While players were not paid for the missed games at the start of the 1972 season, they did earn the right to salary arbitration, which remains a big part of the game more than forty years later.

The ultimate fallout of the 1972 MLB strike was that players gained a realization of how much power they wielded. It would take just four years for them to usher in the era of free agency.

What should be remembered about the historic strike is that it could have been avoided. In his autobiography Miller contended that the last thing he had expected was a players' strike, that it caught him unawares. He also thought the issue said to be the cause of the strike was "only a mask" for the real issue: power.

According to Miller, club owners wanted to bring to an abrupt halt the progress being made by the Players Association. They decided the best way to do this was to either provoke a strike, which they were confident they would win, or force the Players Association to back down and accept what Miller felt was an "unreasonable" position.

By 1972 players' health care costs had climbed by about $500,000 per year since 1969. The Players Association wanted owners to meet that rise in costs. They also wanted increased payments to the pension plan in order that retirement benefits could be adjusted to match the 17 percent increase in the cost of living since 1969. The increase would bring the owners' annual cost to $6.5 million. Miller had a proposal that would ease their financial pain: since the pension plan had amassed a surplus of $800,000, that sum could be applied to the benefits increase. The end result would be that the owners' out-of-pocket costs would be substantially reduced.

Miller and the Players Association felt their requests were modest, particularly since Major League Baseball had just signed a four-year, $70 million deal with NBC-TV for broadcast rights to the *Game of the Week*, the All-Star Game, and the World Series.

Negotiations were glacial, in both mood and movement. Yet Miller did not see signs of trouble. On his annual spring training trip in early March, Miller met with seven major league teams to discuss pension negotiations and never mentioned the possibility of a strike.

Gaherin made an offer of $500,000 per year on health care contributions, but the bosses balked at increasing retirement benefits. Still since surplus income from the pension fund could be used toward retirement benefits without additional cost to the owners, it seemed to Miller a settlement might be within reach.

Instead the situation quickly spiraled downward. As Miller prepared to meet with the Chicago White Sox in Sarasota, Gaherin issued an announcement: "The owners aren't going to increase pension benefits at all," he stated, "and we're going to reduce our offer on health care."

Gaherin pulled the offer of $500,000 and reduced it to $400,000. The perception among the owners was that the union was weak and this was the time to take it on.

Miller felt the owners had reduced a bargaining position they already knew to be inadequate. As far as the union boss was concerned, this amounted to baiting the Players Association into a strike.

Where Miller had earlier seen the possibility of a settlement, he now saw something else. His mindset in meeting with the White Sox the next day was much different than it had been in his prior meetings with clubs that spring. "Negotiations will continue and there's always the possibility we'll reach a settlement," he told White Sox players. "But it's beginning to seem unlikely."

Over the next ninety minutes, Miller informed the White Sox of the importance of keeping the players' retirement benefits on the same level as living costs. If the benefits were not adjusted, he explained, rising inflation over the next 25–30 years, when the players would be eligible for their pensions, would drive down the worth of their benefits to a fraction of their current value.

The options, Miller said, were to stand or fold. He outlined each option, what was involved in a walkout, and the procedures the union would follow until the expiration of the current benefits plan on March 31. Before leaving the Chisox camp, Miller asked club player representative Jay Johnstone to conduct a strike authorization vote.

Johnstone had the reputation of being a clubhouse prankster. He nailed teammates' cleats to the floor, dressed up as a member of the grounds crew and dragged the infield between innings, and climbed on the dugout roof to walk to the concession stands to get a hot dog.

This was no time to clown, however. A strike vote would be baseball's first since 1946, when Robert Murphy, formerly a negotiator for the National Labor Relations Board, attempted to get the Pittsburgh Pirates to engage in a walkout in order to gain collective bargaining rights. Murphy disliked the reserve clause in player contracts that allowed team owners to have control of players' services. Murphy argued that players should have more rights, including the right of salary arbitration and the right of contract.

Murphy's plans were thwarted by Commissioner Albert "Happy" Chandler, a fiscal conservative who had served his native Kentucky both in the

U.S. Senate and as governor and had hoped to be FDR's running mate in the 1944 election.

Passed over in favor of another Midwestern senator, Harry S. Truman of Missouri, Chandler eventually resigned his seat in the U.S. Senate to succeed Kennesaw Mountain Landis, baseball's first commissioner. The Judge—Landis had served as judge of the U.S. District Court for the Northern District of Illinois—had died on November 25, 1944, after being hospitalized in October with a severe cold and then suffering a heart attack while in the hospital.

A multi-sport athlete in his youth, Chandler used his folksy charm to the benefit of baseball during World War II. Major league owners fearful of seeing their players made eligible for the draft during the war wanted a commissioner who had the political skills needed to protect their interests in the nation's capital. With his down-home Southern drawl, his willingness to serenade acquaintances with his version of "My Old Kentucky Home," and his reputation as a "preening politician" and "hand-shaking, baby-kissing practitioner of the [political] arts," Chandler was the perfect man to represent baseball on Capitol Hill.

Nicknamed "Happy" due to his jovial nature, Chandler was generally a friend of organized labor. His approval of Jackie Robinson's contract with the Brooklyn Dodgers that integrated major league baseball and his establishing of the first pension fund led him to be called the "player's commissioner."

In the case of the Pirates' proposed walkout, however, Chandler sided with management. His motives may have stemmed from a situation early in 1946 in which the Mexican baseball league, fronted by Jorge Pasquel and his four brothers, took campaign funds from the impending Mexican presidential election in order to offer signing bonuses and lucrative salaries to American baseball players. Some of the salaries being offered were reportedly three times the major league salaries.

Angered at seeing the American pastime raided, Chandler announced a five-year ban on any major leaguer who jumped to the Mexican League and did not return the majors by April 1, 1946. Some eighteen players ignored the commissioner's ban. Future Hall of Famers Ted Williams, Stan Musial, and Phil Rizzuto were among those targeted by the Mexican League, but each declined the lavish contracts. Sal "the Barber" Maglie and Mickey Owen agreed to play in Mexico but then returned prior to Chandler's deadline.

Aided by labor spies on the Bucs' ball club, Chandler moved quickly to squash the Pirates' walkout. Working with Pirates team officials, the commissioner's office organized a contingency plan that included a team of replacement players should the regulars walk. The team would have included Pirates Hall of Fame shortstop Honus Wagner, who was seventy-two years old at the time.

Twenty-six years after the Pirates' walkout ended before it really began, the White Sox voted 25–0 to support a strike. Miller followed by revisiting over the next eight days the teams with which he had previously met prior to Gaherin's announcement. Miller said that each team voted unanimously to support the strike.

The March 31 deadline was fast approaching, and Miller's hopes for a settlement were fading just as fast. In St. Petersburg, St. Louis Cardinals owner Gussie Busch issued what Miller took as a "war cry" to the press: "We voted unanimously to take a stand," he stated. "We're not going to give them another damned cent! If they want to strike, let them strike!"

While much of the press sided with Busch, the dean of American sportswriters, Walter "Red" Smith, mockingly referred to the petulant beer baron as the "malty proprietor." Smith and *New York Times* colleague Leonard Koppett were considered by Miller to be among the few writers providing accurate and balanced reporting of the strike.

New York *Daily News* columnist Dick Young was seen by Miller as one who was obsessed with the union chief. Young opined at the time that as far as the owners were concerned, the enemy wasn't the players, whom the owners regarded as misled ingrates. The real enemy was Miller, "general of the Union," as Young called him.

By March 29 player support for the strike swelled to 663–10. Of the ten dissenters, four were on the Red Sox. Owner Tom Yawkey had taken care of his boys.

Gaherin downplayed the strike vote. To him it was little more than a public rattling of the sabres. It didn't necessarily mean a strike was really in the works: "Any labor leader who can't get a strike vote," Gaherin said, "might as well quit and go home."

When the players' show of solidarity failed to impress management, Miller suggested an impartial arbitrator be brought in to decide the dispute. He proposed the arbitrator be chosen by former U.S. president Lyndon Johnson, President Richard Nixon, or Chief Justice Earl Warren.

Gaherin declined the proposal. Baseball, he said, was such a unique business that an outsider couldn't possibly understand the issues involved. Miller thought it convenient that owners could magically transform baseball from a "game" into a "business" when it suited their cause.

Miller and Moss mulled their options. The union lacked the financial and public relations resources management had at its disposal. If the players went on strike and didn't sustain it, their capitulation would be disastrous for the Players Association.

On the morning of March 31, Miller; Oakland A's player rep Chuck Dobson; and the club's alternate rep, Reggie Jackson, flew to Dallas. From the A's spring training camp in Arizona, Dobson and Jackson had been following the negotiations in the newspapers. It was their belief that the owners were confident the players were too fearful to strike.

Disembarking from the plane, Miller, Dobson, Jackson, and company were swarmed by reporters and photographers. A labor economist, Miller had been involved in five national Steelworkers' strikes, but the scene at Love Field was unlike anything he had ever seen.

At the meeting Miller reviewed the negotiations with the owners and suggested the strike be delayed until 1973, when the Players Association would be on a more firm footing.

There was a great stirring in the room as numerous hands instantly shot up. The players were more determined to accept management's challenge not to strike than Miller had realized. They were, he thought, "positively militant."

The union boss played the role of devil's advocate. The Players

Association didn't have a strike fund, didn't have a public relations staff to battle a hostile press. None of that mattered. Player after player stood and expressed his dedication to the cause. Of the forty-eight player reps, forty-seven voted for the walkout.

On April 1 MLB players initiated a "lightning strike." When the strike was announced, much of the national press turned hostile. *The Sporting News* editor C. C. Johnson Spink said the walkout marked the "darkest day in sports history." The press in Cincinnati was particularly virulent. It was no surprise, Miller thought, since Reds owner Francis Dale was also the owner of the Cincinnati *Enquirer*. Among those at the forefront of the firestorm of criticism was California Angels owner Gene Autry. The owners, he angrily declared, "ought to close baseball down forever!"

Many fans felt the same way. With the average U.S. income in 1972 at $11,800, most paying customers had little sympathy for the financial plight of players earning an average of $30,000. In New York City angry cabbies told passengers the players were spoiled. "Why are they striking now," some asked, "in the baseball season? It isn't fair." *Time* magazine captured the sentiment of many baseball fans when it led its coverage of the work stoppage with a poem:

> There were saddened hearts in baseball for a week or ever more;
> There were muttered oaths and curses—every fan was clearly sore.
> "Just think," said one, "how much we missed with no one up to bat,
> And ballparks closed throughout the land by an owner-player spat."

As far as many Americans were concerned, unions were in place to protect employees and provide a counterbalance against employers who might abuse their powers. The idea of a major league baseball union was odd to many since making a living playing a game seemed to the public to be a privilege. Certainly being a ballplayer was less rigorous than being a coal miner and more rewarding and glamorous than being a grocery clerk. That the athletes would go on strike and risk losing the favor of their fans was a notion too foreign to many to even entertain.

Reds players were so concerned with negative blowback from fans and the media that team player rep Jim Merritt asked Miller to address the squad on April 5. Roberto Clemente contacted Miller and asked if the union chief would visit the Pirates following his meeting with the Reds. Dave Giusti was Pittsburgh's player rep, but as Miller noted, Clemente was the real leader of the reigning champions' clubhouse.

At the urging of Baltimore player rep Brooks Robinson, Miller followed his visits with the Reds and Pirates by meeting with the Orioles. After the walkout, Orioles owner Jerry Hoffberger called a team meeting and proceeded to rip the players at length. Manager Earl Weaver warned his team the strike would ruin their chances of playing in a fourth straight World Series. Orioles ace Jim Palmer said Miller had brainwashed the union.

Despite the charges emanating from Baltimore, it was clear to keen-eyed observers that the Players Association had been right all along. Roger Angell, an author and writer for the *New Yorker* magazine, is arguably the most passionate and elegant essayist of the American pastime. It was Angell's opinion that from the beginning of negotiations the Players Association had been willing to compromise or submit to arbitration its main point of difference with the owners: the use of accumulated funds in the players' pension plan to increase the benefits being paid out.

The owners, Angell noted, had declared any accommodation to be an absolute impossibility. He blamed the hard-liners, the "more dedicated Cro-Magnons among the owners," whom Angell identified as Busch, Dale, the New York Mets' M. Donald Grant, and the Kansas City Royals' Ewing Kauffman. Minnesota Twins owner Calvin Griffith fit into this group of conservatives. Some said swimming was invented when Calvin Griffith first came to a toll bridge. This group of owners, Angell said, saw the strike as an opportunity to strain, and perhaps crack, their young employees and to discredit their leader, Miller.

Other members of the press came down on both sides. Young used the strike to decry unions. Fellow New York sportswriter Phil Pepe thought the players were getting a bad rap and wondered why the continual citing of the players' salaries was not balanced by a mentioning of the average length of a player's career, which in 1972 was four-and-a-half seasons.

Fans found it hard to bleed for grown men playing a kid's game, but it was the players whom people paid to see. No one, it was noted, ever went to the stadium to watch old Connie Mack wave his scorecard around.

The owners told fans they were standing fast for them, that it was the players who were ruining the game. But many believed the fate of the game rested, as it always had, with the kids. If America's youth devoted its time and energy to baseball, the sport would thrive. If they were playing football or basketball instead, baseball would suffer.

On the scheduled Opening Day, stadiums across the country were fronted by signs reading "No Game Today." New York sportswriter Larry Merchant covered kids in Central Park, East River Park, and Washington Square playing baseball. CBS-TV carried a picture of Blue, Oakland's young southpaw ace and reigning Cy Young winner-turned-toilet fixtures executive, and declared him to be MLB's lone employed player. An Associated Press photographer snapped a picture of an Orioles clubhouse employee disconsolately playing solitaire in a Baltimore locker room filled with uniform tops hanging neatly in their stalls.

To paraphrase the poet Robert Burns, big league baseball had become a world of gathering brows and a gathering storm. One prominent player thankful for the strike was Mets player rep and staff ace Tom Seaver. The sudden death of skipper Gil Hodges in spring training had rocked the Mets. Seaver's roommate on the road, All-Star shortstop Bud Harrelson, said Seaver saw the strike as "a blessing in disguise." The Mets needed time to recover from Hodges's passing before the season started.

At the same time that Jack Nicklaus was about to grab headlines by claiming the fourth of his eventual six Masters titles with a three-stroke victory among the azaleas in Augusta and the New York Knicks and Los Angeles Lakers were on an East-West collision course in the NBA playoffs, American League president Joe Cronin ordered major league stadiums closed to players during the strike.

In Oakland the owner of the A's defied the order and demanded that the Coliseum be kept open so his players could keep fit. Charles O. Finley was about to become the voice of reason in baseball.

CHAPTER FOUR

He was, according to the *Los Angeles Times*, "a self-made man who worshipped his creator."

Charles O. Finley—the "O" stood for "Oscar," but Finley told one of his managers, Dick Williams, the "O" really stood for "Owner"—was a slick salesman, an innovator, and his own general manager. He was baseball's answer to his NFL counterpart in Oakland, the Raiders' Al Davis, and a forerunner to Dallas's Jerry Jones. In its 1975 cover story *Time* magazine called Finley baseball's Barnum, the sport's "Super Showman."

A's All-Star catcher/first baseman Gene Tenace remembers Finley as a "hell of a general manager." Hall of Fame slugger Reggie Jackson said Finley would do anything to make his team better. Jackson allowed that Charlie O. could also be a lot of fun. Finley, he said, knew how to raise a little hell and have a good time. Jackson thought Charlie O. would be a great guy to have as a buddy—if, Reggie added, you didn't have to work for him.

Those who did work for Finley found he could also be a tyrant and a miser. From 1961 to 1975 Charlie O. churned through sixteen broadcasters, twelve team managers, ten publicity managers, seven farm directors, and five scouting directors. He sent his overworked staff scurrying with round-the-clock phone calls and kept tabs on everything from his players' baseball bat orders to press room food in the Oakland Coliseum. A's equipment manager Frank Ciensczyk sometimes took as many as six calls a day from Finley. When Tenace asked for a new pair of uniform pants, Ciensczyk balked. "I'll have to check it with Charlie," he told a startled Tenace.

Alvin Dark, who succeeded Dick Williams as the A's skipper in 1974 and helped guide Oakland to a third straight World Series title and consecutive

Western Division titles in '74 and '75, recalled that Finley was tough to work for. Charlie was rough and tough, Dark said, and at times seemed cruel. A's skippers complained that the boss called them in the dugout, in the clubhouse, and at home. He would make them explain every move and never seemed satisfied with their explanations. He told them whom to play, where to play them, and when to play them.

Still Finley was a winner, and Charlie O. made that plain to his players, who at times benefited from his generosity but also had to fight at times for every penny. By the mid-1970s Finley seemed to be gaining as much satisfaction from winning arbitration battles with his stars as he was from winning world championships. In 1974 Jackson, Bando, and Holtzman won salary increases from Finley. The following season, Bando produced 24 game-winning hits and Holtzman was a 19-game winner, yet neither received a raise.

"Sure, Bando had some clutch hits," Finley said then. "Don't I deserve something for $100,000? As for Holtzman—hell, he won 21 games in 1973. What am I supposed to do, give him a raise for having a worse year?"

When Jackson had held out for higher pay in 1970, Finley had humiliated his twenty-three-year-old star by publicly ridiculing his athletic ability and salary demands. Later that summer Jackson slugged a grand slam, and as he crossed home plate, he looked toward Finley and raised his fist in defiance. An angered Finley responded the next day. Jackson was ordered to write a formal apology in the presence of then manager John McNamara, four coaches, and Bando. Reggie wrote the apology—in tears. Finley, Jackson said later, wanted to show who was boss.

In time A's players came to hate Finley. "Screw that bastard!" they would exclaim with great venom. They grew tired of torn pants and two-year-old shirts serving as uniforms, no stamps for answering fan mail, no free telephone in the clubhouse for local calls, commercial flights instead of charter flights, and cheap hotels on road trips. "Charlie Finley," one A's player told *Time* in 1975, "is the cheapest son of a bitch in baseball."

Finley angrily refuted each charge. The A's, he declared, stayed in the same hotels as other major league teams. The commercial flights were all first class; there was no phone in the clubhouse because it was against major league rules to have a phone handy since gamblers could call. As for stamps, Finley said the players could have all they needed if they brought their fan mail up to the club office. "I know one thing," he told *Time*. "They're so selfish and lazy they won't answer any fan mail. Hell, there'll be so few letters I'll lick 'em myself!"

Charlie O. called the charges against him "ridiculous." To him, his champions had become "a bunch of spoiled brats."

Finley, meanwhile, was seen by some as an insufferable self-promoter. He liked to slip into his chauffeured sleek black Cadillac and order driver Howard Risner to "Get this crate rolling." As the car nosed into traffic, Finley would tell Risner, "Shoot the works." Risner would hit a button and city streets would reverberate to the sound of the Caddie's musical horn. "Now the siren," Finley would say, and a loud wail would startle drivers steering frantically toward the curb. Charlie O. would then switch on a loudspeaker hidden beneath the Caddie's hood and regale pedestrians with his chatter.

Finley was likely the only owner in major league baseball at the time whose bio in the team's media guide took up more pages than those of his star players. He had always wanted to be a player, he said once, but had never had the talent to make the big leagues. "So I did the next best thing: I bought a team."

Charlie O. had charged into the gray-suited world of baseball owners and general managers wearing a dazzling green blazer and matching ten-gallon hat. In 1964, while owner of the Kansas City Athletics, Finley promised the local citizenry he would bring the Beatles to Kansas City's Municipal Stadium during the British rock group's first tour of the United States. He met with Beatles manager Brian Epstein in San Francisco and offered $100,000 if Missouri were added to the Fab Four's itinerary. Epstein declined, telling Finley that the Beatles' lone available open date was September 17, and the group had planned a day of rest in New Orleans.

One week later Finley encountered Epstein again, this time in Los Angeles, and upped his offer to $150,000. For their one-night performance in Municipal Stadium the Fab Four earned a then record $4,687 per minute for the thirty-two-minute concert. The show was billed with the slogan "Today's Beatles fans are tomorrow's baseball fans." On the back of each concert ticket—prices ranged from $2.00 to $8.50—was a photo of Finley in a black wig. Charlie O. had made himself the fifth Beatle.

Finley created his own brand of baseball—Day-Glo orange—and labeled it "The Charles O. Finley Alert Orange Baseball." He also put forth a request to use green bats.

Born in 1918 in Ensley, Alabama (near Birmingham), Charlie was just twelve years old when he organized his own sandlot baseball team. Naturally he installed himself as the manager. He promised himself at the time he would someday either be a major leaguer or own a big league club. Charlie's wheeling and dealing in his boyhood days was not limited to baseball. He would buy rejected eggs for five cents a dozen, carry them to office buildings, and sell them for fifteen cents a dozen. He won prizes for selling thousands of magazines door to door. Baseball and salesmanship ruled his boyhood years. When he was fifteen, his poverty-ridden family moved to Gary, Indiana, where Finley took part in sports. He played baseball and football and was a Golden Gloves boxer. He was a batboy for the Birmingham Barons, receiving fifty cents and a used baseball per day, along with an occasional tip for providing chewing tobacco to players. Charlie loved being close to the game. He saw Dizzy Dean pitch for Houston against Birmingham in the Dixie Series and was awed by the colorful character. "What a pitcher Dizzy was!" Finley exclaimed years later.

To help his family Finley worked as a theater usher and in a butcher shop, and he was considered by classmates the most gentlemanly dresser in school. He met Shirley McCartney, a regular customer in the butcher shop, and Charlie became, in his words, "sweet" on her—so sweet, in fact, that when Shirley came to the shop with three dollars, Charlie would go back into the icebox and wrap up fifteen dollars' worth of meat. The transactions had her father believing she was a great shopper and the butcher believing she was a valued customer.

Upon graduation from high school Finley toiled for six years in Gary's steel mills, following in the footsteps of his father, who spent forty-seven years in U.S. Steel Company mills, and his grandfather, an Irish immigrant steelworker. While earning a starting rate of forty-seven cents an hour, Charlie developed a formula: "S plus S = S." It stood for "Sweat plus Sacrifice equals Success." Shirley Finley would later claim it actually stood for "Shirley plus Sharon [the couple's oldest child] equals Success."

At age twenty-four Finley became an insurance salesman, a job that would change his life and ultimately lead to his dragging the game of baseball kicking and screaming into the modern era.

In his spare time Finley was manager and first baseman for a semipro team in northern Indiana, the LaPorte Cubs. His part-time baseball career ended due to a severe bout with tuberculosis. Hospitalized for twenty-seven months in Parramore Hospital, a Crown Point, Indiana, sanitarium, Finley devised a plan to sell disability insurance to doctors. Here he was, Finley recalled thinking, just a guy in an ordinary job and selling insurance as a night sideline. When TB hit him, Shirley had to work as a proofreader in a Gary newspaper to help make ends meet.

Charlie figured it was a bad enough situation for the average guy, but what a calamity it would be for a fellow with a big income who suddenly found himself without money to meet his high standards of living. Finley asked himself what group of people had such high standards and would be interested in such an insurance program. He thought of doctors. Suppose a surgeon lost a finger or got crippled? His expenses continued, but his income dwindled.

He left Crown Point with an idea that seemed to him "a natural," as he told *The Sporting News* in 1972. The insurance companies weren't buying any such suggestions, but Finley was stubborn. He had practically exhausted the list of companies that might underwrite his program, so he went back and sold it to the first company that had turned him down—Lake County Medical Society.

Finley was among the first to write group medical insurance policies for those in the profession. His big break came in 1951, when Continental Casualty handled his first national plan for the American College of Surgeons (ACS). He borrowed $2,000 for two suits, a manicure, and a plane ticket to the ACS convention in San Francisco. With insurance premiums rolling in, Finley's idea made him a millionaire before the age of forty.

"He was a master salesman, a very persuasive gentleman," Curt Gowdy said.

Finley also prided himself on being an excellent chef. But as Gowdy wondered, "When did he find time to cook?" One other thing about Finley: he never forgot his roots or those who helped him along the way. During the 1972 World Series he would be up until 5 a.m. arranging entertainment and distributing tickets to old friends. A high school classmate from Gary who became a banker and helped finance some of Finley's early investments said Finley always told him he'd be among the guests when the A's reached the World Series. In the Series aftermath a testimonial dinner was held in La Porte, Indiana. Finley insisted that the cost of dinner tickets be just two dollars—he wanted prices within reach of working men and women and children. Christmas at the Finley household would find Shirley shopping for their ever-growing family and Charlie telling her the sky was the limit on funds. When the Christmas bills came due in January, however, Charlie usually hit the ceiling. "I really think," Shirley said then, "that he believes in Santa Claus."

In the 1950s Finley used his accumulated wealth to try and purchase a major league franchise. His first attempt to buy the Kansas City Athletics fell short by one hour. Finley had a 9 a.m. breakfast date with Connie Mack, and Charlie believed there was every indication a deal would be made. But another investor, Arnold Johnson, had an 8 a.m. meeting with Mack that same day, and it was Johnson who wound up with the club.

Finley then bid for the Detroit Tigers and twice came close to acquiring the Chicago White Sox, first from Dorothy Comiskey Rigney and then from the troika of Bill Veeck, Hank Greenberg, and Arthur Allyn. Charlie also pursued the Angels' expansion franchise in Los Angeles. In December 1960, following Johnson's untimely death, Finley bought a controlling interest (52 percent) in the Kansas City Athletics for $1.975 million. Now the principal owner, he also named a new chairman of the board: Charles O. Finley.

"I wanted to get into baseball in the worst way," he joked to banquet audiences when the Athletics were perennial pushovers. "And that's exactly what I did."

To generate interest in his sad-sack squad, which had endured four straight dreadful summers since moving to Kansas City from Philadelphia prior to the 1955 season, Finley formulated publicity stunts. He had a herd of sheep grazing in a zoo beyond the outfield wall, and the team mascot was changed from the symbolic White Elephant of Connie Mack's dynasty teams to a live mule named Charlie O. The mule was given the run of Kansas City's Municipal Stadium, parading around the outfield, hotel lobbies, cocktail parties, and media dining rooms.

When catcher/outfielder Johnny Blanchard was traded from the imperial Yankees, where he had played on clubs that had gone to four straight World Series, to the cellar-dwelling Athletics in 1965, he was disgusted to find a game at Municipal Stadium being delayed so that Charlie O. the mule could be walked, ever so slowly, through the center field fence to home plate, where the Kansas City players were expected to surround the mule and sing happy birthday to him.

This is a long way from the Yankees, Blanchard thought. No way am I going to sing happy birthday to that damn mule. The players weren't the only ones expected to sing to Charlie O. the mule. Catfish Hunter recalled Finley commissioning two team songs, one of which Hunter said was a country and western number titled "Charlie O. the Mule." Finley also demanded A's announcer Harry Caray change his famous "Holy cow!" call to "Holy mule!" Charlie O. the mule was also used to transport Kansas City pitchers, bareback of course, from the bullpen to the mound.

In 1972, after letting Charlie O. the mule meander around the organization for years, Finley demanded Charlie O. join the team. The mule went from grazing in hospitality suites deep in the Oakland Coliseum to grazing in foul territory in left field. The mule had a habit of, in Williams's words, "taking a big crap" down the left-field line. It got so bad that the A's skipper would have to tell the opposing manager during pregame meetings at home plate at the Coliseum, "The mule shits out there, and we can't always be cleaning it. So if a ball rolls in shit, it's still in play."

Charlie O. the mule was just one of the promotions that sprang from Finley's fertile mind. Grounds crews at Municipal Stadium performed their duties dressed in space suits; the fence in right field was moved in to mirror the famed short porch in Yankee Stadium; and "Campy Campaneris Night" was held so that the versatile shortstop could play all nine positions in a single game. Finley's promotions included Bald-Headed Night, Hot Pants Day, Farmers' Night, etc. The A's sponsored Back-to-School Days, Finley buying several thousand dollars' worth of rulers to give to children in attendance.

Like fellow maverick owner Bill Veeck, whose promotional gimmicks included an exploding scoreboard, nameplates on uniform jerseys, and the sending of 3-foot-7 Eddie Gaedel, whose uniform number was "1/8," to bat—Finley bucked tradition at every turn.

Charlie despised major league baseball's bland uniform colors—"eggshell white and prison gray," in his words. To take advantage of the country's switch from black-and-white to color television Finley persuaded the league to allow the Athletics to change the color of their uniforms to a flamboyant green and gold. Critics ridiculed the new uniforms, but Charlie O. didn't care. He knew the trend was to color. He remembered the days when almost all telephones and automobiles were black and TV screens were black and white. Then the switch came to color. He thought the A's attractive uniforms were eye-catching on color TV.

In 1967 Finley outfitted the A's in white cleats rather than the traditional black. He said the cleats were made of kangaroo skin so that the A's could "get a better jump on the ball."

The players were embarrassed by their new accoutrements. They felt like clowns in a circus, and opposing players taunted them by singing the Barnum and Bailey theme song. When New York Yankees great Mickey Mantle first saw the gaudy green-and-gold outfits and white cleats, he suggested the A's come out of their dugout "on tippy-toes, holding hands and singing."

When Williams first put on his A's uniform, he noticed that the coaches' caps were white with a green bill while the players' caps were green with a gold bill. Some of us, Williams thought, have been given the wrong uniforms. Ultimately he realized the mismatched uniforms were another of Finley's innovations. Charlie wanted members of the coaching staff to be able to quickly spot each other. Williams understood that more than he understood what he called the "styrofoam surfboards on my feet—white shoes."

Despite his nonstop promotional gimmickry, diminishing attendance in Kansas City caused Finley to seek relocation more than once. Proposed moves to Dallas in 1962 and Louisville in 1964 were blocked by fellow owners. When Finley did finally move the franchise to Oakland prior to the 1968 season, he was serenaded out of town by irate Missourians. Senator Stuart Symington labeled Finley "one of the most disreputable characters ever to enter the American sports scene."

Charlie O. laughed all the way to the bank. Funded by his giant insurance brokerage and his fertilizer company, he owned the Athletics, and in time would also own the NHL's California Golden Seals, whom he also outfitted in colorful uniforms and white skates, and the Memphis Tams of the American Basketball Association. He got college basketball legend Adolph Rupp to work for the Tams.

Finley ran the A's with a small staff—the smallest, he boasted, in the majors. But that didn't stop him from signing some of the game's best young talents. In 1962 he got future All-Star shortstop Bert Campaneris for just $500. Two years later he landed eighteen-year-old Catfish Hunter. Tenace, fellow future All-Star Joe Rudi, and future Hall of Famer Rollie Fingers were signed fresh out of high school within a year after Hunter.

Finley's tireless pursuits weren't limited to baseball. A football enthusiast, he put out feelers to purchase the Chicago Bears and also the Miami Dolphins. He had season tickets to Bears' games and was an admirer of George Halas, Pittsburgh Steelers owner Art Rooney Sr., and San Francisco 49ers boss Lou Spadia. His college football cronies ranged from Notre Dame's Frank Leahy and Ed "Moose" Krause to Alabama's Paul "Bear" Bryant.

Tenace recalls Finley being so enamored with Bryant that he wore the Bear's famous plaid fedoras and houndstooth hats to A's games and once invited the legendary coach to give the A's a pep talk during a team slump. "We didn't know what the hell was going on," Tenace laughed. "But, hell, he was Bear Bryant and he had some good things to say."

Finley was so obsessed with football that Shirley once stated that if her husband thought it was possible to purchase Notre Dame, "he'd give it a try."

Colorful and controversial, Finley enraged and entertained the baseball establishment. He championed change in a sport that in many ways had stood still for half a century. He campaigned for night World Series games to replace afternoon games so that the working man and schoolkids could see the game. Also there was the benefit of prime-time television and increased revenue from the networks. He lobbied to have the World Series and regular season openers start on Saturday rather than weekdays for maximum exposure. The designated hitter was another Finley folly that was ultimately adopted by American League owners. In 1997 the Lords of the Game would also begin interleague play, some twenty-five years after Finley had first pushed for it. His proudest promotional accomplishment, he said at the time, was Mustache Day. It gave the A's a look and style unique to their sport.

Change was necessary, Finley stated at the time, to keep the game modern. He embraced the role of the prophet in the desert. "If anyone asks me what's wrong with baseball," he said in 1972, "I'd say stupidity on the part of the owners. I've always been aggressive in my thinking regarding baseball, and any time that you become a little aggressive in your thinking you're bound to step on a few toes. And I have no apologies whatsoever for that. If it's necessary to step on a few more, I'll step on 'em!"

Baseball is a great game, he said, but it's faced with a lot of competition, and the people in baseball had to do everything possible to keep the game the nation's number one sport. He pointed to the NFL, NHL, and NBA and said the thing that kept those sports so interesting was the balance between offense and defense. Football matched 11-on-11, basketball 5-on-5. But baseball was nine fielders against one batter. It was time to give the hitter some help.

"We in baseball are like this," Finley said, spreading his hands wide.

"The defense has great advantages over the offense. They say pitching is 75 to 80 percent of the game and how true that is. We've got to take some of the advantages away from the defense."

The average pitcher, he declared, couldn't hit. So the pitcher went into every game facing eight hitters instead of nine. Use a designated hitter, Finley reasoned, and now the pitcher would have to face nine hitters. That would put more action in baseball. The same went for a designated runner, three-ball count, and a twenty-second clock on pitchers. Every other sport had a clock, he reasoned. Why not baseball?

Action—that's what the game needed, Charlie O. declared. "Let's get some action in this sport!"

NFL owners, Finley said, were aggressive in their thinking. They were continuously making rules changes to keep their sport interesting. Get a list of NFL rules changes, he said. "It'll be enough to choke a cow."

He recalled a time in football when a player had to be five yards behind the scrimmage line before he could throw a pass, and if he threw two consecutive incomplete passes, his team was penalized. He remembered when he played high school basketball, and every time a basket was scored, there was a jump ball at center court. "After every damn basket!" he said. If the final score was 23–21, headlines in the paper referred to it as a "free-scoring match."

His point was that while other sports adapted, baseball didn't. "We haven't had one major rules change in 86 years," he said in '72. "Eighty-six years, not one major change."

Three years later Finley was still singing the same tune. He had never seen so many "damned idiots" as the owners in the sport. Baseball, he declared, was headed for extinction if the owners didn't make changes.

But change had come to baseball in the spring of '72. Finley initially stood with his fellow owners in the early days of the strike, even issuing a sound bite that sounded like an ominous warning to his players: "Pigs get fat and hogs go to market."

He soon saw the folly in the owners' position. Finley realized his colleagues didn't know a surplus existed in the pension fund until the players disclosed it. Along with that, the owners hadn't had enough time to properly digest an actuarial report given to them in a meeting in Chicago. Finley understood it, but despite his obvious qualifications given his background, the insurance magnate wasn't a member of the owners' pension committee. Realizing the Players Association had valid points, Finley reversed his hard-line stand.

"The owners didn't understand what it was all about," he said later. "I was adamant in standing pat on our original offer but I was standing pat only because I hadn't been presented with the facts."

Feeling he was better informed than his fellow owners, Finley took charge. A maverick-turned-moderator, he contacted his colleagues via a flurry of long-distance phone calls and, using his gift for salesmanship, convinced them to accept a compromise settlement.

Sportswriter Ron Bergman wrote later that the "voice of reason was heard throughout the land. And the voice belonged to Charles Oscar Finley, owner of the Athletics. And the populace fell over each other in surprise and disbelief."

No one fell harder or faster at the thought of Finley being the voice of reason than one of Charlie O.'s own, his young fire-balling phenom, Vida Blue.

While Finley assumed a conciliatory stance in the players' strike, he stood fast and firm in his contract dealings with *his* holdout, Blue. Vida was one of the game's great young stars in 1971. Having gone 24-8 with a 1.82 ERA and 301 strikeouts in 312 innings, he was the starting and winning pitcher in the 1971 All-Star Game in Detroit. At season's end, the twenty-two-year-old from Mansfield, Louisiana, had earned both the American League Cy Young award and Most Valuable Player honors. In so doing, he became just the fifth man in major league history to that point to record the rare double.

Blue was, according to Williams, "so smooth and so rough he resembled a jewel." Bando compared Blue's 1971 season to Bob Gibson's record-setting 1968 campaign. Reporters likened Blue to great flame throwers of the past—Bob Feller, Sandy Koufax, et al. "I find it astonishing," Vida said of the heady comparisons.

Blue was also astonished by all the attention he was receiving. Vida, Hunter once recalled, didn't like it. To Blue it was "a weird scene." He wins a few baseball games, and all of a sudden he's surrounded by reporters and TV men with cameras asking things about Vietnam and race relations. I'm only a kid, Vida thought. I don't have a whole philosophy of life set down.

What Blue did have was an elaborate and unique windup; "all pretzeled up" was how *Sports Illustrated* writer Roy Blount described it. Blue hid the ball behind a high knee pump of his right front leg. Like the celebrated hurler in Bruce Springsteen's *Glory Days*, Vida could throw his speed ball by you, make you look like a fool. "The way we heard it," New York Yankees All-Star outfielder Bobby Murcer said after facing Vida for the first time at Yankee Stadium, "was that we wouldn't even be able to see the ball."

When the Yankees finally faced Blue, they still weren't sure they had seen his fearsome fastball. Yankees star outfielder Roy White told *Time* magazine that a pitch from Blue "seems to speed up on you and then disappear." The Yankees weren't alone in issuing effusive praise. Kansas City Royals third baseman Paul Schaal swore Vida's heater was otherworldly. "It jumps," he said.

Oakland catcher Dave Duncan believed Blue to be the hardest thrower in baseball. "His ball is on top of a hitter almost before he sees it," Duncan said. Baseball historian and statistician Bill James calls Blue the hardest throwing lefty of his era and the second-hardest thrower of that period behind Nolan Ryan.

Eyewitnesses claimed Vida's blue darter alternately popped, hopped, tailed, sailed, skipped, swooped, sunk, smoked, and whooshed. Some opponents were confident they could catch up with Blue's fastball. "We'll get him," they would say before taking the field. After another dominating performance by Blue, those same opponents would be heard muttering, "Well, we'll get him . . . *next* time."

Blue's success in '71 wasn't totally unexpected. In 1968 he led the Midwest League in strikeouts and in '69 the Southwest League, and in 1970 he topped the American Association with 165 Ks. He joined the A's for the final month of the '70 season, and on September 21, in just his fourth major league start, he no-hit eventual Western Division champion Minnesota. Eleven days earlier he had been four outs away from no-hitting Kansas City when outfielder Pat Kelly singled. Blue finished with a one-hitter.

Vida took the sports world by storm in '71. He was Mark Fidrych before "the Bird," Fernando Valenzuela prior to "Fernandomania," Dwight Gooden before he became "Dr. K," and Tim Lincecum before he became the Freak.

"Instant phenomhood," is how *New York Post* sportswriter Larry Merchant described Blue's summer. The young gun's name was a headline writer's dream. Baseball writer Roger Angell thought "Vida Blue" was the kind of name conjured up by Ring Lardner or Damon Runyon—Lardner or Runyon, Angell wrote, "on a good day."

Blue's surname lent itself to all kinds of possibilities: Rhapsody in Blue; Blue Streak; and in a play on the famous "Spahn and Sain and Pray for Rain," Hunter and Blue and Pray for Dew.

Finley loved colorful nicknames. "Who the hell," Finley would say, "ever paid to see *George* Ruth?"

Early in the 1971 season the boss called Blue into his office. "I'll give you $2,000 if you have [your name] changed legally to 'Vida True Blue.' We'll have them take the name 'Blue' off of your uniform and have them use 'True.' I'll tell the broadcasters to start calling you True Blue.'"

Blue could barely contain his anger. He told Finley he would never consent to changing his name and told a writer he was "humiliated" by the request. "I couldn't believe he was serious," Blue said. "Vida was my father's name. I loved him very much. He was a good, good man. Vida means 'life' in Spanish. I enjoy being Vida Blue. Why would I want to be called 'True Blue'?" If Finley likes it so much, Blue said then, "why doesn't he call himself 'True O. Finley?'"

Vida's success on the mound granted him access to avenues off limits to all but the superstars of sport. En route to leading Oakland to its first division championship and the A's franchise to its first postseason berth since 1931, Blue would do TV ads for milk and aftershave lotion; be cast in the 1972 movie *Black Gunn*, which starred retired Cleveland Browns great Jim Brown; and appear on the TV show *What's My Line?* He was featured on the cover of national magazines; *Time* featured a splashy artist's rendition accompanied by the words "New Zip in the Old Game." President Nixon arranged for the A's to visit the White House so that he could meet the man who was on track to become baseball's first 30-game winner since Detroit's Denny McLain had won 31 in 1968.

In the Oval Office Nixon told Blue, who was making just $13,000 at the time, "I've read that you're the most underpaid player in baseball."

Finley, overhearing the conversation, grimaced.

"Who is the lawyer for this club?" the president asked before turning his attention back to Blue. "I would hate to negotiate your contract next year."

Negotiating on behalf of Blue was his agent, Bob Gerst. A thirty-six-year-old Los Angeles attorney, Gerst had been put in contact with Blue by A's teammate Tommy Davis, a star outfielder for the Dodgers during their championship years in the 1960s. Gerst was a contract lawyer, and he handled the business affairs of Los Angeles Lakers great Jerry West, among others.

On January 8, 1972, Gerst and Blue arrived at the Michigan Avenue office building that housed the insurance offices for Charles O. Finley and Company, Inc. For five hours the three men sought to negotiate a new deal for Vida in Finley's wood-paneled inner office high above Lake Michigan. Blue had hoped to increase his salary to $75,000, but Gerst was aiming higher. The agent wanted a deal that would make his client one of the top ten highest-paid players in baseball. Gerst asked for $115,000.

Finley, who had in mind an offer of $45,000, scoffed. The owner asked the agent what floor of the building they were on. The twenty-seventh, Gerst said. "Mr. Gerst," Finley said, "you have as much chance of getting $115,000 as I have of going out that window and landing on my feet."

When Finley countered with an offer of $50,000, Gerst and Blue lowered their number to $92,000. Finley held firm. He would not raise ticket prices, he said, to satisfy Blue's demands. Nor would he trade him or sell him. "Either he accepts what we have offered," Finley angrily remarked, "or he is through in baseball."

Gerst attempted to justify Blue's request. He called his client one of the ten best pitchers in baseball. Gerst pointed to the salaries of Blue's contemporaries: Bob Gibson, $150,000; Ferguson Jenkins, $125,000; Tom Seaver, $120,000. Gerst also pointed to the increased attendance the A's had enjoyed—both at home and on the road—during Blue's thirty-nine starts in 1971. "He's proven his importance," Gerst stated, "to the financial well-being of his club and to the league."

Finley knew it to be true. Blue's breakout season in '71 had helped the A's increase their attendance over 1970 by 150,000, thereby earning Finley $1.3 million, an increase of $800,000 over the previous year's profits. Vida averaged 23,100 fans per game; "Blue Moon" Odom, 16,183; and Hunter, a three-time All-Star and reigning ace, 14,719. Blue's road starts drew crowds that averaged 85 percent more fans than the rest of Oakland's games. Of the seven A's games that drew more than 40,000, Blue started six of them.

On June 1, when the A's went to Yankee Stadium, fewer than twelve thousand tickets had been sold. When it was announced the *wunderkind* was pitching that night, over twenty thousand fans purchased tickets at the gate. When the A's returned to the Bronx later that summer, the Yankees promoted the game as "Blue Tuesday" and colored the scorecard inserts in their team yearbooks blue in honor of Vida. The crowd for Blue's start at the Stadium swelled to more than fifty thousand.

Finley's awareness of Blue's celebrated status may have cost Vida a chance at becoming a 30-game winner in 1971. Blue was 17-2 at the All-Star break, but he was basically a .500 pitcher (7-6) for the second half of the season. Williams blamed Blue's struggles on his boss's late-season juggling of the pitching rotation. According to Williams, Finley called him into his office and insisted the rotation be juggled so that Blue would start seven of his final games in Oakland. Williams said the move "screwed up Blue."

"The Athletics," sportswriter Larry Merchant wrote, "pitched Vida like he had a terminal disease, trying to get everything they could out of him."

Watching the A's that summer, former major league second baseman Jerry Lumpe thought Finley tried to exploit Blue. Bando believed the same and said Vida pitched a lot of games with very little rest just for the attendance.

Escalating innings—only four pitchers in the majors that season threw more innings than Blue—proved costly. Beginning with an August 20 start against Boston, Blue made seven of his final nine starts at home and won just two of them. After striking out 10 or more batters 11 times through September 3, he fanned 5 or fewer in each of his final five starts.

Glenn Schwarz, the dean of Bay Area sportswriters, believed the A's overuse of Blue in 1971 irrevocably damaged the pitcher's career. In one game Vida worked eleven innings of shutout ball, striking out seventeen. He would have great games and good seasons in years to come, but he would never again be as dominant.

Finley would tell Blue after the season, "So you won 20 games? Why didn't you win 30?"

In his negotiations with Gerst, Finley countered comparisons with Gibson, Jenkins, and Seaver by bringing up Blue's limited service time in the bigs. "I don't mind paying a player that has proved himself," he said, "but a player can't prove himself in one year."

He had to be firm on paying Blue $50,000 for 1972, Finley stated. The owner likely had another reason for refusing to go higher. In his most recent contract negotiations with his other ace, Finley had haggled with Hunter, a 20-game winner for the first time in 1971. They had finally agreed on a deal calling for the Catfish to earn $45,000 for his pitching and $5,000 for his hitting.

Finley also promised Hunter he would not pay Blue more than he was earning. Finley, however, didn't tell Gerst and Blue about his promise to Hunter. Instead he stated that based on the fact that Vida had just one full year in the majors, "I think [$50,000] is a fair offer."

Blue and Gerst thought otherwise, and the Western Division champs opened spring training minus their golden arm. Gerst took his client's case to the court of public opinion. He set up an aftershave commercial in which Blue referred to himself as "baseball's lowest paid superstar." A's players backed Blue in his holdout but only up to a point. Curt Blefary said Blue was foolish for giving up $50,000. "He could have made $100,000 with endorsements," Blefary said.

First baseman Mike Epstein blamed Gerst for Blue's not being in camp. "I'm sorry for Vida," he said. "He obviously hooked up with the wrong guy."

Bando said that while he was all for a player's earning his worth, he felt Finley had offered Blue a fair contract. The only Oakland teammate to speak on Blue's behalf was Davis, also a Gerst client. He would love to see Vida in uniform, Davis said, "but I respect his decision."

Gerst told Finley that Blue would accept the offer of $50,000 if his client could be a free agent at the end of the 1972 season. When Finley laughed off the notion, Gerst countered that Blue was considering jumping to the Japanese League. Finley knew that wouldn't happen since an agreement between Major League Baseball and the Japanese League stated that no player could jump from one continent to the other without the permission of the owner.

Keeping up public pressure on Finley, Blue appeared at a press conference with Richard Roundtree, the star of *Shaft*. It was announced that Blue had signed a deal with MGM to star in a sequel to the highly successful movie. Blue and Gerst then called another press conference in which Vida, reading from a prepared statement, said he had accepted a position as vice president of public relations for Dura Steel Products. Based in Santa Fe Springs, California, it was a company specializing in bathroom and toilet fixtures and located just down the freeway from the picturesque pastel surroundings of Dodger Stadium. Few members of the assembled media took him seriously since Blue chuckled throughout his statement, which included his announcement that he was leaving baseball.

"Hold it," he said at one point. "I'm serious."

He was not serious enough, however, to stop from meeting again with Finley. Following another failed face-to-face with Blue, Finley asked A's equipment manager Frank Ciensczyk over drinks in a motel bar if he had any ideas on how to settle the situation. Ciensczyk was startled. "I'm just a sock-and-jock man, Mr. Finley." When Ciensczyk suggested that Finley send one of the players to talk to Blue, the boss seized on the idea.

He ordered Tenace and Blefary to make separate trips to Oakland to persuade Blue to return. Some saw the sending of "goodwill ambassadors" as eccentric, but it fit right into what had become a bizarre and near deadly offseason for the AL's defending Western Division champions.

On January 6 Odom tried to prevent a burglary at his neighbor's house in Macon, Georgia, and was shot in the left side of the neck and the right side of his chest by a man wielding a .38-caliber pistol. Both bullets missed Odom's muscles, bones, and vital organs.

In spring training Finley scheduled his A's for an exhibition game against a Japanese team in which the rules of the game were altered so that a batter would walk on three balls and strike out on two strikes. Finley had long been in favor of the three-balls-and-two-strikes innovation, much to his manager's dismay. So what if baseball had used different rules for seventy-five years? The boss thought the innovation would catch on, but Williams recalled his pitchers walking about twenty Japanese hitters and the A's getting the hell kicked out of them. Williams called Finley's proposed innovation an "invention defeated by defeat."

Finley also had his club fooling around with orange baseballs, which would be used in an exhibition game in 1973. Former A's outfielder George Hendrick, who had been dealt to Cleveland, drove three of Finley's orange baseballs beyond the outfield wall for homers. Hendrick then told Commissioner Kuhn he couldn't pick up the spin on the ball. Williams figured Hendrick had told Kuhn that just to get back at Finley and said the orange baseballs experiment had been killed by a grudge.

Throughout the spring Williams handled Blue's holdout like he dealt with all contract matters involving his players. He told his players he didn't give a damn who was right, he just wanted them to be ready for the season. To that end Williams secretly supplied Blue with baseballs and equipment.

With Blue holding out and with Odom recovering from gunshot wounds and fellow pitcher Chuck Dobson nursing an elbow injury, the A's were in desperate need of pitching. Following their three-game sweep by Baltimore in the ALCS the previous October, Finley heeded Williams's call for another reliable starter and acquired stylish southpaw Ken Holtzman from the Chicago Cubs in exchange for outfielder Rick Monday. Holtzman was only twenty-six years old and had authored two no-hitters, the first in 1969 against Henry Aaron and the eventual NL Western Division Atlanta Braves and the second in 1971 against the Big Red Machine in Riverfront Stadium.

With the A's still needing another arm Finley pulled the trigger on a deal for Denny McLain.

"When you haven't got your big starter in camp and it's been open for two weeks, you've got to take action," Williams told the press. Privately he had reservations. Since winning a combined 55 games over the 1968–69 seasons for Detroit, McLain had won just 13 games over the 1970–71 campaigns. He was still weeks shy of turning twenty-eight at the time of his arrival with the A's, but his appearance left Williams unimpressed. The former star looked overweight and out of shape.

In his first spring start, McLain was manhandled by Milwaukee and bombed for ten runs. San Diego pummeled him for seven runs on fourteen hits. Four days later McLain flashed his old form, shutting out Cleveland for five innings and earning a spot in the rotation as the A's broke camp and headed to Oakland for the belated season opener against the Twins.

One player not heading to Oakland was Davis. He had hit .324 for the A's in 1971 while playing in 79 games, .464 as a pinch hitter. On the morning of March 24 he had climbed aboard the team bus for the trip to Yuma for the game against San Diego. Davis was nursing a sore left leg but was still batting .563. Shortly after the bus arrived at the clubhouse, he was called aside by Williams. The man who had introduced Blue to his agent had been given his unconditional release.

Though the A's would claim that injuries had scuttled the aging star's career, Davis believed it was Finley's way of seeking retribution. Finley wanted a scapegoat, Davis thought. Charlie didn't want to get rid of Blue, but he wanted to show "how strong he could be."

Davis insisted he had introduced Gerst merely to look after Vida's endorsements and personal appearances. But if his introducing Blue to Gerst was the reason they had cut him, the gentlemanly Davis said, there was nothing he could do about it. "If it is [the reason]," he said, "it's very childish."

Opening Day on Saturday, April 15, brought a crowd of just 9,912 to the

Coliseum for a game matching two teams that had combined to win the AL's first three Western Division titles since the beginning of the divisional format in 1969. The small turnout wasn't limited to Oakland alone. Only 17,401 fans showed up at Wrigley Field as the Phillies' new ace, lefty Steve Carlton, donned the team's powder blue double-knit uniform and launched his historic season with a 4–2 win over ace Ferguson Jenkins.

In Shea Stadium a crowd of 15,893 cheered Seaver's 4–0 shutout of the champion Pirates and booed Commissioner Kuhn. After having waited out the strike, baseball fans watching at home were greeted with NBC cameras panning cloud-shrouded "Big Shea" while play-by-play man Jim Simpson provided the voice-over. It was a raw, windy, cold day at Shea, but as Simpson warmly intoned, "The strike is over and major league baseball is back with us today."

Simpson's broadcast partner and color analyst Sandy Koufax, newly elected to the Baseball Hall of Fame, compared the players' late start in '72 to the celebrated holdout he and teammate Don Drysdale had undergone prior to the 1966 season.

Following a solemn ceremony honoring the late Mets manager Gil Hodges, Seaver stared in at Rennie Stennett and fired his customary first-pitch fastball.

"It is bitterly cold here in New York," Simpson told his viewers, "but what a thrill it is to be back and have the 1972 season underway."

The thrill was also evident in Cincinnati, where the Reds were engaging in their eighty-eighth season opener. The Western Division rival Los Angeles Dodgers were in town and amid leaden skies and a threat of rain a crowd of 37,895 watched Jack Billingham duel Don Sutton.

Longtime Dodger voice Vin Scully thought it "rather fitting" that the Dodgers and Reds paired off in the '72 season opener. In 1962 the Dodgers had opened their new ball park in Chavez Ravine against the Reds, and Frank Robinson had been in a Cincinnati uniform that day. Here the two teams were ten years later on Opening Day, and Scully said it was ironic that Robby was now wearing Dodger blue and playing against the Reds.

One more difference to this Opening Day was that the Dodgers and

Reds were debuting their new double-knits. The designs of the uniforms were different. The Dodgers were still sporting the button-down jerseys, while the Reds had adopted the pullovers with no buttons and no belts popularized by the Pirates and Cardinals. Montreal outfielder Ken Singleton thought the new form-fitting uniforms looked great on Bench, Morgan, Rose, et al. "Of course, on those guys any uniform would have looked great," he added.

American League umpire Ron Luciano thought the form-fitting double-knits a perfect fit for television as long as the player had good form. There were some forms, he added, over which even a tent would not have looked good. Some players welcomed them; Singleton was allergic to wool, so he became one of the first Expos to don the double-knits. The home uniform double-knits had a much brighter glow to them; alongside teammates still wearing the somewhat dull flannel uniforms, Singleton was said to look like a light bulb turned on. Others, like veteran Jim Kaat, had their reservations about the stylish uniforms. Kaat noted that on hot days the blousy flannels afforded some ventilation. The double-knits, tapered to the body as they were, did not.

Scully's longtime partner on Dodger broadcasts, Jerry Doggett, welcomed listeners on the team's flagship station, KFI AM 640. Doggett, who was working the first three innings, opened the broadcast, and Scully took the mic in the top of the fourth: *"Opening Day 1972 and thank goodness it's here. . . . Despite the weather, despite the dismal forecast, the enthusiasm was certainly not dimmed by any means."*

Outside of Cincinnati fans were less enthusiastic. In Chicago's Wrigley Field fewer than eighteen thousand seats were sold for the Cubs' opener. In St. Louis, one of the best baseball cities in the country, only 7,808 fans showed up for the opener against Montreal. Conspicuously absent was Cardinals owner Gussie Busch. Those who were on hand heckled Bob Gibson as he struggled through the first inning. "Hurry up," one person shouted. "I've got to go to a union meeting!" When Cardinal center fielder Jose Cruz misplayed a single, another fan yelled, "Put a dollar sign on it!"

Oakland fans, however, quickly warmed to Holtzman, who in his first official start for the A's held a lineup featuring future Hall of Famers Rod Carew and Harmon Killebrew to three hits over eight innings. He left with a 3–2 lead, but the Twins reached reliever Rollie Fingers for a run in the ninth to send the game into extra innings. Rudi doubled off Dave LaRoche to open the bottom of the eleventh and was sacrificed to third by Jackson. Bando drew an intentional walk, bringing Tenace to the plate. A's announcer Monte Moore made the call:

> *Wouldn't you know it, the A's are starting this season on an exciting note. . . . In rides the pitch. Tenace swings. There's a bouncing ball, right side of the infield. Rudi's gonna try to score! Carew picks the ball up, here's the throw to the plate, it's gonna be close. . . . Mitterwald's got the ball. Rudi crashes into him and the ball is knocked loose! Rudi is safe at the plate and the A's win, 4–3!*

The finale of the brief two-game series was almost as dramatic, the Twins winning 3–2 when Carew beat the Catfish with a two-out RBI double in the eighth. Two nights later McLain opened a three-game series against Kansas City by not allowing an earned run over seven innings, and the A's won by another 3–2 final.

Afterward, a beaming Williams greeted reporters. "McLain was fabulous," he said, "just fabulous."

Attendance, however, was anything but fabulous. The series opener against the Royals drew a paltry crowd of 4,494, and when Oakland drew fewer than 15,000 fans combined for a two-game series in Yankee Stadium one week later—a series punctuated by Stadium fans chanting, "We want Vida!"—a summit conference was convened in Chicago on Thursday, April 27, involving Finley, Blue, Gerst, and Kuhn.

The group met at the Drake Hotel, and their twenty-two hours of marathon negotiations to get one of baseball's meal tickets back on the field were highlighted by Finley's storming from the room and Blue's leaving to take a nap. A compromise settlement was finally reached. Finley's offer of $50,000 was agreed upon, but Blue would receive a $5,000 retroactive bonus for his 1971 accomplishments and another $8,000 to be put in a reserve scholarship fund should the pitcher decide to return to college. The latter was part of the original contract Blue had signed in 1967.

While Finley wanted to announce Vida's salary as $50,000, Blue and Gerst wanted it listed as $63,000. Finley withdrew his offer. Kuhn returned to his New York office and issued a statement: "I feel a fair offer has been made. And I am urging [Blue] to reflect upon this. And I am ordering Finley to keep the offer open. . . . I have the authority to do what I'm doing under my general powers, which includes actions that are in the best interest of baseball."

Finley fumed, then issued a statement of his own: "It's ridiculous for the commissioner to get involved and I resent it very much. . . . Should he call another meeting I will not attend."

A fed-up Kuhn ordered Finley and Blue to meet with Cronin at the Boston office of the American League president. Finley told Kuhn to go to hell. Kuhn countered forcefully: "Charlie," he said, "either you show in Boston and sign a contract with Blue or I will make him a free agent. Take your pick."

Blue decided to sign. Gerst arranged for Vida to make his official announcement May 1 on Howard Cosell's Monday night ABC-TV show. In the interim President Nixon was asked to comment on the situation. Unaware that the two parties had already reached a deal, Nixon said at a Sunday barbecue on the Texas ranch of Treasury Secretary John Connolly that Blue "has so much talent, maybe Finley ought to pay."

The next night, Blue announced that he had ended his holdout. He hopped a plane bound for Boston, and the following day he and Finley met with reporters at American League headquarters. "I'm happy and ready to play," Blue said.

In truth he was neither happy nor ready. He stated that Finley had soured his stomach for baseball—"He treated me like a damn colored boy," Blue spat—and that after months of press conferences and contract negotiations, his body was not in shape.

At the time of his signing, Vida's mood was, in fact, true blue.

CHAPTER FIVE

Sparky Anderson always referred to it as "the Deal."

Baseball writer Roger Kahn considered it closer to larceny.

On November 29, 1971, Bob Howsam pulled off one of the most celebrated trades in baseball history, the Reds general manager acquiring second baseman Joe Morgan, outfielders Cesar Geronimo and minor leaguer Ed Armbrister, right-handed pitcher Jack Billingham, and infielder Denis Menke from Houston for first baseman Lee May, second baseman Tommy Helms, and utility man Jim Stewart.

There had been many good trades in baseball during his years in the game, but the one Howsam engineered with Houston GM Spec Richardson was to Anderson the best ever.

Cincinnati fans decried the Deal initially. Howsam had surrendered the right side of the Reds' infield. A few thought it was a great trade, Reds radio announcer Al Michaels said at the time, but many Reds fans thought the big trade was a big mistake. Some bumper stickers in and around Cincinnati read, "Trade Howsam." What everyone agreed on was that the Deal was one of the most startling moves in franchise history.

Along with Pete Rose, May had been one of the few bright spots of the Reds' offense in '71. He was a popular slugger, and in '71, the Big Red Machine's best run producer, rapping 39 homers and driving in 98 runs, both career highs. Only Hank Aaron and Willie Stargell hit more homers than May in the National League that season. From 1969 to 1971, May had 111 homers and 302 RBIs. His towering three-run shot in Game Four of the 1970 World Series in Baltimore allowed the Big Red Machine to escape the embarrassment of a sweep. With Rose, Bobby Tolan, and Johnny Bench batting in front of him, May was often denied his rightful share of publicity. "They got all the handshakes," May would say, "and I got all the knockdown pitches."

With Bench slugging 45 home runs in 1970, Perez 40, and May 34, the Big Red Machine was the most devastating National League club since the Mays-McCovey-Cepeda San Francisco Giants of the early 1960s. That October Curt Gowdy called May the "Big Bopper from Birmingham, Alabama." A free swinger, May often went for the first pitch. "If he hits it right," Gowdy said, "it's gone." Despite his power May was, according to Gowdy, "one of the less glorified thumpers" of the Red Menace. Still Baltimore Orioles' 20-game winner and future Hall of Famer Jim Palmer called May the "quickest bat this side of the Mississippi" during the '70 Fall Classic.

As critics of the Deal noted, May had it over Morgan when it came to offensive production. May had hammered 38, 34, and 39 homers each of the previous three seasons and knocked in around 100 runs each of those years. Morgan at the time was a .263 hitter who had never hit more than 15 homers or driven in more than 56 runs in a season.

Helms, meanwhile, was a Gold Glove winner who was viewed by Cincinnati fans as the second coming of Rose and Morgan's equal at second base. Stewart was the team's super sub, and along with May and Helms, Ol' Stewball, as his friend Bench called him, was a favorite among fans and teammates.

Morgan, on the other hand, was believed by some to be a troublemaker, a reputation stemming from acrimonious dealings with Astros manager Harry "the Hat" Walker. Morgan knew that in baseball, a reputation can be as indelible as a birthmark, but Howsam knew better than to believe the bleating of others. He wouldn't rely on rumor mongering when it came to rebuilding the Reds. Like the character in Dickens's *Great Expectations*, the GM would take nothing on its looks; he would instead take everything on evidence.

For the better part of the 1971 season Howsam had Reds scout Ray Shore follow Morgan and the Astros. The GM's orders were to the point: find out what kind of player Morgan was and what kind of presence he was. The

Reds were a conservative team in a conservative town. Their Queen City was a quiet city, as American as apple pie, and the Reds knew the kind of men they wanted on their club.

When Shore filed his report, he answered all of Howsam's questions. The Reds had a need for speed, and Morgan's quickness could help the club. On whether Morgan was a troublemaker Shore said he didn't think that was the case.

Howsam believed May could be replaced at first base by the younger Perez, who had been playing third. The rebuilding of the right side of the infield continued with the addition of the Mercury-quick Morgan, who excelled at scoring runs in bunches; he had 131 steals in 166 attempts over the previous three seasons. The teaming of "Go-Go Joe" with Rose (a.k.a. "Charlie Hustle") and Tolan at the top of the order would restore the lightning to Cincinnati's attack and complement the thunder from the booming bats of Bench and Perez. Anderson knew Bench and Perez were strong enough to power the Machine. What Sparky wanted was another sparkplug.

The genesis of the Deal came in the twilight of the summer of '71. The Reds' move in 1970 from Crosley Field to Riverfront Stadium required Cincinnati to stock itself with different ballplayers, different *kinds* of ballplayers. The Astroturf field in Riverfront made speed an essential ingredient. The deeper distances from home plate to the outfield walls meant that power hitting alone would not suffice. The Big Red Machine would need to become a sleeker, quicker, more athletic squad.

The Reds were not alone in their realization. Dodgers speedster Maury Wills knew the game was changing, knew the new ballparks put as much stress on speed as power. The big parks with their artificial turf demanded speed. If you have to choose between speed and power, Wills said, you have to take speed because power alone won't do the job as it did in the days of the great Yankee teams.

Wills had stolen pennants for the "Tap Ball" Dodgers of 1965–66; Lou Brock had done the same for the Cardinals in '67–68. In the final months of the season, with his team out of contention, Howsam began calling for regular meetings in his office with his advisers: Chief Bender; the Bowen brothers, Rex and Joe; Shore; Anderson; and Reds coaches.

The GM peppered his lieutenants with questions: Should we deal Helms, a solid second baseman but one who lacks speed? Could the club afford to keep both a slow May at first base and a slow Perez at third? Could a modern team be successful with no speed at the corners?

All parties at the meetings agreed: either Perez or May would have to be dealt. The synthetic surface dictated that the Reds couldn't keep both. Anderson recalled there being "100 percent agreement" that May was more expendable than Perez. Perez, the Reds' brass reasoned, could be moved from first to third. He had, after all, joined the Reds in 1964 as a first baseman. He switched to third in 1967 to make room for May, but Perez had always preferred playing first base.

Team speed dominated the discussions in Howsam's office. San Francisco had unseated Cincinnati atop the West due in part to a lineup that took advantage of its new carpeted field in Candlestick Park, a lineup that included speedy young outfielders in Bobby Bonds and Ken Henderson, who flanked the legendary Willie Mays in center.

Shore had watched intently early in '71 as the Giants' ground-eating outfielders seemed to run down every fly ball that didn't leave the stadium. He shook his head when watching the Giants' fleet-footed fliers. One howling liner down the right-field line convinced the batter to make the turn at first before abruptly jamming on the brakes, but a throw from Bonds was already on its way to second base. Shore gasped; he couldn't believe it.

Three innings later another foul-line hugger headed for the left-field corner. Before the batter could dig for second, Henderson had unleashed a laser from the shadows. The runner continued his mad dash for a double, but Henderson's speed and strong arm made the outcome at second base inevitable.

In the eighth inning Mays gunned down another runner's bid for extra bases. Shore stood to leave; the super scout had seen enough. "Now I know," he stated, "where base hits go to die."

The flash and dash of the Giants' outfield, which would come to include a young Garry Maddox and Gary Matthews, left a lasting impression on the Reds. It was agreed in Howsam's office that Cincinnati simply had to get quicker to compete.

The Reds also needed another good left-handed hitter in their lineup to counterbalance Bench and Perez. In 1971 the switch-hitting Rose and Bernie Carbo had often been the club's only lefty bats against right-handed hurlers. In addition, the Reds' rotation was in need of a solid starting pitcher to complement southpaw Don Gullett and right-hander Gary Nolan.

During the 1971 World Series between Baltimore and Pittsburgh, rumors made the rounds the Astros were preparing to trade Morgan to Los Angeles for first baseman Wes Parker. Morgan, meanwhile, heard he was heading to Philadelphia in a trade. Privately he told his wife Gloria he was prepared to give up the game rather than go to a last-place club. Houston hadn't fared much better in the West, finishing fifth in a six-team division, but Morgan felt he had invested too much of himself in the Astros' organization to be treated, as he told Gloria, "like a piece of meat."

When Howsam heard of the trade rumors during the Series games in Pittsburgh, he sent Shore and Anderson to find Richardson and tell him the Reds were prepared to put together a package deal the Astros would find "very interesting."

The Deal was worked out, but the original trade didn't include Geronimo. It was May and Helms for Morgan, Menke, Billingham, and Ed Armbrister, whom the Red Sox would rue in the 1975 Fall Classic.

Howsam wasn't satisfied. He had heard good things about a speedy young Astros outfielder who had originally been found in the Dominican Republic by the Yankees. It was said he could flip the wall switch and be in bed and under the covers before the room was dark. Anderson wasn't impressed. What the hell do I care, he thought, about Cesar Geronimo?

Geronimo joined the Astros as a twenty-one-year-old in 1969 and played sparingly for Houston, making just 133 plate appearances in three seasons. His batting average dipped from .243 in 1970 to .220, and from what Anderson had seen of Geronimo in an Astros uniform, he wasn't convinced Cesar could hit big league pitching.

Among the Cincinnati coaches, Ted Kluszewski believed Geronimo had the kind of batting stroke that could eventually deliver a respectable batting average. Based in part on "Big Klu's" opinion, Howsam was persistent in his pursuit of Geronimo.

Anderson grew concerned. "Let's not lose the deal," he told his boss, but Howsam assured him everything would be all right. Eventually the Astros agreed to include Geronimo in the swap.

The day the Deal was consummated at baseball's annual winter meetings, a beaming Anderson told Howsam the Reds had just secured the 1972 pennant. The GM knew it was a controversial trade and braced for feedback from the fans. But in the weeks that followed, the Reds' front office didn't receive nearly as many letters of criticism as it expected—only about sixty from a fan base that drew nearly 3.5 million in 1970. The front office patiently answered each letter, explaining that there were four reasons May and Helms had been dealt: to acquire speed, get left-handed hitting, add depth to the pitching staff, and strengthen the defense. Once the Reds stated their reasons, 60 percent of the letter writers who had been critical of the trade wrote back saying they agreed with it.

Anderson thought the Deal indicative of the length to which Howsam and the brass would go in fine-tuning the Big Red Machine. They knew Morgan and Menke would be on base more than May and Helms. While Big Klu had green-lighted Geronimo, it was another Reds coach, Alex Grammas, who had pushed hard for Morgan. Grammas had grown impressed watching Morgan's range at second base, especially on the artificial turf of the Astrodome. Nicknamed "Little Joe," the 5-foot-7, 160-pound Texas native and Oakland product was known as "Go-Go Joe" for his quickness on the base paths.

Morgan knew he wasn't as fast on the bases as Wills or Brock. What Morgan did was rely on his quickness in breaking away from the bases. He would single or draw a walk, take his lead off first base, then dig his cleats in the dirt and take off for second. At times his speed would force the catcher to make a hurried throw to second. Anderson knew that like Bobby Bonds or Cesar Cedeno, Morgan could control a game from the base paths.

Despite Morgan's ability to get to second base on the field, he could never get to first base with Walker. That led to Little Joe's being thought of as big trouble.

Morgan's problems in Houston were due primarily to his disagreements with Walker. Morgan believed the Hat was a bigot, believed this son of the South and World Series star for the 1946 Cardinals felt he was more intelligent than any black or Latino player, and he pointed to Walker's conflicts with the Astros' Bob Watson, Jimmy Wynn, and Jesus Alou as proof. Walker went to the front office and spoke bitterly of Morgan's "attitude." Jim Bouton would praise Walker in his book, *Ball Four*, as a knowledgeable field boss, a compliment Wynn would later scoff at. Wynn said Walker often ignored what was going on out on the field, instead walking up and down the dugout talking about hitting. It would get to the point where Wynn would finally say, "Harry, pay attention to the field."

Wynn also resented Walker's trying to alter his batting style and change him from a power hitter into a .300 hitter. The "Toy Cannon," as Wynn was known, told Walker he was too far along in his career to change. He was a pull hitter, having hit between 26 and 37 homers every season from 1967 to 1970, and he had hit that way too long to suddenly change.

Morgan had his disagreements with Walker as well and knew in 1971 his days were numbered on any team managed by the Hat. But Morgan also considered the idea of leaving Houston a one-way ticket to Siberia. Initially the trade to Cincinnati left him anything but happy. When he turned up at the Reds' camp, Morgan's attitude was that he couldn't care less about his clouded reputation; he was there to just play ball and help his new club win. In time Bench would come to regard Morgan as the finest player he had ever played with, a man who could win more ball games in more ways than anybody.

Anderson, a former minor league infielder, helped speed Morgan's development on defense. NBC sportscaster Tony Kubek noted on a *Game of the Week* telecast in 1972 that Morgan was turning the double play better than he ever had. In 1973 Morgan would win the first of five consecutive Gold Glove awards.

Figuring Morgan shared the same assets of great players like Rose, Anderson went to Bernie Stowe, the Reds' delightful clubhouse man and equipment manager, and suggested he put Morgan's locker next to Rose's. Anderson felt that what made Charlie Hustle baseball's most exciting player might rub off on Morgan.

Rose was the ignition switch for the Big Red Machine. He was the Cincinnati Kid, and his "Charlie Hustle" nickname had been applied by Yankee veteran Whitey Ford during a spring training game in the early 1960s. Ford's teammate, Mickey Mantle, recalled that Rose gained the nickname after Ford had watched him trying to climb a fence in spring training to catch a homer that was sailing far beyond the outfield wall.

Rose took the insult and turned it into a badge of honor. He knew he didn't have the natural skills of Willie Mays or Roberto Clemente, so he compensated by playing hard and fast all the time. Even though Anderson's naming Rose team captain in 1969 bothered Bench for years, the Reds' catcher acknowledged that Rose always led by example, that Pete's enthusiasm and concentration were something to behold.

Los Angeles Times columnist Jim Murray called Rose the Reds' "cloud of dust." Murray said it was legend in Cincinnati that Rose had once hung his uniform on a railing to dry and it had promptly stolen second. Watching the Reds' captain draw a walk against the Dodgers and sprint to first base, announcer Vin Scully told his audience, "Pete Rose just beat out a walk." Gowdy noted that Rose didn't hit many homers, but when he did give a pitch a ride, he ran it out. "He's the fastest home-run hitter in the game," said Gowdy. Atlanta Braves traveling secretary Don Davidson said Rose "plays the game like it should be played." Reds announcer Waite Hoyt, a Hall of Fame pitcher for the 1927 Yankees, considered Pete a throwback to earlier eras. "Rose even runs out his strikeouts," Hoyt said. *The Sporting News* declared Rose "Baseball's Best Ad."

Rose's reckless abandon on the field turned him into a human grass stain and caused longtime observers to compare Pete to Jim Rivera, an outfielder for the Chicago White Sox in the 1950s. Nicknamed "Jungle Jim," Rivera gave fans an exciting show by executing head-first slides and diving catches a decade before Rose arrived with the Reds. Hall of Famer Rogers Hornsby said at the time that Rivera was "the only man I would pay admission to see."

Longtime National League umpire Shag Crawford said the same of Rose. He thought it a pleasure to be on the same field with Mays, Aaron, and Clemente, but the guy who stood out most was Rose. An MLB umpire from 1956 to 1975, Crawford thought Pete the greatest player he'd ever seen. Quite a few players had more talent, but Crawford considered Rose the total player and thought the effort Pete put into every game incredible.

Ed Sudol, a National League umpire from 1957 to 1977, believed that for a good, steady hitter there was none better in his era than Rose. Pete didn't hit with much power, but Sudol knew Rose could be counted on to make contact.

Some fans and opposing players saw Rose as a showoff. His mannerisms made him the player opponents loved to hate. Assuming his unique batting crouch—"an unorthodox stance that makes him look as if he is squatting to milk a cow," Dayton *Daily News* sportswriter Hal McCoy wrote—Rose followed each pitch into the catcher's glove and then turned and glared into the umpire's face for the call. He sprinted to first base following a walk; executed head-first, belly-flopping dives on the base paths; and caught routine fly balls in the outfield with a snapping, downward slice of his glove.

Rose was all out all the time. In the bottom of the twelfth inning of the 1970 All-Star Game in Riverfront Stadium, Rose separated American League catcher Ray Fosse's shoulder with a body check that would have made Gordie Howe proud. Some criticized Rose's running into Fosse as an over-aggressive play that damaged the catcher's career and prevented him from reaching his full potential. Pitcher Clyde Wright of the California Angels was just one of the AL All-Stars angered by the play. Wright yielded the single that allowed Rose to reach base in the twelfth and stated afterward he believed Pete could have scored with a conventional slide and hadn't needed to shatter Fosse. "Why did he do that?" Wright asked reporters. "I guess that's how he plays. But from where I was standing, it looked like he could have gone around him."

Few remember that Fosse played the next ten games while Rose sat out three straight games and only pinch-hit in the fourth because of injuries incurred in the collision and that Fosse returned to the All-Star Game in 1971 and won his second straight Gold Glove. Rose never apologized for the play, never felt a need to. Fosse, he said, was a stride up the line and had the baseline surrounded. Rose said he didn't feel it was his obligation to apologize because he was just trying to win.

Fosse was trying to win as well and four decades later recounted how the play had gone from his vantage point: "I positioned myself where the ball was being thrown by Amos Otis," he said. "I was up the line." Had he not been, Fosse said, he would have missed the throw by three feet and people would still be asking him, "Why did you ole it?"

Rose has spent the intervening years defending his collision with Fosse, saying that nobody had told him that they had changed it from hardball to girls' softball between third and home. In a twist of fate, when Rose went to prison for tax evasion, he was sent to the penitentiary in Marion, Illinois, Fosse's hometown.

New York Mets manager Gil Hodges, who skippered the 1970 NL All-Star team, told reporters Rose made the only play he could. Fosse had the plate blocked, but Pete was going to score, Hodges said, "one way or another."

Anderson also defended Rose's play. Pete had to play that way for two reasons, the skipper said. One, Rose loved baseball, and he showed it by putting all his energy into it. Two, Rose was not a natural ball player. He succeeded with hard work and hustle. Baseball was Pete's job and his hobby. It was everything to him.

Reggie Jackson admired Rose because Pete hustled. To Jackson, Rose was like Mantle, Mays, and Frank Robinson in that each was a living definition of the word "determination." They could go to a movie, Jackson said, and stand out even with the lights out.

Bench thought Rose had that "Charlie Hustle" spirit from the moment he walked on the field until the stadium lights went off. Where Bench would be so exhausted following a game that all he could do was go to sleep, Rose would stay up to listen to a West Coast night game. Rose had a kid's devotion to the game; he reminded Bench of little boys who hung their caps on their bedposts at night and slept on their baseball gloves.

Solidly built at 5-foot-11 and 192 pounds, Rose was a model switch hitter and leadoff man. He had sturdy forearms—"Have you seen Rose's arms?" Bench asked a reporter. "I'd like to have them"—and could muscle up on the ball and hit a home run when needed. If Rose wanted to go for home runs, Anderson said he could hit twenty-five a season.

Mostly Rose preferred to line the ball with authority to all areas of the field. He was a human hitting machine, a model of consistency. He would hit .300 or better 16 times in his 24-year career; bang out 200 or more hits 10 times; lead the National League in hits 7 times; author a league-record 44-game hitting streak; and, on an emotion-packed night in Cincinnati on September 11, 1985, eclipse Ty Cobb as the all-time hits leader.

Knowing observers made it a point to stand by the batting cage and watch Rose hit. Reds teammate Andy Kosco, a veteran of seventeen stops along the minor and major league trail, believed most guys used batting practice to see how far they could drive the ball or how many homers they could hit. Not Pete. Rose sprayed the ball around the field, went with the pitch—"Just like in a game," Kosco said.

Rose served as the role model for Reds baseball not only on the field, but in the clubhouse as well. This was particularly true in the case of Morgan. For the seven seasons they were teammates in Cincinnati, Rose and Morgan were the sparkplugs that would set the Big Red Machine into motion. Pete called the pair "salt and pepper."

One of the first things Morgan did following the trade was to buy "Big Red Machine" T-shirts to wear under his uniform every day. Wearing the shirts helped make him feel like he belonged. He was proud to be part of such a powerhouse team and imagined it was the same kind of pride once felt by the members of the Yankees of the 1950s and '60s.

Gathering in spring camp, the Reds were put through a rigorous regimen. Anderson believed the country club atmosphere of the previous spring had contributed to a summer-long slump. Bench thought the Reds took things for granted. Rose was blunt. In '71 the Reds didn't field, couldn't bunt, and left runners in scoring position.

"Hell," Rose roared a year later, "we should have been put in jail." Looking around at the Spartan surroundings of the Reds' camp, Bench managed a faint smile. "We have been," he said.

Rose would joke that the Reds had gone from being the Big Red Machine to the Little Red Wagon. The joking ended, however, as training camp turned into what Reds players described as "Stalag 17." Morgan called it a "concentration camp." Anderson banned TVs from the clubhouse, set weight limits for each player, fined each man $50 for every pound over his limit, curtailed postgame food spreads, and set an 11 p.m. curfew.

Anderson kept his watch in his back pocket as drills at Redsland—a complex of four diamonds arranged with an observation tower in the middle in a cloverleaf—ran up to five hours. The Reds grunted and growled through camp, but Anderson didn't care about ruffling his player's feathers. What he did care about was how the team was representing the Reds organization, and part of that was what Sparky saw as the players' fixation on fashion and food. The mod squad members of his club worried about their bell-bottom pants? Then let them join the navy, he snapped.

The Reds had been bigger hits on the banquet circuit following their National League pennant than they would be on the field the following summer. After one particularly poorly played loss, Anderson followed his team into the clubhouse. What he witnessed disgusted him. Rather than seeing his players slumped on their stools figuring out why they were struggling, they kept peeling in front of him, headed for the food room. The next day Anderson watched as one of his players approached clubhouse man Bernie Stowe: "Hey Bernie, what's to eat after the game?"

That did it as far as Anderson was concerned. Near the end of the season he drew up a list of playing weights for his players: Bench, 202; Perez, 195; Gullett, 185, and so on.

It was Rose's habit to arrive in camp five pounds over his playing weight and then burn it off. He would run twenty wind sprints at day's end, making sure that the last three or four hurt. For Pete it was more important to be stronger at the end of the season than at the beginning. Otherwise Rose showed up with the same goals he always had: hit .300, get over two hundred hits, collect thirty-five doubles and close to ten triples. To Rose a .300 average was the secret to a lot of things. It meant he would have around two hundred hits; he would be scoring around one hundred runs; and, most important, it meant the Reds would be winning.

Anderson played another hunch in the spring of '72 and asked Pete if he would move from right field to left. Bernie Carbo, the Reds' number one pick in the inaugural 1965 major league free agent draft, had played left field for Cincinnati since his Rookie of the Year season in 1970. But the free-spirited Carbo had slumped badly in the 1970 postseason and '71 regular season and was a spring training holdout in '72 due to a contract dispute.

The newly acquired Geronimo had a gun for a throwing arm, and right fielders are required to have stronger and more accurate arms since they have to make the long throw from the outfield to third base. Rose responded that while he wasn't Clemente or Carl Furillo, right fielders renowned for their rifle-like throws, he had thrown out 13 base runners the season before.

"I'm asking you," Anderson said, "for the good of the team." If it was for the good the team, Rose said, he would make the switch.

Morgan found Rose inspirational, and Little Joe was also inspired by the large amount of talent surrounding him in Cincinnati. Bench and Perez provided the power; Morgan and Tolan provided the speed; Rose, Morgan, Tolan, and Perez hit for average; Morgan and Perez hit for average and power. The hitting skills of the first five batters in the Big Red Machine's order were in perfect harmony.

Rose, a switch hitter with power, led off and annually led the team in hits. The left-handed hitting Morgan hit second, and with a first baseman holding Rose on at first base, there was more room for Morgan to pull the ball, which he did extremely well. Because of his speed Morgan wouldn't likely be doubled up on an infield grounder, meaning there would still be a runner on for the big boppers. In 1972 Morgan proved to be the toughest player in the NL to double up; he hit into a DP once in every 110 at bats.

Tolan hit third. He was faster than Morgan and, like Morgan and Rose, could hit for average and power. Tolan was a good fastball hitter, a plus for the Reds since he saw a lot of fastballs from pitchers who grew anxious when Morgan got on base.

Bench, batting cleanup, and Perez, hitting fifth, provided power. In 1972 they would combine for more RBIs (215) than any other 4–5 punch.

Cincinnati had a solid starting staff headed by Gullett, Nolan, and Billingham and a deep bullpen keyed by the rubber-armed Clay Carroll. The Reds also owned the gift of grab; they would become one of the best defensive teams in history. From 1974 to 1977 the men who comprised the middle of the defense—Bench, Morgan, shortstop Dave Concepcion, and Geronimo in center field—each won four consecutive Gold Glove awards.

The Reds would have been a powerhouse in any era, but they were a perfect match for 1970s baseball, which emphasized speed due to the emergence of synthetic surfaces. The wide reaches of Riverfront Stadium, Candlestick Park, the Houston Astrodome, Three Rivers Stadium, Veterans Stadium, and Busch Stadium allowed the Reds to take full advantage of their abilities.

Previous pennant winners, like the 1959 "Go-Go" White Sox, the 1963–66 Dodgers, and the 1964–68 Cardinals had emphasized speed as well. But the Reds were the first team to put an end to "station-to-station" baseball, where runners advanced one base at a time and the game itself was played at a much slower pace.

Because the Reds ushered in a new era, they were not only a team of the present, but also a team of the future. A decade later the '82 Cardinals followed Cincinnati's lead and fielded a club whose players—Lonnie Smith, Willie McGee, Ozzie Smith, Tom Herr—were greyhound quick and took advantage of Busch Stadium's carpeted interior. The "Runnin' Redbirds" led the league with 200 stolen bases in '82 and six of their starting eight posted double-digit steals.

Managed by Whitey Herzog, a.k.a. the White Rat, the Cards' dash and daring was dubbed "Whiteyball." They delivered a World Series title that fall by beating Harvey Kuenn's Milwaukee Brewers, a.k.a. "Harvey's

Wallbangers," a team that played old school power ball and featured six regulars with double digits in home runs. From 1982 to 1987 Whiteyball won three NL pennants.

Michaels called the '72 Reds the "New Red Machine." Yet when the season started April 15 against ace Don Sutton and the division rival Los Angeles Dodgers in Riverfront Stadium, the Machine sputtered. Sutton went seven solid innings in a 3–1 win, spoiling Billingham's debut as a Red.

New additions Morgan and Menke helped even matters the next day, combining for 4 hits, 3 runs scored, and 3 RBIs in a 10–1 romp that saw Nolan get the win and Carroll claim the first of his major-league-record 37 saves that season. But the Reds lost five of their next six and went just 5-8 in April. By May 10 the New Red Machine looked in need of an overhaul.

Anderson was worried. The clubhouse was funereal; rather than the good-natured needling of Rose, Morgan, Bench, and Perez, one could hear a pin drop.

"We're going to win this thing," Anderson suddenly announced. "So why don't you guys quit worrying?"

Sparky's statement sparked his squad. Morgan and Perez drove in two runs apiece in the Reds' next game to trim St. Louis 5–4, and the Reds ripped off nine straight wins. The highlight of Cincinnati's streak was a doubleheader sweep of defending division champion San Francisco in Candlestick Park on May 16. Reds reserve Julian Javier hit a three-run homer in the opener, and Billingham hurled a three-hitter in the second game to earn his first win in a Reds uniform.

But the day really belonged to Rose. In the opener Giants southpaw Ron Bryant tried to intentionally walk the Reds' switch-hitting captain to get to left-handed hitters Morgan and Tolan and set up a double play. Rather than take an intentional walk, Rose reached out and slapped a sharp single that skidded along the bright green synthetic turf and past third baseman Jim Ray Hart.

The clean ocean breezes that swept through Candlestick Park during Cincinnati's four-game sweep of the champs might have been seen by the Reds as winds of change. There was symbolism in Rose's aggressive at-bat; it represented the spirit of the New Red Machine. All summer long Cincinnati would attack opponents, constantly applying pressure. During the course of its nine-game win streak the Machine motored from fifth place to third in the West.

We're on our way, Anderson thought.

CHAPTER SIX

"We can win without Blue," Oakland third baseman Sal Bando told reporters during Vida's celebrated holdout. "It would be harder, but we can."

To a man, the A's agreed. As Catfish Hunter said, when Captain Sal spoke, even E. F. Hutton listened.

The worth of Bando's words could be seen in Oakland's uneven start. By the time Blue signed on May 2, the reigning Western champions were 7-4 and in second place behind the Chicago White Sox. It would be another three weeks before Blue appeared in a game and another year before he would begin to resemble the superstar he had been in 1971.

With their ace out of action, the A's relied on the rotation of Hunter, Holtzman, and McLain. Hunter was the A's Mr. Automatic: author of a perfect game in 1968, the first in the American League in forty-six years, and a 21-game winner in 1971.

"The first thing you think about when you reach the majors is winning 20," Hunter said. "The thing about winning 20 is that it makes you hungry to win 20 again."

The Catfish won 20 or more games five straight seasons, becoming the fourth and most recent AL pitcher to accomplish a feat previously recorded only by Walter Johnson, Lefty Grove, and Bob Feller. In 1974 Hunter won 25 games and the AL's Cy Young Award. In 1976 he became the fourth pitcher in history and the first since Johnson in 1915 to have 200 career wins before the age of thirty-one; the others were Cy Young and Christy Mathewson.

Despite being the Cat-alyst of the A's great staff of the seventies, Hunter was an underappreciated star. Writer Dan Schlossberg noted at the height of Hunter's powers that the quiet Carolinian was often overlooked when great pitchers were discussed.

Unlike other members of the A's, including owner Charlie Finley, Hunter did not have a flamboyant personality. It was Finley who gave him the flashy nickname "Catfish" because the boss thought Jim Hunter just too plain a name.

Hunter didn't possess a flaming fastball like Blue or outsized personality like McLain. The Cat, however, was a prankster—he incurred the wrath of manager Dick Williams in an incident with a stolen megaphone—and had a sharp tongue at times. He and Bando sat in the back of the A's bus and when necessary—usually during a losing streak—broke the team's tension by insulting each other and their teammates. They would rip Reggie for his showboating and erratic throwing arm, Holtzman for wearing similar clothes every day, and Darold Knowles for his mismatched outfits.

No one on the club was safe, and before long, Rollie Fingers, Dick Green, Blue Moon Odom, Mike Epstein, and the entire team would be in on it. The whole point, Hunter said, was to make sure there were no prima donnas on the team. Meanwhile, the bus, and the A's, kept right on rolling along. So too did the Catfish, who continually went out and gave masterful but low-key performances on the mound.

"Nothing mysterious about Hunter," Baltimore Orioles manager Earl Weaver, an admiring rival, once said. "He just throws strikes."

There were critics. After Hunter beat the Brewers, Milwaukee boss Dave Bristol called a clubhouse meeting and told his players, "If you can't hit Catfish Hunter, you can't hit anybody." Because he relied on control rather than power, Hunter didn't generate excitement among writers. Following a 2–1 win against the Angels in 1971, a writer rose from his seat in the press box and said mockingly, "Well, folks, another exciting game pitched by the Catfish."

But Alvin Dark, who coached the Cat during two stays with the A's and also managed against him when Dark skippered the Cleveland Indians, recalled Hunter's being such a great pitcher that Dark expected him to throw a shutout every time the Cat took the mound.

Stuffing his jaw with chaw and tugging on the gold bill of his oversized A's hat between pitches, the Catfish changed speeds and consistently worked the corners of the plate. Like his boyhood idol Robin Roberts, Hunter was a control artist, a thinking man's pitcher. He wore his A's hat a size too big for a reason: if he had to resettle it too much following each pitch, he knew he was overthrowing.

The solidly built Hunter threw an above-average fastball that would ride and another that would sink. His sweeping curve had downward movement, and he had a hard slider and an off-speed slider. He also changed speeds on all of his pitches. At his best he could pinpoint his fastball, slider, and curve, and he pitched in an "X" pattern—up and in, down and away, etc.—changing it from batter to batter and inning to inning as he engaged in a game of mental gymnastics with hitters.

Trying to judge Hunter on his fastball alone would be missing the point, said A's pitching coach Wes Stock, who considered Catfish an "artist on the mound." Hunter was almost always ahead of the hitter because he almost always had his control. Usually the Cat wouldn't show his fastball until he had the batter off balance. Then, Stock said, the Catfish would pop one and it was strike three.

Hunter excelled at throwing strike one as well. He would establish his control and command at the start of the game, and by the seventh inning he had expanded the width of the plate in the umpire's eyes from seventeen inches to as much as twenty-one.

Hunter told writer Larry Bortstein at the time that he would rather be out there on that mound than anywhere. "That's my business and my pleasure," Hunter said, "and I work at it."

Indeed Jim Hunter may have been unassuming, but the Catfish was a ferocious competitor. When told by Williams during the 1971 season he was being passed over in the rotation to give Blue additional starts, Hunter responded by walking out of the skipper's office and tossing a chair in the clubhouse. It was the Cat's turn to start on July 4, 1971, against the Angels, but he was passed over ostensibly so that Vida could be ready for the July 13 All-Star Game in Detroit. As *Sport* magazine writer Pat Jordan later stated, the move was really made so that the Angels would be guaranteed a huge holiday crowd. As a reporter said then, "Who the hell will pay to see Catfish Hunter pitch?"

The slight angered Hunter, who had a combative attitude when it came to his craft. He carried that combativeness to the mound. Though not a strikeout pitcher, Hunter liked to go at batters with his fastball. Weaver admired the way Hunter challenged hitters, and Stock called Catfish as much a competitor as Pete Rose, who was known to slide on his belly even in an exhibition game.

Reggie Jackson said he had seen Hunter surrender six runs in the early innings and grind out a 7–6 win. Getting roughed up doesn't bother Catfish, Jackson said then. "He just comes right back at you."

When Epstein was with the Washington Senators, he faced pitchers who had better stuff than Hunter but were afraid to challenge him. Catfish was never afraid to challenge him, said Epstein, who called Hunter a "helluva competitor."

NBC's Tony Kubek remarked during a 1972 *Game of the Week* Saturday telecast from Boston's Fenway Park, in which Hunter was dueling fellow mound artist Luis Tiant, that the Cat was something special. "He has good control and I don't mean just getting the ball in the strike zone," Kubek said. "He hits the corners, doesn't throw many balls down the middle of the plate. . . . He spots his pitches pretty well."

Hunter spotted his pitches so well A's coach Vern Hoscheit barely had to move his glove in bullpen warmups; Hunter's fastball, curve, and slanting slider continually hit the exact spot Hoscheit placed his catcher's glove.

Like Kubek's former teammate, Yankees ace Whitey Ford, Hunter won with guts and guile. In retirement, Ford said Hunter was one of the pitchers he most enjoyed watching. Like Whitey, the Catfish excelled in big games. He was the A's go-to guy in must-win situations. Williams called Hunter the best clutch pitcher he ever coached and said the A's liked to see the Catfish climb the mound in big games. Bando said that if he had one game to win and one pitcher to throw it, "I'd want Catfish Hunter." Jackson saw Hunter not only as the A's most valuable pitcher, but also their most valuable player. "We can't win without the Catfish," Reggie said at the time. "The Fish is automatic."

Reliever Paul Lindblad, Hunter's roommate with the A's, called the Cat pressure-proof. Hunter just pushed pressure aside, Lindblad said. Hunter's wife, Helen, said once that when her husband took the mound in a big game, she was certain he was the calmest person in the stadium. Knowles, another member of the Oakland bullpen, had never seen a man pitch with more determination than Hunter. To Knowles the Cat was a "deadly professional."

After Ray Fosse replaced Dave Duncan as the A's starting catcher in 1973, he came to consider the Catfish a "bulldog," a baseball term for a pitcher who grinds it out every fourth or fifth day and gobbles up two hundred-plus innings per season. Decades later, as an A's color analyst, Fosse traveled with the team to Citizens Bank Park in Philadelphia in June 2011. Fosse thought Philadelphia Phillies ace Roy Halladay, then at the peak of his powers with a recent perfect game and just the second no-hitter in postseason history, was cut from the same cloth as Catfish.

Oakland in the early 1970s featured three aces—Hunter, Holtzman, and Blue—and Fosse thought Hunter the easiest to catch of the three. Against right-handers, Hunter had what Fosse called a "super slider." The Catfish also came up with a change-up he used against left-handers. In his first season behind the plate for the A's, Fosse said Hunter didn't shake him off when it came to pitch selection more than three times. Dave Duncan, who shared Oakland's catcher's duties with Gene Tenace in 1972, said if he called for a curveball and the Cat was thinking fastball, rather than shake Duncan off, Hunter would just reprogram himself to throw the curve. It made him an easy man to catch, Duncan said.

Hunter and Holtzman liked to work fast to stay in the groove. They wanted to get the game over as quickly as possible. Blue was different, Fosse said. He had a little bounce on the mound; Vida wanted to have a little fun out there.

The differences extended to the Big Three's personal lives as well. Blue said the three aces weren't of the same mind when it came to off-the-field activities. The reason was simple, Blue said. "We weren't that much alike."

Still the A's aces talked pitching constantly at a time when a lot of pitchers, as Hunter pointed out, didn't talk to each other. In that way the Big Three were like a brotherhood, a feeling that was familiar to Hunter, who had grown up in Hertford, North Carolina, as part of a farm family that included nine older children.

Hunter recalled that baseballs were rare down on the farm when he was growing up, so they made due with potatoes, corncobs, or anything else that was round and firm. When they did get a new ball, they wrapped and rewrapped its cover, ultimately slipping an old sock over it. They may not have had much money, but they always had the game of baseball.

Hunter and his family and friends played in cow pastures and yards. Hunter's father, Abbott, had been a catcher, and he never lost his love for the game. He would drive his youngest son to Baltimore to watch the Orioles, and Hunter recalled Robin Roberts pitching for the Birds in many of the games they attended in the early 1960s. As soft as Roberts was throwing, Abbott would say, he was sure he could get a hit off of him.

No, Jim would tell his father. Roberts knows where the ball is going, and the batter doesn't. Hunter would adopt Roberts's strategy as his own. "My philosophy for pitching," Catfish said, "is to make them hit your pitch."

He would throw strikes, try to get ahead of the hitter, and try not to nibble too much. Because he was always around the plate with his pitches, Hunter surrendered his share of home runs. Some of the drives he gave up were legendary. The Cat recalled a moon shot by Mickey Mantle in the 1960s and a similar sky-scraping blast by Dave Kingman in the 1970s. There was a memorable drive by Frank Howard that Hunter joked must have landed in a Third World country.

When asked about all the homers he gave up, Hunter would shrug. That's usually just one run on one pitch, he reasoned. Give up three hits and a run, and that's a lot of pitches and wear and tear on the arm.

Though he was just twenty-six years old in 1972, Hunter had already been around the big leagues for eight seasons. At the time, he was one of the few major leaguers to have never played in the minors. Like Blue, Hunter had been a multi-sport star in high school. He was all-state in football; he won the state 440-yard dash; and his teams won state titles in baseball and football. His junior year in high school he struck out 29 batters in a twelve-inning game.

His triumphs over adversity weren't limited to the playing field. His senior year at Perquiman High in Hertford, he rose with the sun on Thanksgiving Day and went wading through a swamp with his brother Pete, the pair armed with shotguns and looking for small game. Pete's shotgun went off accidentally and got Jim in the foot. "He had the nerve to faint on me," Hunter recalled. "I had to slap him to wake him up."

At the time, Hunter thought he might never pitch again. He had gone 13-1 his junior season and pitched his team to the state championship, but some major league teams stopped following him once they learned of his hunting accident. After his right foot healed, Hunter pushed off the pitching rubber the way he always had; he didn't have to change anything in his delivery.

Finley didn't change either. The Athletics owner and one of his scouts, former major league catcher Clyde Kluttz, still believed Hunter could become a major league pitcher. Kluttz had taught Hunter how to grip a baseball so that his fastball sank a good six inches and how to hold it across the seams so that the pitch rose like it had a mind of its own.

Finley visited the Hunter family in June 1964, on the eve of Jim's second straight appearance in a state title game. Finley described Abbott and Lillie Hunter's dwelling as a "sharecropper's home with a tin roof." When Finley arrived, Lillie was hoeing the weeds in a peanut patch; Abbott was in the smokehouse turning bacon and hams.

Hunter remained a country boy at heart. When he was a star with the A's, he would wear Edwardian sport coats, white twill bell bottoms, and blousey-sleeved body shirts. But he still spoke with a down-home Carolina drawl and spent his off-seasons doing the same things he had done as a kid—walking in the woods for as much as thirty miles on a given day hunting squirrel, raccoon, quail, and deer; fishing for trout and, yes, catfish; spraying his peanut crops; harvesting corn; and loading melons onto trucks. As a boy, he loaded watermelons for twelve hours a day; once he worked from sunup to sundown and then pitched the next afternoon. He said farm life had made him twice as strong at age eighteen than he was in his mid-twenties, when he was only working forty days a year as a starting pitcher.

His baseball future was on the line when Finley arrived at his home. After talking with the family for an hour, Finley asked about Jim's injury. When Hunter took off his boot, Finley almost fell over. The top of Hunter's right foot was loaded with buckshot. Others had backed off in their pursuit of Hunter, but Finley would not. He later told the *New York Times* he had fallen in love with the Hunter family. Finley told the Hunters that even if Jim never pitched again, he could keep the $75,000 signing bonus and he would personally see to it that Hunter got the best medical treatment available.

Hunter signed, and Finley asked about a nickname.

"What do you like to do?" Finley asked. "Hunt and fish," Hunter replied.

Fine, Finley said. When you were six years old you ran away from home and went fishing. Your mom and dad had been looking for you all day. When they found you about four o'clock in the afternoon, you'd caught two big catfish and were reeling in a third. "And that," Finley said with some satisfaction, "is how you got your nickname."

Finley, like St. Louis Cardinals minor league manager Blake Harper before him, loved nicknames. Legend has it that Harper handed one of his fiery, feisty players the moniker "Pepper" because his birth name, John Martin, was just too ordinary. "Catfish," like "Pepper," looked good in headlines and was another way for Finley to add color to his club.

The newly named Catfish spent the 1964 season recovering from his accident and was ticketed for the minors in 1965 when an injury to an A's pitcher opened a spot for him on the Athletics' major league roster. He had just turned nineteen. Also on the club that summer was Satchel Paige, soon to be fifty-nine years old. A publicity photo was taken of the youngest and oldest pitchers in the majors in 1965: Hunter, the bonus baby, sitting on the grandfatherly Paige's lap. It was an experience, Hunter said, to be around a mound master like Paige. Hunter and Paige sat in the bullpen, and Satchel talked about the old days. Hunter watched in fascination as Paige and his "hesitation" pitch surrendered just one hit—a Carl Yastrzemski single—in three innings against the Red Sox.

Hunter won a combined 17 games over his first two seasons and on May 8, 1968, pitched the major league's first perfect game since Sandy Koufax had shut down the Chicago Cubs in 1965. In what may be the best-pitched game in major league history, Koufax outdueled Bob Hendley, who surrendered just one hit and one walk in going the distance. Hunter's gem, a 4–0 final against a Minnesota lineup boasting Rod Carew, Harmon Killebrew, and Tony Oliva, would be the majors' last perfect outing for the next thirteen seasons.

Al Helfer, teamed with Monte Moore, made the call on the Athletics' radio station: *"Jim Hunter comes again with the 3-2 delivery. . . . Fastball in there. . . . Strike three! The boy has pitched a no-hitter! . . . He pitched a perfect ball game and goes into the record books [with] the immortals."*

Hunter wasn't the only member of Oakland's Big Three to make baseball history. Blue threw a no-hitter in 1970 and would combine with Lindblad and Fingers to no-hit the California Angels in 1975. Holtzman threw *two* no-hitters, both with the Cubs. The first came August 19, 1969, and the 3–0 win was made more impressive since it came against the eventual Western Division champion Atlanta Braves and a lineup listing Hank Aaron, Orlando Cepeda, Rico Carty, and Felipe Alou.

Holtzman had to survive a pulled drive to left by Aaron in the seventh. Cubs longtime announcer Vince Lloyd made the call: *"Aaron swings, look out, that baby is hit. . . . It is way back there. . . . Billy Williams, back to the wall . . . back to the corner. . . . He grabs it!"*

Holtzman's second no-hitter came two years later in Cincinnati's Riverfront Stadium, a 1–0 victory over the reigning league champions. Jack Brickhouse, the Cubs' colorful television announcer, provided the call on Chicago's WGN: *"Here is Lee May. . . . Here we go, two out in the ninth. . . . Ball two, strike two, everybody on the edge of their seat here at Riverfront Stadium. . . . Strike three! It's a no-hitter for Kenny Holtzman! He did it again!"*

It was close to being Holtzman's third or even fourth no-hitter. He had one-hit eventual Western Division champion San Francisco in 1971 and five years earlier had nearly done the unimaginable: no-hit the great Koufax and the champion Dodgers. Holtzman took a no-hitter into the ninth against Los Angeles on September 25, 1966, before third baseman Dick Schofield singled to center field. Holtzman finished with a complete game two-hitter and outdueled Koufax 2–1.

The Holtzman-Koufax matchup had come the day after Yom Kippur, and Holtzman's mother, Jacqueline, was torn between rooting for her son and rooting for Sandy, whose name was being extolled in Jewish households as the "New Patriarch." "Maybe," Ken's mother reportedly told him, "you can get a no-decision."

Holtzman's mother was a housewife; his father, Henry, worked in the machinery business. Ken played for the University City High School team, earning Most Valuable Player honors on a state championship team. He graduated from the University of Illinois in 1967 with a Bachelor of Arts degree in business administration. Originally told at a Minnesota Twins tryout camp that he was too small to play professional baseball, Holtzman was taken by the Cubs in the fourth round of the Amateur Draft and signed for a $65,000 bonus. The bonus was important, Holtzman knowing that if he opted for a career in baseball, by the time he turned thirty he would be ten years behind guys with whom he had graduated college. He had to be assured he would earn enough money in baseball to make it financially worthwhile to him. He believed his signing bonus did that.

Holtzman began his baseball career in 1965 in the Pioneer League and, after going 4-0 with a 1.00 ERA, was promoted to the Northwest League, where he went 4-3 with an ERA of 2.40.

Called up to the Cubs that September, he made his major league debut September 4 at age nineteen. Entering the game against San Francisco in the ninth inning, Holtzman allowed a home run to the first hitter he faced, Jim Ray Hart. He made three relief appearances at the end of the season and then became a starter in 1966.

Jewish and a stylish southpaw, Holtzman was called the "next Koufax."

He is the winningest Jewish pitcher in major league history, his 174 career victories surpassing the 165 recorded by Koufax, who at age thirty was forced into early retirement by an arthritic elbow following his 1966 Cy Young–winning season.

Holtzman said once that of all his baseball accomplishments—winning three straight World Series with the A's; hurling two no-hitters for the Cubs; being remembered as the all-time winningest Jewish pitcher—his biggest thrill came the first time he walked into Wrigley Field in a Cubs uniform. That moment validated the sacrifices and hard work necessary to reach the majors. The no-hitters, championships, and personal accomplishments were anticlimactic. Nothing, Holtzman said, surpassed realizing a childhood dream.

Armed with a looping, roundhouse curve, Holtzman established himself as the number two man in the Cubs' rotation behind right-hander Ferguson Jenkins. Until he joined the A's, 1969 had been Holtzman's best shot at reaching the playoffs. It was a fun summer on Chicago's North Side. The Cubs featured future Hall of Famers in Jenkins, Ernie Banks, Billy Williams, and Ron Santo. They were the beasts of the East, leading their division by as many as nine games as late as August 16. But as the summer wore on, the Cubs wore down. With the signature ivy on Wrigley's walls turning from bright green to light brown as fall descended, the Cubs were overtaken by the "Miracle Mets" in the race for the division title and finished eight games back.

"Once we got caught," Jenkins said, "we just couldn't keep the pace."

Throughout his Cubs' career Holtzman kept a remarkable pace. He was talented and durable, throwing an eleven-inning complete game against the Dodgers in 1967 and going twelve innings against the eventual world champion Pirates two years later. In '71 he set a Cubs record by being the club's first pitcher since 1884 to toss two no-hitters. That same summer Holtzman tied a league record when he struck out the first five New York Mets he faced in a September 5 outing.

By 1971 Holtzman was unhappy with the Cubs and with manager Leo Durocher. True to his nickname, Leo "the Lip" had criticized Holtzman publicly for not using his fastball more and relying on what Durocher disparagingly described as a "lollipop" curve. At the close of the season, Holtzman walked into the club's front office and asked general manager John Holland to trade him. Holtzman said it was Durocher's handling of the team, rather than the Lip's public criticism, that prompted him to seek a trade.

Holtzman knew Durocher was from the old school; he had been a player on two of the greatest teams of all time, the Babe Ruth–Lou Gehrig "Murderers' Row" Yankees of the 1920s and the Dizzy Dean–Pepper Martin "Gashouse Gang" Cardinals of the 1930s.

Baseball, however, had changed a lot by the 1970s. The major leagues weren't just getting a lot of players from small towns in the South anymore. The modern players, Holtzman pointed out, were more educated; they had college degrees, even master's degrees. He didn't think Durocher understood that.

Chicago had been the site of some happy times for Holtzman. He met his wife Michelle in the Windy City. At the time of the trade some of his family and friends lived there. His biggest issue was that while the Cubs had the talent to win, something always seemed to prevent them from reaching the postseason. Even when leading the East, they expected the worst to happen. Holtzman felt the Cubs played defensively because of Durocher; they were afraid to get yelled at by Leo the Lip.

Holtzman noted in 1972 that he had *asked* to be traded, not *demanded*. When Holland called Holtzman to tell him he had been dealt to the A's, Ken's response was simply to say, "Fine, thank you." By his own admission, he wasn't that familiar with the American League, but he realized the A's must be good since they had been in the playoffs the season before. Now, he thought, he had a chance to pitch in the postseason.

The timing of the trade was fortuitous for Holtzman and the A's. He was a seasoned, talented front-line lefty in search of a new team, and the A's were a team in search of a seasoned, experienced front-line lefty. Williams figured another southpaw on the A's starting staff would help neutralize some of the league's better portside swingers: Yaz, the Yankees' Bobby

Murcer, Baltimore's Boog Powell, and (in the A's own division) the Twins' Tony Oliva and Rod Carew. On November 29 the A's and Cubs agreed, and Holtzman was dealt to Oakland for outfielder Rick Monday.

A's catchers found Holtzman almost as easy to catch as Hunter. Holtzman's theory was to challenge hitters. He wasn't going to give a game away by walking batters. One of the top control pitchers of his era, he ranked among the league leaders in fewest walks four times in his career. There were times Holtzman didn't have his pinpoint control, but he never gave up or gave in. Some pitchers in similar situations would start fighting themselves, but Holtzman didn't. It hadn't always been that way. When Holtzman was younger, he would get down on himself if he started a game pitching poorly. By 1972 he knew he had to work to adjust. It was a matter of maturity.

Like Hunter, Holtzman constantly looked to get ahead of the hitter. Both were pattern pitchers in that each pitch was connected to the one before and after. They thought in terms of two or three pitches at a time, putting one pitch in one spot to set up the next two pitches. Holtzman might start a hitter with an inside pitch to let him know he had it; another time he might throw a couple of pitches outside to set up the hitter for an inside pitch. Concentration is the biggest part of pitching, Holtzman once said. When he struggled, it was often because he was not thinking in sequence.

Holtzman learned how to pitch from Bill Hands when both were with the Cubs. Hands told Holtzman to get that first strike, and Ken learned to avoid walks while pitching in Wrigley Field. Hands taught Kenny there was more to pitching than physical ability, taught him how to adjust on days when he didn't have his best stuff.

It all came together for Holtzman in 1968, and it happened from one game to the next. One game he was a thrower, the next he was a pitcher. Before that he had just thrown as hard as he could. He didn't like to talk about pacing because he felt most fans would think that meant throwing half-speed pitches in the early innings. What it really meant was working so that if you had to reach back for something extra in the later innings, it would be there.

The scouting report on Holtzman was that he had different fastballs and would take something off of them. Holtzman also had what Fosse thought was a "real easy delivery." Having batted against him, Fosse knew Holtzman's fastball could suddenly be on top of the hitter. Opposing batters believed they could wait on Holtzman's offerings, but that wasn't true. "The ball would be on them," Fosse said, eating them up.

Fosse found out the same was true for the catcher. Sometimes he would give Holtzman a sign, and before he could get down in his catcher's stance, here came the pitch. Fosse would have to ask Holtzman, "At least let me get down there before you throw the ball."

It was all part of Holtzman's pitching in rhythm. It wasn't uncommon for him to throw a complete game in two hours; he once beat Texas 4–1 in 1:39.

Holtzman was not only quick on the trigger, but he was a quick study as well. He read books whose subjects would deter some of his teammates and led to his being called "the Thinker." When the A's went on the road, Holtzman would buy four or five paperbacks in the terminal so that he would have something to read in his hotel room rather than going out on the town. He preferred to read Proust in the original French. Sportswriters found that Holtzman, like Hunter, seldom answered questions quickly. The Cat was given to long pauses and would at times answer questions only after staring for long moments at the floor. Kenny, too, thought over his answers, almost savoring them, as the smoke from his cigarette swirled past a wispy mustache.

Holtzman didn't see any conflict in being an intellectual and a baseball player. He knew baseball was an instinctive sport in which "book smarts" were seen by some as only useful in winning clubhouse bridge tournaments. Holtzman knew intelligence was relevant to the game because it was needed to make the day-to-day adjustments necessary to compete with the best players in the world. To stay in the majors one had to have knowledge of the game's strategy and techniques. Holtzman believed his earned run average should be roughly equal to what his grade point average had been in college, and it was. His career ERA is 3.49, and his GPA was right around 3.4.

Holtzman was an intellectual but not aloof. On plane trips he played bridge with Fingers, Knowles, and Green. He got along well with his new teammate and roommate, the blustery McLain. Unlike McLain, who was a gambler and liked to play golf for money, bowl for money, etc., Holtzman thought of money during his playing days as a tool to better one's self, not a status symbol. Holtzman said he was a free spender at times, but he made sure the immediate needs of his family were met first.

McLain helped smooth Holtzman's transition to a new team. Holtzman was quiet, and the reason he was reserved at times, he said, stemmed from concentrating so much. Still Holtzman had a dry humor. When the A's acquired Art Shamsky, a member of the Miracle Mets, on June 28 to replace Curt Blefary as a left-handed pinch hitter, it gave Oakland three Jewish players—Holtzman, Epstein, and Shamsky. Holtzman said he heard the A's were "going to have Golda Meier as a shortstop."

Holtzman could joke about his Jewish heritage, but since his retirement from the game he's revealed he had to endure a fair amount of anti-Semitic remarks during his career. The insults came from fans, players, and others associated with the game. Jackson has claimed that Holtzman's troubled tenure with the New York Yankees in the mid-1970s was due to the fact that manager Billy Martin was anti-Semitic. Others have refuted that charge and said that it was not Martin who held Holtzman back but team owner George Steinbrenner, who believed Holtzman was underperforming. Hunter recalled Steinbrenner's confronting him in 1975, the Catfish's first season in New York, and accusing the Cat of not pitching up to expectations.

When he encountered antisemitism, Holtzman did not let it distract him. He was dedicated to his craft and believed that if he allowed insults to affect him, he was not being fair to himself, his teammates, management, or the front office.

Holtzman, however, would not run from a challenge. He stood up to bigotry when necessary. In an amateur league in St. Louis, Holtzman was the lone Jewish player on a team playing a game in a very rural part of the state. An opposing player shouted anti-Semitic remarks and challenges at Holtzman from the dugout. Finally the player got up to bat. Holtzman glared at him, then threw a slow curve on the first pitch. The idea, Holtzman said, was to get that player leaning out over the plate so that he could drill him with a subsequent pitch. Holtzman issued another slow curve, then came back with a pitch that the batter tapped weakly back to the mound. As he was running toward first base, the hitter threw his bat at Holtzman. For a second Holtzman believed he might become the first pitcher to deliver a knockdown pitch against a hitter who was already running to first base. Before Holtzman could react, his catcher, who was Catholic and a friend, tackled the runner. Holtzman's father was at the game, and he came out of the stands and tried to get at the hitter as well. All hell broke loose, and the police had to restore order.

Some forty years passed and Holtzman was working at the Jewish Community Center in St. Louis when the same player who had thrown his bat at him showed up and apologized for his behavior that day. They talked, shared a beer, and continued to stay in touch.

It didn't take long for Hunter see why Holtzman won 17 games two years running and had two no-hitters to his credit. All Holtzman ever threw, Hunter thought, was the fastball and changeup. Hunter said Holtzman would only show the hitter the curve in the dirt, never up in the strike zone. He moved his fastball around—in and out, up and down, showing it and then taking it away.

Stock had never seen a pitcher who threw as fast as Holtzman have the control Ken had. Time after time Stock saw him throw the ball exactly where he wanted it. Hitters kept waiting for Holtzman to miss in the strike zone, but he almost never did. Stock thought Holtzman machine-like.

Holtzman credited his control to his change in home ballparks. Wrigley Field is a hitter's park, and Holtzman always had the feeling that if he made a mistake in the strike zone, it would end up a home run. Even when the wind was blowing in, Holtzman still thought Wrigley a hitter's paradise. Because the stands were so close to the field, it was difficult to get batters to foul out. The Oakland Coliseum was the opposite of Wrigley, a pitcher-friendly stadium with acres of foul territory. After joining the A's, Holtzman found that while a bad pitch in the Coliseum could still hurt him, it wasn't nearly as easy to put one in the seats as it was in Wrigley.

Holtzman won four of his first five decisions in '72; Hunter, six of his first eight. Along the way, they beat some of the top guns from their division rivals—Holtzman topping ageless knuckleballer Wilbur Wood and the Chicago White Sox; Hunter downing the Angels' new acquisition, the young flamethrower from the Mets, Nolan Ryan.

By the All-Star break, Holtzman had 13 wins, Hunter 12, and Odom, who had replaced McLain in the rotation, was 9-2. Oakland owned a six-and-a-half-game lead in its division. The A's were looking golden in the West. McLain was convinced this was the most fundamentally sound team he had ever been on, and he had been on Detroit's 1968 championship team. McLain thought the A's execution flawless. They hit the cutoff man, made the double play. "They do just about everything they're supposed to," he said.

Oakland's relief corps of Fingers, Knowles, Bob Locker, Diego Segui, and Joe Horlen was doing everything it was supposed to. Williams called it the best in baseball. Through the first seventeen games of the season A's relievers allowed just one run in thirty-three and a third innings.

Blue became part of the bullpen and saw his first game action of the season on May 24 against California. Vida made his first start four days later against the Chicago White Sox and finally earned his first win on June 18 with a complete-game shutout of Cleveland. As the summer heated up, so did Blue. He went 3-1 in July, posting a 2.72 ERA.

Bolstered by a strong mound corps and a lineup that saw left fielder Joe Rudi ranked second in the AL in batting; Bando in the top five in runs batted in; and Jackson, Epstein, and Duncan among the AL leaders in home runs, the A's won seven straight in June. After beating the Yankees July 4, Oakland boasted the best record in baseball at 46-24.

With their long, unkempt locks, Charlie O.'s Mustache Gang may have looked like extras from the Broadway musical *Hair!* or liberals at the Democratic National Convention in Miami Beach that July who included the "right to be different" in their platform. The convention, which saw future NBA commissioner Larry O'Brien mentioned as a possible vice presidential replacement during the Thomas Eagleton affair, was so contentious that George McGovern's acceptance speech—which he called "the best speech" of his life—didn't occur until 2:48 a.m. EST, after most of America had gone to bed.

The Swingin' A's knew all about discord, but they also knew how to play hardball. Williams had to fight and scrape for everything he had earned as a player, and he coached the A's in his image: chippy and combative. A's broadcasters Monte Moore, Jim Woods, and Jimmy Piersall provided Bay Area fans with a soundtrack for their summer:

Last half of the 19th inning, the longest game ever played by the A's here in Oakland. The Chicago White Sox and the A's went five hours plus last night, 17 innings, didn't decide a thing. Tonight, it's the 19th as they continue last night's suspended game. . . . A base hit by Rudi could give the A's a big win. Campy Campaneris is on at second. Joe Rudi is ready, Bahnsen pitches. . . . There's a long drive to center field, that one's got a chance, it's really got a charge in it. . . . And theeerrreee she goes! The A's win!

Bottom of the fourth. . . . Fans would like nothing better than to see Bando put a charge in one and light up the scoreboard. The A's and the Yankees, nothing-nothing. The bases are loaded for the A's captain. . . . [Mel] Stottlemyre goes into the windup, around goes the arm, in rides the pitch. . . . Bando swings. . . . There's a long drive, Sal hit this ball deep and that one's got a chance to set off the Finley fireworks on the Fourth of July. . . . It is gone!

Top half of the 10th inning, Campy Campaneris leading off against Gaylord Perry. . . . Game tied 2–2. . . . Perry into the windup, here's the pitch. . . . There's a line drive to left! That ball's got a chance to go! A home run for Campaneris.

There's a drive to deep right-center field, Reggie Jackson's going to have to go to come close to this one. Reggie with the dive. . . . An unbelievable catch for Jackson!

The pitch. . . . Swinging strike three! And Catfish on 10 pitches strikes out the side!

Oakland was rewarded for its fast start as seven members of its squad—Hunter, Holtzman, Jackson, Rudi, Williams, Bando, and Campaneris—were named to the AL All-Star team for the July 25 Midsummer Classic in Atlanta.

The Mustache Gang was having hot fun in the summertime. The A's were thinking the West had already been won, but they thought wrong.

Led by Wilbur Wood and the rejuvenated Richie Allen, the White Sox were about to make it a noisy summer on Chicago's South Side.

CHAPTER SEVEN

Knowing baseball minds, when they revisit the 1972 All-Star Game in Atlanta, will pay particular attention to the pulse-quickening mano a mano matchups involving legendary hitters and pitchers. One such showdown saw Reggie Jackson digging in against Bob Gibson in the opening inning.

Gibson was one of the premier power pitchers of the 1960s; Jackson, one of the premier power hitters of the 1970s. Gibson's St. Louis Cardinals had been a dominant team the decade before, winning three National League pennants and two World Series from 1964 to 1968. Reggie's Oakland A's would dominate the early to mid-1970s, winning three consecutive world championships and five straight division titles from 1971 to 1975. In the game's history, "El Birdos," as the Cardinals of the 1960s are known, and the A's Mustache Gang of the 1970s are two of the greatest teams ever.

Jackson's at-bat versus Gibson helped encapsulate a collision of eras. It was also the only time these two dominant personalities and future Hall of Famers would engage in a battle on the national stage.

More than any other team sport, baseball is a game in a game, individual matchups in a team concept. Jackson-Gibson is the kind of vivid and classic confrontation the All-Star Game has created since its inception in 1933.

Created by *Chicago Tribune* sports editor Arch Ward to be part of the 1933 World's Fair in Chicago and also created in part to take the public's mind off the Great Depression, the major league All-Star Game was intended to be a one-time event. It was the "Game of the Century," a midsummer classic matching the game's greatest players and two aging but legendary managers—Connie Mack, the "Tall Tactician" of the Philadelphia Athletics, and the recently retired "Little Napoleon," John "Mugsy" McGraw, formerly of the New York Giants. McGraw's Giants and Mack's "White Elephants" had gone head to head in the 1905, 1911, and 1913 World Series, and the famed field bosses were enlisted to skipper the National and American League squads respectively.

Played in Chicago's Comiskey Park on July 6, that first game featured Babe Ruth, Lou Gehrig, Al Simmons, Lefty Gomez, and Lefty Grove for the American League and Pepper Martin, Frankie Frisch, Pie Traynor, Bill Terry, and Carl Hubbell for the National League. Won by the AL 4–2, the game proved such a success—Ruth christened it with a home run off "Wild" Bill Hallahan of the soon-to-be-named "Gashouse Gang" St. Louis Cardinals—it became an annual event.

Through the years, the All-Star Game has provided some of baseball's most memorable moments: Hubbell fanning five future Hall of Famers—Ruth, Gehrig, Jimmie Foxx, Simmons, and Joe Cronin—in succession in 1934; Pete Rose running over Ray Fosse; Pedro Martinez dominating an NL lineup of Barry Larkin, Larry Walker, Sammy Sosa, Mark McGwire, Matt Williams, and Jeff Bagwell in 1999.

Until the advent of interleague play in 1997, the All-Star Game and World Series were the only stages in which fans' fantasy matchups—Joe DiMaggio versus Dizzy Dean; Whitey Ford versus Willie Mays; Derek Jeter vs. Tim Lincecum—could be realized. Yet it wasn't just the fans' dreams becoming reality.

In the aftermath of the inaugural classic in 1933, Hallahan spoke of the National League team's immense respect for Ruth: "We wanted to see the Babe," he said. "Sure, he was old and had a big waistline, but that didn't make any difference. We were on the same field as Babe Ruth."

Six decades later, Ted Williams echoed those sentiments when he spoke of All-Star competition. He always liked the All-Star Game because he wanted to see the best pitchers, Williams said in 1999. "I got a big kick out of that."

Fans got a big kick from seeing Bob Feller firing fastballs from atop a National League mound and Jackie Robinson running the bases in American League stadiums. By the 1950s and '60s, the Midsummer Classic had become must-see TV. Since there was no interleague play save the World

Series, the All-Star Game was the only time fans could see something as rare as Sandy Koufax pitching in Fenway Park and Mickey Mantle hitting in the Houston Astrodome.

The National League won every All-Star Game from 1963 through 1970, and it was during this time that the classic took on deeper meaning. For years Mays, Koufax, Gibson, Aaron, Clemente, et al. represented a rising tide of talent for which the American League had no answer. Rose, by 1970 a perennial All-Star, picked up where his predecessors had left off and, as one of the young guns of the National League, set a tone with his physical play.

Paced by the power hitting of Jackson and the power pitching of Vida Blue, the American League responded in 1971. By 1972 a palpable dislike had grown between the stars of the two leagues. They didn't mingle as they would in later decades, and since there wasn't as much cross-pollination of players, the familiarity and complacency that has led to the manufactured stimulus that marks the modern All-Star Game didn't exist then.

What did exist was a rivalry based on a fierce sense of league pride and competitive passion, and because of that, the All-Star Games of the 1960s, '70s, and '80s were, for baseball fans, magical days that would be marked on every fan's calendar.

Such was the case on July 25, 1972, when the American and National League All-Stars took the field in Atlanta. Koufax, serving as a color analyst for play-by-play man Jim Simpson on NBC Radio, captured the mood of the evening during the early innings when he spoke of the pride and passion players felt when they represented their respective league in the Midsummer Classic: "It's interesting that the All-Star Game has taken on a new complexion," Koufax told his audience. "For years it seemed like it was just an exhibition game; the best players in baseball, both leagues wanting to win, but nobody out there [going] that hard. But this year it looks like both leagues want to win very badly. It's a different situation, a different feeling."

Personifying the passion and pride of the National League was the man on the mound for the senior circuit. A ferocious competitor, Gibson's demeanor defined the Cardinals' championship squads of the 1960s. He was revered and feared. Gibson stood 6-foot-1 and weighed 195 pounds, and he put every inch and ounce of himself into every pitch.

Gibson intimidated opponents. Called "Hoot" after the old-time cowboy Hoot Gibson, the Cardinal ace brought his own brand of frontier justice to the field. Surly, brusque, and unsmiling on the mound, he eyed batters from sixty feet, six inches with a squinty-eyed stare. Some hitters thought they were being stared down, and Gibson let them think that. Baseball, he knew, was as much a psychological battle as a physical one. It was only in retirement that Gibson revealed the reason for his fixed glare: he sometimes had difficulty seeing the signs from his catcher.

Regardless, Gibson got a lot of mileage out of looking angry and was deliberately unfriendly to opponents, refusing to even say hello to enemy hitters. When Gene Clines, a young Pittsburgh Pirates outfielder, approached Gibson before a game and asked him to autograph a baseball, Gibson tossed the ball over his shoulder into left field.

To Gibson it was important to maintain an air of mystery. He didn't want opponents to know him, to know what he was thinking or what he was like personally. He wanted hitters to be wary of him, to be uncertain—to be, he said, intimidated. Slugger Dick Allen said Gibson was so mean on the mound that he would knock you down and meet you at home plate to see if you wanted to make something of it.

Gibson's ferocious competitiveness came in part from his background. He was born into a black ghetto in Omaha, Nebraska, the youngest of seven children to a widowed mother. His father had died of pneumonia shortly before his birth, and his mother worked in a laundry to support her family. "Maybe mom needed a new dress or a new pair of shoes," he said, "but she would get by with her old dress and her old pair of shoes so she could give us something."

Gibson was a sickly child; he nearly died of the same disease that claimed his father. An older brother, Josh, coached Bob in sports to help him improve his health and strength. Sports eventually helped Gibson escape the ghetto. He was an outstanding basketball player—he would play for the Harlem Globetrotters—but was turned down for an athletic scholarship by Indiana University because he was told by the school that it had "fulfilled [its] quota of Negroes."

It was not the first time Gibson experienced racism. Growing up in the ghetto, he had endured racial slurs from white kids from the other side of the housing projects; fights were a near daily occurrence. As late as 1961, when he was in his second full season with the Cardinals, Gibson, his wife, and two daughters drove from Omaha to St. Petersburg for spring training. What should have been a pleasant family experience became, in Gibson's words, "disgusting and degrading." The young family found they could not stop for the night despite being tired because most hotels would not accommodate them. They had difficulties finding places to eat because many restaurants would not serve them. Hungry and tired, they were forced to drive miles out of their way to the black section of town. Stopping at a service station for gas, Gibson asked the attendant if his daughters could use the restroom. The attendant directed the girls to a room in the back of the station, above which hung a sign: *Colored Only*. Angered and humiliated, Gibson told the attendant, "Forget the gas," put his family in the car, and left.

In 1964 Gibson beat the Mickey Mantle–Roger Maris Yankees in Game Seven of the World Series, then established his legend three years later when he defeated the "Impossible Dream" Red Sox three times in the Fall Classic, including another route-going Game Seven performance. Gibson's greatest season came in 1968, when he set a modern record with a 1.12 earned run average, threw 13 shutouts—a stunning 5 in succession—and in one ninety-two-inning stretch surrendered a grand total of 2 runs. In the process, he pitched the Redbirds to another pennant.

Along with Koufax, Drysdale, Marichal, McLain, et al., Gibson thrived in the era of the high mound and high strike, an era in which fierce pitcher-hitter confrontations made every game seem like high noon. Gibson's dominance during the Year of the Pitcher led to what has become known as the "Gibson Rules" in 1969: the lowering of the pitcher's mound from fifteen inches to ten and the reduction of the strike zone from the batter's armpits to his jersey letters.

Still Gibson remained dominant despite the rules changes. He won 20 games again in 1969, posted a 2.18 ERA, and threw an "immaculate inning" against the Dodgers, striking out the side on nine pitches. In 1970 he struck out a career-best 274 batters and won a career-high 23 games and another Cy Young award. On August 14, 1971, he no-hit the eventual world champion Pirates 11–0. By the time he climbed the hill for the Midsummer Classic, he had won 11 straight.

The AL All-Stars in Atlanta were well aware of Gibson's greatness and persona. The scowling right-hander retired leadoff hitter Rod Carew on a groundout to second baseman Joe Morgan to start the game and Bobby Murcer on a pop foul to catcher Johnny Bench. That brought Jackson to the plate.

A student of baseball history, Jackson was aware of the moment when he dug in against Gibson. Rather than jockey the count, Reggie roped the first pitch—a hard breaking ball—for a line drive double to deep right-center field. "Jackson took dead aim," Simpson told listeners. Thirty-seven years later Jackson and Gibson got together again, collaborating on an insightful book about the battle between hitter and pitcher.

There were other notable matchups that starry night—Jackson versus Steve Carlton; Jim Palmer versus Aaron and Mays, the latter subbing for the injured Clemente. The abundance of future Hall of Famers on both sides promised a close contest, and that's precisely how it played out. The AL led 1–0 early, following Carew's RBI single off Steve Blass, but the NL rallied to take the lead in the sixth on a two-out, two-run homer by the hometown hero, Aaron.

The AL came back in the eighth to take a 3–2 edge on a two-run homer by Cookie Rojas. The NL tied it in the bottom of the ninth on a Lee May groundout off Wilbur Wood that scored Billy Williams. In the tenth San Diego's Nate Colbert drew a leadoff walk from Baltimore's Dave McNally. A sacrifice bunt by San Francisco's Chris Speier put Colbert in scoring position, and Joe Morgan ended the exciting evening with a single to right-center that scored Colbert for a 4–3 finish.

For Colbert, crossing the plate with the winning run was not the only time that season the Atlanta ballpark would provide one of his more memorable career highlights. One month later Colbert had what Braves manager Lum Harris called the "greatest night any player's ever had." Colbert had arrived in Atlanta that August for a series with the Braves nursing an ailing knee. He had suffered the injury the previous week while sliding into home plate. Despite being hobbled, Colbert was not about to miss out on playing in Atlanta.

Nicknamed the "launching pad," the Braves' ballpark annually led the league in home runs hit within its confines. In the opening game of a doubleheader, Colbert hammered two homers and drove in five runs in a 9–0 victory. In the nightcap he plated eight more runs and hit three homers, including a grand slam, to power an 11–7 win.

Don Zimmer, in his first season managing the Padres, said years later that Colbert's cloudburst was one of the greatest days in baseball he had ever witnessed.

Colbert's totals for the twin bill were a major league record 13 RBIs, 22 total bases, and a record-tying 5 home runs. It is interesting that the home run record Colbert tied had been set May 5, 1954, by Musial in a doubleheader against the Giants. In the stands that day was one particular eight-year-old named Nate Colbert, who, like most young baseball fans growing up in the Gateway City, idolized Stan the Man.

Zimmer recalled Colbert's being a big, imposing hitter. The Padres had a lot of good, hard-working players, Zimmer said. They just didn't have enough of them. San Diego's feast-or-famine experience in '72 was further exemplified in a pair of pitching exploits. On July 18 San Diego starter Steve Arlin, who was leading the majors with 21 losses, was one strike away from no-hitting the Phillies when light-hitting Larry Bowa chopped a bouncer over the head of third baseman Dave Roberts, who was playing in in an eventual 5–1 win. On September 2 the Padres were no-hit by the Cubs' Milt Pappas, who lost his bid for a perfect game with two outs in the ninth when Larry Stahl drew a controversial walk.

Just as Colbert was one of the NL's young stars, so too was Houston's Cesar Cedeno. Just twenty-two years old in 1972, the native of Santo Domingo in the Dominican Republic was called by Astros field boss Harry Walker the best young hitter in the major leagues. As late as August 28, Cedeno was leading the league in batting with a .343 average, and the Astrodome was being called Cesar's Palace. He was eventually overtaken by Braves teammates Ralph Garr and Dusty Baker, but Cedeno concluded the season with a .320 average that represented a fifty-six-point jump over his 1971 mark.

Pitchers who made a mistake in the strike zone paid the price of rendering unto Cesar, who was part of the rising tide of Latino talent. As baseball writer George Vass asked at the time, baseball was the national pastime, but which nation were we talking about? Mexico, Panama, Venezuela, and the Dominican Republic were among the Latin American countries turning out superstars named Clemente, Cedeno, Marichal, and Oliva. Before them had come Minnie Minoso, Camilo Pascual, Zoilo Versalles, Roberto Avila and Chico Carrasquel. The influx of impact players from Latin America included Luis Aparicio, Bert Campaneris, Orlando Cepeda, Mike Cuellar, Tony Perez, and Luis Tiant, and it was continuing with younger standouts Cedeno, Cesar Geronimo, and Jorge Orta.

White Sox general manager Roland Hemond, a veteran Latin talent scout, thought the number of Latin Americans in the majors hadn't yet peaked. Latin countries would be a rich source of talent in the coming years. At the start of the 1972 season, 9 percent (84) of the 960 players listed on the rosters of the twenty-four MLB teams were Latin American. Hemond expected that number to jump to 11 percent in '73, considering that the quality of Latin players was improving every year.

During an NBC-TV *Game of the Week* telecast in the summer of '72 Tony Kubek marveled at the way Latin American ballplayers exuded their love of baseball. Curt Gowdy used to fish in Cuba and spent some time in Havana before Fidel Castro came to power. Gowdy saw how popular the game was in Cuba, and he knew that in Venezuela, the Dominican Republic, and Puerto Rico, baseball was "the" game. He wondered how many major league players there were in Cuba in '72 and estimated "20 or 30" could play major league ball if Castro allowed them to leave the imprisoned isle.

Better education, better playing conditions, and a greater hunger to succeed were the driving forces behind the success of Latin players. The driving force behind the Astros was a talented lineup. Despite playing in the dead air of the Astrodome, Cedeno and Doug Rader slammed 22 homers apiece to pace the Glasshouse Gang. Jimmy Wynn blasted 24, and Lee May, swirling his bat like a swizzle stick, had a team-high 29 homers and 98 RBIs. Bob Watson batted .312, and on June 18 twenty-three-year-old lefty Jerry Reuss carried a no-hitter into the ninth against the Phillies before Bowa broke up yet another bid at baseball history.

The Astros battled the Reds and Dodgers throughout the summer and owned first place in late June. With Colbert's acrobatic catches in the deep recesses of the outfield robbing Mays and Willie Stargell of home runs and Rader performing larceny with his glove; with Johnny Edwards beating the Cubs with a blast in an eleven-inning thriller and Wynn clubbing his two hundredth career homer; and with Reuss, Dave Roberts, and Larry Dierker having moments of excellence on the mound, it made for an exciting summer in the Lone Star State:

Astros play-by-play man Gene Elston on April 24: *"Here's the 2-2 pitch and Edwards slams a long drive to right. It's gonna go! Home run, Edwards, and the Astros win it 3–2 in 11!"*

Astros announcer Loel Passe on July 3: *"The pitch, swung on, hit down past third . . . Doug Rader with the grab, gets up, throws to first, he got him out with an unconscious play! . . . I wouldn't be surprised if the Atlanta Braves stand up in the dugout and give him an ovation!"*

Passe on July 18: *"Cedeno drives it deep to right-center field, way back it goes, up against the wall! . . . He may score . . . Here he is, coming around, being waved on. Here's the throw to the plate. . . . He scores! An inside-the-park home run for the superstar of the future!"*

The future did indeed look golden for the West's young stars and for talented players like San Francisco's Speier, Bobby Bonds, and Dave Kingman; Los Angeles' Steve Garvey, Bill Russell, and Bill Buckner; and Atlanta's

Baker and Garr. The depth in the division was a big reason the Big Red Machine was not a consensus choice to win the West.

San Francisco was the reigning champion, and the Giants, awash in fresh ocean air and sunny optimism, returned an All-Star cast headed by future Hall of Famers Willie Mays, Willie McCovey, and Juan Marichal. Charlie Fox's crew was an interesting mix of experience and youth, and they had won the West in '71 by storming from the gate with a 12-2 record, winning nine straight and eight in a row at Candlestick Park. Even a sub-par season by Stretch McCovey—the big slugger with the scythe-like swing who was slowed by arthritic knees—had failed to stop San Francisco.

Dazzling in their white uniforms with black-and-orange trim and taking full advantage of Candlestick's slick, sea-green synthetic surface, the Giants emerged as one of the most exciting teams in baseball. Mays hit the first pitch thrown to him in 1971 over the wall, the 629th homer of his career. Suddenly it was 1951 again—Russ Hodges was behind the mic, and Willie was the eager and energetic "Say Hey Kid," playing an exhilarating brand of baseball that writer Peter Schrag said "brought jazz" to the grand old game.

With Mays and Marichal seemingly sipping from the Fountain of Youth and with McCovey, Bonds, Speier, Ken Henderson, Dave Kingman, and the flamboyant Tito Fuentes all contributing, the Giants appeared primed to defend their title.

Marichal would be a key. The Dominican Dandy blanked Houston 5–0 on Opening Day. With his face often creased in a smile, Marichal was called by some "Laughing Boy." Gus Triandos, a catcher for the Phillies in the 1960s, said it all seemed too easy for "Manito" Marichal.

It was one thing to go hitless against Gibson, Koufax, or Drysdale, Triandos thought. You could see the cords standing out on their neck; they looked like they were working. Marichal, Triandos said, just stood there laughing at you. Scout Dewey Griggs noticed the same. Marichal, he thought, never seemed to exert himself. Throwing what Griggs saw as a very good live fastball, Marichal seemed to toy with hitters.

Giants Hall of Famer Carl Hubbell called Marichal a "natural," and Branch

Rickey thought no pitcher made such magnificent use of his arm as Juan did. The way he used his arm may have had something to do with Marichal's unique mound delivery. It's been said that if all the great pitchers in history were placed behind a transparent curtain, Marichal's silhouette—his left leg thrust high in the air, his right hand holding the ball and nearly touching the mound—would be the easiest to identify. He was the best right-handed hurler in the 1960s; Bob Gibson said Marichal was not only better than he, but he was also better than Koufax. Pete Rose thought Marichal the greatest pitcher he had ever faced.

Marichal and the Giants began the season eager for another opportunity at the brass ring, but this was not the same San Francisco squad as the season before. Perry had been dealt to Cleveland for southpaw smoke-thrower Sam McDowell, one of two deals made around that time that would haunt the franchise for years. McDowell never fully recovered his fastball or his All-Star form and lasted less than two full seasons in San Francisco. Perry played twelve more major league seasons and won two Cy Young awards and a plaque in Cooperstown. The previous season, the Giants had traded one of their talented young outfielders, twenty-two-year-old George Foster, to the Reds. Foster went on to become a big bopper for the Big Red Machine. San Francisco also parted ways with Dick Dietz, its All-Star catcher in '71, who was claimed off waivers by the Dodgers.

Early in the season McCovey suffered a broken right forearm in a collision with Padres catcher John Jeter and missed two months. Before long Bonds would suffer a broken spirit due to the dealing of his close friend, Mays. He sulked and slumped his way through the season. Marichal, suffering from a lumbar disc in his spine that robbed him of his trademark high left-leg kick, lost eight straight. The Giants spent the first four days of the season in first place but slipped to 9-16 and six games behind when Mays was traded to the New York Mets on May 11 for reliever Charlie Williams and cash.

The blockbuster deal was made for several reasons. Mays was batting just .184 at the time, and the Giants had young outfielders like twenty-two-year-old Garry Maddox and twenty-one-year-old Gary Matthews they could bring up to the big club. The defending champs quickly fell from contention, but young Jim Barr hurled himself into baseball's record books when he retired the last 20 Pirates he faced in an 8–0 win on August 23 and the first 21 Cardinals in his next start on August 29, an eventual 3–0 win. The 41 straight batters set down is an MLB record that stood until 2009, when Mark Buehrle broke it.

Economics played a part in the Giants' transformation. Owner Horace Stoneham was losing money, the team losing more than $600,000, and for the first time in team history not paying a stock dividend. Stoneham simply couldn't guarantee Mays a job once the longtime superstar's playing days were over.

As the sun was setting on a singular icon in San Francisco, it was rising for what would become an iconic foursome in Los Angeles. The durable Dodger infield of Garvey, Russell, Lopes, and Cey had come together in Chavez Ravine.

There have been other famous infields in major league history: the Chicago Cubs of 1906–10 featured Joe Tinker, Johnny Evers, Frank Chance, and the less publicized Harry Steinfeldt; the Philadelphia Athletics of 1911–14 had their celebrated "$100,000 infield" of Eddie Collins, Frank "Home Run" Baker, Jack Barry, and Stuffy McInnis; the Brooklyn Dodgers' "Boys of Summer" had squads of Jackie Robinson, Pee Wee Reese, Gil Hodges, and Billy Cox.

The Tinker-to-Evers-to-Chance double play combination was immortalized in a 1910 poem by Franklin Pierce Adams titled "Baseball's Sad Lexicon":

These are the saddest of possible words:
"Tinker to Evers to Chance."
Trio of bear cubs, and fleeter than birds,
Tinker and Evers and Chance.

Decades later, writer Bill Schroeder penned a poem honoring a Dodger infield that set a major league record for longevity by playing together nine years and is now considered one of the greatest in history.

The '72 season was the first in which Garvey, Lopes, Russell, and Cey—all products of the Los Angeles farm system—wore Dodger Blue at the same time. Russell, a sandy-haired twenty-three-year-old, was the first of the four to solidify his position when he moved from the outfield to shortstop to replace the retiring Maury Wills in '72. Garvey, a clean-cut All-American who had bulging forearms like Popeye; Lopes, a fiery, mustachioed road runner; and Cey, nicknamed the penguin because he seemed to waddle when he ran, all saw playing time for manager Walter Alston in '72.

If the Robinson-Reese-Hodges-Cox Dodgers of the '50s were the celebrated "Boys of Summer," the '72 Baby Dodger Blues were the Boys of Spring. Over the next nine years "The Infield" would start 833 games together; combine for 21 All-Star selections, with each man earning at least three; earn five Gold Gloves; produce one league MVP, one NLCS MVP, and one World Series MVP; and win four division titles, four NL pennants, and one world championship.

From 1973 to 1981 the Dodgers were 498-335 in games started by The Infield, a .598 winning percentage. In games in which at least one member of the four didn't start, the record dropped to 306-267-1, a .534 percentage. Over a full season, Los Angeles averaged 97-65 when The Infield started, 87-75 when it didn't.

In their final game together—Game Six of the 1981 World Series in Yankee Stadium—Dodger manager Tommy Lasorda penciled the four in at the top of his lineup: Lopes, Russell, Garvey, Cey. Russell thought it unusual that Lasorda would do that since it wasn't very often that those four were at the top of the batting order. Just a fluke, Russell surmised. Considering The Infield's place in baseball history, it was entirely fitting.

The components for the Dodgers' dream infield arrived in '72, and so did Don Sutton, another of their building blocks for future championship seasons. The NL's Rookie of the Year in 1966—he debuted on April 14, the same day that fellow future Hall of Famer and 300-game winner Greg Maddux was born—and won 12 games for a sterling staff that boasted Koufax, Drysdale, and Claude Osteen and won the NL pennant. Sutton endured losing seasons the next three years despite posting respectable ERAs. He was also prone to surrendering gopher balls at an alarming rate—25 in 1969, 38 in '70.

An exasperated Alston sent Sutton to the bullpen in '68 and wondered aloud if Sutton would ever learn to pitch. By late May 1971 Sutton was suffering the same crisis of confidence. Nursing both a sore elbow and a 1-5 record, he considered walking away from the game. Only two people at the time knew Sutton's state of mind—he and his wife Patti. Sutton had never been more dejected.

Two things turned the twenty-six-year-old right-hander around: he went to an arm specialist, and Dodgers coach Red Adams straightened out Sutton's pitching form after watching films of Sutton's starts from 1966 on. Adams told Sutton he had been pitching more from the side rather than coming over the top, and that was putting a strain on his elbow.

Sutton made adjustments to his mechanics and developed a hard curve and a screwball to throw when he fell behind in the count and hitters were sitting on his fastball. A most artful Dodger, he won his first four starts in awesome fashion—beating the Reds in the season opener on a three-hitter, shutting out Atlanta on a two-hitter, spinning a five-hitter against Montreal, and blanking the streaking Mets. Sutton was undefeated in seven games overall, had three shutouts, and owned a ridiculous 0.89 ERA.

He was particularly effective at home in Dodger Stadium, pitching amid the warm sunshine and pastel surroundings of Palazzo O'Malley and beneath a Dodger Blue sky. For the '72 season he would go 11-4 with a 1.76 ERA in Dodger Stadium and 8-5 with a 2.49 ERA away from the friendly confines of Chavez Ravine.

Sutton meticulously kept two books during the early years of his career. One was a diary in which he detailed each of his mound outings; the other was a personal scouting report on opposing hitters. Some say Sutton kept something else: a block of sandpaper, which he allegedly used to doctor baseballs. He was supposedly nicknamed "Black and Decker" by grease ball artist Gaylord Perry, who is said to have handed Sutton a bottle of Vaseline and received sandpaper in return. When Sutton was being searched one night on the mound, the umpire found a note in Don's uniform pocket: "You're getting warm, but it's not here."

What Sutton did have was a variety of four pitches, each with varying velocity. His screwball acted like a change-up and nosedived when it approached home plate. He also developed a one-fingered curve, fully extending his index finger around the ball while the nail of his middle finger dug into the ball. Sutton called it a "slurve"—half slider, half curve. With a good fastball, sinker, and excellent slider and the ability to change speeds on his curve very well, Sutton had roughly the same assortment of pitches as Jim Palmer in the American League. Sutton didn't have the same style of delivery as Palmer; the Dodger ace's motion was a little shorter and quicker, not as long a motion as his Orioles counterpart.

Dodgers broadcaster Vin Scully described Sutton as a "stiff-backed pitcher." In other words, he didn't curl his leg in his windup and delivery. He drove off the rubber well with his back or right foot, but if he kept his front leg too stiff, his pitches had a tendency to sail high. Dodgers coaches wanted him to bend his leg a little but keep it firm. Scully likened it to the "fulcrum principle," where you get a stiffness to challenge you, and that's how you push off.

The Dodgers got a great push to start the season. Unlike their pitch-and-putt predecessors of the 1960s, Wes Parker, Willie Davis, Frank Robinson, and Jim Lefebvre banged baseballs toward the teal-colored walls of Dodger Stadium. After splitting with Cincinnati to open the season, they marched through Georgia like Sherman's troops, their offense afire and their pitching putting down enemy retaliation. Thirtysomethings Maury Wills, Manny Mota, Claude Osteen, and Jim Brewer joined with fortysomething Hoyt Wilhelm and younger types like Tommy John to put the Dodgers atop the division into early June.

While the Dodgers, Reds, and Astros battled for the division lead the first three months of the season, an aging Aaron was in the midst of his relentless pursuit of Ruth. The Hammer had hit a career-high 47 homers in '71, bringing his total to 639 as the season began.

Aaron had several of Ruth's and Ty Cobb's career marks in sight, but it was the Babe's home run record—714—that represented the Mount Everest of baseball. One of the ironies of Aaron's career is that he was not a home run hitter to begin with. When he broke in in 1952, he wasn't even a power hitter. He weighed 160 and hit a total of nine home runs at Eau Claire, Wisconsin.

Aaron helped the Indianapolis Clowns win the Negro League World Series in '52, when Braves scout Dewey Griggs purchased his contract for $10,000. He had another offer from the New York Giants, who had just had another former Negro League star, Willie Mays, debut for them the previous May. Aaron had the Giants' contract in hand, but when the Braves offered fifty dollars a month more, he signed with Milwaukee. That fifty dollars was the only thing that kept Mays and Aaron from being teammates.

It's intriguing to think of a Mays-Aaron pairing in a dream outfield from 1954 to 1973. But while the Giants missed out, so did the Braves. Prior to signing with the Giants, Mays had been scouted by the Braves. He had also been scouted by the Dodgers, and had Brooklyn acted more quickly, Mays might have been one of the fabled "Boys of Summer" and later a teammate of Koufax, Drysdale, Wills, et al. on the Los Angeles Dodgers of the 1960s.

At the time of his signing, Aaron was an infielder, playing second and short, and owned a cross-handed batting style that defied the rules of hitting. Along with the Cubs' Ernie Banks, Aaron ushered in the era of the slim sluggers—"wrist hitters" who used very light bats in the 30–32 ounce range. Two years after his signing Aaron broke into the big leagues with the Milwaukee Braves when outfielder Bobby Thomson suffered a broken leg in spring training. Aaron took Thomson's position in left field and stayed in the Braves' starting lineup for the next twenty seasons.

Atlanta spent the entire 1972 season under .500 and eventually fell as far as twenty-five games off the pace in the West, but the thirty-nine-year-old Aaron continued to play with machine-like consistency. He overcame assorted injuries through the years—a knee injury in '70, nagging back pain in '71—to become the only player in National League history to that point to hit 40 or more home runs seven times, and his 34 homers in '72 allowed him to set a major league record for most seasons topping the 30-homer mark—fourteen.

Like Gibson, Aaron grew up in a poor family; he spent a good portion of his youth in Alabama picking cotton. Also like Gibson, Aaron experienced racism. As he closed in on the Babe, Aaron received hate mail and death threats. The threats were serious enough for *Atlanta Journal* sports editor Lewis Grizzard to quietly compose an Aaron obituary. In August 1973 *Peanuts* creator Charles Schultz penned a series of cartoons in which Snoopy attempted to break Ruth's record, only to be besieged by hate mail.

Also that summer, *Sports Illustrated*'s William Leggett asked if this was to be the year in which Aaron took "a moon walk above one of the most hallowed individual records in American sport . . . ? Or will it be remembered as the season in which Aaron, the most dignified of athletes, was besieged with hate mail and trapped by the cobwebs and goblins that lurk in baseball's attic?"

Ruth's widow, Claire Hodgson, denounced the bigotry aimed at Aaron and believed the Babe would have enthusiastically supported the historic chase. Ruth, an unprejudiced man, had been the subject of racial taunts by those who believed the Babe had black features.

Aaron maintained that he wasn't attempting to eclipse Ruth's status as the game's all-time slugger. "He'll still be the best, even if I pass him," he said at the time. "Even if I am lucky enough to hit 715 home runs, Babe Ruth will still be regarded as the greatest home run hitter who ever lived."

While Aaron spent the summer chasing Ruth's ghost, the rest of the West was chasing the vapors of the Big Red Machine. Cincinnati took first place for good with a 5–4, ten-innings victory over Houston on June 25. At the same time that the Nixon administration was seeking to suppress protests by the Gainesville Eight and other anti–Vietnam War activists at the Republican National Convention in Miami in August, the Reds were suppressing all challenges as well. The NL West had been baseball's most competitive division in '71. By late summer of '72 the Reds were turning the race into a runaway. One of the anthems of the era was Sly and the Family Stone's "Hot Fun in the Summertime," and the Big Red Machine could relate.

Cincinnati's style not only made the club a cinch to win the West, but it also captured the imagination of fans. The Reds reached one million in paid attendance faster than any time in the 104-year history of professional baseball in Cincinnati, and their success at the turnstiles was due in part to their 5-foot-7, 150-pound second baseman. No story unfolded at a faster pace than that of the Cincinnati speedster. By early August Go-Go Joe was leading the league in runs scored and was reaching base a remarkable 43 percent of the time.

Speed and power were a big part of the Reds' success, but so was pitching. Armed with an arsenal of good off-speed pitches, Gary Nolan took the mound for a July *Game of the Week* against the Cubs sporting the lowest ERA in the NL at 1.90. By game's end he had passed eventual NL Cy Young winner Steve Carlton and Mets ace Tom Seaver as the first NL pitcher to reach twelve wins.

"I think the best description we can use of Gary Nolan," Gowdy told his audience, "is he's now a 'finished pitcher.'"

The Big Red Machine looked to be a finished product as well. Tom Hedrick was a Reds broadcaster in 1971–72, and he recalled the team's turnaround. "That trade was made for one guy—Joe Morgan," said Hedrick, who teamed with Yankees Hall of Fame pitcher Waite Hoyt on Reds broadcasts. "Morgan was the one Bob Howsam wanted. Howsam put together that trade and it was very controversial at the time. The Reds actually got four players out of that trade and that was the genius of Bob Howsam. He was the architect, a guy who was very shrewd on trades. . . . When you hit on turf you have to have a bunch of gap hitters and that's precisely what the Reds had. That team, with its speed at the top [of the lineup] was built for that stadium."

Hedrick recalled the first day of spring training in 1972, when Morgan approached Cincy's pitchers and told them how he had stolen bases off them in the past. Morgan kept a book on every pitcher in the league. "He was a thinking man's player," Hedrick said.

So too was Rose, who also kept a book, his rating the throwing arms of every outfielder in the NL. Hedrick said Pete made it a point to know everybody, including Hedrick himself, the guy who when Rose joined the Reds had been Sportscaster of the Year in 1970 and a broadcaster for (among other teams) the champion Kansas City Chiefs squads of the American Football League. He broadcast three Super Bowls and nine Cotton Bowls for CBS Radio.

Hedrick said, "When I first came to the club in '71 he came across the field and said, 'I'm Pete Rose. If you need anything just ask me.' He was a great guy who led by example. He played hard and he expected you to play hard. He also had a big heart and helped a lot of people. Those two guys [Morgan and Rose] played off each other."

Hedrick got to know the Reds players. Like others, he was amazed at the huge paws of Johnny Bench—"The biggest set of hands I've ever seen," he said. He called Bench and Yogi Berra the two best catchers he's ever watched work. Bench, he said, completely revolutionized the position with his one-handed style, and he could do that because he had such big hands.

"Bench was an amazing talent," Hedrick said. "He had maturity and charisma. I don't know what charisma is, but Bench had it."

Hedrick thought Tony Perez a great leader. "Pete could be up and down [emotionally] but Tony was always the same," Hedrick said. "Tony was the 'good ol' Dawg,' as he called himself."

The leader of the Big Red Machine, Sparky Anderson, was a baseball genius, according to Hedrick: "Sparky always said he was dumb but he was dumb like a fox. He always wanted to make sure he put his players in the best position to win. He was perfect for that club. He was able to put the egos in the background."

Hedrick was impressed by Anderson's dealings with people. "He always said, 'It doesn't cost you a dime to be nice.'"

Hedrick joined the Reds the same year as Al Michaels, and when Hedrick first heard Al broadcast, he told producer Ken Fouts that Michaels "sounds just like Vinny [Scully]." That wasn't a coincidence. Until he found his own voice, Michaels emulated the Dodgers' legendary broadcaster. "If you're going to imitate somebody," Hedrick said, "imitate Vinny because he's the best."

Hedrick had emulated Curt Gowdy because the Cowboy was whom Hedrick heard growing up in Massachusetts at a time when Gowdy was in the midst of his fifteen years as the radio voice of the Boston Red Sox.

"I loved Curt Gowdy," Hedrick said. "He was my mentor and my idol. He and Vinny and Ernie [Harwell] and Lindsey Nelson were great people who happened to be broadcasters."

When Hedrick moved to the Midwest, he emulated Monte Moore, whom he heard all the time on Kansas football and basketball. Moore, who broadcast the A's in 1972, the team Hedrick's Reds would face in the Fall Classic, was another mentor for Hedrick.

"When I did baseball games I sounded like Monte," Hedrick said. Seeking advice on finding his own voice in his early broadcasting years while working for KWBW, a small station in Hutchinson, Kansas, Hedrick phoned Moore. "He told me, 'You have to be yourself.'"

Moore advised Hedrick not to listen to him for three or four weeks and to keep working. Somewhere along the line, Moore told Hedrick, you'll find your own style. Driving home one night after broadcasting a high school game in El Dorado, Hedrick was listening to the tape of the game when he had a breakthrough. He finally sounded like himself.

Michaels would find his own voice as well, and along with broadcast partner Joe Nuxhall—the latter had the signature signoff phrase, "This is the old left-hander, rounding third and heading for home"—made memorable calls in Cincinnati's memorable summer:

Pitch on the way, that ball's drilled to deep left. If it's fair it's gone and it is a . . . fair ball! Hit the foul pole! Johnny Bench hits the foul pole in left for a three-run homer!

Two down and that will bring Denis Menke to the plate. . . . Pitch to Menke, swung on and hit along the left field line, could be extra bases, it's down in the corner! Perez could score, he's being waved in, here he comes. . . . The Reds win it in 10, 5–4!

Breaking pitch grounded up the middle, Morgan great stop! Flips to Chaney, they get him at second! What a play! Joe Morgan takes a base hit away from Bonds on a sensational play!

[Glenn] Beckert swings, line drive into right field, a base hit. . . . [Joe] Pepitone coming home, here's the throw and he's out by a mile! And now the Cubs have met Cesar Geronimo. As we go around the league they all try him one time and that's all.

On August 8 the Reds beat the Dodgers 2–1 in nineteen innings, and on September 1 Rose became Cincinnati's all-time leader in hits in a 1–0, twelve-innings win over the Expos. Michaels provided a word picture for Reds fans: *"The strike-two pitch to Rose. . . . Pete hits a checked-swing chopper toward second. . . . And there's the record-breaking hit, an infield single by Pete Rose!"*

On September 22 in the Astrodome, Carroll, who set a then major league mark for most saves in a season with 37, clinched the Reds' second division title in three seasons.

Michaels made the call: *"The Reds are now a strike away from the Western Division championship. . . . The strike-two pitch on the way. . . . Swung on, grounded to short. . . . Chaney goes to Morgan and pop the corks! . . . The Cincinnati Reds are the champions of the National League West!"*

In the American League the race to be best in the West was a little wilder.

CHAPTER EIGHT

With his team trailing by two runs in the bottom of the ninth inning, it didn't take Chuck Tanner long to pick a pinch hitter.

"Okay, Dick," the Chicago White Sox skipper said to Dick Allen. "Go in and hit."

It was late in the day on June 4, 1972, the second game of a doubleheader against the New York Yankees. The Sox had won the first game 6–1, Allen contributing two hits and a run scored as Chicago improved to 24-17 to stay in second place in the West, half a game ahead of Minnesota and three and a half games behind Oakland.

The doubleheader drew 51,904 fans to Comiskey Park and left another 8,000 hopefuls stranded on the sidewalks surrounding the jam-packed stadium. The crowd inside Comiskey was the old ball park's largest in eighteen years, lending a festive atmosphere to the proceedings. Thousands had come to see Allen, who was in the midst of an MVP campaign that would see him hit .308 and lead the league in home runs (37), RBIs (113), walks (99), on-base percentage (.420), slugging percentage (.603), and on-base plus slugging percentage (OPS, 1.023). He did all of this while playing his home games in pitcher-friendly Comiskey Park.

Each of Allen's homers seemed to come with a story, and June 4 provided one of his more memorable moments: the "chili dog homer."

Tanner had chosen to let Allen sit out the second game. "He's played every inning this year," Tanner explained at the time, "and he deserves a rest."

But as soon as the lineups were posted on the scoreboard—sans the Sox superstar—team owner John Allyn placed a call to his manager. "Where," the boss asked, "is Allen?"

Tanner's response was unruffled: "I'm saving him for late in the game," he said. "I'll send him in to pinch-hit with a couple men on base so he can hit a homer and win the game for us."

With left-hander Mike Kekich in control through eight and a third innings, the Yankees led 4–2 in the bottom of the ninth. But when Bill Melton worked a one-out walk and Mike Andrews singled to left, New York manager Ralph Houk emerged from the dugout and waved in southpaw reliever extraordinaire Sparky Lyle.

Tanner responded by sending a batboy to the clubhouse to summon his slugger. Allen was eating a chili dog when he heard Tanner wanted him to hit. He had chili all over his shirt, so he put on a new one and a pair of pants with no underclothes.

As Allen hefted his bat—at forty ounces it weighed a half-pound more than those used by other sluggers his size in the early 1970s—Tanner sent Jorge Orta in to pinch-run for Andrews. When Allen was announced as a pinch hitter, Andrews, who had been Lyle's roommate on the Red Sox, shouted at Lyle, "Sparky, you're in deep shit now!"

Allen strode to the plate, took a strike and then a ball. The next pitch was one he'd remember the rest of his life. Yankees announcers Phil Rizzuto and Frank Messer made the call on WABC radio:

> **Rizzuto**: *Lyle against Richie Allen, what a battle. The two top men facing each other. . . . The pitch. . . . Oh, he creamed one! And the ballgame is over! Holy cow! I don't believe it! Richie Allen pinch-hits a three-run homer and the White Sox beat the Yankees.*
>
> **Messer**: *It's a fantastic finish for the White Sox and you could just feel the drama building up for that possible moment. Then when they got the two men on, the league's top hitter and the league's top reliever confronted each other and that was the result.*

Sparky Lyle threw him a slider, Allen said, "and it wound up in the seats." It wound up some 370 feet away in the left-field grandstand, winning the game for the White Sox 5–4. It was the ninth walk-off home run of Allen's career.

For the Sox and their delirious fans, it was a giddy, heady moment not seen on Chicago's South Side since the Sox were contenders in 1967. So much so that the crowd refused to leave Comiskey Park and spent the next thirty minutes after the game standing, cheering, and hollering.

To Allen it was a memorable moment, one of many for the Sox that summer. In a year when Seals and Crofts scored a top hit with "Summer Breeze," winds of change were gusting through the Windy City. Yet unlike the changes that had caused other major cities in the Midwest to falter, Chicago had made the difficult transition from manufacturing to a modern economy due in part to the vision of its mayor, Richard Daley.

Daley was called by biographer Adam Cohen an "American Pharaoh", and just as the pyramids in Egypt reflect the vision of leaders of long ago, much of modern-day Chicago is a testament to Daley's dogged determination. The Sears Tower, O'Hare International Airport, McCormick Place, and Dan Ryan Expressway were all built at the behest of a boss who stood astride his city's politics like a colossus for more than two decades.

Like New York's Fiorello LaGuardia and Philadelphia's Frank Rizzo, Daley was a larger-than-life figure whose impact on his city has lasted longer than his terms in office. Daley was also a White Sox fan, and like his fellow South Siders in the summer of '72 he watched as Allen, Tanner, Wilbur Wood, Carlos May, Jay Johnstone, Stan Bahnsen, "Beltin'" Bill Melton, Walt "No Neck" Williams, Rich "Goose" Gossage, and Terry Forster produced a season of excitement that built over the course of the hot summer, thanks in part to the enthusiastic radio calls of new Sox broadcaster Harry Caray on WTAQ/WEAW.

On May 21 the Sox trailed California 8–6 in the bottom of the ninth. With two out and two on, May faced reliever Alan Foster.

> *Caray*: *There's the pitch. . . . There's a long drive. . . . Way back! It may be. . . . White Sox win! . . . Listen to the crowd. . . . How about that! Holy cow, what a thrill! . . . This puts the White Sox in first place in the Western Division! This crowd is wild! Everybody's screaming. . . . I'm the only calm guy in the ball park!*

May's upper-deck shot completed a stunning comeback that served to put Chicago one half-game ahead of the A's. Much to the delight of their fans, the White Sox and Caray were just hitting their stride.

On July 23, in another Sunday doubleheader, the Sox beat the Indians in the opener at Comiskey but trailed 3–1 in the bottom of the eighth in the nightcap. Once again the Sox showed a flair for the dramatic. Ed Hermann's home run and Allen's RBI groundout combined to tie the game, setting the stage for May's leadoff at-bat in the ninth. On the mound for the Indians was reliever Ed Farmer.

> **Caray**: *There's a long drive.... Way back.... It might be.... The Sox win a doubleheader! Carlos May just hit his second home run of the game! ... What a blast! High into the right-center field stands and the Sox have won this doubleheader!*

Eight days later the Sox were in Minnesota's Metropolitan Stadium for a two-game set with the Twins. Both clubs were in need of a win to keep pace with the A's, whose .622 winning percentage was the best in the league. The Met was a big ballpark with power alleys that seemed as wide as the Grand Canyon.

Assisted by physical and judgmental errors by Twins center fielder Bobby Darwin, Allen became just the second man in major league history to that point to hit *two* inside the park home runs in the same game. Both homers came off future Cooperstown inductee Bert Blyleven. In the top of the first inning Allen roped a drive to right-center. As Darwin took his angle on the ball, his feet slipped out from under him on the grass, and the ball took a strange hop over him and rolled to the fence. Pat Kelly, Luis Alvarado, and Allen all scored for a quick 3–0 lead.

Jack ("Let's go the races!") Drees made the call on WFLD, the Sox's television network: *"He now has a 15-game hitting streak that was interrupted [by] a couple of pinch-hitter appearances where he failed to hit.... He's got this one, lined to center, Darwin over and he falls down! Ball bounces over him, goes back to the screen.... Allen is coming to third, they're waving him in! C'mon Dick, get an inside-the-park home run.... He's got it!"*

In the fifth Allen followed Alvarado's RBI single with a sinking liner to left-center. Darwin tried to make a shoe-top catch, but the ball got by him. Allen, who was quick as well as strong and had 19 steals on the season, raced around the bases for his major league record-tying second inside-the-park homer in a single game, and Chicago romped 8–1. While Allen's feat was rare, it has happened since, and Blyleven was once again involved. On October 4, 1986, Minnesota's Greg Gagne hit a pair of inside-the-park homers to back Blyleven, the same man who had surrendered Allen's twin blasts.

It wasn't just that Allen was thrilling Sox fans with a level of baseball many on the South Side had never seen, but it was also the way he was doing it that gripped their imagination. Almost one month after his record-tying afternoon in Minnesota, Allen made history again. On August 23, in the seventh inning of a tight game, Allen unloaded on a 2-0 offering from the Yankees' Lindy McDaniel and sent it soaring into the center-field bleachers directly under the Comiskey Park scoreboard.

Caray, who was broadcasting the game from that area (as was his custom for Wednesday afternoon games), came close to catching the ball in his famous fishing net, which he kept for just such an occasion. Holding a microphone in his right hand and the fishing net in his left, he reached for it but missed. Fans who were in Comiskey that day remember the shirt-sleeved crowd being sent into a state of shock and awe. Caray, screaming into his mic, was stunned by Allen's blast, which cleared a wall that was 20 feet high and 445 feet from home plate and provided a pair of insurance runs in an eventual 5–2 win.

> **Caray**: *Richie Allen hit one into the center field stands. . . . I almost got it with my net! It hit a fan's hands right in front of me!*

Allen's power was prodigious. His sky-scraping homers exceeded even the most distant reaches of stadiums and sometimes even their rooftops. Willie Mays once said Allen could hit a ball farther than anybody he'd seen.

Allen was the "Chisox Colossus" to some, the "Wampum Walloper" to others. A native of Wampum, Pennsylvania, and graduate of Wampum

High, Allen was one of nine children of Mrs. Era Allen. Three of his brothers were all-state basketball players, and during Dick's playing days Wampum High, despite being one of the smallest schools in the commonwealth and boasting an enrollment of just thirty boys, won 82 consecutive games and two state championships. Allen was offered numerous basketball scholarships, but since baseball offered a quicker route out of poverty, he took it.

It was during his three-plus seasons in the minors that Allen began using his forty-two-ounce bat. When the big bats first arrived in the clubhouse, Allen figured someone had forgotten to take the roots off. They're tree trunks, he thought. Who's going to swing that?

During batting practice it dawned on Allen that he should handle the big bat the same way he would handle a heavy log, by picking it up at one end rather than in the middle. Allen altered his swing so that he was throwing the end of the bat at the ball. The bat became his trademark—its weight alternated between forty and forty-two ounces during his career—and while it looked like a log, he swung it like it was a toothpick.

In his fourth year in the minors, Allen was sent to Little Rock, Arkansas, a small town torn by racial tension. In the fall of 1957 President Dwight D. Eisenhower had sent one thousand U.S. Army paratroopers from the 101st Airborne Division to Little Rock to enforce integration and protect nine black students enrolling at the city's all-white Central High School. Allen, who had just turned twenty, was the first black player assigned to Little Rock. The target of racial slurs, taunts, and crank phone calls, Allen felt dehumanized, as if he was playing baseball inside a prison.

Disheartened and frightened by the threats, Allen feared for his safety even on the playing field. He would hear the taunts, look around the stands, and be so frozen with fear that he would pray that a ball wasn't hit to him. When it was, Allen sometimes found it difficult to move, to raise his arm to catch a liner, or to run and chase it down.

He considered quitting and returning home, but Era Allen wouldn't hear of it. He couldn't come home a quitter, his mother told him. Allen stuck it out and by season's end had won many of the fans over by batting .297 and belting 33 homers. Little Rock fans even named him "Most Popular Player."

Allen made his major league debut at age twenty-one on September 3, 1963, becoming the first black player to wear a Phillies uniform. In 1964, his first full season, Allen powered the Phils' pennant chase with 13 triples, 29 homers, 91 RBIs, and a league-leading 125 runs scored. He was a unanimous choice for Rookie of the Year but couldn't prevent Philadelphia from faltering in the stretch and suffering a collapse that allowed St. Louis to surge to the league title and beat the fading Yankees in the World Series.

The bitter Philly faithful found fault with their superstar on a number of levels. Allen had played outfield, shortstop, second base, and first base in the minors. The Phils, needing to find a place for their young slugger, put him at third, the "hot corner." It is one of the more demanding defensive positions in baseball and one that was unfamiliar to Allen. He made 41 errors, and Phillies fans didn't forget. Nor did they forget he fanned a league-leading 138 times. In 1965 he fought teammate Frank Thomas, a fan favorite. Thomas hit Allen with a bat and within hours was released by the club. Phillies brass forbade Allen from telling his side of the story to the media under threat of a fine. When Allen showed up at the stadium that night, fans hurled both angry insults and assorted items at him.

Everything Allen did seemed to become a *cause célèbre*. He was accused of paying more attention to his horses than to the horsehide, of drinking, of refusing to take batting practice. Phillies' fans feud with Allen lasted for five seasons before he was dealt to St. Louis in 1970. Allen would later say he could play anywhere—first, third, left field—anywhere, he added, except Philadelphia.

In '71 Allen was traded again, this time to Los Angeles. He collected 23 homers and 90 RBIs and batted .308 in September to help fuel the Dodgers in their division race with San Francisco. Despite the Dodgers' finishing just a game out of first, Allen was traded yet again, this time to the White Sox for Tommy John, a talented southpaw starter who went 13-16 in '71, and infielder Steve Huntz.

Allen was called by some a clubhouse cancer; he wasn't that, but he was a nonconformist. Dodgers shortstop Maury Wills said Allen was one of those guys who couldn't go along with the group in everything. Los Angeles teammate Willie Davis thought there was something in Allen's makeup that made him fight certain things. Davis said he shuddered to think how great Allen could have been had he simply conformed.

As it was, Allen was great and on his own terms. The late Hall of Fame baseball writer and official baseball historian Jerome Holtzman called Allen "as gifted a ballplayer as there ever was in the major leagues." There has been a long-running debate whether Allen belongs in baseball's Hall of Fame. Some consider him the best player not in Cooperstown. Mays said Allen was a Hall of Famer as far as he was concerned.

The debate over Allen's Hall of Fame candidacy is one more aspect of a man sabermetrician Bill James rated as the second most controversial player in baseball history, Rogers Hornsby ranking number one. Gossage sees little controversy when it comes to Allen. In his Hall of Fame induction speech, the Goose praised Allen: "In 1972, I had the privilege of playing with Dick Allen. I didn't know it at the time, but in retrospect, he was the greatest player I ever played with. That's quite a statement because I played with a lot of great ones. He taught me how to pitch from a hitter's perspective. He took me under his wing and we would talk for hours on end about pitching. It was amazing."

Another former teammate, Phillies third baseman Mike Schmidt, wrote in his autobiography *Clearing the Bases* that baseball writers claimed Allen divided the clubhouse along racial lines. "That was a lie," Schmidt wrote. "The truth is that Dick never divided any clubhouse."

Caray said the same back in '72. Despite what Caray referred to as "all this junk about Richie Allen being so tough to get along with," the slugger had proved to be an asset to the club not only by what he did on the field, Caray said, but also because of his positive influence on teammates.

There was nothing controversial about Allen's talent and raw power. In an era marked by great pitching and low batting averages, he posted a .534 slugging average. Enormously strong and quick, he put the full power of his shoulders, chest, and biceps into every blow. Much of the secret of his swing was in his wrists. He would snap it at the ball like a man cracking a whip, as writer William Barry Furlong observed at the time.

Stories of Allen's prodigious power sound like tall tales:

He hit a ball that struck an obstruction one hundred feet high when the
 ball was 360 feet from home plate and another over a scoreboard
 fifty feet high and 408 feet from home;
His drives measured at times between 500 and 565 feet;
He hammered a home run over the left-center field roof of Connie Mack
 Stadium. The drive prompted the Pittsburg Pirates Willie Stargell to
 state, "Now I know why they boo Richie all the time. When he hits
 a home run, there's no souvenir."

Yankees fans, fearful of Allen's power in a game at Yankee Stadium,
unfurled a banner that read, "Save our monuments! Walk Allen!"

Gene Mauch, who was Allen's manager with the Phillies in the early
1960s, said once he wouldn't be surprised if Allen homered to both left and
right field *at the same time*. "He'll split the ball in half with his strength,"
Mauch said.

Another manager, Tanner, was at the wheel when Allen in 1972 had
arguably the most dominating season by an American League slugger
since Babe Ruth. Tanner thought Allen was doing more for the White Sox
than any player he had ever seen do for another team. "He's doing it all,"
Tanner said, "at bat, in the field and on the bases."

A native of New Castle, Tanner, like Allen, was a product of western
Pennsylvania. The two men, whose home towns were just ten miles apart,
were family friends, and the slugger once considered surly thrived under
Tanner's laid-back leadership.

Opposing players paid the price for Allen's serenity, and American
League pitchers were soon scrambling for an effective strategy. Detroit
Tigers ace Mickey Lolich thought Allen a scary figure at the plate. When
Allen came to bat, he had your attention, Lolich said. Mickey wanted to
forget a couple of line drives Allen had hit off him but couldn't because
"they almost killed me."

The Sox played ball with a vengeance. It was a hot time, summer in the
city, and the backs of the necks of fans on the South Side weren't the only

things getting dirty and gritty. The White Sox were getting down and dirty in the division fight with defending champion Oakland, and Windy City headlines trumpeted the daily battles:

SOX WIN, ALLEN SLUGS PAIR
SUPERMAN ALLEN HERO AGAIN
ALLEN, WOOD LEAD SOX INTO FIRST PLACE

Forty years later, Roland Hemond, the architect of the Allen trade that was one of the more pivotal in franchise history, remembered Allen's transformative season with special fondness. Everything a ballplayer could do or should do, Allen did, Hemond said: hit, field, or run the bases. Plus he was terrific with the young players on the team. Hemond called it "one of the most impactful seasons a player ever had."

As magnificent as Allen was, he was not alone in leading the White Sox. Wood tied Gaylord Perry for the league lead in wins with 24 and led the AL in starts (49) and innings pitched (376.2). Bahnsen won 21 games in his first season with the Sox; Tom Bradley won 15. Gossage, a future Hall of Famer, and Forster comprised a young righty-lefty fireman tandem that combined for 13 wins. Forster fronted the bullpen with 29 saves. May contributed power and a .308 batting average; Pat Kelly had a team-best 32 steals.

Gossage debuted on April 16 in Kansas City, and it wasn't until September 1 that he would make his first mound appearance in Yankee Stadium. Born and raised in Colorado, he was the son of ardent Yankees fans. When it came time to take the mound in Yankee Stadium, Gossage recalled in 2014 that his legs were shaking so badly, he felt he might "keel over." Six years later, he was the ace reliever on a Yankees squad that won its second straight World Series. In June 2014 he was on a Yankee Stadium mound again, throwing out the ceremonial first pitch on Old-Timers' Day at the modern Bronx ballpark and being honored with a plaque in Monument Park.

"This," he told the sellout crowd, "is the greatest day I've ever had."

Gossage and the Sox had many great days in '72, and the team's turnaround had actually begun the season before. After dropping 95 games in 1968, 94 in '69, and 106 in '70, the franchise was not only losing games, but it was losing fans as well. Home attendance of under 500,000 in 1970 was some 600,000 less than the league average.

In 1971 Hemond and Tanner collaborated in their first full season together, and the result was an exciting, hustling ball club. Beltin' Melton belted 33 homers to become the first White Sox player to lead the league in that department, and the Sox finished just four games under .500. By the end of the season they were winning not just games, but also the hearts of a previously disheartened fan base. Attendance at Comiskey Park increased by 340,000, and the positive-thinking Hemond and Tanner went into the winter meetings believing they were only a couple of impact players away from contending for a title.

They acquired both pieces they needed on December 2, 1971, one of the landmark dates in franchise history. Bahnsen was brought over from the Yankees for talented infielder Rich McKinney, and Allen was obtained from the Dodgers.

Initially both Allen and Chicago sports fans were wary of the deal. Allen idolized Jackie Robinson and wanted to remain a Dodger. Sox fans were fully aware the nomadic Allen was now with his fourth team in as many seasons and that he was said to be nonchalant toward some of the game's time-honored traditions.

There was one other thing that gave the veteran Allen pause in the spring of '72: the Sox's youth at key positions. The Sox were seventeen years old at second, eighteen years old at shortstop. Allen thought "This is a high school team."

When the Sox lost their first three games, Allen told Tanner he was ready to pack his bags and head home. Tanner pulled Allen into his office for a pep talk. "We'll do it together," Tanner told Allen, meaning the two men would help mentor the young players—Gossage, May, Orta, et al.

Tanner recalled years later how Allen became the leader of the team, the manager on the field. "He took care of the young kids, took them under his wing," Tanner said. "And he played every game as if it was his last day on earth."

And so did the entire team, leading Allen to believe the Sox did more with enthusiasm than experience. "We became tighter than pantyhose two sizes too small," he said.

That magical summer on the South Side saved the Sox franchise. There had been talk that the Windy City Sox could be gone with the wind. Hemond's wheeling and dealing helped bring the buzz back to the old ball park. Home games at classic Comiskey saw the Sox take the field in equally classic uniforms—bright red pinstripes with the iconic "Sox" script over the chest, red numbers front and back, a White Sox patch on the sleeve, a red cap with a variation of the Sox script, red belt, and red cleats.

Also classic were Caray's radio calls. Harry Christopher Carabina broadcast Cardinals games during their glory years in the 1960s, was fired following the 1969 season, and spent 1970 with the A's before he and owner Charlie Finley parted ways. Finley didn't care for Caray's broadcasting style—"That [crap] he pulled in St. Louis didn't go over here," Finley spat—and Caray grew tired of his boss's meddling.

Hired by the White Sox in 1971, Caray quickly became a fan favorite among the South Side faithful, who saw him as one of their own. Like Bob Prince in Pittsburgh and Russ Hodges with the Giants in New York and then San Francisco, Caray was considered a fan's broadcaster. Like many of the masses, he was a bleacher creature; on hot days he would broadcast afternoon games bare-chested from Comiskey's center-field bleachers, his trusty fishing net by his side to snare home runs.

Caray held a lifelong fascination with unusual names. Speaking one day of the Dodgers' Manny Mota, Caray informed his audience that "Mota spelled backwards is atom. . . . And that's where he hit, right at 'im." His offhanded insights, garrulous voice, and oversized glasses became part of his legend and made for good-natured fodder for impersonators, the most famous being Will Ferrell in skits on *Saturday Night Live*.

While Cubs fans reveled in Wrigley Field, with its brick walls and ivy in the outfield, White Sox supporters streamed into Comiskey Park, the oldest baseball stadium in use at the time. Opened on July 1, 1910, predating Fenway Park by two years and Wrigley by six, Comiskey Park—later renamed White Sox Park—was home to the Sox for eighty-one years until their final game on September 30, 1990.

Original plans called for Comiskey to have a Romanesque design with a cantilever upper deck. Construction costs, however, led to a more conservative two-tier grandstand extending down both baselines and a single level of wooden bleachers beyond the outfield wall. A red-brick façade made the stadium look from the outside like a factory. Through the years Comiskey Park was altered in various ways—its seating capacity was enlarged, an exploding scoreboard complete with fireworks and aerial bombs was installed, and moveable box seats were added and removed as home plate was moved back and forth to increase the number of home runs.

One of the more startling renovations came in 1969, when Astroturf was installed in the infield to cut field maintenance costs. Comiskey became the only park in the majors with an Astroturf infield and an outfield of God's green grass.

Allen, known for his dry quips, uttered what remains the most cutting criticism of artificial grass: "If a horse won't eat it," he said, "I don't want to play on it."

The Sox infield may have been artificial, but the challenge to the A's was authentic. Even with Beltin' Melton sidelined by a back injury suffered the previous November when he fell from his roof protecting his three-year-old son Bill, Chicago still owned a lead of one and a half games over Oakland as late as August 26. Wilbur Wood was a big reason why.

Winning over twenty games for the second straight season, the wily knuckleballer owed much of his success to his mentality. He was still a relief pitcher at heart, he said, pitching one batter at a time rather than one game at a time.

Despite a physical appearance that *Chicago Sun-Times* sports columnist Jack Griffin once compared to "the guy who just won the beer frame," Wood was remarkably resilient. In 1971, after beginning the season as a reliever and spot starter, he moved into the rotation and worked twelve straight weeks on a two-day rest basis; in one stretch in '72 Wood threw in four games in ten days. Making an AL record-tying 49 starts, completing 20 of them, and throwing 376 $^2/_3$ innings, Wood put up numbers not seen since the deadball era. He became a modern-day Big Ed Walsh, who had started a record 49 games for the White Sox in 1908, had won 40 of them, and had hurled 464 innings.

Wood's reliever mentality and rubber arm allowed Tanner to do something unprecedented in modern times: work with a three-man starting staff. The "Great Trio"—Wood, Bahnsen (43 starts) and Bradley (40 starts)—combined for 132 starts in '72. The rest of the staff combined for all of 24 starts.

The quick-start system was not new to Chisox strategists. Chicago pitching coach Johnny Sain helped hurl the Boston Braves to the 1948 pennant by working nine complete games with only two days' rest between each. Sain won 24 games, and the Braves won the pennant. He shared the heavy lifting with another famous iron arm, Warren Spahn, and the Braves became known for their "Spahn and Sain and two days of rain" strategy.

"There's nothing I have to do for Wilbur," Sain said then, "except give him a ball before the game and give him a cigar after it."

Wood's cigar concealed the gap left by a missing tooth. At 6 feet, 180 pounds, the thirty-year-old southpaw wasn't lean or muscular. He was a little old and a little portly. With his shirttail protruding from his pants, his wheat-colored hair receding beneath his bright red cap, and his casual throwing motion, the man nicknamed "Wilbah" could have passed for a father playing catch with his son in the yard.

Wood had an indestructible temperament. When the Indians retaliated against the White Sox's hazing of Perry by asking the umpires to shake down Wood—"Cut off his knuckles!" Tribe third baseman Buddy Bell shouted—Wilbur was unfazed. He carried that mindset to the mound and, armed with a dancing knuckle ball that he first began throwing in junior high, baffled batters. Wood had just one high-caliber pitch, but he threw it relentlessly.

"He throws that knuckleball nice and easy," Tanner said then. "It's no strain on his arm."

Wood had learned to throw the knuckleball by mistake. He was twelve years old, watching his father throw a palm ball. Like the knuckler, the palm ball approached the plate without rotating. Wilbur wanted to do everything his dad did, so he tried imitating his palm ball. Because the twelve-year-old Wood's hands were too small to wrap around the ball as completely as his father's could, the younger Wood's pitch came out a knuckle ball. It eventually carried him on its fluttering, unpredictable wings to the big leagues.

When his knuckle ball was working, Wood believed there wasn't anybody who could beat him. When it wasn't working, there wasn't anybody he thought he could beat. Wood won three straight decisions against the A's in '72, outdueling Catfish Hunter, Rollie Fingers, and Vida Blue in succession.

Chicago and Oakland were clearly the best in the West, but the division was not without its stars. In Minnesota, Rod Carew—holding his thin bat so lightly it seemed to dance in his hands—led the league with a .318 batting average while Harmon Killebrew's compact swing powered the Twins with a team-high 26 homers. Carew became the first AL player to win the batting title without benefit of a home run.

The 1972 season saw the end of Minnesota's celebrated brand of hardball played on the prairie. The Twins finished 77-77, and though Carew was the best hitter in the league, Killebrew was in his final season as a feared slugger and former star Tony Oliva was limited to just ten games due to an injured right knee that cut short a potential Hall of Fame career.

The plight of Tony O., the Killer, and Carew in '72 was captured by Terry Cashman in his song "Talkin' Twins Baseball: Tony, the Killer and Carew."

Nicknamed "Killer" and "Hammerin' Harmon," Killebrew was one of the most prolific power hitters in history. At the time of his retirement in 1975 he had hit more homers (573) than any right-handed hitter. A thirteen-time All-Star in his twenty-two-year career and the AL's MVP in 1969, Killebrew was a 5-foot-11, 210-pound man mountain who looked to have enough strength to squash a small bear.

Hoisting his "Oregon Slammer" bat, which was made of maple rather than ash since maple was said to last longer, Harmon was a frightening sight for opposing pitchers and managers. Former Baltimore Orioles skipper Paul Richards said Killebrew could "knock the ball out of any park—including Yellowstone."

Killebrew credited his prodigious power to the chores he had growing up in Idaho in the 1950s. For four years, beginning in 1950, when he turned fourteen, he lifted and hauled ten-gallon milk cans full of milk. That, he said, would put muscles on you even if you weren't trying.

Soft-spoken and humble, Killebrew's quiet dignity was a hallmark of a man who embodied not only Minnesota Twins baseball, but also baseball in the Midwest. At the time of Killebrew's death from cancer in May 2011, Carew issued a statement in which he called his fellow Hall of Famer "a consummate professional who treated everyone from the brashest of rookies to the groundskeepers to the ushers in the stadium with the utmost respect. I would not be the person I am today if it weren't for Harmon Killebrew."

Oliva said it was difficult to describe how nice Harmon was. Like Carew, Oliva described the man called "Killer" as being nice to everyone and always willing to help people. To play with Killer, Oliva remembered, was a privilege.

In Kansas City, John Mayberry, a twenty-three-year-old wallbanger playing his first full season of big league ball, plated 100 RBIs for the Royals and was called the Chauffeur for driving so many men home. Traded from Houston to Kansas City in 1971 after the Astros acquired Lee May from Cincinnati, Mayberry struggled at first to learn American League pitchers. After forty-one games his batting average (.222) was the same as the title of a popular TV show at the time, *Room 222*.

Mayberry wasn't worried. He was going bad but making good contact. Big John was a fast learner and an intelligent hitter. Royals hitting instructor Charlie Lau said at the time that he had never seen anyone Mayberry's age know the strike zone as well as he did. Opponents knew it and were baffled on how to pitch Big John. Red Sox rookie catcher Carlton Fisk found that Mayberry didn't swing at many bad pitches and that although Boston pitchers tried to set him up for a pitch, Mayberry didn't go for setup pitches. Fisk tried mixing pitch selection but finally admitted the Red Sox were stymied.

Mayberry ended his initial AL campaign with 25 homers and a .298 batting average. The Royals' neighbor in the new-look West, the Texas Rangers, were led by skipper Ted Williams. The Rangers lost 100 games in their first season in Texas, but another newcomer, California Angels fireballer Nolan Ryan, was trending upward.

Ryan's fastball, clocked at a then Guinness World Record 100.9 m.p.h., was dubbed "the Express" after the 1965 World War II action movie *Von Ryan's Express*. It's been suggested that Ryan reached 108 m.p.h. in his career, but no official reading exists. Still he is the man most consider the fastest throwing pitcher in history, faster even than celebrated fireballers like Aroldis Chapman of the Reds, who in 2013 set the MLB record for fastest pitch ever recorded at 105.1 m.p.h., and Rapid Robert Feller, who was timed at 107.9 m.p.h. in 1946, a mark MLB doesn't recognize because it can't verify its accuracy.

Traded by the Mets to California on December 10, 1971, for third baseman Jim Fregosi in one of the more infamous deals in Mets' history, Ryan blossomed on the West Coast, winning 19 games and pitching 20 complete games. He hurled a league-high 9 shutouts, tying Don Sutton and Steve Carlton for the most in the majors, and rang up 329 Ks in 284 innings, a ratio of 10.4 strikeouts per nine innings that ranked second all-time to Sam McDowell's 10.7 in 1965. He blew away the powerful Twins with 17 strikeouts to tie a major league mark for most Ks at night and twice whiffed 16.

Ryan was at his best in a July 9 game against the Red Sox. He struck out eight straight to tie another league record and retired 26 in a row in his second straight shutout.

Mere stats, however, fail to do justice to the Express. Killebrew said if he was ever hit by Ryan's heater, he would have the pitcher arrested for manslaughter. Oakland's Sal Bando said Ryan threw him one pitch he didn't even see. Reggie Jackson called the Express faster than instant coffee and remarked that Ryan was the only pitcher he feared.

Jeff Torborg, an Angels catcher in 1972 who had previously played for the Dodgers and caught Koufax, thought Ryan as fast as Sandy. Catching Ryan caused Torborg to develop a bone bruise on his hand after just three pitches. The last time that had happened was when Torborg had caught Koufax the night of his perfect game.

Former Koufax battery mate and Angels coach John Roseboro believed Ryan every bit as fast as Sandy. The difference was that Ryan didn't mind knocking down a hitter. That was something Koufax wouldn't do, Roseboro said.

Before terrorizing American League batters, Ryan had been on a Mets staff that included Tom Seaver, Jerry Koosman, and Gary Gentry and that had upset Baltimore in the 1969 World Series. For four seasons in New York Ryan was never able to get into a pitching rhythm; locked in a cycle between starting and relieving, he remained a wild-flinging flame thrower. In 1971 he walked seven batters every nine innings. Met management had seen enough and with the chance to snare an All-Star third baseman, sent Ryan to California.

Angels GM Harry Dalton was so enamored with Ryan, he told those approaching him about a trade that the young ace was as much an "Untouchable" as Eliot Ness. Thriving on regular work, Ryan progressed from thrower to pitcher. In his final start of the season he went for the coveted twentieth win in a game against the A's. Ryan pitched well, but Blue Moon Odom and Oakland won 2–1.

The A's run to a second straight division title wasn't easy. They had to fight off a fierce challenge by the White Sox, and A's skipper Dick Williams had to contend with injuries and a revolving door at second base, where eight different men played the position for Oakland during the '72 season. A's announcer Monte Moore said the situation at second seemed to be a takeoff on the classic Abbott and Costello bit: "Who's on First?" In Oakland's case, it was "Who's on Second?"

Williams also had to juggle an ever-changing roster, Finley making more deals than Monty Hall. The Oakland owner made sixty-two transactions that season.

Still the A's trailed the White Sox in late August, but Hunter's 1–0 win over Cleveland in the Coliseum on August 29 put Oakland in first place for good. As late as September 19 the White Sox trailed the A's by five games when they arrived in Oakland for a two-game series that marked their final meeting of the season.

Prior to the opener Caray told his radio listeners this series was crucial for the Sox and "almost a must for the White Sox to sweep this series in order to have a chance." Allen told Caray the Sox hadn't given up yet. "This has been a scrappy club all year," he said.

Chicago's scrappy side was on display in the opener, the Sox outlasting the A's 8–7 in fifteen innings, with Gossage getting the win in relief thanks to a home run by rookie Jorge Orta. The A's lead was cut to four, and if the Sox could sweep, they would leave Oakland trailing by three games with eleven to play and a more favorable schedule than the A's. The second game of the series matched southpaw aces Holtzman and Wood. Neither proved particularly sharp, but Holtzman got the win with relief help from Fingers and homers by Jackson and Bando.

The A's would go 18-10 in September while the White Sox went 14-13. Hunter and Holtzman each went 5-0 in the season's stretch run, Holtzman twice beating the rival White Sox. Holtzman had turned into one of Finley's shrewdest acquisitions, and two other veterans, Matty Alou and Dal Maxvill, proved to be key late-summer additions. Another Finley addition was pinch-running specialist Allan Lewis, the "Panamanian Express," who stole key bases in the drive to the division title.

The A's won the West on September 28 and did it in what was typically dramatic fashion for the Mustache Gang. With their magic number at one, Oakland trailed Minnesota 7–0 in the Coliseum. The swingin' A's battled back and eventually tied the score in the seventh on Angel Mangual's two-run single.

Sal Bando led off the bottom of the ninth and was hit by a pitch, bringing Maxville to the plate. Moore called the title-clinching hit:

Maxville swings, hits a line drive, deep left-center field, it's going all the way to the fence! Here's Bando rounding third, he's heading home and the A's win the West! The fireworks are blasting away!

It looked for a long time today as if it would never happen, but that's not the way the A's play. They make it happen!

The war in the AL West was won. In the NL East, Roberto Clemente and the Pirates were making things happen as well.

CHAPTER NINE

Wilver Dornell Stargell was a Pirate treasure.

A big man with a buttery, baritone voice, Stargell's windmilling of his bat in looping, rhythmic circles between pitches is as enduring an image of signature batting styles from the summer of '72 as Felix Millan's hands-halfway-up-the-bat grip and Dick McAuliffe's "foot-in-the-bucket" stance that stirred memories of Mel Ott.

Bob Skinner, an outfielder with the Bucs when Stargell broke into the big leagues in 1962, said Stargell's calling card was a timing device. Stargell would stand on the port side of the plate and get his bat going—one, two, three times around. But once the pitcher went into his delivery, Stargell's bat was very still and in a cocked position. His record shows what happened after that, said Skinner.

What happened in '72 was that Stargell hit .293 and a team-high 33 home runs and 112 RBIs. It wasn't his best season; the year before he had led the National League with a career-high 48 homers and in 1973 would post league-high numbers in homers (44), RBIs (119), doubles (43), slugging percentage (.646), and OPS (1.038).

Stargell was a big bat, but the Bucs knew he was much more than that. Danny Murtaugh, who piloted the Pirates to a world title in 1971, thought Stargell was a lot like Roberto Clemente in that he led by example. He ran every play out and played hard all the time. The younger Pirate players would watch the thirty-two-year-old Stargell do things the right way and would try to follow in his footsteps. Pirates center fielder Al Oliver said the Bucs had so much respect for Stargell that if he asked them to jump off the Fort Pitt Bridge, their only question would be what kind of dive he wanted.

"I think of Willie and those Pirate teams and we really had some good people," Oliver remembered. "Dock [Ellis] and [Bob] Robertson and I came up and blended with [Roberto] Clemente and Stargell and [Steve] Blass, and we all got along so well. We had diversity—we were white and black and Spanish—and we all got along."

The previous September 1, the Pirates had made major league history by fielding a lineup made entirely of men of color: Rennie Stennett, second base; Gene Clines, center field; Clemente, right field; Stargell, left field; Manny Sanguillen, catcher; Dave Cash, third base; Oliver, first base; Roberto Hernandez, shortstop; Ellis, pitcher. Stargell was one of the leaders of this diverse team, but his road had not been an easy one; four years earlier he had stood at the crossroads of his career. There was a time when Stargell thought all there was to baseball was to show up at the stadium a couple of hours before game time, go through the usual routine, play nine innings, and go home. He talked to Willie Mays, Hank Aaron, and Stan Musial to find out what it took to give a good performance every game. Always give 100 percent, they said.

Stargell did, at the plate and in the field. His prodigious power allowed him to own seven of the eighteen baseballs hit out of the Pirates' old park, Forbes Field. When the team moved to Three Rivers Stadium, Stargell reached the upper-right-field deck several times. But he refused to be defined by home runs. He was embarrassed when people talked about his tape-measure drives. Stargell would reply that he was just as happy if his home run landed in the first row of seats.

What counted even more than reaching the seats, Stargell thought, was driving in runs. Even after hitting a game-winning homer, he would announce in the clubhouse, "You take the home runs; I'll take the RBIs." He had seen guys hit a lot of homers and not provide maximum production. Stargell didn't want to be that kind of hitter. He wanted to be a guy who hit with men on base. To him earning the RBI crown was more important than being the home run champion.

He didn't regret playing in Pittsburgh's spacious stadiums as opposed to cozy ball parks like Atlanta's. If he had played in a bandbox, he might have developed an arch in his swing and would have been a home run hitter rather than a line-drive hitter. If he allowed himself to think in just one direction—hitting home runs—he would be forgetting other important parts of the game. Stargell wanted to do his best in every department.

Stargell was an outstanding fielder with a fine arm. Few who witnessed it will forget his laser-like throw from left field that cut down Baltimore's Davey Johnson at home plate in the '71 World Series or his leap against the wall in that same Series. Blass thought the latter was one of the great leaps for a big man. Stargell was moved back and forth between the outfield and first base several times in his career and was named an All-Star at both positions. Physically he preferred playing first base because he saved wear and tear on his knees, which didn't have to carry his 225-pound frame around the Tartan Turf of Three Rivers Stadium. Mentally he liked playing the outfield because it meant he was involved in fewer plays than at first base and could concentrate more on his next at-bat.

Stargell played a pivotal role in the Pirates' pennant drive in '71 but struggled in the postseason, going 0 for 15 in the NLCS against San Francisco and batting .208 against Baltimore. He remained cool under pressure, calm amid adversity. He had always been even tempered. He remembered his father telling him to never feel too good when things were going well and never too bad when things were going badly.

It was sage advice for a guy whose career ran hot and cold. The summer game could be as fickle a friend as the summer wind Frank Sinatra famously sang of in the 1960s and '70s. Stargell's career was proof of that. He once struck out seven straight times; on another occasion he lashed five doubles in a doubleheader.

Stargell was unchanged either way. A product of the gritty Oakland, California, ghetto, he had experienced too much to be affected by ups and downs. His father had worked at the naval air station; his mother worked as a hair dresser and in the local cannery. Growing up in Alameda on the waterfront, Stargell was exposed to temptation. He could have easily taken the wrong road; a lot of his friends did.

Stargell's road led him to sign at age seventeen with the Pirates for a

$1,200 bonus. A year later he was leaving home and heading for the Deep South for his first pro baseball camp. The plane had a stop in Jackson, Mississippi, and when Stargell and another black player, Art Blunt, headed for the airport restaurant, they were subjected to racial taunts by the man behind the food counter. The trip, and the indignities, continued. In Jacksonville, Florida, Stargell couldn't stay with white players in the comfortable accommodations on the beach; instead he was relegated to "black bottom," an inland apartment house hot as a sauna. The second floor was equipped with army cots but no other furniture. Stargell said once the lights went out, he fought roaches for his bed.

He also battled racial intolerance. He was called "pork chop" by fans in minor league parks. He often lay in his cot at night crying. In Grand Forks, North Dakota, a small girl pointed to Stargell and Elmo Plaskette, a Virgin Islander, and told her mother she wanted a teddy bear for Christmas as black as the two men were.

"We weren't really human," Stargell once said of some people's perception of blacks. His belief was reinforced when he and Plaskette walked into a barber shop in Grand Forks and were looked at by the other customers like invaders from another planet. When the barber asked what they wanted, Stargell said they wanted a haircut. The barber looked at their tightly curled hair. "I can't cut that stuff," he snapped.

Stargell found the Steel City more to his liking. James Parton once described Pittsburgh as "Hell with the lid off," and there was a time when the Steel City—or Smoky City as some called it because the smog was so thick that street lights burned by the day—lived up to its reputation. Powered by the Irish, Italians, Germans, Hungarians, and Poles who flocked to its three riverbeds, Pittsburgh's mills and fiery furnaces forged the steel for the Industrial Revolution; victories in World Wars I and II; and the nation's skyscrapers, including the Empire State Building. Enough carbon and soot was coughed and belched from its processing plants that the white collars of the robber barons that ravaged its mines for coal were turned black by noontime.

By 1970 Pittsburgh was enjoying a renaissance. The territory that had once served as a remote outpost for George Washington and was later the first Gateway to the West had become a steel-and-glass manufacturing monster, home to U.S. Steel and Pittsburgh Plate Glass. Three Rivers Stadium and the U.S. Steel Tower, the final building projects of a Pittsburgh urban renewal program called Renaissance I, were completed in 1970.

"It was a great time to be in Pittsburgh," Oliver recalled. "One thing about Pittsburgh people, they never forget you. I was in Germany and I heard someone call, 'Scoop!' [It was Oliver's nickname for his defensive abilities at first base]. I go back to Pittsburgh today and it's like I never left."

Just as the Steel City was forced to reinvent itself in the 1970s due to the collapse of the steel industry, Pittsburgh's professional sports teams reinvented themselves as well. In 1970 the Pirates ended a ten-year postseason drought. In 1972 the Steelers made the playoffs for the first time in team history and stunned Oakland with Franco Harris's "Immaculate Reception."

Turning out teams as hard and unyielding as the coal and steel that emanated from its mines and mills, Pittsburgh saw the Pirates dominate the Eastern Division throughout the decade and win two World Series. The Steelers, coached by Chuck Noll and boasting a balanced offense and its famous Steel Curtain defense, swept to four Super Bowl titles in the '70s.

When the Pirates and Steelers won world championships in 1979—a rare MLB-NFL double claimed by the Yankees and Giants in 1927, '38, and '56; Tigers and Lions in 1935; Mets and Jets in 1969; Orioles and Colts in 1970; Mets and Giants in 1986; and Red Sox and Patriots in 2004—Pittsburgh had gone from being "Hell with the lid off" to the "City of Champions."

The man who by 1979 would be called "Pops" by his teammates and was the patriarch of the Pirates' "We Are Family" World Series winners championed causes in and outside Pittsburgh. Stargell did charitable work for sickle-cell anemia, visited the state penitentiary and spoke with convicts, rapped with kids on the street, and met with junkies. He flew to Vietnam during the war and talked to wounded servicemen. He sat with a soldier who had burns over 97 percent of his body and watched the man die; he visited a triple amputee.

Pressure playing the game of baseball? Stargell scoffed at the notion.

He kept things in perspective by reminding everyone that the umpire's words to start every game were "Play ball!" not "Work Ball."

"Willie was definitely a leader on the club," recalled starting pitcher Bruce Kison. "He wasn't afraid to voice his opinion, and he did what he thought was right. And he was a visible leader. He wouldn't necessarily say, 'Get on my shoulders,' but that's what he meant."

By 1972 the soft-spoken giant had learned to deal with the emotional and physical battering life can deliver. He had been beaned in Grand Forks and with the Pirates had overcome neck spasms, debilitating headaches, and double vision incurred when he had run into the scoreboard at Forbes Field. Doctors told him another blow to the head could be fatal. He tore a thigh muscle while legging out a double, taped the injured leg, and played the next day in Houston, where he got involved in a collision at first base that tore a muscle from his rib cage. He underwent knee surgery following the 1971 season.

Stargell soldiered on. With the Pirates fighting the Mets, Cubs, and Cardinals for first place in the East in '72, he hit .320 in July and .344 in August and collected 18 homers and 56 RBIs over those pivotal months. No one man carries the Pirates in hitting, he said at the time. There wasn't pressure on any one Pittsburgh hitter because they had so many good hitters.

Four Pirates regulars (Clemente, Richie Hebner, Vic Davalillo, and Oliver) hit .300 or better in 1972; Sanguillen was at .298 and Stargell five points behind. Gene Clines's .334 paced Pittsburgh's super subs, which included Stennett, Milt May, 1971 postseason hero Bob Robertson, 1960 October legend Bill Mazeroski, Richie Zisk, Gene Clines, Jackie Hernandez, and Jose Pagan.

In olden days pirates rattled their swords, but Pittsburgh's buccaneers were lifting heavy lumber. With so much firepower in a lineup known as the Pittsburgh "Lumber Company," to go along with a dependable defense and deep pitching staff, many Pirates, including Kison, believed the '72 club better than the '71 World Series champs. "Guys had more experience," Kison recalled.

The Bucs' all-around strength took pressure off the club's individuals and put pressure on rival pitchers. The enemy hurlers in the East were a fearsome group. Tom Seaver was in New York, Bob Gibson in St. Louis, Ferguson Jenkins in Chicago, and Steve Carlton in Philadelphia. Pittsburgh's pitching staff didn't have a singular superstar, but Ellis, Kison, Blass, Bob Moose, Nelson Briles, Dave Giusti, and company strong-armed the competition.

And what competition it was. As a boy Kison had collected baseball trading cards of Willie Mays, Hank Aaron, and others. "These were people who impacted my youth," he recalled. Now he was playing against them. "Holy crap," he remembered with a laugh, "now I'm facing Mays and Aaron."

The defending world champions opened the season in Shea Stadium on NBC-TV's *Game of the Week*. Seaver, who the season before had set a National League record for strikeouts by a right-hander with 289, fanned Stennett to start the game. He struck out the side, getting Clemente and Stargell swinging, and the Mets—wearing a mourning band on their left arm in memory of Gil Hodges—went on to beat Ellis and the Bucs 4–0, setting a tone for both clubs in the early stages of the race.

"If Seaver got you to chase his high fastball, you couldn't touch him," Oliver recalled. "His fastball rose. You had to get him when his pitches were low [in the strike zone]."

LEAVE IT TO SEAVER was a sign held aloft in those heady days early in the season by Queens resident Karl Ehrhardt, better known to fans as the "Sign Man." A commercial artist, Ehrhardt was a fixture from 1964 to 1981 at Big Shea, the Flushing Meadows ballpark distinguishable by the multicolored blue and orange panels on its façade. In his field-level box seat behind the third base dugout the Sign Man would hold aloft one of the sixty block-lettered, 20-by-26-inch black cardboard placards he brought to dozens of home games every season. In his home he had a collection of some twelve hundred signs, each carrying white or orange upper-cased characters, and he would "crystal ball" what might happen on game day by reading newspapers to find out which players were streaking and which were slumping.

Like Hilda Chester, the cowbell clanger who was a fixture at Ebbets

Field during the days of Brooklyn's "Boys of Summer," Ehrhardt loved Dem Bums. As a Mets fan, he was a part of the happening that Big Shea became. When left-fielder Cleon Jones gloved the final out of the World Series on October 16, 1969, Sign Man responded with THERE ARE NO WORDS. It may have been the lone time Ehrhardt didn't have the appropriate verbiage. "I just called them the way I saw them," he told the *New York Times* in 2006. He greeted great plays with placards asking, "BELIEVE IN MIRACLES?" Colorfully clad in a black derby rimmed with a blue-and-orange band, he was a favorite not only of fans, but also of TV cameras, which zoomed in on his signs:

AMAZIN!

MET POWER!

TOOTHLESS CUBS JUST A LOTTA LIP

With Seaver winning seven of his first eight decisions to set the stage for a 21-win season; with young left-hander Jon Matlack starting 6-0 en route to 15 victories and National League Rookie of the Year honors; and with energetic relief ace Frank Edwin "Tug" McGraw saving games the starters didn't finish, new manager Yogi Berra had his Mets in first place in July. The off-season acquisition of red-headed slugger Rusty Staub from Montreal for power-hitting prospect Ken Singleton, pepper-pot shortstop Tim Foli, and slick-fielding first baseman Mike Jorgensen added one of the league's best left-handed bats to the Mets' offense. "Le Grand Orange" batted .298 in his first month as a Met and .336 in May, when he rapped 5 homers and drove in 28 runs to help fuel a fast start that saw New York go a major league-best 24-7 and open a lead of six and a half games.

Staub was ably assisted by the remaining Miracle workers of '69. On May 7 Tommie Agee's single in the bottom of the ninth tied San Diego, and his homer in the tenth won it as the Mets rallied from a six-run deficit. New York had the National League "Mets-merized" but the "Amazin' Mets" truly became "A-Mays-in'" on May 11. The news that the Mets were bringing Mays back to New York sent shock waves through the sports world.

Mets owner Joan Payson had coveted Mays for more than a decade, but every overture to pry him loose from San Francisco had been rebuffed by Giants boss Horace Stoneham. In the spring of '72 the Mets started to sense a fissure in San Francisco's stonewalling. On May 5 the forty-year-old Mays went 0 for 4 in the Giants' 3–2 loss in Philadelphia. His average dipped to .167, the lowest in San Francisco's batting order. Jack Lang of the *Long Island Press* contacted Mays by phone in Philadelphia and asked Willie if he had heard anything about a possible trade to the Mets. Mays replied that he hadn't heard, but that if the Giants wanted to trade him, they could.

The next day was Mays's forty-first birthday, and stories of a possible deal were everywhere. Stoneham and the Mets' board chairman, M. Donald Grant, acknowledged the possibility of such a move. A report circulated that trade talks between the two teams had intensified when the Mets were in San Francisco for a three-game set May 1–3. On Wednesday, May 10, two days before San Francisco was to begin a three-game weekend series in New York, it was reported that Stoneham's demands for multiple players in return for Mays had prevented the trade from happening.

"MAYS DEAL OFF" was the headline on a United Press International story. Grant told reporters Stoneham wanted players, not money, for Mays. The Mets' chairman of the board consulted with Berra and his general manager, Bob Scheffing, and then told Stoneham it was "improbable the Mets could provide the personnel he needs."

Mired in last place in the West, San Francisco had reportedly asked for versatile utility player Ted Martinez and a pitcher, either Matlack or right-hander Jim McAndrews, in exchange for their aging superstar. Since Martinez and Matlack had helped fuel the most impressive start in franchise history and since the Mets knew Mays's days as a player were dwindling, they thought the Giants' request out of line and out of the question. Both sides agreed to leave the door open for negotiations, however, and both stated that a deal would not be consummated unless Mays agreed to finish his playing days as a Met.

Grant and Stoneham went so far as to invite Mays to the trading table to clear up any concerns Willie had. Mays, for his part, always had affection for New York. He had broken into the big leagues with New York in 1951 and had played there until the Giants moved west for the 1958 season. At the time of the trade talks Mays said he would like to finish his playing career in San Francisco but had no objections to being dealt to the Mets.

Finally on Thursday, May 11, Mays officially became a Met. Lang was credited in the New York media for spurring the trade, and even though it had been rumored for days, the news had a "wow" factor to it. Mays was one of the game's legends, a giant in reputation if no longer a Giant in uniform. *New York Times* sportswriter Joseph Durso told readers the "$165,000-a-year folk-hero" was traded "after one of the most complex series of negotiations in baseball history."

The deal called for Mays to join the Mets in exchange for young minor league pitcher Charlie Williams and an undisclosed amount of cash that was later reported to be $50,000. From a headlines standpoint it was the biggest trade in sports in 1972. The strangest deal, however, would occur just over two months later, when the NFL's Baltimore Colts and Los Angeles Rams swapped owners, Carroll Rosenbloom going west and Robert Irsay heading east. Colts fans would come to rue the day the deal was made. In the four years before Irsay took command of the Colts, Baltimore had gone to two Super Bowls and won one. Twelve years later Irsay shepherded the beloved team out of town under the cover of darkness to Indianapolis.

Bright lights greeted Mays's meeting with the media at the Mets head-quarters at the Mayfair House. Grant stood to the right of Mays. Stoneham, blinking behind dark-rimmed glasses, was on Willie's left side. Berra and Scheffing were also present, and because it was Mays who was being traded, commissioner Bowie Kuhn was there.

"It's a wonderful feeling being here," Mays said. "I'm very thankful I can still play at the age of 41 and play in New York. If used in the right way, I can do a very good job."

When a reporter asked Mays what he meant by the "right way," the intellectual sharks in the audience took note. It was common knowledge that in San Francisco Mays had written his name into the lineup when he wanted to. Prior to his trade to the Mets, Mays and Berra met, and the manager made it clear who was boss. Berra would make out the lineup card, he would play Mays in the outfield at times and at first base at times, and the decisions would be Yogi's.

There would be plenty of decision making for Berra to do since New York already had Eddie Kranepool, an original Metropolitan, at first base and their own Shea Hey Kid, Agee, in center field. All Agee was doing in the month of May was hitting .340. He was flanked on both sides by a trio of similarly hot bats—Staub in right and the tandem of Cleon Jones and John Milner, a.k.a. "the Hammer," in left. Milner and Matlack were both twenty-two years old and the latest products of a rich farm system operated by Whitey Herzog.

At his press conference, Mays said he was looking forward to contributing to what the Mets believed would be another A-Mays-in' season. "I can still swing the bat, I can still run," he told reporters in his pealing voice. "Teamwork is very important to me."

May 11 was a bittersweet day for Gotham's sports fans. At the same time they welcomed their prodigal son home to New York, their beloved Rangers bowed to rival Boston in Game Six of the Stanley Cup finals. Despite the continuous cheers of Rangers fans, who packed Madison Square Garden (MSG), the Broadway Blue Shirts couldn't hold off Bobby Orr, Phil Esposito, Gerry Cheevers, and the Big Bad Bruins in a 3–0 final.

It was a heady spring for New York's pro sports teams. As Ricky Nelson reminisced of a "Garden Party," there was a Garden party going on in Manhattan's MSG. While the Rangers rode their famous GAG (Goal-a-Game) line of Vic Hadfield, Jean Ratelle, and Rod Gilbert and the goal tending of Ed Giacomin to a Stanley Cup showdown with Boston, the Knicks of Walt "Clyde" Frazier, Earl "the Pearl" Monroe, Bill Bradley, Dave DeBusschere, Willis Reed, Phil Jackson et al. responded to chants of "Dee-fense!" inside MSG as the NBA playoffs heated up. The Knicks would meet Wilt Chamberlain, Jerry West, and the rest of the record-setting Los Angeles Lakers in the finals.

The deal for Mays added to the sports fever in the city and marked the Mets' third big trade in the past half-year. The official story line was that the Giants wanted to do right by Mays by sending him to New York to bring his career full circle. The truth was more complex. Mays was at the end of his Hall of Fame career, and his best years were behind him. He was also thirty years older than the franchise to which he had been traded and was viewed by many as the most expensive substitute in major league history. It was written at the time that Mays was being paid $165,000 to sit on the bench, and as *Sports Illustrated*'s William Leggett noted, those were wages even Supreme Court bench sitters didn't get.

The Giants had young outfielders they were anxious to work into the starting lineup, and Mays was benched at times in favor of a youth movement. San Francisco was also unwilling to guarantee Mays a high-paying coaching position when his playing career ended. Mays asked Stoneham for a ten-year retainer at $75,000 per year to work for the Giants in any capacity. Stoneham balked. The attendance-challenged Giants couldn't afford it. San Francisco had won the West in '71, but in the course of winning the battle it was losing the war. Attendance at Candlestick Park in '71 was 1,106,043, some 800,000 less than the club drew on the road and close to a million less than the 2,064,594 the Dodgers drew in Chavez Ravine. When San Francisco dropped eleven of thirteen at Candlestick early in '72 and lost slugger Willie McCovey for three months to an injury, the Giants' boss decided it was time to trade Mays and build for the future. "The Mets are the only club that could take care of him," Stoneham said. "Don and Mrs. Payson are as much in love with Willie as I am."

Berra drove to Shea Stadium following the press conference, walked into the clubhouse where his team had learned about the trade from radio broadcasts, and sought out equipment manager Nick Torman. "I guess you'd better get No. 24 off Beauchamp," Berra told Torman.

Jim Beauchamp, a utility outfielder–first baseman who had worn Willie's number with the Mets, was given number 5 instead.

The deal for Mays paid immediate dividends for the Mets when Willie made his debut in a Met uniform on Sunday, May 14. On a gray, rain-swept Mother's Day afternoon, with the crowd full of women wearing the straw bonnets management had given away, Mays played first base and batted leadoff against Giants fireballer "Sudden" Sam McDowell. Amid a thunderous ovation from Mets fans, Willie walked in his first at-bat and scored on Staub's grand slam.

San Francisco tied the game with four runs off Ray Sadecki in the fifth, and Mays led off the bottom of the inning against reliever Don Carrithers. Willie worked the count to 3-2 and Lindsey Nelson provided the play-by-play: *"Payoff pitch to Mays. . . . It's way back in left field, could be. . . . It's going, going and it is a home run! A home run for Willie Mays! Willie Mays gets a great ovation from the crowd and in the dugout from the Mets as he belted a 3-2 pitch over the left field wall."*

Shea Stadium shook as the aging Say Hey Kid circled the bases. Every Met stood to greet Mays after he crossed home plate and returned to the dugout. One of the foremost among them was Kranepool, the man Mays had replaced at first base. Mays, the longtime Giant, had turned Giant killer. His dramatic homer proved to be the game winner. "It just seemed like the stage was set and I had to do something," Mays told reporters.

The near-mythical play was vintage Mays. This was the superstar who had more than six hundred career home runs to his credit and had a flair for artistry in the field as well, the guy who was known for robbing Vic Wertz in the 1954 World Series and running down a Ted Williams drive in Milwaukee's County Stadium in the '55 All-Star Game.

Mets fans who had been bubbling for days over the trade for Mays thought Willie's debut was all that it was supposed to be. It was, New York poet Joel Oppenheimer wrote, as if a script had been written.

Much to the delight of Mets' fans, Willie went on to hit .375 in May, and despite occasional clashes with Berra over playing time, Mays's return read like a storybook tale. Along with the Mick and the Duke, the Say Hey Kid was part of New York folklore. The trio of legendary center fielders was further immortalized in Terry Cashman's song "Talkin' Baseball" (Willie, Mickey, and the Duke).

What a thrill it was for Mets fans, Mets announcer Bob Murphy said, to see Mays patrolling center field in the Mets' blue pinstripes. New York fans were Mets-merized. They streamed into Big Shea. The Mets were the only team in the majors in 1972 to surpass the two million mark in home attendance.

Once inside Shea Stadium, fans were treated to the lilting, optimistic sounds from Jane Jarvis. The organist for Mets games at Shea from 1964 to 1979, Jarvis's in-game repertory included "Singin' in the Rain" for rainouts, "There'll Be a Hot Time in the Old Town Tonight" for homers, and "Just One of Those Things" for a Mets batter who struck out with runners in scoring position.

Jarvis serenaded Seaver with "Mr. Wonderful," greeted McGraw's entrance from the bullpen with "When Irish Eyes Are Smiling," and played "My Buddy" for Mets shortstop Bud Harrelson. When the Mets lost, she boosted the mood of departing fans with "Pack Up Your Troubles in Your Old Kit Bag and Smile, Smile, Smile." She had a song for when the Mets took the field, and she had the "Mexican Hat Dance" for the seventh-inning stretch when the home team needed to pick up the pace.

At the time, Jarvis was to Mets fans at Shea what Eddie Layton and his Hammond Organ and then Toby Wright were to Yankees fans in that era. Her music reached beyond baseball. At the height of the Vietnam War protests she played excerpts of her composition, "A Prayer for Peace." Blogger Joe Dublin said Jarvis's music provided the "semblance and comfort of things staying the same as life otherwise all around us changed too quickly."

When New York City was darkened by a blackout in July 1977, Jarvis was credited with calming the fears of more than twenty-one thousand fans in Shea Stadium by playing non-stop on her Thomas Organ for ninety minutes a series of relaxing tunes from her collection of American songs. During the Mets' heated 1973 National League Championship Series against Cincinnati, Jarvis's music helped calm an enraged crowd following Pete Rose's hard slide into Harrelson. Mets announcer Ralph Kiner said Jarvis in those years "was the Mets."

So too was the broadcasting team of Nelson, Murphy, and Kiner, the last hosting a postgame show, "Kiner's Korner." Fans in the New York area tuning into Mets' broadcasts on WOR Channel 9 from the late 1960s into the early 1970s were greeted with a one-minute montage of highlights and accompanied by an up-tempo instrumental of the team's theme song, "Meet the Mets."

Penned by Port Chester native Ruth Roberts, the lilting melody was recorded as the Mets' fight song following their inaugural 1962 season. It didn't help the fledgling Metropolitans in their early years, but it became a hit with fans and grew into an iconic anthem. "Meet the Mets" has also made its way into modern TV series *Seinfeld* and *Everybody Loves Raymond*. Roberts, who died in 2011 at the age of eighty-four, grew up in a baseball home whose favorite team was the New York Giants. Somewhat ironically, two of her songs—a 1956 ode to Yankees superstar Mickey Mantle ("I Love Mickey!") and "It's a Beautiful Day for a Ballgame," played at Dodger Stadium prior to every game, were favorites of two of the Giants' traditional rivals.

Since the Mets were a light-hitting team, the clips shot by Winik films for the annual highlights featured mostly pitching, defense, and base running. Nelson provided the voice-over at the conclusion of the clips, introducing the sponsors for New York Mets baseball: Rheingold, Manufacturer's Hanover, Getty, and White Owl cigars.

"Kiner's Korner" followed every Mets' home game. Kiner, the former Pirates slugger and Hall of Famer would issue a series of questions to his guests, who were usually Mets but were sometimes opposing players. The plain set, awkward questions, and camera screw-ups made for quirky and popular viewing. It was great sports entertainment, far removed from the slick, high-gloss look of modern-day programming.

From the Mets' inception in 1962 through 1978, Kiner, Nelson, and Murphy made for a tremendous TV and radio broadcasting trio. Nelson was known for his colorful sports jackets, but he was a versatile broadcaster who did national broadcasts of pro and college football and, on Sunday mornings in the fall, Notre Dame highlights ("We move ahead to further action later in the second quarter . . .").

Kiner wasn't as polished a broadcaster as his two colleagues. He once said of the sport he covered, "That's the great thing about baseball. You never know what's going on!" Kiner was prone to tongue-twisting malapropisms and mispronunciation, but he provided great insight. In 1973 Kiner was doing a Mets-Phillies game and predicted young Mike Schmidt had a bright future. Schmidt went on to have a Hall of Fame career. He also said of Garry Maddox, the Phils' ground-eating center fielder, "Two-thirds of the earth is covered in water. The other third is covered by Maddox."

As a teen Kiner had shaken hands with Babe Ruth and had talked baseball with Ty Cobb. His A-list friends included fellow baseball enthusiasts Bing Crosby and Frank Sinatra. He golfed with Bob Hope and Jack Benny and dated Liz Taylor and Janet Leigh. He had an easygoing charm and engaging personality, and his trademark home run call—"Going, going, gone, goodbye!"—was one of the staples of Mets broadcasts. Kiner, Nelson, and Murphy were living room companions for generations of Mets fans.

The procession of planes from nearby LaGuardia Airport sometimes drowned their comments, but Kiner, Nelson, and Murphy had much to talk about in '72. There were the additions of Staub and Fregosi, at the time the forty-sixth man to play third base for a Mets franchise just starting its second decade; young guns Matlack and Milner; Seaver and McGraw; Jerry Koosman, Jim McAndrew, and Buzz Capra; Berra's first season at the wheel; and of course Mays, who would have a solid season for the Mets, with a team-best on-base percentage of .402 and a .446 slugging percentage that was second on the club.

While Mays provided magic, Seaver provided muscle. The Giants' Bobby Bonds said Seaver's fastball took off "like a 747 going up." Reds manager Sparky Anderson thought Seaver the best pitcher in baseball.

Nicknamed "the Franchise," Seaver reached the twenty-win plateau for the second straight season and for the third time in four years. He struck out ten or more in a game six times in '72, including an overpowering performance against the Pirates on September 20 in which he fanned 15. Nine days later Tom Terrific tamed the Bucs again, whiffing 13 in a two-hit, 1–0 win. Another gem that summer was a 5-hit, 2–1 win over the Big Red Machine in Riverfront on June 18.

Seaver was a student of the game—he copied Sandy Koufax by loosening his jersey beneath his pitching arm to remove restrictions—and was a student of history as well. He read *Rise and Fall of the Third Reich* and *Bury My Heart at Wounded Knee*. He liked French wine and would arrive at the clubhouse early to read fan mail and work crossword puzzles. He was a practical joker, once goading his roommate, 5-foot-10, 155-pound shortstop Bud Harrelson, into shadow-boxing 6-foot-5, 250-pound NFL star Deacon Jones.

Facing San Diego in the first game of a July 4 doubleheader at Shea, Seaver pitched one of the finest games of his career. He struck out six over the first four frames and was staked to a 2–0 lead in the third following Fregosi's disputed bases-loaded walk that brought Padres manager Don Zimmer storming from the dugout. Many of the more than forty thousand fans on hand mocked the mustard-gold uniforms the Padres wore. "Hey Zimmer," one man shouted from the box seats. "You look like a pregnant canary!"

Seaver had eleven strikeouts through eight innings and nursed a no-hitter into the ninth. With the holiday crowd buzzing, left-handed hitting Leron Lee stepped in with one out.

> **Kiner**: *Here's the pitch to Lee. . . . It's a bloop hit, a broken-bat base hit into center field and Seaver's no-hit game goes out the window. . . . Listen to the ovation for Tom Seaver.*

His bid to make history over, Seaver got a double play to end the game. It was the fourth one-hitter in as many seasons for Tom Terrific.

Lee would come to be known for more than just ending Seaver's bid to make history. He played eight years in the majors before helping revolutionize Japanese baseball in 1977, when he became one of the first American players to play in Japan while still in his prime. Lee went on to become the batting coach for the 1989 world champion Oakland A's and is uncle to Yankees great Derek Jeter.

Oppenheimer, who wrote a book about '72 titled *The Wrong Season*, believed the Mets' loss in the second game of the doubleheader was the one that said it all about the club. "We are hurt bad," Oppenheimer wrote in his diary. The Mets' storybook season had begun to fall apart back on

June 3, when Staub was hit by a pitch by Atlanta reliever and future Mets teammate George Stone. Staub continued to play despite the injury but went on the disabled list when it was revealed he had a broken hand. At the time of his injury Le Grand Orange was grand indeed, batting .313 and helping the Mets to a 31-12 mark and five-game lead over the Pirates. When he went on the DL on July 18, Staub's average had dipped to .297, and New York was 47-35 and five games behind Pittsburgh.

To paraphrase P. F. Sloan's protest song of the era—"Eve of Destruction"—the eastern world in the NL was exploding, and the absence of Staub's bat was crippling the Mets' attack. Seventy-one NL batters had at least one hundred hits in '72, but none of them were trimmed in Mets' orange and blue. Tommie Agee led New York with ninety-six hits, and the Mets batted a league-low .225.

Seaver struggled on the mound as well. On June 13 he surrendered a three-run lead in the eighth inning at Atlanta. The Braves won it in the bottom of the tenth on Hank Aaron's 650th career homer. Seaver dropped five straight decisions from late July into early August. On June 24 he was driven from the mound in the fifth inning of an eventual 11–0 loss to St. Louis on a rainy Saturday afternoon *Game of the Week* telecast, prompting Tony Kubek to murmur, "This isn't the Tom Seaver we're used to seeing. He hasn't thrown a fastball with real good stuff on it." Curt Gowdy agreed. "He doesn't have that little extra mustard [on his fastball]." When Seaver lost July 23 in San Francisco on Bobby Bonds's three-run homer, Mets fans like Oppenheimer exploded in anger. "Tom Seaver," an irate Oppenheimer wrote, "has no goddamned right blowing a goddamned ballgame proving his goddamned machismo throwing a goddamned fastball to goddamned Bobby Bonds."

Seaver reached his nadir on September 16 at Wrigley Field, surrendering eight runs in just two and a third innings in an eventual 18–5 loss. Seaver bounced back in his next start with fifteen strikeouts against division-leading Pittsburgh, fanning Clemente and Stargell three times each. It was the first of four consecutive victories that allowed him to close out the season with his third twenty-win campaign in four years.

Staub's injury was one of several that struck the Mets. Jones, Harrelson, Fregosi, and catcher Jerry Grote missed games due to a string of injuries that decimated the team. His troops depleted, Berra was forced to move players around like pieces on a chessboard. Martinez saw playing time at second base, third, short, and the outfield; Grote and fellow catcher Duffy Dyer patrolled the outfield; Fregosi played third, short, and first.

Despite the versatility of their "Bandage Brigade" the Mets fell from contention in the second half of the season and ultimately finished third in the East behind the Pirates and Cubs. Ernie Banks, "Mr. Cub," had retired the year before at age forty following a nineteen-year career that would take him to the Hall of Fame. But Chicago still had a solid corps of talented players, including a collection of gritty holdovers from their bittersweet summer of '69—Jenkins, Beckert, Santo, Don Kessinger, Jim Hickman, Randy Hundley, Bill Hands, and of course Billy Williams.

A native of Whistler, Alabama, Williams was known as "Sweet Swingin' Billy from Whistler," and even at age thirty-four in 1972, Williams still had that sweet swing. He led the majors with a .333 batting average and a .606 slugging percentage, both career bests. Lean and muscular, Williams was the most overlooked hitter of his era.

Stargell called Williams the best left-handed hitter he had ever seen. He recalled playing first base in a game and Williams stinging the ball so hard through Stargell's legs that Willie didn't even have time to move his glove.

Pirates second baseman Dave Cash said that when he got to Pittsburgh, he found out there were guys who weren't half as good as he had heard they were. But when he saw Billy Williams, Cash thought this man is a ballplayer, and nobody writes about him.

Why was Williams overlooked? His manager, Leo Durocher, figured it was because Williams wasn't controversial. Williams never got mad, never threw a bat. Durocher would write Williams's name in the same spot in the lineup card every day—batting third and playing left field. To Durocher, Williams was "a baseball machine."

He was a machine largely ignored by fans. As late as midsummer, Williams was fourth among National League outfielders in the fans' balloting for the All-Star team, despite the fact he was in the midst of a campaign that would see him named Player of the Year by *The Sporting News*, earn the National League Batting Trophy, be named to the Associated Press All-Star team, and gain the Fred Hutchinson Memorial Award for typifying the "character and competitive spirit" of the late Reds manager.

Sweet Swingin' Billy took the lack of attention in stride. He knew it wasn't always the good player who got all the stories. If someone was a .250 hitter and was suddenly batting .340, everybody wondered, "Hey, where did this guy come from?" The writers rushed to find out what changes he's made and how to account for his hot streak.

On May 19, 1972, Williams was a .250 hitter—.254 to be precise—and was trailing the league leaders by 150–190 points. He didn't panic; he'd had slow starts before. "Every spring!" he told reporters with a laugh.

Williams knew he would come around, knew that among starting players who had the 600–700 plate appearances he managed every season, the difference between batting .250 and .330 was two additional hits each week throughout the summer.

His turnaround began in June, when he hit .326 with 9 homers and 23 RBIs. In July he batted .438 with 9 homers and 29 RBIs. In one two-week stretch that month, he hit .458 with 5 homers and 13 RBIs. Included in that period was his best day in baseball—an 8-for-8 outing in a doubleheader against Houston in which he collected 5 singles, 2 homers, 1 double, and 4 RBIs. In that one day, Williams raised his average eighteen points to .328. Durocher called it "a week's work in one day."

Such improvement was made possible by Sweet Swingin' Billy's near-perfect stroke. There was beauty in its brevity. Sharp and economical, Williams's artistic swing relied on the wrist-snapping power in his hands and forearms. When he connected, the ball was lined with startling speed and power. Onlookers still recall the day a Williams drive to the wall was hit so hard that it bounced back to the infield before Billy made the turn at first base.

Tony Kubek said on an NBC telecast in '72 that Williams owned a picture-book swing, one you would like your Little Leaguer to emulate. But there was more to Williams than his sweet swing. He was a student of his sport; he studied opposing pitchers, watched how their pitches moved, and observed which pitches they used in certain situations.

Williams's physical and mental approach combined to earn him a reputation as the finest number three hitter in baseball. He was fast enough to outrun double plays, and he hit for power and for average. He also hit in the clutch; he was one of the few in baseball at the time to hit .400 with runners on base.

Williams was a natural at the plate but not in the outfield. He had been an infielder growing up, but after signing with the Cubs for a "bonus" of a one-way ticket to Ponca City—a team in the Class D Sooner State League—and a fifteen-cent cigar for Billy's father Frank, eighteen-year-old Billy was converted into an outfielder. The transition was a work in progress. He made 25 errors his first year in pro ball. He had to learn how to judge fly balls and to compensate for not having a strong arm.

Williams worked to improve his all-around defense and learned to deal with the demands of playing the outfield amid the unpredictable winds and the ivy-covered brick walls of Wrigley Field. He proved instrumental in no-hitters thrown by the Cubs' Ken Holtzman, Burt Hooten, and Milt Pappas, making sensational catches in each of those historic games.

Pappas's no-hitter came on September 2, 1972, against San Diego. Legendary Cubs announcer Jack Brickhouse provided the call: *"Milt Pappas, trying not only for a no-hitter, he's trying for a perfect game. . . . [John] Jeter is in the batter's box. . . . There's a well-hit ball, deep to left-center, back goes [Bill] North, he slips and falls. . . . However, it's Billy Williams coming from nowhere to save that play! Oh, brother!"*

After retiring the first twenty-six hitters, Pappas worked a 1-2 count on the pinch-hitting Larry Stahl. Leaning forward from the waist and swinging his arms back and forth between pitches, Pappas was one strike from baseball immortality. Home plate umpire Bruce Froemming called the next two pitches—both of which were close—balls.

Brickhouse: *Now here comes one of the most fateful pitches of the year. . . .*
Ball three, strike two, two out. . . . Perfect game on the line. . . . No-hitter
on the line. . . . It's a ball! And Pappas is enraged.

Stahl's walk ended Pappas's bid for MLB's first perfect game since Catfish Hunter's in 1968. Pappas retired the next batter, former Cub Garry Jestadt, on a pop-up to second, and the Cubs won 8–0. It remains the only perfect game bid to be broken up by a walk to the twenty-seventh hitter.

Froemming's call incensed Pappas, who shouted at Froemming from the mound. Froemming, in his second season as an MLB umpire, told Cubs catcher Randy Hundley that if Pappas walked toward home plate, "Tell him to keep walking," because Froemming was going to run him out, no-hitter or not.

Pappas later referenced Don Larsen's perfect game in the 1956 World Series in which umpire Babe Pinelli called a game-ending third strike on a pitch that appeared to be high and outside.

It's a home game in Wrigley Field, Pappas said later. He's pitching for the Cubs, and the score is 8–0 in his favor. What does Froemming have to lose by not calling the last pitch a strike to finish a perfect game?

Froemming's response was he was not aware a perfect game was on the line. Besides, he said, he was an umpire, not a fan. Froemming would call ten more no-hitters in his career.

The date—September 2—has been a historic one in Cubs' history. Pappas's no-hitter was preceded in 1970 by Williams's setting an NL record by playing in his 1,117th straight game. Williams ended the streak the next day, when he asked Durocher to sit him down. In 1955 Banks set a record for shortstops on September 2 when he slammed his fortieth home run, eclipsing the mark set by Vern Stephens of the Red Sox.

Banks was "Mr. Cub," "Mr. Sunshine," and his "Let's play two!" attitude was infectious. Upon Banks's passing in January 2015 Dick Allen wrote movingly of his first meeting with Banks in 1958. Allen was a high school sophomore, and scout John Ogden took Allen and other prospects to Pittsburgh for a game against the Cubs. Banks allowed Allen to hold his bat—a thirty-ounce Louisville Slugger S2 model. Allen thought the bat very light. But as Allen recalled, Banks "could do some damage with that toothpick."

Six days after Pappas's gem Jenkins threw another notable game in Cubs history, beating the Phillies 4–3 to win his twentieth game for the sixth straight season. Jenkins credited his Gold Glove catcher, Randy Hundley, for much of the success enjoyed by Cubs pitchers, including rookie Rick Reuschel, who went 10-8 and at 6-foot-3, 215 pounds inspired comparisons to former American League pitcher Mike "Big Bear" Garcia.

While Pappas and Jenkins made headlines, Williams continued to go overlooked—difficult to do for a guy whose durability allowed him to take the field every day. Playing in the sometimes stifling heat and humidity in an era before night games were inaugurated in Wrigley, Williams in 1970 became the only man in major league history to that point to play seven consecutive seasons of 161 games or more. But he learned to pace himself. Tempted to try for the Triple Crown in 1972—he led the league in batting and trailed slightly in homers and RBIs—he decided to rest rather than let fatigue warp his play.

The acknowledgment of the wear and tear baseball inflicts on the mind and body lent insight into this man-within-a-machine. A Chicago writer in the summer of '72 suggested Williams wasn't "easy to get close to. . . . Definitely a case of 'still waters running deep,' he must do things on his own time, in his own way, for he's quite independent."

The same could be said for Philadelphia Phillies ace Steve Carlton. "Lefty" was as much a man of mystery to the media in the City of Brotherly Love as Williams was to writers in the Windy City. Carlton baffled not only those who carried a ballpoint pen, but those who hoisted a bat as well. Working behind a hard slider, sharp curve, and fastball, Carlton owned the league after being obtained from St. Louis for right-hander Rick Wise.

Dominating on the mound in a manner not seen in Philadelphia since another Lefty—Robert Moses Grove—had dominated the American League as the ace of the Philadelphia Athletics, Carlton had the most wins (27), strikeouts (310), complete games (30), starts (41), innings pitched (346), and lowest earned run average (1.97).

These were video game numbers before video games were invented, and they were more remarkable considering Carlton accomplished what he did in a strike-shortened season. When he beat the Cubs on a cold, gray day in October to claim his twenty-seventh victory, it was the most wins since Sandy Koufax had won the same amount in 1966. The difference was that Koufax's victories had come for the pennant-winning Dodgers and that Sandy's total represented 28 percent of Los Angeles' 95 wins. Carlton's wins represented 46 percent of the Phillies' paltry 59 wins, Philadelphia finishing last in the East.

Carlton went on to become the greatest clutch pitcher in Phillies history, leading the Fightin's to five division titles, two World Series, and in 1980 their first world championship. But he would never have become the best "money" pitcher in the Phils' long history had he not asked for more money prior to the '72 season. At the same time Carlton was seeking a substantial raise from the Redbirds, Wise went to the Phillies' front offices and asked for a hike in pay.

Carlton had been a member of the Cardinals' World Series staffs in 1967 and '68 and in '71 won 20 games for the first time. Cardinals owner Gussie Busch reminded Carlton that he had lost 19 games in 1970. Deciding a change of scenery was necessary for Carlton and Wise, the Cards and Phils swapped pitchers. Wise went 16-16; Carlton had a season that is arguably the most dominant by a pitcher in MLB history.

From June 7 to August 17 Carlton won fifteen straight; the Phils, meanwhile, were futile in games Lefty didn't pitch, going 2-22 in that same span. Carlton's win streak was finally snapped on August 21, when he lost 2–1 to Atlanta before an overflow crowd of 52,600 in Veterans Stadium. In one sixty-three-inning stretch Carlton surrendered one earned run while pitching five shutouts and five one-run games. En route to winning the NL Cy Young award in '72, Carlton was the focal point of the Philadelphia Story.

It was a story colorfully told by Bill Lyon, who in 1972 was in his first year as a sports columnist for the *Philadelphia Inquirer*:

I came here [to Philadelphia] from Illinois in the summer of '72; a friend of mine had gone to work for the *Inquirer*. I heard Philadelphia is a great sports town, nothing but winners, winners, winners. Steve Carlton was on his way to winning 27 games and the rest of the team won about three. He was overpowering. Before the slider became the pitch of choice his was just devastating. It was like a Frisbee in a high wind."

Longtime Phillies public relations director Larry Shenk believes Carlton in 1972 was the best pitcher he'd ever seen in a career that spanned some six decades. "He was unhittable," Shenk said. "I never saw a pitcher focus on the mound like Lefty. He was in his own world. [Roy] Halladay came close in [2010–11]. Lefty was not focused on records, he was focused on winning."

One thing Carlton wasn't focused on was media relations. "Carlton was a thoroughly disagreeable person, kind of surly," Lyon remembered. "It was a shame because I don't know if he ever got the recognition he deserved."

Shenk said the tipping point was provided by the city's sports scribes. "They started to turn on him, they started to get personal with him," he remembered. "One day he came to me and said, 'My quotes were taken out of context. I don't want to talk with them anymore.'"

Whatever his wars with the writers, Philly's faithful still believed Lefty was all right. "The two great attractions in Philadelphia in the summer of '72 were the Great Wallendas and Steve Carlton," Lyon said. "They sold a lot of tickets those days [Carlton pitched]. The rest of the times [the Vet] was like a ghost town."

Shenk remembers the vivid difference on days Carlton climbed the mound at Veterans Stadium. "The excitement, the enthusiasm from the fans was unbelievable," he said.

Before he had a falling out with the media and became "Silent Steve," Carlton explained that his entire attitude about pitching had been changed by a series of letters from a man he had never met or even responded to, a Tucson, Arizona, night watchman who stressed the value of positive thinking. The watchman's first letter to Carlton ran ten pages and stated that he was tired of seeing a man with so much talent lose so much.

"Those letters were beautiful stuff," Carlton said at the time. "He talked in depth about applying positive thinking. It changed my whole outlook on things."

The Phillies were changing too. Just as the Dodgers cast the die in '72 for a team that would win four Western division titles, four pennants, and one World Series from 1974 to 1981, the Phils were putting in place the pieces for a club that would dominate the East from 1976 to 1983. While the Dodgers had their Baby Blue infield of Steve Garvey, Davey Lopes, Bill Russell, and Ron Cey, the Phils had the "Sesame Street Gang," so dubbed by the *Philadelphia Inquirer* to characterize the young corps that would be fixtures in Philly for years to come.

Schmidt believes the '72 foursome of young guns (Schmidt, Greg Luzinski, Larry Bowa, and Bob Boone) compares favorably to the Core Four of Ryan Howard, Chase Utley, Jimmy Rollins, and Carlos Ruiz, who helped highlight the Golden Era in 2007–11.

"Ours was sort of the first championship run," Schmidt recalled. "We had two runs and [the modern Core Four] had one. Theirs was pretty strong, there's no question. I thought both eras were great. I guess it depends on how old you are whether you say one was stronger than the other, but there are some similarities."

The season got off to a strange start for the Phillies' kiddie corps. In the April 17 opener at the still new Veterans Stadium—the "Crown Jewel of Philadelphia," as its architectural firm, KlingStubbins, called it—Kiteman attempted to throw out the first ball but instead crashed into the center-field seats. Almost a month to the day later Luzinski, the Bull of Broad Street, gave a glimpse of the future when he bull-rushed a pitch five hundred feet into the Liberty Bell monument atop the Vet.

Schmidt and Boone debuted in September, and the exploits of the Sesame Street Gang became the sounds of summer as described by play-by-play men Byrum Saam and Harry Kalas and color analyst Richie Ashburn.

Saam is recognized as the first full-time voice of baseball in Philadelphia, broadcasting games for the Philadelphia Athletics and Phillies. He was also behind the mic for the Philadelphia Eagles and Philadelphia Warriors of the NBA and was one of the broadcasters for Wilt Chamberlain's historic hundred-point game in 1962. Saam suffered the occasional slipup behind the mic—"Hello Byrum Saam, this is everybody speaking!"—but Kalas and Ashburn thought so highly of him, they invited the retired Saam into the broadcast booth to call the final half-inning of the Phils' Eastern Division–clinching game in 1976. The Phils also added him to the club's broadcast team for the NLCS.

"By was a basic play-by-play announcer, a facts-and-figures kind of guy," Shenk recalled. "That's the way it was then. No humor, no color, no personality. Harry and Richie were entertainers."

Over the next two decades Kalas and Ashburn became as much of a beloved treasure in Philadelphia as the Liberty Bell or Billy Penn's statue. Kalas often referred to Whitey as "His Whiteness," and Ashburn, in between plugs for Celebre's Pizza, would punctuate some strange happenstance on the field below with "Hard to believe, Harry!" Kalas's signature call—"Swing and a long drive. . . . Watch that baby, outta heeeere!"—was inspired by Bowa's commenting at the batting cage one day that a Luzinski drive was "way outta here!" "It had a unique ring to it," Kalas remembered. As did Kalas's leathery tone, a product of the Parliament cigarettes he favored. Just as Vin Scully's voice is revered in Chavez Ravine, Harry the K was what baseball sounded like in Philadelphia.

What baseball sounded like for the Phils on the penultimate day of the regular season was Harry the K calling Carlton's twenty-seventh win, an 11–1 victory over the Cubs in Wrigley.

Winning was all Carlton's ex-mound mate in St. Louis, Bob Gibson, was doing from May 25 to July 21. After starting the season 0-5, Gibson won eleven straight. Catcher Tim McCarver joked that his battery mate was the luckiest man in baseball, that Gibson always pitched on days when the other team didn't score any runs.

Gibson's summer gave Cardinals voice Jack Buck ample opportunities to punctuate St. Louis victories with his trademark phrase: "That's a winner!" When he broke in with the Cardinals in 1954, Buck teamed with Harry Caray in the broadcast booth. Because of their contrasting but complimentary styles, Buck later called his pairing with Caray the greatest broadcasting team ever. Along with his "That's a winner!" Buck issued famous calls on injured Kirk Gibson's 1988 World Series Game One homer that beat Dennis Eckersley and the A's in the bottom of the ninth ("I don't believe what I just saw!") and another bottom-of-the-ninth postseason walk-off homer involving the Dodgers: Ozzie Smith's stunning drive that beat Los Angeles in Game Five of the 1985 NLCS ("Go crazy, folks! Go crazy!").

Aside from baseball, Buck called two of the more iconic games in NFL history: the celebrated "Ice Bowl" on New Year's Eve 1967 ("Third-and-goal. . . . Quarterback sneak! Touchdown Green Bay!") and in 1981 "The Catch" ("Montana lines up at the five. . . . He rolls right, looking to throw. . . . And he throws into the end zone. . . . Touchdown!")

The '72 baseball season was Buck's first with his new broadcast partner, Mike Shannon, a third baseman for the great Cardinal squads of the 1960s. Buck and Shannon would broadcast St. Louis baseball for the next twenty-eight summers.

Gibson won 19 games for a squad that finished fourth, far below expectations for a team returning the league MVP in mutton-chopped Joe Torre; speedster Lou Brock, who was on the fast track to baseball's Hall of Fame; and fellow .300 hitters Matty Alou and Ted Simmons. St. Louis's "MOmentum" from a second-place finish the season before failed to sustain the Cards.

With their team finishing fifth Montreal Expos fans didn't have an overabundance of success to cheer about. Playing in the charming but rinky-dink Jarry Park, the major league's lone team north of the border had All-Star pitcher Bill Stoneman, who on October 2 no-hit the Mets for his second career no-hitter and the first outside the United States, along with fan favorites Boots Day, John Boccabella and Coco Laboy.

If the Expos' play on the field was forgettable, their distinctive uniforms remain memorable. Their red, white, and blue pinwheel caps were designed to reflect and carry on the carnival atmosphere of Expo '67. Debuting in

1969, MLB's first international franchise was named "Expos" following the hugely successful festival of 1967. Montreal's caps and jerseys were adorned with an equally distinctive and often misinterpreted logo—a lower case "e" in red on the left; a capital "M" half in white, half in blue; and lower case "b" in blue on the right. It was a combination of the team initials when spoken in French, the eMb representing "[les] Expos [de] Montreal baseball."

Montreal's most recognizable player, Staub, had been dealt to the Mets, but the Expos did boast talent in outfielders Ron Fairly and ex-Met Ken Singleton; infielders Bob Bailey, Ron Hunt, and Tim Foli; and starting pitcher Mike Torrez and closer Mike Marshall. Yet the biggest attraction for Montreal fans may have been Jarry Park. Known as Parc Jarry to Quebec's French-speaking population, the tiny wooden stadium seated just 28,456, and that was only after renovations added 3,000 seats. One of the last major league parks to have a single deck, the closeness of spectator seats to the playing field provided intimacy larger stadiums lacked.

Contributing to the ambiance at Jarry Park was public address announcer Claude Mouton and his unique delivery. Al Oliver was Hal Holiver, and Montreal columnist Ted Blackman wrote that Mouton could really roll the "r" in Angel Hermoso's last name and dramatically pause between syllables when announcing Boccabella—"Bocca-bellaaaaa." Mouton, Black-man wrote, was "part of the color of the joint."

The joint also had attractive usherettes, who, upon being issued their blue uniforms, shortened the skirts. Organist Ferdinand "Fern" Lapierre was so entertaining even visiting players praised him. A's owner Charlie Finley said LaPierre was the most valuable member of the Expos, and the organist inspired another Jarry Park fan favorite, the Dancer. Claude Desjardins, a hospital cook, was the Dancer, who entertained patrons between innings. Like Jackie Gleason, he was a big man with nimble feet.

The Fiddler on the Dugout Roof; bleacher fans in Jonesville, named after the Expos' first hero, left-fielder Mack Jones; and the fan who brought a duck (some said goose) to a game added to an atmosphere akin to a country fair. Spectators created a racket by drumming their feet on the metal bleachers. Former Dodgers great Maury Willis, who played part of the 1969 season in Montreal, compared Jarry Park patrons to passionate Latin American fans. It was said by natives that Parc Jarry was one of the few places left in Montreal where the French, English, Italians, and Jews could get together and have fun. Among the faithful was Steve Shutt, a defenseman on the dynastic Montreal Canadiens teams of the late 1970s. Shutt and other fans of Nos Amours—"Our Beloveds"—would pack Parc Jarry and give their players standing ovations.

The Expos were a season away from serious contention, but it was a September to remember for the city's sports populace, riveted as it was by the historic first Summit Series between Team Canada and the Soviet Union. Almost every Canadian old enough to recall can remember where he or she was on September 28, when legendary hockey announcer Foster Hewitt exclaimed, "[Paul] Henderson has scored for Canada!" Henderson's shot late in the third period of the eighth and final game slipped past goalie Vladislav Tretiak and won the series for Team Canada. It was the goal heard round the world, and Canadians celebrated in a style likened by some to that at the end of World War II.

Late summer found Steel City fans in a celebratory mood as well; it was clear the Battlin' Bucs were still the beast of the East. Powered by a near endless array of hot hitters (Cash hit in nineteen straight games, Oliver and Richie Hebner in sixteen, and Sanguillen in fifteen), the Pirates posted a torrid .739 winning percentage (34-12) from May into July.

The Bucs had built a modern Murderers' Row along the Monongahela. Blass, who opened the season with an NL-best 9-1 record en route to a 19-8 season, said Pittsburgh's hitters were so awesome that it frightened him to watch them take batting practice. Reliever Bob Miller called the Pirate lineup deeper than the Pacific Ocean.

Blass fronted a deep and versatile array of arms that boasted double-digit winners in Ellis, Nelson Briles, and Moose, along with the clutch Kison. A staff that ranked second in the league in ERA and saves helped pace the Pirates to a major league-best 96 wins. Pirates general manager Joe Brown thought the 1972 staff the best the Bucs had fielded in his nineteen years with the team to that point.

Kison's 7–4 win over the Cubs on July 2 allowed Pittsburgh to seize the lead for good. The Bucs became the first team to clinch when they beat the Mets 6–2 on September 21. With a third straight title secured and a chance to defend their world championship guaranteed, the only remaining drama for Steel City fans resided in Clemente's slashing his way toward the magical three-thousand-hit plateau.

Fittingly the confluence of Clemente and baseball history took place in a Pittsburgh stadium built on the confluence of three rivers. Legendary Pirates announcer Bob Prince, "the Gunner," provided the historic call as Clemente faced Matlack and the Mets on a steel gray afternoon on September 30: *"Everybody's standing and they want Bobby to get that big Number 3,000. . . . Matlack on the oh-and-one, Bobby hits a drive into the gap in left-center field. . . . There she is!"*

As the crowd roared and Clemente raced around first base in his signature style, the Pirates' great had become just the eleventh player in history to record three thousand career hits.

No one could have known it was the last regular-season hit of Roberto Clemente's life.

1. Oakland A's slugger and showman Reggie Jackson was a lightning rod for the colorful Swingin' A's.

2. Pete Rose, sliding into second base against the rival San Francisco Giants, personified the all-out style of the rollicking Big Red Machine.

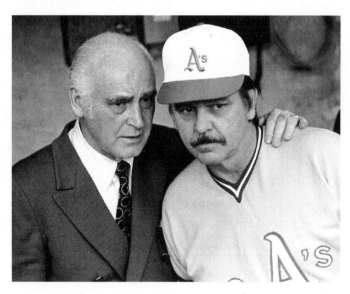

3. A's maverick owner Charles O. Finley, left, and embattled manager Dick Williams won World Series titles in 1972 and 1973 before a fed-up Williams walked away.

4. Charlie Finley's mechanical rabbit Harvey came out of the ground to supply umpires with baseballs. Harvey was one of several gimmicks—along with Charlie O. the Mule, Finley Fireworks, and Hot Pants Day—that the A's P. T. Barnum–like owner used to liven up home games.

5. From left, A's aces Jim "Catfish" Hunter, Vida Blue, and Ken Holtzman gave the Mustache Gang a starting rotation unmatched in the majors. In 1973 Hunter, Blue, and Holtzman each won at least twenty games, the last trio to achieve the feat.

6. A's skipper Dick Williams, far right, and his team exult as Gene Tenace scores the winning run to beat the Detroit Tigers in Game One of the 1972 American League Championship Series in Oakland. Tenace went on to greater glory in the World Series against the Cincinnati Reds.

7. Cincinnati shortstop Dave Concepcion leaps high to avoid the takeout slide of Oakland captain Sal Bando in Game Four of the hotly contested 1972 World Series.

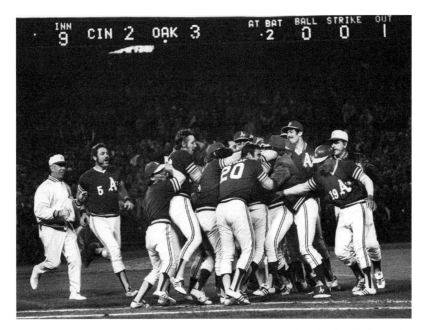

8. The Oakland Coliseum scoreboard tells the stunning story after the A's rallied past the Reds in the bottom of the ninth inning to win Game Four of the 1972 World Series.

9. With his long hair, Salvador Dali–style mustache, and wicked slider, A's ace reliever Rollie Fingers presented a fearsome picture to opponents.

10. Reds third-base coach Alex Grammas (right rear) grimly watches the underdog A's celebrate their 1972 Game Seven victory on the Riverfront Stadium Astroturf.

11. Reds star second baseman Joe Morgan, left, congratulates Oakland Game Seven starter John "Blue Moon" Odom following the A's shocking victory in Cincinnati in 1972.

12. From left, Mustache Gang members Mike Epstein, Dave Duncan, Joe Rudi, and Sal Bando enjoy a champagne celebration following the A's Game Seven win over the Reds in 1972. Epstein's New York disco T-shirt was a sign of the times.

CHAPTER TEN

Battling Billy Martin never backed away from a fight, on or off the field.

He one-punched Matt Batts, Jim Piersall, Clint Courtney, and Jim Brewer and demolished Dave Boswell with two punches. At the time of their fight in 1969, Boswell was in the midst of a twenty-win season for Martin's Minnesota Twins, who went on to win the West that season. Upon winning his twentieth, all Boswell did was rush to the dugout and plant a kiss on Billy the Kid's forehead.

By '71 the two combatants were reunited in Detroit. One year later the Tigers, having taken on Battling Billy's persona, were fighting for their playoff lives in a four-way battle with New York, Baltimore, and Boston in the bustling American League East. The ferocious free-for-all for the division flag had fans in each of the four contending cities following Motown giant Marvin Gaye's lead and asking, "What's going on?" as the Tigers, Orioles, Yankees, and Red Sox daily fought for position in the fluent standings.

It was Martin's kind of race, a gut fight in which guile counted as much as skill. Battling Billy could be a brilliant manager but also a study in contrasts. He went to Mass on Sunday mornings, loved to hunt and fish with his then eight-year-old son Billy Joe, and would excuse his wife Gretchen from a night of cooking by taking over the kitchen and preparing veal parmigiana. A sincere man, overly sensitive and thus easily offended, Martin owned a medieval code of honor that he enforced with a murderous right hook. He coached old-school baseball but was forward-thinking when it came to race relations. Half Portuguese and half Italian, Martin had an easy rapport with African American and Latin American players. "I'm a minority too," he would say.

Like many minorities, Martin scraped and scrapped for everything he got. He grew up in poverty in Berkeley, California, the son of a single mother, Joan "Jenny" Martin. His father, Alfred Martin Sr., deserted the family, and Jenny, not wanting her son to share the same name of the man she referred to as the "jackass," began calling her son "Billy" upon hearing her mother refer to him as "Bello," Italian masculine for "beautiful."

Martin was an undersized eighteen-year-old when Yankees skipper Casey Stengel gave him a tryout. Stengel liked what he saw in the scrawny kid, a middle infielder who attacked the game with a zeal writer Ed Linn once likened to a "holy war on every ball hit down to him."

Stengel, in time, became a father figure for Billy the Kid. The Ol' Professor taught Martin to take charge on the field, and it was Stengel who brought him up to the Bronx in 1950 over owner George Weiss's objections.

Billy the Kid was often called the best .260 hitter in baseball because he delivered so many clutch hits. He batted .333 in twenty-eight World Series games and in 1952 made his famous catch of Jackie Robinson's infield fly when Brooklyn had the bases loaded in the seventh inning of the seventh game. The following October, Martin's twelve hits in a six-game Series win over the Dodgers were as much as anyone in history had managed even in a seven-game series. His final hit that fall came in the ninth inning of Game Six and delivered a second-straight Series title to the Bronx Bombers.

Martin spent five full seasons with the Yankees before being traded to Kansas City in June 1957. Feeling abandoned again, he refused to speak to Stengel for the next eight years. Billy the Kid's sensitivity was punctured again when another paternal figure, Twins boss Calvin Griffith, fired him following the 1969 season. He had taken the reins of a talented but fractured club. The Twins had lost to the Dodgers in seven games in the 1965 Fall Classic and in 1969 boasted future Hall of Famers Harmon Killebrew, Rod Carew, and All-Star Tony Oliva. But the team was being torn apart by racial tension. Martin eased the strife, and his managerial fire and fury fueled Minnesota's run to its first postseason berth in four years.

Battling Billy was fired at season's end because of his feuding with other members of the organization—namely, traveling secretary Howard

Fox and assistant farm director George Brophy. Martin had been out of baseball for a year before taking over the Tigers. Many questioned the Martin-Motown marriage. Billy the Kid's brassy brand of ball—hit and run, steal and double-steal, suicide squeeze—seemed ill suited to a Tigers team whose key players were comfortably into their thirties and who had always relied on the long ball.

Detroit had won a World Series three years earlier, and the stars from '68—Mickey Lolich, Al Kaline, Norm Cash, Bill Freehan, Willie Horton, et al.—were aging. Critics said doddering Detroit wasn't the kind of young team Martin could mold in his image. Tigers general manager Jim Campbell wasn't so sure. Mayo Smith had skippered Detroit to a World Series title, but by 1970 the Tigers had been tamed; finishing four games under .500, they bore the demeanor of a demoralized club. If they seemed complacent under the laid-back, laissez-faire style of Smith, Campbell figured Battling Billy was a guy whose fierce temper could wring one final season of splendor from his aging veterans.

"What am I going to do, hire a man for what he is and then try to change him?" Campbell asked at the time. "I think [anger is] definitely one of his assets."

Prior to the start of his first season, Martin met with his players and laid out his expectations for the team.

Detroit went 91-71 in Martin's first season and jumped from fourth to second in the division. The summer of '72 saw the Tigers spend more than half the season in first place. Under Martin they had become a model of consistency, leading by as many as four games and never trailing by more than two and a half, winning as many as five straight and not losing more than four in a row.

Hold those Tigers? No way.

"Billy was a heck of a manager, you couldn't find any better," recalled Ike Blessitt, a late-season call-up for the Tigers. "Strategy-wise he was one of the best. Between those white lines he was dynamite."

A year later, however, Blessitt would have what he described as "an incident"—a fight—with Martin that Blessitt said caused him to be black-balled from baseball. A four-sport star at Hamtramck High in Michigan, Blessitt was a solid prospect when he was drafted as a seventeen-year-old in 1967. He spent the next six years in the U.S. Army Reserve, shortening each season to complete his military duty.

Blessitt remembers his eventual arrival at Tiger Stadium as "one of the biggest days of my life. It was a great thrill for me. Tiger Stadium was one of the great stadiums to play in. The fans were right on top of you and they were into the game. You would be in the on-deck circle and you could look up in the stands and damn near touch everybody."

Joining a team with legends like Kaline and Cash, Lolich and Freehan, Blessitt almost had to pinch himself:

Coming up to a team in a pennant race, knowing I'm going to put that uniform on and playing in my hometown in front of my mom and dad, it's a feeling I can't express," he said. "Walking into the clubhouse, it was something to see. Kaline was always a gamer. A pitcher would throw at him and he would get up, dust himself off and hit a line drive back through the box. Lolich would go out [to the mound] time and again and never get a sore arm. All those years in the majors he never missed a start [because of injury] but one. He should be in the Hall of Fame. He never said 'Billy, I can't pitch, get some one else.' You put the ball in his hand and he went out there and threw that damn ball.

The Tigers were close, really close; they grew up in the minor leagues together. That's where they jelled. They believed in each other. We stuck together and Detroit pulled together.

With Kaline and Cash carrying the offense, Lolich and Joe Coleman keying the mound corps, new additions like slick-fielding infielder Tony Taylor providing additional veteran experience, and Tiger Stadium's ancient confines crowded with fans—Detroit led the league in attendance—the "Ti-guhs," as the team's radio voice Ernie Harwell called them, became a hot ticket.

Campbell's acquisition of Taylor, the former Phillie, paid big dividends for Detroit. Martin platooned the right-handed hitting Taylor with left-handed

hitting Dick McAuliffe, and the thirty-six-year-old Taylor responded by batting .303. He was versatile in the field; able to play second base, third, and
first; and as NBC's Curt Gowdy declared, "a good man to have in a tough
pennant race." Indeed. Taylor was a contact hitter who could move runners along. He was smart and had experienced pennant pressure before.

Every Taylor plate appearance was notable for his making the sign of
the cross prior to batting and also for his attire. He was one of two Tigers,
Cash being the other, who wore just a cloth cap at the plate. MLB had made
batting helmets mandatory in 1971, but the rule had a grandfather clause,
meaning that veterans could continue to wear their caps rather than their
helmets if they chose. Many, like Pittsburgh catcher Manny Sanguillen,
wore their helmets on top of their caps. Taylor teamed with McAuliffe,
Gates Brown, Duke Sims, Ike Brown, and big Frank Howard to give the
Tigers one of the best benches in the league, and they played a vital role
in the knock-down divisional race.

Howard had been a World Series hero in the Dodgers' sweep of the
Yankees in 1963. In Game One at Yankee Stadium he hammered a Whitey
Ford fastball some 460 feet to center field. The drive reached the famed
monuments and is remembered as the longest double in the Stadium's
forty-one-year history. In Game Four in Dodger Stadium Howard crushed
a slow curve from Ford into the upper deck in left field. Dealt to the Senators in December 1964, the 6-foot-7, 255-pound Howard, whose nickname
was "Hondo," also became known as the "Washington Monument" and the
"Capital Punisher" for his size and prodigious power. In 1972 the Senators,
now relocated to Texas and renamed the Rangers, sold Howard to the Tigers
on August 31. He was brought to Detroit to platoon at first base with the
thirty-seven-year-old Cash, whom Martin wanted to keep fresh by saving
him for the big games. Howard hit .242 in September and provided a big
win over Baltimore on September 13 when he homered and drove in four
runs to beat Dave McNally 6–5.

The Taylor/McAuliffe tandem teamed with Brinkman to turn the double
play beautifully. Brinkman was a tall and willowy shortstop in the manner of Marty Marion (known as "Slats" when he played in St. Louis) and

contemporary Mark "the Blade" Belanger of Baltimore. Like the 6-foot-2, 170-pound Marion, who was also known as "the Octopus," Steady Eddie played his position as if he had suction cups rather than hands. Brinkman paired with third baseman Aurelio Rodriguez to make the left side of the Tigers infield air tight. Rodriguez, like his counterpart in Baltimore, boasted a magnetic mitt.

Detroit fans appreciated defense; their Lions had been fielding great defenses for decades. Joe Schmidt, Night Train Lane, Roger Brown, Alex Karras, Dick LeBeau, and Lem Barney played hardball too and thrilled fans on cold, snowy Thanksgiving Days in Tiger Stadium. The fans' appreciation extended to the summer game, and they hung banners in Tiger Stadium lauding their "Dynamic Duo" at third and short. Curt Gowdy said the theme for the left side of the Detroit defense was "Thou Shall Not Pass."

Brinkman had come to Detroit in another of Campbell's shrewd deals that also brought Coleman to Motown for Denny McLain. Martin could not have been happier. He saw some of his scrappy self in Brinkman and played him regularly. Brinkman was the lone Tiger to play in each of the team's 156 games in '72. What Steady Eddie lacked in offense he more than made up for in defense. He set an MLB record for shortstops by going seventy-two consecutive innings without an error, a mark that stood until Cal Ripken Jr. surpassed it. Brinkman's streak caught the attention of the nation's fans, including President Richard Nixon. Nixon sent Brinkman a congratulatory message in midsummer, and by summer's end, Steady Eddie's .990 fielding percentage had earned him ninth place in the AL MVP voting. The Detroit chapter of the Baseball Writers' Association of America named Brinkman "Tiger of the Year" over Lolich, Kaline, Cash, and Freehan.

At age thirty-seven, Kaline shared elder statesman status with Cash. Kaline was aging, but he proved more than once how difficult it still was to slip fastballs past a great hitter. Martin knew Kaline had just so many games left in him and used him wisely, playing him in just 106 games to conserve his energy and allow him to be fresh for the big games.

Harwell, a.k.a. "the Voice of Summer," provided the play-by-play and Ray

Lane the color commentary on WJZ. A Hall of Fame broadcaster who was the voice of the Tigers from 1960 to 1991 and from 1993 to 2002, Harwell was a native of Georgia known for his charm, southern accent, and low-key style. He was also known for his classic calls:

That one is looong gone!
Two for the price of one for the Tigers!
Strike! And he stood there like the house by the side of the road and
watched it go by!

Harwell was a part of the family for many Tigers fans. Via radio, they took him into their homes, took him, as Harwell would note in his heartfelt farewell broadcast in 2002, "to that cottage up north, to the beach, the picnic, your workplace, and your backyard . . . sneaking your transistor under the pillow as you grew up loving the Tigers."

And Detroit loved Harwell. Blessitt said Harwell could have run for mayor of Motown. "Everybody loved that man."

For the second time in four years, pennant fever gripped the city. In 1968 Detroit's downtown department stores had sold everything from Tiger T-shirts to Tiger milk. As fast as cars rolled off the assembly lines of the "Detroit Big Three"—Chrysler, Ford, and General Motors—it seemed Tigers fans plastered them with bumper stickers that read, "Go Get 'em Tigers!" In 1972 Motown was magical again. Fans took transistor radios to restaurants, movie theaters, and Tiger Stadium to tune in Harwell and Lane.

The Tigers' whirlwind rise to contending status was set against a backdrop of a city in a downward economic spiral. Detroit's decline, like its rise, was directly linked to the auto industry. Automobile magnates, Henry Ford among them, had developed an industry that for decades would serve as an engine driving the middle class and bringing boom times to Detroit while helping define American creativity.

During World War II Detroit became the "Arsenal of Democracy" demanded by U.S. President Franklin D. Roosevelt. Yet a race riot in 1943 proved a forecast of postwar problems to come. From the mid-1950s into the late 1960s Detroit lost more than a hundred thousand factory jobs.

Many white people fled the city for the suburbs; factories followed suit, abandoning the city's black neighborhoods.

Tensions exploded in the infamous 1967 Detroit riots. For a frightening five days in July, rioters roamed the city setting fires and looting stores and businesses. Some thirteen hundred buildings were destroyed; forty-three people were killed and more than seven thousand arrested.

The riots accelerated the exodus of people and employers from Detroit. In 1972 Motown, the city's renowned record label, left for Los Angeles, leaving behind both its ten-story headquarters and the city identified with its enormous success. Crime became commonplace, and Detroit became the homicide capital of the country. The Motor City was now "Murder City."

Like its Rust Belt compatriot Pittsburgh, Detroit in the 1970s sought reinvention via a Renaissance Center mega-project. Yet while it was supposed to revive the city, the Renaissance Center failed for the same reason it was supposed to succeed. Isolated from downtown Detroit, the center did little for the city and surrounding neighborhoods, both of which continued to decay.

If the Renaissance Center on the outskirts of the city was a monstrous failure, the Oakland Hills Country Club, situated in a suburb northwest of Detroit and the site of the 1972 PGA Championship, was simply a monster. So named during the 1951 U.S. Open, for which it underwent a drastic redesign by Robert Trent Jones Sr., the grueling course was finally conquered on the final day by master shot-maker and strategist Ben Hogan. It took Hogan playing perhaps the greatest round of golf in history—a 3-under 67—to bring down the monster. "I'm glad I brought this course, this monster, to its knees," said Hogan in what remains the most famous quote in golf's history. In early August 1972 Gary Player slayed the monster, which had been tamed by another redesign but still had teeth, as evidenced by Player's winning score of 1-over par 281.

The Tigers were looking to slay their own monsters that summer, and their success softened the harsh realities of Detroit's dilemma. They became part of that something special that defines September baseball. To be in position to make a final push for the playoffs brings a different feel to the entire month. The summer heat has softened, there's a sharper slant to the shadows extending across sun-lit fields, and the sights and sounds associated with the sport—the deep green of the outfield and contrasting dark brown of the infield, the multicolored outfits of fans filling the ballpark, and the deepening roars of the crowds—are more vibrant and vivid.

John Donne, an English poet, once wrote of autumn's splendor: "No spring nor summer beauty hath such grace as I have seen in one autumnal face."

Nowhere in 1972 was this changing of the season more evident or symbolic than in Detroit, where the Tigers had gone from a team that had been pushed around just two years prior to one that was now pushing back—much like Martin, their dirt-kicking leader, was known to do. If somebody popped him, Martin said at the time, they'd better know how to fight because he was going to "beat the hell out of them."

While Martin was a mighty mite, John Wesley "Boog" Powell of the rival Baltimore Orioles was a 6-foot-3, 260-pound gentle giant, a man given to simple pleasures. Life, however, wasn't always so plain and simple for Powell, and when the Booger wasn't battling twelve-pound bonefish in Biscayne Bay, he was dealing with problems that sometimes seemed as massive as the man himself.

Born in Lakeland, Florida, Powell was the oldest of three boys. His mother died when he was just nine years old; his father, Charles, worked as a salesman to support the family. It was Charles who bestowed the nickname "Boog" on his first-born. It's a custom in parts of the South for parents to call mischievous sons "Buggers." Charles shortened it to "Boog," and the nickname stuck. Hardly anybody ever called him John, he said. Powell didn't know if he'd even turn around if somebody called him by his given name.

As a professional, his prowess was as a hitter, but Powell's early success in baseball was as a pitcher. He pitched Lakeland to the prestigious Little League World Series in Williamsport, Pennsylvania. It was a family affair for the Powells—Boog's younger brothers Carl and Charlie started at catcher and in the outfield respectively. Carl Taylor was a stepbrother who joined the family when Boog's father remarried. Lakeland lost its opener to Schenectady, New York, but the Powell brothers continued their upwardly mobile move. Carl played in the majors for six years, from 1968 to 1973, primarily with Pittsburgh and Kansas City. Charlie played in the minors for the Orioles.

But it was Boog who had the greatest impact. The first baseman for Baltimore from 1961 to 1974, Powell became the triggerman of the Orioles' offense, according to Harry Dalton, general manager and architect of the Birds' dynasty. Quite a statement, considering Baltimore had future Hall of Famers Frank and Brooks Robinson in its lineup during the dynasty years of 1966–71.

When Boog was hot and hitting well, Dalton said then, the offense jelled. It wasn't a one-man show, but the O's success seemed at least partly related to his performance. Baltimore's success was considerable, and the three-time defending league champions opened September 1972 on top of the standings and in search of another title. Their first had come six years prior, when they had stunned the reigning world champion Dodgers with a four-game sweep in the World Series. In 1969 Baltimore won another Eastern Division title and swept Martin's Twins in the inaugural American League Championship Series before running into the "Miracle Mets" in the World Series. In an outcome more surprising even than their 1966 win over the Dodgers, the favored Orioles fell to the Mets in five games.

Baltimore was embarrassed; its seemingly invincible Colts had been shocked by another New York underdog, Joe Namath and the Jets, the previous January in Super Bowl III. In the spring of 1970, Gotham made it three straight over the Charm City in postseason competition, the Knicks beating the Bullets in seven games.

The Orioles returned with a vengeance in 1970, winning 108 games, sweeping the Twins for the second straight year in the ALCS, and returning the favor to the National League by routing the Reds in five games in the Fall Classic. In 1971 Earl Weaver's Orioles won over one hundred games and swept their third straight ALCS—this time against the up-and-coming A's. Baltimore boasted arguably the greatest single-season rotation in history, four 20-game winners in the persons of Jim Palmer, Dave McNally, Mike Cuellar, and Pat Dobson. But the favored Birds stumbled again on the game's biggest stage, falling to Roberto Clemente and the Pirates in seven games after taking a 2–0 Series lead.

Still the Orioles' accomplishments were impressive. To that point, they were the first team since the 1960–64 Yankees to reach three straight World Series and just the seventh team in AL history to claim three consecutive pennants. From 1969 to 1971 they won 318 games in the regular season, still an AL record, and nine straight ALCS games.

Powell had been a big part of Baltimore's success and would be again in '72 as the Birds battled Detroit, New York, and Boston. He had come a long way from his early years in the majors, when he recalled facing Ford and striking out three times on nine pitches—all curveballs. No shame there since Powell considered Ford the best he had ever faced.

What did bother Powell was his 1967 season, when he hit 13 homers and batted .234—this just one season after he had been voted AL Comeback Player of the Year and was touted by some as the next Mickey Mantle. Hall of Fame hurler Robin Roberts had predicted Powell would hit fifty home runs a season.

Like Johnny Bench during his slump in 1971, Powell in the 1967 season was targeted for heavy criticism. "Everyone ripped me," Powell said, "the fans, the press, the club."

He tried to adjust, but nothing worked. He just couldn't figure it out, he said. He estimated he had ninety-two different stances that season and (with just slight exaggeration) took "one million rounds of extra hitting." The booing from Birds' fans became so intense that Powell's wife, Janet, bolted from her seat in Memorial Stadium and cried hysterically as she ran from the park. Powell was benched, but when Weaver took over as manager in 1968, he restored the big man's confidence. "You bat third or fourth, depending who is pitching," Weaver told Powell, "and you play every day."

Powell responded by hitting 22 homers and driving in 85 runs in '68, the first of five straight seasons with 21 or more homers and at least 81 RBIs. He matured as a player and as a person. Powell adjusted to what opposing pitchers were trying to do. A lefty hitter, he still had trouble with southpaws, particularly when they threw breaking balls low and outside. But when they made mistakes, Powell wasn't missing those mistakes the way he once had. He became more patient at the plate, no longer swinging at the first pitch. He became a thinking man's hitter, punching outside pitches to the opposite field and no longer trying to pull the ball all the time.

By the early 1970s Powell had overcome assorted injuries and nagging self-doubt to become, in Dalton's opinion, "the most feared hitter in the American League."

Powell was indeed an imposing figure on the field. With his thick, bare biceps jutting from his Orioles jersey, with his black-and-orange Orioles helmet covering a crew cut, and with eye black smeared on both cheekbones, he presented as much a challenge to pitchers as the bonefish in Biscayne Bay did to him. When you're as big as Powell, former Yankees third baseman Clete Boyer once said, you intimidate a lot of pitchers.

Despite his size, Powell was anything but awkward of hands or feet. Yankees coach Elston Howard thought Howard "one hell of a glove man." Dalton called Powell "The Goalie" because of all the saves the big man made at first base. "How many saves for The Goalie tonight?" Baltimore players would ask. Shortstop Mark Belanger said Powell made thirty-six "saves" of potential throwing errors in 1970. Belanger wasn't counting the low, short throws that are easy to trap. He was counting the high throws where Powell had to tag the runner and the low throws that bounced 12–15 feet in front of first base.

Many observers, including Mantle, credited the Birds' air-tight infield for part of their pitchers' great success. Belanger, third baseman Brooks Robinson, and second baseman Davey Johnson were all multiple Gold Glove winners. Powell never won a Gold Glove, but his defensive contributions weren't lost on his teammates.

Brooks Robinson, the Houdini of the Hot Corner and the man Curt Gowdy called "Baltimore's greatest discovery since crab cakes," said he sometimes made blind throws to first because he knew Powell would catch them. Brooks recalled his famous play in Game One of the 1970

World Series, when he robbed Bench of a hit with a blind throw to first. Robinson said his throw skipped some fifteen feet in front of Booger, a tough chance, but "he made the play and I got the applause," Brooks said then. He called Powell one hell of an underrated fielder.

Johnson, a three-time Gold Glove winner, said that where Powell had once played conservatively at first base, lining up right behind the bag, by 1972 he was moving twenty or twenty-five feet off the bag. That adjustment allowed the Oriole infield to have more movement. Johnson could play closer to second base, Belanger deeper in the hole at short, and Brooks closer to the left-field line.

While Powell helped orchestrate the Orioles' famous infield, away from the game he enjoyed the orchestrations of various kinds of music. His father was an avid collector of record albums, mainly big band types like Benny Goodman. Powell preferred country. He and Roy Clark were good friends and neighbors in Miami, and the country singer's "Yesterday, When I Was Young," written by French singer Charles Aznavour, was a favorite among Powell's collection of some six hundred LPs.

When he wasn't playing baseball, fishing, or barbequing, Powell would pull Clark's "Yesterday, When I Was Young" from his collection, light up what writer John Devaney said was Powell's forty-third or forty-fourth cigarette of the day, and listen to lyrics the Booger believed to be the most beautiful he had ever heard.

The song was also a favorite of Mantle's, and like Powell, Mickey counted Clark among his good friends. Mantle asked Clark to perform the song at his funeral, and Clark did.

The song was a personal anthem for both Powell and Mantle; by 1972 it could have been a team anthem for the thirty-year-old Boog, the Birds, and Billy Martin's Tigers. Their time was indeed running out. The two proud champions had combined to win four straight pennants and five of the previous six, but by the summer of '72 they were lions in winter.

Because they had Don Baylor waiting in the wings, the Orioles had dealt thirty-six-year-old Frank Robinson and his $130,000 salary to the Dodgers in a sudden and surprising six-player deal on December 2, 1971.

From the standpoint of consistency Frank and Brooks were Baltimore's version of death and taxes. Lamenting the trade, one O's teammate said Frank won five or six games by himself in the late innings every season. Oakland's Reggie Jackson, comparing the O's to Popeye, said the dealing of his mentor to Los Angeles meant the three-time reigning AL champs had lost the "can of spinach in their shirt."

The Birds' offense suffered a dramatic dropoff in '72. Brooks still had a magic mitt but like many of his teammates wasn't waving a wand at the plate. Wearing his trademark cropped-bill batting helmet—there were fewer uniform dress codes in the 1970s so Brooks was free to customize, and he had the team's equipment manager saw an inch off the visor so that there was nothing in his line of vision—Robinson hit just 8 homers in '72. It marked the first time since 1961 that he hadn't reached double figures in homers.

Powell also struggled—he did not surpass .200 until mid-July—and even donned glasses during games to better see the pitches. The glasses didn't last long, and Powell's slump came to an end as well. Over the final three months he slammed 17 of his eventual 21 homers, drove in 61 of his 81 runs, and raised his average to a more respectable .252.

With Powell supplying the power and Palmer, McNally, Cuellar, and Dobson the pitching—the staff ERA of 2.53 was number one in the league—the Birds spent forty-three days in first place and still owned the lead as late as September 4, when they split a home doubleheader with the Yankees to fall into a first-place tie with the Tigers.

The Orioles, oddly, never seemed at home in '72 amid the poplar trees and gray cinder of the "Old Gray Lady of 33rd Street," Memorial Stadium. The Birds went 38-39, a stark contrast to the 53-24 home mark they had enjoyed the year before. What did remain constant was Baltimore's broadcast team of Chuck Thompson, Bill O'Donnell, and John Gordon. Thompson, a Hall of Fame sportscaster, and O'Donnell called Orioles games from 1966 to 1981 on WBAL and then WFBR Radio and from 1966 to 1977 on WJZ-TV. The pair also broadcast Baltimore Colts games on the radio. Thompson's descriptive style and deeply resonant voice was punctuated when something good happened for the hometown team by his trademark calls—"Ain't the beer cold?" and "Go to war, Miss Agnes!"

Thompson often spoke his sentences backward—"Bats from the left side, does Boog Powell"—a quirk that further endeared him to his many followers. Gentlemanly and quick with a kind word, Thompson was beloved in Baltimore. He was "Uncle Chuck" to many fans and like other sportscasters of his era was more than an announcer.

As writer Frank Deford, who grew up in Baltimore listening to Thompson, once said, these men were the voices of summer, of good times, of baseball, of hometown. You listened to them at night while pretending to be asleep, the radio beneath your pillow. You listened while driving or sitting on the beach, and they were as much a sound of summer as crickets, lawn mowers, and the Good Humor Man's bell. They spoke with a tone and rhythm unique to each man, painting word pictures with clarity and crispness. Sometimes, Deford said, "the games we heard from their lips were better than the games we saw with our eyes."

What many witnessed away from baseball as August melted into September was the triumph and tragedy of the Summer Olympics in Munich. The Munich Massacre—a September 5 attack by Palestinian terrorists on members of the Israeli Olympic team—overshadowed the exploits of Mark Spitz, Olga Korbut, Dan Gable, Dave Wottle, Frank Shorter, Vasiliy Alekseyev, and Teofilo Stevenson. The Munich Games are also remembered for the U.S. loss to the Soviet Union in the men's basketball final, a game USA Basketball calls "the most controversial in international basketball history."

Unlike the gold medal game in men's basketball, the American League's East championship would be settled without controversy. As the Orioles faded in the final month, the Yankees found themselves deadlocked with their longtime rivals, the Red Sox, just a half-game back in what was easily the most exciting race of the summer.

When New York beat Baltimore September 5 on a second straight save by Sparky Lyle, the Orioles fell from first to fourth. The Birds were just a game behind, and they did rally in mid-September, when Boog's five RBIs in two games backed complete-game victories by Palmer and Cueller in

Yankee Stadium. But the dynastic O's could not reclaim their dominance in the East and eventually finished five and a half games off the pace.

The foursome of Palmer, McNally, Cuellar, and Dobson, which had gone a combined 81-31 in '71, went 68-57 in '72. Palmer was the lone 20-game winner, and Cuellar claimed 18 victories; McNally and Dobson finished with sub .500 records. But these marks are misleading; the renowned mound staff suffered from meager run support. This was still a great staff, as evidenced by the fact that three of the four aces—Palmer, Cuellar, and Dobson—had lower ERAs in '72 than in '71 and all four were 2.95 or under. In 1971 the fearsome Palmer-McNally-Cuellar-Dobson rotation had accomplished a feat that hadn't been done since 1952 and hasn't been done since: it recorded consecutive seasons with three or more 20-game winners. The 1903–1904 Boston Americans, 1904–1905 New York Giants, and 1951–52 Cleveland Indians are the only staffs in history to stand with the Orioles in that regard. The 1920 Chicago White Sox, who one year after their infamous "Black Sox" scandal flashed four 20-game winners in Red Faber, Lefty Williams, Dickie Kerr, and Eddie Cicotte, are the only rotation that can match the '71 O's. In the Bronx the Yankees' late-summer resurgence was led in part by the inimitable Lyle. Obtained from Boston for first baseman Danny Cater in March 1972 in one of the most lopsided deals in baseball history, Lyle thrived on the extra work afforded him in New York, hurling a then personal-best 107 $^2/_3$ innings and appearing in 56 games, tops among AL pitchers. By season's end, Lyle had set an American League record with 35 saves while fashioning a 1.92 ERA. Just as Roger Kahn felt the Reds had committed grand larceny in getting Joe Morgan from the Astros, Bobby Murcer believed New York had stolen Lyle from Boston in one of the all-time great trades for the Yankees.

New York rallied from a season-high eight-game deficit on July 27 to within a half-game of the lead on September 12 following Lyle's save in a 3–2 win in the Stadium.

An eccentric known to sit on birthday cakes in his birthday suit, Albert "Sparky" Lyle was a star in the Bronx Bombers' grand tradition: colorful, cocky, and commanding respect. Amid the roiling race, Lyle would step from the pinstripe-painted Datsun that brought him from the bullpen to the bump, and, with his jaw bulging with Red Man chaw, stride to the mound as Stadium organist Toby Wright played "Pomp and Circumstance" and Yankees fans chanted "Dee-fense!"

Despite being called upon to rescue his team time and again, Lyle resisted pressure by not thinking about it. He didn't listen to the crowd or care who the batter was. He simply threw fastballs and sliders inside to right-handers and outside to left-handers.

Against Milwaukee, he was called on in the ninth to protect a one-run lead with two on and nobody out. He slammed the door on six pitches. Against Texas, he relieved starter Mel Stottlemyer in the eighth with the Yankees leading 3–2, runners on second and third, and no outs. Lyle intentionally walked Frank Howard to load the bases and then struck out the next three hitters on a total of ten pitches. In a key series against Detroit in August he twice entered games in the ninth to preserve one-run leads.

Yankees manager Ralph Houk thought the breezy lefty had the perfect temperament to be a reliever. Houk, a hard, cigar-smoking army man whose nickname was "the Major," called the durable Lyle a "throwback to the old-timers." As far as Houk was concerned, Lyle, a product of western Pennsylvania, seemed as much at home amid the rattle of the IRT trains, the emerald expanse of the outfield, the monuments in center, and the famous façade as any of his illustrious predecessors in pinstripes.

Even so, after Lyle had contributed to eight of nine wins in mid-August, Houk rested his workhorse. New York lost its next four games. Lyle improved to 9-5 when he beat the Tigers 3–2 in twelve innings on September 28, the victory keeping the Yankees' hopes alive.

The dramatic victory over Detroit symbolized baseball in the Bronx in '72. Presaging their epic playoff battles with Kansas City from 1976 to 1980, the Yankees split wild, 7–6 decisions with the Royals in late summer. On August 15 in Municipal Stadium, Thurman Munson lashed three hits, but future Yankees teammate Lou Piniella's single capped Kansas City's game-winning three-run rally in the ninth. Twelve days later at the Stadium it was New York's turn to rally, coming back from a 6–0 deficit. On August

29 Murcer hit for the cycle against Texas, blasting the tying homer in the bottom of the ninth to set the stage for Johnny Callison's decisive hit in the eleventh in another 7–6 finish.

It all made for an exciting and memorable summer in the city: the IRT rumbling from the tunnel to reveal iconic Yankee Stadium and the initial view of the expansive green outfield through your window as your train lurched into the 161st Station; public address announcer Bob Sheppard welcoming fans to the Stadium in his precise, distinctive baritone; Wright playing the Stadium organ; Robert Merrill singing the National Anthem, his words echoing throughout the Cathedral-like ballpark. These were some of the reasons American League umpire Jim Honochick, who worked the junior circuit from 1949 to 1973, thought Yankee Stadium the best AL park to call games in.

New York in the 1970s bears little resemblance to the refined Big Apple of the twenty-first century. New York then was far more Frank Sinatra's gritty 1979 depiction than the gentrified Gotham that Alicia Keys soulfully sang of thirty years later. The city had a fiscal crisis in the mid-1970s, the likes of which had rarely been seen before in an American metropolis. It led to New York City mayor Abe Beam's leaving a desperate, one-word note—"Help!"—at the Wailing Wall in Jerusalem.

From Times Square to Park Slope, prostitutes and drug dealers plied their trade in full view. Heroin and cocaine were commonplace, and with them came increased street violence. Like Detroit, New York suffered from economic decline and ultimately white flight. In the summer of '77, New York City descended into darkness during a terrifying twenty-five-hour blackout in July. The chaotic event led to widespread looting and rioting in the Bedford-Stuyvesant section of Brooklyn; the devastation of neighborhoods from East Harlem to Bushwick; more than 1,000 fires and 1,600 damaged stores; 3,700 arrests; and a total cost to the city that exceeded $300 million. The trauma of those two days in mid-July symbolized the growing malaise gripping America's major cities.

The sense of uneasiness shared throughout the five boroughs was felt by Yankee fans as well. Murcer and Munson led a modestly talented team that included Callison, Horace Clarke, Gene Michael, Celerino Sanchez, Roy White, and Ron "the Boomer" Blomberg. These Yankees were far removed from the fearsome Mantle-Maris-Ford clubs of the early '60s; comedian Joe E. Lewis famously compared rooting for the lordly Yankees to rooting for U.S. Steel. Boxing writer A. J. Liebling of the *New Yorker* said at the time of the Yankees' second straight World Series title in 1962 that those Bombers were the least popular of all baseball clubs "because they win, which leaves nothing to 'if' about."

Clarke, a leadoff man and second baseman, is often recalled as the front man and fall guy for the era that extended from 1965 to 1975, a time referred to, unfairly it seems, as the "Horace Clarke Era." Clarke was a solid player for a squad that in 1970 won 93 games—second-best in the AL East and the fourth-highest total in baseball that season—and in '72 was in the playoff chase until the final days.

Nicknamed "Hoss," Clarke was a durable player who averaged 151 games over a seven-year stretch from 1967 to 1973 and twice led the AL in at-bats. He had good range at second base, a fact recognized by Mickey Mantle, who, playing first base at the end of his career because of bad legs, told the young Clarke in 1967, "Take anything you can reach!" A deft bunter and contact hitter, Clarke twice led the American League in singles. The switch-hitting Clarke had a signature style at the plate. In a July 23 game at the Stadium against California, Angels announcer Dick Enberg noted that when the 5-foot-9 Clarke batted out of his signature deep crouch, "he doesn't give that pitcher much of a strike zone between the knees and letters. . . . Little guy spreads [his feet] out as much as any hitter."

Fans who couldn't make it to the Stadium tuned in to WPIX Channel 11 in New York. There they were greeted by a rapid montage and the Yankees anthem.

Composed by Bob Bundin and Lou Stallman of Columbia Records and recorded by the Sid Bass Orchestra and Chorus, the song had been the Bombers' theme since 1967. It ushered in each game's broadcast by the announcing team of Phil "Scooter" Rizzuto, Frank Messer, and Bill White. The trio would work together from 1970 to 1984, endearing themselves to generations of Yankees fans in the New York–northern New Jersey area with their "Welcome to New York Yankee baseball" introduction. Rizzuto, Messer, and White's broadcasting Yankees baseball on WPIX 11 and WMCA Radio became for many as much a part of the team's tradition as pinstripes, monuments, and the Stadium's famous frieze.

The Scooter's stream-of-consciousness style of broadcasting and lively play-by-play, with the occasional malapropisms, was adored by his fans but irritating to his critics: *"Deep to left-center, nobody's gonna get that one! Holy cow, somebody got it!"*

Rizzuto's "Holy cow!" was his catchphrase, punctuating his calls of some of the most famous moments in Yankees history: Roger Maris's sixty-first home run in 1961 and Chris Chambliss's bottom of the ninth blast to beat Kansas City in the fifth and deciding game of the 1976 ALCS, among others. His "Holy cow!" would be featured in Meat Loaf's "Paradise by the Dashboard Light" and in an episode of *Seinfeld*.

The Scooter's frequent digressions on the air led to his reading recipes sent in by listeners and viewers, speaking well of restaurants he frequented or the cannoli he ate between innings, wishing fans happy birthday or happy anniversary, and sending get-well wishes to fans in hospitals. He would joke about leaving the game early, issuing an on-air statement to his wife: "I'll be home soon, Cora!"

Rizzuto was also known for calling his broadcast partners by their last names—"White" rather than "Bill"—a habit that stemmed from his Hall of Fame career as the Yankees shortstop from 1941 to 1956.

White: And here's Phil Rizzuto....
Rizzuto: I'm doing play-by-play? White, you're doing play-by-play!

By mid-September, Rizzuto, White, Messer, the Yankees, and their fans were concerned not only with the play-by-play at the ballpark, but also with watching the scoreboard for games involving Boston and Detroit. Fritz Peterson's 3–2 win over Tiant September 12 in the Bronx brought New York to within a half-game of the lead. With seventeen games to play, the Yankees were within reach of making the playoffs for the first time since '64.

The elevated IRT trains on the Third Avenue El weren't the only cause of the rumble coming from the Bronx. Pinstripes were back in style in Gotham, and for a time it seemed as if the Bombers might turn back time to the days when the Yankees were winning pennants in waves. Even Wright got swept up in the excitement, banging out "It Seems Like Old Times" on the Stadium organ.

It was a dramatic change for a club that seemed to be better known in the early '70s for off-the-field news—muggings in the Bronx; poor parking at the Stadium; the Mike Kekich–Fritz Peterson family trade that had its origins in a July 15, 1972, party but wasn't announced until March '73.

Apart from the Lyle deal the Kekich-Peterson swap was the Big Trade in the Bronx in '72. It's ranked by ESPN.com as the sixth most shocking moment in baseball history. The two couples had grown close and came to realize they were married to the wrong people. The introspective Kekich, once regarded in the Dodger organization as the second coming of Sandy Koufax because of his blinding fastball, became Peterson's roommate when dealt to the Yankees. He gravitated toward the thoughtful Marilyn Peterson, while Fritz, a man who lived in the moment, was drawn to Susanne Kekich, an ex-cheerleader.

"Don't make anything sordid out of this," Peterson, a 20-game winner in 1970, said at the announcement of the Big Trade. Mike Kekich concurred. "Don't say this was wife swapping because it wasn't."

Kekich said it was a matter of swapping lives more than wives. The Big Trade began in mid-July, and the couples moved in with each other's spouses that fall. Yet by spring training 1973 Peterson and Kekich were barely speaking. Fritz and Susanne were happy; Mike and Marilyn, not so much. Years later Kekich said his career went into a "black hole" after the Big Trade. He and Marilyn split, and he was dealt to Cleveland in 1973 and then moved on to Japan. Fritz and Susanne, meanwhile, remained married and had children of their own.

Recently Peterson was said to be living in "semi-hiding." Kekich, reportedly "panic-stricken" over word of a Matt Damon–Ben Affleck film about the Big Trade, was said by New York writer Mark Jacobson to have assumed a new identity.

As summer cooled, so too did the Yankees. A 7–2 loss to Boston on September 13 started a spiral that saw New York lose six of its next seven. Two of the more damaging blows were delivered by Indians ace Gaylord Perry, the first coming September 22 in Cleveland and the final shot, it turned out, on October 1 in New York. Despite being in the presumed twilight of his career, the thirty-three-year-old Perry had gone to the American League after ten years in San Francisco and dominated, compiling an AL-leading 24 wins, 29 complete games, and a 1.92 ERA and winning the league's Cy Young award.

Perry's productivity on the mound hadn't made for an Indian summer in the East, but he had proved to be the best, and most controversial, pitcher in the league that season.

A lanky right-hander, the 6-foot-4 Perry was both the son of a North Carolina tobacco farmer and the father of the modern-day spitball. By the age of seven, Gaylord and his ten-year-old brother Jim were behind a mule plowing the fields of the twenty-five-acre spread owned by their parents, Evan and Ruby. As a student, Gaylord was more into sports than books. In high school he was all-state offensive and defensive end in football and averaged almost thirty points and twenty rebounds in four years of basketball. But his favorite pastime was chucking baseballs in and around the southern hamlet of Williamston. In time Perry developed an extensive repertoire of pitches; writer Ray Robinson described Perry's arsenal in the early 1970s as an "express train fastball, a sinuous curve, a rollercoaster sinker, a mystifying forkball and a teaser of a slider." There was one other pitch in Perry's weaponry: his celebrated spitball.

The "greaser," as Perry called it, has a long and colorful place in the game's history. Big Ed Walsh of the Chicago White Sox popularized the pitch during the game's deadball era. After Indians shortstop Ray Chapman was struck in the temple and killed by a spitball thrown by the Yankees' Carl Mays in August 1920, the spitball was banned. Use of the pitch persisted, and in the mid-1950s and 1960s baseball commissioner Ford Frick advocated its return to the game. It was a great pitch, the commissioner stated, and apparently forgetting Chapman's death, added that "there was nothing dangerous" about it. Frick was not alone in his thinking. American League president Joe Cronin; Cal Hubbard, the supervisor of umpires; and baseball's bible, *The Sporting News*, all believed the rule banning the spitter should be abolished since it was not enforceable.

The pitch remained outlawed but not out of practice. In 1968 MLB took additional steps to sideline the spitter when it instituted what is known as the "Gaylord Rule," which forbid a pitcher from putting his hand to his mouth anywhere on the mound. Perry had picked up his myriad of motions on the mound—touching his belt, his cap, his neck—by watching Don Drysdale, who Perry thought made a big thing of tugging at his hat.

Until 1974, when Perry authored a book, *Me and the Spitter: An Autobiographical Confession*, he claimed innocence. Despite the allegations against him through the years, the sweet-drawling man who, like Sal Maglie before him, cultivated a mountain man's beard between starts, would issue a sly smile when asked about the spitter.

Perry once told ump Ron Luciano during a search on the mound, "Look at my left shoulder but don't look under my hat!" Gaylord giggled during another search, telling Luciano he was tickling him, and he once asked Luciano if he gave massages.

In his book Perry claimed he threw his first important illegal pitch on May 31, 1964, in the second game of a doubleheader against the New York Mets at Shea Stadium. The game would last twenty-three innings and a record seven hours and twenty-three minutes. A mop-up reliever at the time, Perry entered the game for the Giants in the bottom of the thirteenth. Up to that point he had thrown spitters in meaningless situations—spring training games and batting practice—but he and catcher Tom Haller decided it was time to try the pitch with the game on the line. With the aid of the spitter and his other new pitch, a slider, Perry pitched ten innings to earn both the win and the confidence of manager Alvin Dark.

Perry won 12 games that season and 21 in 1966, the first of his five twenty-win seasons. As he raised his win totals, he also raised the ire of opponents. During the '72 season, Oakland's Mike Epstein pointed his bat at Perry and threatened to charge the mound. A's skipper Dick Williams protested so vigorously that Perry was strip-searched and ordered to change jerseys. Billy Martin brought bloodhounds to a game in order to sniff baseballs for illegal substances like Vaseline. Despite the ban, Martin insisted Perry still threw spitters, especially to good hitters.

One such hitter was Murcer, whose hot bat helped fuel the Yankees' surge. With his dark hair flowing from the back of his helmet, Murcer would take a slight crouch from the portside of the plate and punch hits to all fields. He caught fire in the heat of the summer, hitting .367 in June, .283 in July, and .331 in August.

He had always been a streak hitter, but Murcer's *modus operandi* was to start fast and then tail off. He reversed form in '72. On May 15 he was hitting just .183 with two homers and six RBIs in twenty-two games. On June 1 he lit the fuse on his bat by lashing four hits in Milwaukee. On the twelve-game road trip he went 21 for 46 to raise his average to .273.

Murcer, who was then wearing number 1, matched that numeral by reaching career-highs to that time in all extra-base hit categories. He did so by *not* being a Bronx Bomber in the traditional sense. It wouldn't have been surprising at the time to hear Yankees fans paraphrasing Marvin Gaye's 1971 hit as "Murcer, Murcer Me."

In the aftermath of his 1970 season, which had seen his home run total fall to 23 and his batting average dip to .251, the Oklahoma kid, who had been touted as the "next Mantle" while still a teenager, had stopped trying to conform to the Yankees' power-hitting image, stopped trying to pull every pitch into the inviting right-field porch.

Like a lot of boys who had grown up in the 1950s fascinated by the Mick, Murcer idolized the Yankee demigod. Unlike Mantle, whose favorite player growing up was not the man who preceded him in center field but St. Louis's Stan Musial, Murcer thought his predecessor the best player he'd ever seen. Murcer's connection to Mantle was closer than most. Both were born in Oklahoma; both had been signed by legendary scout Tom Greenwade; both were shortstops at the time of their signing and were later converted into center fielders. When he reached the majors, Murcer was given Mantle's Yankee Stadium locker.

Murcer realized in 1971 that while he occupied the Mick's locker, he didn't own Mantle's raw strength. Despite hitting four homers in four official at-bats in a 1970 doubleheader—something not even Ruth had done—Murcer realized at season's end that he was a line-drive hitter, not a home run hitter. Sacrificing power for average, Murcer choked up on the bat and cut down on his swing. If the pitch was outside, he would go with it and hit it to left. He began bunting more, a tactic that eventually brought the infield in and gave him more room to spray hits.

Murcer's average in 1971 jumped to .331, his RBIs improved from 78 to 94, his hits from 146 to 175, and his home runs to 25. To paraphrase Shakespeare, the quality of Murcer had been strained, but now it droppeth as the gentle rain from heaven upon the place beneath: a Yankee Stadium crowd thirsting for a pennant.

Like Joe DiMaggio, Mantle, and Earle Combs, Murcer became a fixture at the most glamorous position in baseball—center fielder for the New York Yankees. It was comparable to being a running back for the Cleveland Browns and following in the footsteps of Marion Motley, Jim Brown, and Leroy Kelly or being a Montreal Canadiens goalie and joining the royal lineage of Jacques Plante, Gump Wormsley, Rogie Vachon, Tony Esposito, and Ken Dryden.

That the Yankees didn't know they had a future star in their midst was evident in their initially handing him uniform number 17. New York's star sluggers always wore single digits: Ruth, 3; Gehrig, 4; DiMaggio, 5; Mantle, 7. Roy White broke into the bigs on September 7, 1965, one day before Bobby, and was handed number 6, a clear indication of who the Yankees believed would be the next man up on the monuments. Murcer was happy with his number 17; at least it had the Mick's number 7 in it. But when second baseman Bobby Richardson retired and asked Murcer to take his number 1, he obliged.

A five-time All-Star, from 1971 to 1975, Murcer joined Mets ace Tom Seaver as one of New York's baseball icons. The two represented their respective teams in the 1971, '72, and '73 Midsummer Classics but didn't face each other. Two decades before regular-season interleague games, confrontations between New York's baseball clubs were largely limited to the Mayor's Trophy Game.

Played once a year every season from 1963 to 1979 and again in 1982–83, the Mets-Yankees Mayor's Trophy Game was an annual in-season exhibition that alternated between Shea Stadium and Yankee Stadium and benefited sandlot ball in New York City. From 1946 to 1955 it had been a three-cornered series among the Yankees, Mets, and Dodgers, and the Yanks and Dodgers would meet one final time in '57 before the Dodgers moved west.

When the Mayor's Trophy Game resumed in 1963, a crowd of 50,742 was on hand in the Bronx as former Yankees skipper Casey Stengel, now managing the Mets, returned to the scene of his greatest triumphs. Even if the Mayor's Trophy Game was an exhibition, New York fans took their hardball seriously. Whether they were hopping on the F Train at 15th Street, riding it to the Roosevelt Avenue–Jackson Heights station and transferring to the 7 to Willets Point in Queens, or taking the F to West 4th and the D train to 161st and River Avenue in the Bronx, they crammed into Shea Stadium and Yankee Stadium for the one-game Subway Series. It was the rare occasion they could see Murcer and Seaver on the same field or Ed Kranepool shaking hands with Horace Clarke. The game's outcome would settle, for that summer at least, the endless comparisons made by Mets and Yankees fans: Agee or Murcer, Grote or Munson, Jones or White, McGraw or Lyle.

On August 24, 1972, 52,308 were in Yankee Stadium to see Yankees rookie Doc Medich beat the Mets 2–1. John Ellis, who in 1973 would become the first designated hitter in Cleveland Indians history, slugged the game-winning homer in the sixth inning off Bob Rauch. The victory marked the Bombers' third straight over the Amazin's.

The Yankees' drive to the playoffs was eventually ended by key members of the Tribe who would be future teammates in the glory years from 1976 to 1978—Chris Chambliss, Graig Nettles, and AL rookie and Pitcher of the Year Dick Tidrow. And by Perry, whose 1972 season has been called by baseball historian Bill James the best by an American League pitcher since Lefty Grove's 1931 season. Perry provided sensational pitching for a Cleveland club that was struggling both on the field and financially. Prior to the season the Indians, seeking greener pastures, had proposed to play half their home games in New Orleans. But new owner Nick Mileti outbid, among others, Cleveland shipping magnate George Steinbrenner, and after purchasing the team on March 22, 1972, for $9 million kept the club in Municipal Stadium.

The Yankees' failure to win the division didn't diminish the solid summers enjoyed by Murcer, Peterson, Steve Kline, and in particular Lyle. Lyle was given the pinstriped Datsun that had been delivering him curbside all season. The little car, a sportswriter in the press box cracked, must have twenty thousand miles on it. Lyle, Murcer, and Munson were the pride of the new Yankees, and in 1972 they gave baseball fans in the South Bronx solid reason to believe better times were ahead.

By the close of the regular season, Red Sox right-hander Luis Tiant was sporting some serious mileage as well. In August and September the venerable Cuban veteran won 11 of 12 games and sparked the Red Sox' rapid surge from fourth place to first. At age thirty-one and having already traveled a long and winding road, he would finish 15-6, post the best winning percentage (.714) among Boston's starting pitchers, lead the league with a 1.91 ERA, author one of the great comeback stories of his era, and be the Comeback of the Year in the American League.

Born in 1940 in Marianao, Cuba, Tiant broke into professional baseball in 1959 with the Mexico City Tigers. Over the next seven years he made stops in Jacksonville, Charleston, Burlington, and Portland before getting called up by the Cleveland Indians. He earned double-digit wins over the next four seasons and in that memorable pitcher's season of 1968 won 21 games and led the league in ERA (1.60) and shutouts (9).

Tiant had also set career-highs to that point in games started, complete games, and innings pitched. Changes in the strike zone and to the mound played a role in Tiant's losing 20 games in 1969 and seeing his complete-games total drop from 19 to 9. Traded to Minnesota in December 1969 in a six-player swap that brought Nettles and Dean Chance to Cleveland, Tiant was diagnosed during the season to have a crack in a bone in his right shoulder. His injuries mounted. In the spring of '71 he pulled a muscle in his rib cage and was released by the Twins on March 31. He bounced to the Atlanta Braves' Triple-A farm team in Richmond. When Richmond failed to promote him following a thirty-day trial, Tiant signed with Boston's Triple-A affiliate in Louisville.

Brought to Boston on June 3, Tiant went 1-7 with a 4.88 ERA in '71. Following one loss, *Boston Globe* baseball writer Cliff Keane began his game story with, "Enough is enough."

Titan's father, Luis Eleuterio Tiant, was a legendary left-hander who had starred in the Cuban and Negro Leagues. Giants great Monte Irvin once opined that Luis Sr. would have been a "great star" had he been able to pitch in the majors. Nicknamed "El Tiante" as a tribute to his Cuban roots, Luis bridged the gap between great Cuban pitchers past and future—El Maestro Martin Dihigo, a twelve-year veteran of the Negro Leagues, and El Duque Orlando Hernandez, who helped anchor the dynastic Yankee staffs of 1998–2004.

By 1972, however, Luis Jr. had the look of a journeyman. Many were surprised to see him at the Red Sox's spring camp in Winter Haven prior to the season. But the trade of Lyle to the Yankees likely saved Tiant's career in Boston. Tiant had seen time as a reliever in '71, and with Lyle gone to New York, manager Eddie Kasko figured he could bring Tiant in from the pen.

Tiant was used in a variety of roles—spot start, long relief, and short relief. But when Boston's "twin aces," Sonny Siebert and Ray Culp, struggled with inconsistency and injury respectively, Kasko turned to Tiant. Inserted into the rotation following the All-Star Game, Tiant earned a complete-game victory over the Orioles in Fenway Park on August 5 and then twirled a three-hitter against the Birds one week later. Following an August 12 win in Baltimore, Kasko announced Tiant was in the rotation to stay.

Luis Sr. was known for his variety of pitches and pirouette delivery, and Luis Jr. followed suit. Wiggling his glove prior to his elaborate delivery, El Tiante whirled and twirled atop the mound, delivering a myriad of pitches from a multitude of angles. Reggie Jackson, reacting to Tiant's gyrations, referred to him as the "Fred Astaire of baseball." As Tiant turned his back on hitters during his delivery, Curt Gowdy said Luis's head went one way and his body another. Tony Kubek added that a hitter seeing Luis look down at the ground, up in the air, and then out toward center field while pitching had to be wondering, "Where's he going to throw it, behind me?"

Tiant said he came up with the idea for his unique delivery in 1972. The first time he did it was against Cleveland. When he had pitched for the Indians, he had thrown 98 m.p.h., but he couldn't throw that hard any more, so he started using his body better.

El Tiante succeeded in lifting the Red Sox from fourth place into a ferocious four-team struggle for the lead. He also succeeded in raising the hopes of the Fenway faithful, who crowded into their little gem of a park. Gowdy broadcast there for fifteen years and said a game was never over at Fenway because of the left-field wall, "the Green Monster," which Gowdy likened to a "giant handball court" because of the many different caroms a ball took off it. Fans were right on top of the action; they could almost reach out and touch the players. "They're a part of the game," Gowdy said of the faithful.

There was no parking at Fenway, but fans love their little ballpark as much as they love their "Sawx." Gowdy described Fenway as "a little jewel set right in the heart of Back Bay, a lovely region downtown." For years the only sign owner Tom Yawkey allowed in Fenway advertised the Jimmy Fund. Fans send money to the Jimmy Fund, and the donations are used for research to help children with cancer. The fund started in the late 1940s for a little boy named Jimmy, an alias to protect the privacy of twelve-year-old Einar Gustafson. He was under the care of Dr. Sidney Farber, a father of modern chemotherapy and founder of the Dana-Farber Cancer Institute. Gustafson's cancer went into remission, and he lived to age sixty-five. He died January 21, 2001, of a stroke.

When the Red Sox won the pennant in 1967, they voted a share of their World Series money to the Jimmy Fund. Ted Williams worked for years behind the scenes for the Jimmy Fund, and the late Cardinal Cushing called the Jimmy Fund the "little people's charity." During Gowdy's years broadcasting Red Sox games he would get sacks of money sent to him for the Jimmy Fund.

Teddy Ballgame and the Jimmy Fund were at the center of one of the most celebrated—and least remembered—moments of the Red Sox '72 season. On August 25 Fenway Park was filled with an overflow crowd—33,551, 172 above capacity—for a game with the Texas Rangers. The pregame festivities focused on a hitting contest to raise money for the Jimmy Fund. Former players and local media types took part, but one notable absentee was Williams, who was the Rangers' manager. Ted was five days short of his fifty-fourth birthday, and the former Splendid Splinter was wearing a warmup jacket to hide his expanding waistline. Fenway fans knew Williams was in the visitors' dugout and began to chant, "We want Ted!" and added to the uproar by slamming their wooden seats up and down. Williams, reluctantly it seemed, headed to the Rangers' bat rack and pulled out a piece of lumber belonging to Tom Grieve. The bat—a W183 model—was familiar to Williams. The "W" stood for Williams and had been his preferred bat.

On the mound was Red Sox pitching coach and former major league hurler Lee "Stinger" Stange. The Stinger lobbed a couple of pitches, and Williams growled to put some heat on them. Stange obliged, and Williams proceeded to lash fifteen line drives on fifteen swings. One drive just missed clearing the wall in right field.

It had been twelve years since Williams retired, twelve years since Teddy Ballgame had stood in the batter's box on the left side of the plate at the

Fens and twisted his body into that familiar and iconic swing—a barber's pole twisting unto itself, someone once observed; twelve years since Red Sox fan John Updike had penned his classic short story—"Hub Fans Bid Kid Adieu"—about Williams's final swing in Fenway, a drive that resulted in a home run. It was a moving tribute to a hero in twilight. On that day, the Kid, as Williams was known, had refused fans' exhortations to come out of the dugout and acknowledge their "We want Ted!" pleadings. Updike understood. "Gods," he wrote, "do not answer letters." In '72 Hub fans had bid the Kid redo, and he responded. Williams, as much a god in Boston as John Kennedy or Paul Revere, had finally answered the letters from the faithful. More than one Fenway fan had tears in their eyes.

What few realized was that Williams had prepared for the day. According to Grieve, Rangers coach Nellie Fox said Williams had spent the previous six weeks in the batting cage in case he decided to hit. "You didn't really think he'd go out there and embarrass himself?" Fox asked Grieve.

Tiant beat Texas 4–0 and was aided by another Luis — Aparicio — the little shortstop hitting what was for him a rare home run. Tiant's shutout was his second in a startling string of four straight. From August 5 through September 7 Tiant won seven straight. A narrow 3–2 loss in New York stopped his streak but only momentarily. Teaming with young catcher Carlton Fisk, who in 1972 became the American League's first unanimous choice for Rookie of the Year honors, Tiant won four straight complete games from September 16 to 29.

Tiant's September 20 win over the Orioles in the second game of a doubleheader was a night to remember. Boston's baseball fans had been subjected that summer to what writer Roger Angell described as a "petty and senseless campaign of vilification" against Kasko by local sportswriters and radio broadcasters. Pushing that feud aside, the Fenway faithful fell in love with their mound maestro, filling the fall air with chants of "Loo-eee! Loo-eee!" as he walked to the bullpen to warm up for his duel with Cuellar.

Red Sox superstar Carl Yastrzemski, who had thrilled the city with a Triple Crown summer five seasons before, said he had never heard anything like it in his life. Forty years later, in June 2012, El Tiante was celebrated at Fenway prior to a game with the Washington Nationals. The chants of "Loo-eee! Loo-eee!" from that long ago September night were replaced by "Louie, Louie," the Kingsmen cover that had climbed the charts in 1963.

Tiant's 4–0 win helped bury the Birds, and nine days later in Baltimore, his 4–2 victory over Palmer, a 21-game winner, ended the Orioles' reign in the East and kept Boston's lead over Detroit at a game and a half with five to play. Just as it had in the Impossible Dream season of '67, revelry rose from the railway bridge and Kenmore Square.

Yaz's 2 homers and 4 RBIs provided the difference in Boston's close—and crucial—late September wins in Baltimore. It was a fast finish following a slow start for the Red Sox star, whose first home run of the season hadn't come until the afternoon of July 22, when he caught hold of a Catfish Hunter offering at Fenway. Gowdy called Yaz's home run drought "one of the most confounding statistics of the year." Yaz hit just 12 homers all season, and his sudden power outage was shared by the rest of the Red Sox. Rico Petrocelli's May 5 homer was the club's first of the season and Boston's first in 220 days. The Red Sox would hit 124 round-trippers in '72, Fisk leading the way with 22 and Reggie Smith following with 21 and a team-leading 74 RBIs. By season's end, Fisk owned a team-best .293 batting average and a Gold Glove.

With Tiant, Smith, and Fisk fronting their charge, the Red Sox took over first place on September 7 and held it for all but one day through October 1. The trading of the 1967 Impossible Dream ace Jim Lonborg to Milwaukee for centerfielder Tommy Harper and starting pitcher Marty Pattin had signaled a transition year in Boston. Sporting the second-worst ERA in the league, the Red Sox could have used Lonborg's 14 victories, 2.38 ERA, and big-game experience, but a far worse trade had occurred in March, when Lyle was sent to the Yankees. It was one of the most impactful deals ever and likely cost the Red Sox playoff berths in 1972 and '77 and a world title in '75 while allowing the Yankees to end their postseason drought in 1976 and world championship drought in '77.

Boston didn't make its move until August but then engaged on the greatest ride the town had seen since Paul Revere—or at least since the

1967 squad. Pattin helped anchor the starting rotation, and Harper set a Red Sox standard for steals that wouldn't be matched until Jacoby Ellsbury came along four decades later. Along with Fisk, the young talent included Dwight Evans, who debuted in September and would be in the lineup for the crucial season-ending series in Detroit; Ben Oglivie; and Cecil Cooper.

From September 1 on the division lead was always less than two games. In the division era that began in 1969, the '72 AL East race ranks with the NL East races in 1973 and '80 as the wildest and more memorable multi-team races of the pre–wild card years. Boston split its next two games with Baltimore and was just a half-game up heading into Detroit, into the Tigers' den, for the final three games of the regular season.

Called "the Corner" because of its location on Michigan and Trumbull Avenues, Tiger Stadium in the last days of the 1972 season was the Hot Corner. Built in 1912 and opened on the same day as Fenway Park in Boston, it was originally called Navin Field for Tigers owner Frank Navin. Following Navin's death in 1935, the stadium was renamed Briggs Stadium in 1938 after new team owner Walter Briggs. The Detroit Lions took up residence in the stadium, which served as their home field through 1974 and was the site of several championship games as well as the annual Thanksgiving Day classic.

In 1961 owner John Fetzer renamed the ballpark one final time: Tiger Stadium. In 1972 the American League was known for its antiquated sites—Fenway Park, Yankee Stadium, Comiskey Park, Memorial Stadium in Baltimore, Cleveland's Municipal Stadium, and Metropolitan Stadium. And Tiger Stadium, with its time-worn facilities, green wooden seats, steel support beams, and obstructed view seats fit into that category. But like its brethren, the Corner was beloved by Detroit fans due largely to its historic feel.

Ty Cobb had played there, and visitors could point to the area around home plate and recall "Cobb's Lake," created on the order of the Georgia Peach, who told groundskeepers to water the dirt so his bunts would die in the mud. The Corner was where Babe Ruth hut his 700th career homer; where Lou Gehrig, the "Iron Horse," voluntarily ended his Iron Man streak;

and where Ted Williams won the 1941 All-Star Game with a dramatic upper-deck homer. Bobby Layne buggy-whipped the Lions to NFL titles there, and Roger Brown, Alex Karras, Joe Schmidt, and Detroit's defense sacked Green Bay's Bart Starr eleven times and ruined Vince Lombardi's perfect season on Thanksgiving Day in '62.

With the American League East the only race still undecided, Tiger Stadium was the center of the baseball universe on Monday, October 2. Detroit sent Lolich, its ace and 21-game winner, to the mound for the series opener. The Tigers by this time were minus the services of Bill Freehan, a career eleven-time All-Star catcher who had suffered a hairline fracture of his thumb and would miss the final eleven games of the regular season.

It was a three-game series reminiscent of prior playoffs to decide the NL title: in 1962 (Giants-Dodgers), '59 (Dodgers-Braves), '51 (Giants-Dodgers), and '46 (Cardinals-Dodgers). Because of the schedule imbalance there was no chance of a one-game playoff such as had occurred between Boston and Cleveland in 1948 and would occur again between the Red Sox and the Yankees in '78 and Houston and Los Angeles in '80.

Much to the delight of the 51,518 customers crammed into Tiger Stadium on October 2, Lolich was immediately staked to a 1–0 lead when Kaline clouted a home run off John Curtis. The Red Sox tied it in the third on Yaz's RBI double, but a base-running mishap may have cost Boston the title. Harper and Aparicio had lined consecutive singles to left when Yaz dug in against Lolich. A line-drive double to center scored Harper, but Aparicio, storming home, slipped and fell on the wet turf while rounding third. Luis retreated to third only to find Yaz flying toward the bag. Yaz, criticized in some accounts for not looking at third base coach Eddie Popowski, was caught in a rundown, and the strangeness of the play was reflected in the putout (8–6–2–5).

Just as strange is that Boston's base-running gaffe on October 2 mirrored a play that cost the Red Sox in a 3–2 decision to Detroit in the season opener on April 15. Again Lolich was on the mound in Detroit, and again the Boston hitters were Harper, Aparicio, and Yaz. Each lined a single in succession, and following an out, Petrocelli stroked a single to center. Harper scored from third, but as Aparicio rounded the bag heading home, he was held up by Popowski. Luis headed back to the bag just as Yaz stormed into third. Just as he would be months later, Yaz was called out, and the Sox lost by a run.

The impact of that play and resulting loss—the Red Sox would have led Detroit by a game and a half—was still being felt six months later, when another Detroit homer, this by Aurelio Rodriguez in the fifth, put the Tigers in front to stay. Rodriguez added two-out, run-scoring singles in the sixth and eighth innings to make it 4–1, and Lolich finished it off, fanning a season-high 15 to put Detroit back in first place by half a game and clinch at least a tie for the title. Lolich may have been dominant enough to survive the early Red Sox rally—he fanned Smith and would have faced Petrocelli had Boston still been batting—but the debate lingers. Aparicio's falling remains part of Red Sox lore.

The Tigers took their title the next night, October 3, the penultimate day of the regular season. Their summer running out, the Red Sox reached Woodie Fryman for a run in the first on Smith's RBI fielder's choice. Whirling and spinning on the mound, Tiant silenced Tiger bats until the sixth. Cash opened the inning with a walk, was sacrificed to second by Horton, and scored on Jim Northrup's line-drive single to right.

Kaline's single to left in the seventh made it 2–1 and ended Tiant's great comeback season. An infield error cost his successor, "Spaceman" Bill Lee, a run. Armed with a 3–1 lead, Fryman pitched into the eighth and then gave way to reliever Chuck Seelbach, who sealed the deal in the ninth when he retired a trio of future stars—Evans and then pinch hitters Cooper and Oglivie—in order.

To borrow from English poet William Blake, these were Tigers, Tigers, burning bright/In the forests of the night. A continuous chant coursed through Tiger Stadium as Harwell made the game's final call: *"Photographers have lined each side of the Tigers' dugout. . . . Here's a fly ball to right field, here comes Kaline. . . . He's got it! The Tigers are the champions of the East!"*

CHAPTER ELEVEN

Dickens wrote that nature gives to every time and season some beauties of its own. This is particularly true in sports. There is something transcendent about the tradition of March Madness, its ecstasy, agony, and frenzy gripping millions of fans; the Masters played amid the sweet scent of Augusta's azaleas in April; the scarred ice of the Stanley Cup playoffs in May; the NBA finals amid the sweltering heat of June; the sacred lawns of Wimbledon in early July; the big-city spotlight of U.S. Open hard courts in mid-September; college football on crisp fall afternoons; and NFL playoff games beneath snowy skies in December and January.

"To everything there is a season," The Byrds sang in 1965, quoting both King Solomon in the Book of Ecclesiastes and Pete Seeger's "Turn, Turn, Turn." A time to every purpose under heaven.

October has been heaven for baseball fans. Many of the game's most hallowed moments have come in October: Babe Ruth's Called Shot and Bobby Thomson's "Shot Heard 'round the World"; Enos Slaughter's "Mad Dash" in Sportsman's Park and Willie Mays' catch in the Polo Grounds; Don Larsen's perfect game in Yankee Stadium and Roy Halladay's no-hitter in Citizens Bank Park; Bill Mazeroski's Game Seven blast in Forbes Field and Game Six homers by Carlton Fisk in Fenway and Joe Carter in Toronto; Bucky Dent's shot over the Green Monster; Reggie Jackson's three home runs in New York and Pablo Sandoval's three homers in San Francisco; Kirk Gibson limping around the bases in Dodger Stadium and Derek Jeter racing across the infield in Oakland to execute his flip toss.

Along with the moments there are the memories: Pepper Martin running wild on the bases; Whitey Ford perfectly still on the mound; Sandy

Koufax's flame-belching fastball; Bob Gibson's scowl; Andy Pettitte's stare; Pedro Martinez's glare; Catfish Hunter's flowing motion; Tim Lincecum's flowing hair; Lou Brock's legs; Dave Parker's arm; Dizzy Dean's windup; Pete Rose's crouch; Mickey Mantle's bloodied pant leg and Curt Schilling's bloody sock; Joe DiMaggio's elegance; Jackie Robinson's defiance; Roberto Clemente's grace.

Be it soft, intoxicating afternoons amid sun-streaked fields or frigid nights beneath the lights, October has been a time to laugh, to weep, to dance, to mourn, to gain, to lose.

Reputations have been gained and lost in October, dynasties born and died. Some players and teams embrace the intense, pressure-cooker moments played out against a backdrop of howling zealots; others turn away from them.

Adding to the anticipation in 1972 was the fact that the A's, Tigers, Reds, and Pirates were terrific teams playing beautiful baseball. They were as keenly aware as the fans that there was something special about playoff baseball. Johnny Bench, still dealing with the spot on his lung found earlier in the 1972 season, was convinced as the Reds prepared to meet the Pirates that a man could be half dead or dying at the beginning of the baseball postseason but that his adrenaline would get him through.

As the Reds gathered in Pittsburgh's Three Rivers Stadium early in the overcast afternoon of Saturday, October 7, for the start of the second season, Bench knew the playoffs had what he called a "different kind of intensity" about them. Joe Morgan, making his first postseason appearance, looked across the Tartan Turf at the Pirates and thought Cincinnati's playing Pittsburgh for the pennant was what baseball was all about.

The Reds had known well before the All-Star break that they were on their way to the Western Division title. The Reds weren't cocky, but they did have the attitude all great teams have. When they took the field, they expected to win. Their opponents, Morgan thought, only hoped to win. They knew some opponents were beaten before the first pitch because they feared the Reds' power, speed, and skill.

The Pirates would not be intimidated, and the Reds knew it. Morgan believed Pittsburgh was the only team in the National League that gave Cincinnati cause for concern. The reigning World Series champions were loaded with big-time talent. In catcher Manny Sanguillen the Bucs had a backstop many believed to be the equal of Bench. The Reds' catcher believed it and many were looking forward to the battle between the two All-Stars. That summer Bench had told Curt Gowdy and Tony Kubek on an NBC *Game of the Week* telecast that Sanguillen was as good a catcher as there was in the National League.

The comparisons between Bench and Sanguillen were centered as much on their differences as their similarities. Bench was an Oklahoman; Sanguillen, Panamanian. Bench was cool; Sanguillen, fiery. Bench was power; Sanguillen, quickness. In 1970 Bench was considered a throwback to the greatest catchers in history—Mickey Cochrane, Bill Dickey, Josh Gibson, Gabby Hartnett, Roy Campanella, and Yogi Berra. But in 1971 Sanguillen rose up to challenge Bench as the best backstop in baseball. Bench had led the Reds to the 1970 World Series; Sanguillen and the Pirates had won it all in '71. Bench had won the Reds' only previous playoff encounter, a three-game sweep in '70.

Sanguillen was the more consistent hitter; Bench, the more powerful. Johnny was a better run producer, but Manny was faster afoot and a superior base runner, a throwback to Cochrane, the Hall of Famer with the Philadelphia Athletics and Detroit Tigers. Teammates called Sanguillen the "Roadrunner"; he was adept at legging out doubles. Both he and Bench could throw well, and while Sanguillen was quicker behind the plate and better at handling balls in the dirt, Bench had a quicker release and a more accurate peg. On a personal level, Manny was married; Johnny was single. Yet whatever their differences, they were alike in many ways. Both were relentless in their work ethic, and both excelled at handling pitchers. From the first, Bench was a take-charge guy behind the plate. Reds pitchers called the rookie "the Little General." Sanguillen, a former infielder and outfielder, took longer to develop, but by 1972 Bucs boss Bill Virdon was telling reporters Sanguillen was as good an all-around catcher as any, including Bench.

By October '72 the two stars shared a mutual admiration. Sanguillen called it an honor to be compared to Johnny Bench. He said Bench was the best catcher he had ever seen. He couldn't watch himself play, so he left it to others to compare. Of the comparisons Bench said if some believed he was the best, he was proud. But if someone said Sanguillen was better, Bench wasn't offended. It made him work harder to make everyone believe he was best.

Pittsburgh had won the East by eleven games; Cincinnati, the West by ten and a half. Bench believed the Bucs the strongest team in baseball, besides the Reds. The Pirates, with 96 victories, and the Reds, with 95, were the two winningest teams in the majors. The Reds knew Pittsburgh's strengths, and that only added to the pressure Cincinnati felt going in despite having won eight of the twelve meetings between the two teams that summer.

The book on the Bucs, as provided in part by Baltimore scout James Russo the previous October, was that runners could take liberties with Pittsburgh's arms in the outfield, the exception being Clemente, who Russo said had the greatest arm in baseball. During the '71 Series Gowdy was moved to comment on Clemente's "beautiful, whirling throws." Base stealers were advised not to take chances with Sanguillen unless they could get a jump on the pitcher. Pirate pitchers had the respect of opponents, Steve Blass being considered the ace. Opposing hurlers concentrated heavily on stopping the Bucs' big hitters yet considered Clemente essentially scout-proof.

The Pirates were a steel-tough team in a steel-tough town, and their home, Three Rivers Stadium, with its cylindrical shape and carpeted interior, mirrored the Reds' Riverfront Stadium. Gowdy thought Three Rivers "magnificent" and Riverfront "breathtaking." Bench said the two clubs shared another similarity. The Battlin' Bucs and Big Red Machine believed these were the two best teams, and it was all going to come down to a best-of-five series. "They knew they were good, and we knew we were good," Pirates pitcher Bruce Kison said.

Unlike its sister stadium in Cincinnati, Three Rivers initially had dirt base paths rather than cutouts around the bags, but Pittsburgh's Tartan

Turf made for truer bounces than did the grass in its predecessor, Forbes Field's "House of Thrills." It also made for some hard sprints in the outfield.

"A ball off this synthetic turf really comes off quickly," Pirates radio voice Bob Prince told NBC viewers during the 1971 World Series. "Anything hit on a line in between those outfielders, they don't run to cut it off; they run to just catch up to it."

Pirates second baseman Dave Cash recalls the artificial turf being "lightning fast." When it got wet, he added, "it got faster." But that helped the Bucs because, as Cash says, "We were a team built for speed. But if you were a team that had guys in the outfield who couldn't run, it was going to be a long day."

The battle for the National League pennant and Ohio River bragging rights commenced under leaden skies. Oddsmakers opted for Cincinnati, but Bench didn't think the Reds should be favored. On the eve of Game One the Reds were still seeking to smooth out some pitching problems—Don Gullett was recovering from hepatitis, and Gary Nolan had developed an abscessed tooth that had to be pulled just prior to the playoffs. On top of that, no one outside the Reds' clubhouse knew how tense this team was. Cincinnati's players had not forgotten the 1970 Fall Classic.

To the 50,476 who strolled across the Fort Duquesne Bridge and into the stadium perched at the confluence of the Ohio, Allegheny, and Monongahela Rivers, the Game One mound matchup offered a startling collision of contrasting styles.

Gullett hailed from Kentucky; Blass, from Connecticut. Gullett was a compact southpaw who Bench said could throw a ball through a car wash and not get it wet. Bench knew what to expect from Gullett: Don would take the mound and deal.

Blass, a right-hander, delivered his pitches in a scattering of arms and legs that ended with a lurching move to his left. The book on Blass was that he was a good but not overpowering pitcher. While Gullett relied primarily on his fastball, Blass's repertoire included sinking and riding fastballs, an excellent slider, and a good curve and change-up. Gullett was all about power. Blass was a control pitcher whose electric slider was effective if he could hit his location. Orioles skipper Earl Weaver had said the previous October that while Blass was quick for the first four or five innings, he would "fold like a suitcase" in the late innings. Blass proved Weaver wrong when he went the distance to win Games Three and Seven.

Blass and Gullett were intelligent pitchers who knew how to win. Because of his health issues in '72, Gullett's 9-10 record was misleading. In '72 the Reds won each of the three games he had pitched against the Pirates. In the 1970 NLCS he had closed out two victories, including the series clincher, in Cincinnati's sweep of Pittsburgh.

Blass had learned a valuable lesson after getting roughed up by San Francisco in the 1971 NLCS opener in Candlestick Park. It was his first postseason appearance, and he thought he had to be a different pitcher in the playoffs, had to be better than in the regular season, when he had gone 15-8 with a 2.58 earned run average and had tied Bob Gibson for the league lead in shutouts with 5. Blass tried to overpower the Giants and was instead overpowered, Tito Fuentes and Willie McCovey hitting home runs in a 5–4 win.

The lesson learned was "Be yourself and go with what got you there." It was a lesson he carried into '72. A 19-8 record with a 2.49 ERA established Blass as the ace of the Pirates' deep staff. He was selected for the All-Star Game, allowed a run in one inning of work, and went on to complete 11 of his 32 starts while averaging seven and a third innings each time out.

Blass considers '72 his most consistent campaign. He had a chance to win twenty in his final start but took a John Milner line drive off the tip of his elbow in the first inning of a game against the Mets. The play scared Blass, who knew that a drive like Milner's could break a bone. Blass went to the hospital for X-rays, and though they revealed no broken bones, he nonetheless had team trainer Tony Bartirome bandage him head to toe prior to meeting the press. When the reporters arrived in the clubhouse, Blass was bound like a mummy. He laughed off his practical joke. He had to entertain; it was what he did.

"Steve had a great sense of humor," Al Oliver recalled. "He was always laughing. But he was also a great competitor and a heck of a pitcher."

Blass believed he might have won twenty-five games in '72 if Bucs boss Bill Virdon had stayed with the four-man rotation predecessor Danny Murtaugh had used. Instead Virdon went to a five-man setup, which was something of a novelty in 1972. Virdon believed Blass would have won the NL's Cy Young award had it not been for Steve Carlton's historic season. As it was, Virdon gave Blass the ball for the opening game of the playoffs, and following his first pitch at 1:11 p.m., he retired Pete Rose on a leadoff fly to left.

As a player and as a fan of the game, Blass enjoyed battling the Big Red Machine. The Reds felt the same way about the Pirates, and Rose would tell Blass in later years that the Reds-Pirates games of the early 1970s represented the best baseball he had ever been around. Going into the playoffs, Pittsburgh didn't just hope it would do well; the Pirates knew they would play well because of their postseason success the year before. They had won the World Series in '71 and felt they matched up favorably with Cincinnati.

"Our team in '72 was better than it was in '71," Oliver stated. "With all the talent we had all Bill had to do was post the lineup, take a nap for seven innings, and then bring in Giusti from the bullpen. The rest was up to us."

Gullett, meanwhile, believed the Reds were also a better team than the one that had swept Pittsburgh in the 1970 NLCS. "We had retooled," he remembered. "We picked up Morgan, [Jack] Billingham, [Cesar] Geronimo, and that translated into becoming the Big Red Machine."

Blass was confident. He had pitched against the Reds for years. He knew what they were capable of doing, knew they were a great fastball-hitting team.

The second batter Blass faced was Morgan, who was making his playoff debut. Cincinnati's little big man took his stance at the plate—hands holding his bat high above his ear, feet spread shoulder width—and began pumping his left elbow, as if he were a cardinal, writer Al Hirshberg noted, rather than a Red. Morgan's distinctive wing-like movement had been taught to him by Nellie Fox in Houston in 1967, when he was still an Astro. Fox believed Morgan could be a better hitter if he kept his left elbow away from his body when he swung. Pumping his left arm was Morgan's method for reminding himself to do that. It served as his trademark: Go-Go Joe never stops moving.

Gowdy said Morgan pumped his arm so furiously that he expected him to "take off and fly right over the infield." Kubek noted that Morgan "flaps [the elbow], keeps it away from his body. He's freer with the bat than having [the elbow] tied up close to his body."

Blass delivered a sinking fastball, and Morgan turned on it, pulling a home run to right-center on the first pitch he saw in a postseason game. The run typified Morgan's season in '72. The Pirates, in particular, were wary of him. He had beat them during the regular season when he had scored from third base on an infield pop-up. Pittsburgh second baseman Rennie Stennett had handled the pop fly easily, almost casually, putting his head down once the ball was in his glove. When Stennett looked up Morgan, was halfway down the line. The startled Stennett threw home, but Go-Go Joe slid in with the winning run.

Bobby Tolan followed Morgan's homer with a lineout to Oliver in center, and Bench continued the Reds' hard hitting with a deep drive to center. Blass was shaken. Is this what they're going to do with my fastball today? he wondered.

Realizing he didn't have his good fastball, Blass switched gears and by his estimation threw the Reds only five fastballs over the next five innings. The pitch to Morgan had been low and away. It had been a good pitch, and Blass knew it. When Morgan hit it out, Blass was surprised. If they hit your best fastball, he thought, you had better try some curves.

Blass relied so heavily on feeding the Machine off-speed pitches—"slop," Blass called it—that it brought an enraged Rose to the top dugout step. "Eat a f—— steak!" Rose shouted at the Reds' tormentor. "Throw the ball like a man!"

When Gullet took the mound in the bottom of the first inning, he began firing what Bench called "all smoke." With legendary umpire Augie Donatelli staring over his shoulder, the Reds' catcher put down one finger—the traditional sign for a fastball—put up his mitt, and listened for what he called "the sizzle."

Bench knew there was no other way for Gullett to get past the Pirates than to overpower them. The Bucs, wearing their home whites with gold and black trim, accepted the challenge. Rennie Stennett stroked a leadoff single to center, then scooted to second base on a passed ball. Oliver followed with a triple to left-center. Gullett got Roberto Clemente looking, but Willie Stargell slammed an RBI double to deep right. After an out, Richie Hebner hammered a single to right to score Stargell for a 3–1 lead.

Cash recalls that Blass had "good stuff." Steve, he said, had a good slider and worked both sides of the plate. Cash added that Pittsburgh's offense took pressure off its pitchers because of the Pirates' ability to score. "They knew if we could hold opponents under five runs, we would win," he says. "We were never out of a game. Once we started hitting, everybody wanted to join the party."

The Pirates teed off on Gullett, but Bench figured the Reds would get the runs back on Blass. It didn't happen. Blass, delivering his pitches from the first-base side of the pitching rubber, had the Reds overstriding and overswinging. When a member of the Machine finally connected—Cesar Geronimo smoked a line drive off the backside of first base ump Ken Burkhart in the fourth inning—the ball was ruled foul. Reds manager Sparky Anderson had had a postseason run-in with Burkhart before, in the 1970 World Series following a pivotal play at the plate.

Burkhart was known for his emphatic calls. Ron Luciano wrote that in umpiring school Burkhart used to stand in front of a mirror for hours practicing "safe" and "out" calls. It would be 3 a.m., Luciano wrote, and Burkhart would be screaming "Safe" and "Out" in front of his mirror. When Burkhart called "Foul ball" on Geronimo's drive, Anderson emerged from the dugout. "Fair ball!" he shouted, then argued and kicked some dirt.

Burkhart took umbrage. "I can run you for that!"

"Why don't you?"

Burkhart did. It was the first time all season Sparky had been run.

"I didn't curse him," Anderson said afterward. "He missed the call, and I let him know it. But I didn't curse him. Sure I kicked dirt. But what's this game coming to when you get kicked out for just that in a playoff game?"

Dust-raising rhubarbs between umpires and managers so common in the seventies are all but a memory in the modern game. Heated disputes between Anderson and Burkhart or Earl Weaver and Steve Palermo are reminders of a dying baseball tradition. Rarely do you see skippers charging from the dugout to kick dirt on home plate or on umpires' shoes or managers flipping their lids and their caps as they go nose-to-nose with the game's arbiters. No more raising a little hell—and a lot of dust—with umps like Larry McCoy. No more spittle-spraying disputes. In today's game managers merely meet with umpires and wait out the replay review. It's more efficient but far less entertaining.

Playoff pressure in Pittsburgh brought heightened intensity from both sides. Virdon and third baseman Hebner argued a foul call the following afternoon with ump Harry Wendelstedt, who was patrolling the left-field line and declared a drive by Tolan to be a double rather than a foul ball; Clemente argued a called third strike with Donatelli.

Uncoiling out of his unique arms-and-elbows-akimbo delivery and firing his out pitch with considerable body language, Blass shut Cincinnati down the rest of the game. He was staked to two more runs in the fifth, when Stennett slapped a single and Oliver followed with a homer. Another fastball that was just too fat, Bench thought, and Oliver crushed it.

Oliver relishes the memories of that Game One meeting of Blass and Gullett, two men he now counts among his close friends. Blass was his teammate; Gullett is close to being his neighbor. Oliver said in 2014:

> I live in southern Ohio and Don lives in Kentucky. We get together and I kid him about Game One. He's a great guy and he was a great competitor. That home run was a fastball down. Nobody could hit Don's high fastball. He was like [Tom] Seaver. You could only hit his pitches if they were down. I remember when they called him up [to the majors]. He blew people away. I thought, "OK, this is the guy everybody's been talking about."
>
> Steve had great control. And he wanted the ball. To me, that's a pitcher, a guy who wants the ball. That's like a hitter who wants to

be at the plate in tight situations. Steve wasn't afraid of being in that situation. I'll tell you honestly, his Game Seven in Baltimore was one of the best pitched games in World Series history, but no one ever talks about it. He was dotting the I's, and it was great to watch him pitch in that game.

Oliver lived in the shadow of Clemente and Stargell, but Tom Seaver thought Oliver the toughest out in the Pirates' lineup. Pittsburgh coaches agreed; they thought it uncanny how often Oliver got good wood on the ball. By Oliver's count, he had just "six or seven hits" in '72 that weren't hit hard.

Virdon believed Oliver's weight loss—a steak-and-grapefruit diet in 1971 helped him go from 220 pounds to 202—had also helped him bulk up his average. He thought Oliver could swing a quicker bat at his lighter weight, and that allowed him to handle the high inside pitches that had previously caused him problems.

Oliver's success didn't surprise him. His father, Al Sr., knew his son would succeed. "My father always had confidence in me," he said. "He felt I would become a big league ballplayer, and I never doubted it either."

Al Sr. was a bricklayer in Portsmouth, Ohio. When his wife died in 1958, he raised his two boys and his girl. In 1964, when Al Jr. was seventeen, he was being scouted by both Pittsburgh and Philadelphia. He signed with Pirates scout Sid Thrift for a small bonus, then found out the Phillies had been prepared to sign him for much more. "I lost $20,000 by not signing with the Phillies," Oliver said.

Oliver lost much more than that on September 14, 1968, the day Al Sr. passed away. It was also the same day Al Jr. was called up to the big leagues.

Oliver was a first-rate first baseman, but when Bob Robertson became ready for the majors, Oliver was switched to center field. When spring training began in '72, Oliver wasn't guaranteed a starting position. Gene Clines had hit .308 in '71, and Oliver needed a solid finish to reach .282.

Oliver had always been a strong finisher but a slow starter. He turned it around in '72, batting over .300 early and stringing together an eighteen-game hitting streak. He also had a sixteen-game hitting streak, and his 89

RBIs were second on the team to Stargell's and highly respectable for a guy who was hitting second in the order.

Oliver's batting number two in the lineup helped make the Pirates number one in the East, and he raked Reds' pitching in the series opener.

Blass worked eight and a third innings in a 5–1 win that took just 1:57 to play. When a reporter asked if he was ready to be taken out when Ramon Hernandez relieved him in the ninth, Blass said that if Virdon had stuck him with a fork, "he'd have known I was done." Blass saw Game One of the 1972 NLCS as a good example of his ability to adapt to a good fastball-hitting team. The Reds trudged to their clubhouse concerned. They had lost the opener, and Morgan though the defeat was doubly tough because Cincinnati had used its best pitcher.

Prince would have agreed. He punctuated his broadcasts with, "We had 'em all the way," one of his many trademark phrases. A broadcaster for the Pirates from 1948 to 1975, Prince was nicknamed "the Gunner" for his quick tongue and colorful commentary. He and Nellie King, a Pirates pitcher from 1954 to 1957, broadcast on KDKA Radio what Prince later referred to as the "Halcyon Days" of Pirates baseball. Prince was an unabashed Bucs fan, and while some listeners loved him and others hated him, all were amused by the Hall of Fame broadcaster and his "Gunnerisms":

"Arriba!": Prince's cry to Clemente to hit one over the wall;
"The bases are FOB": Full of Bucs;
"Kiss it good-bye": The most famous Gunnerism, his much-copied home run call;
"Rug cuttin' time": Crunch time.

It was rug cuttin' time in the American League as well, the Championship Series opening in Oakland later that Saturday. As similar as the Reds and Pirates were, the A's and Tigers were as different as their uniforms—the A's outfitted in California gold jerseys, Kelly green undershirts, and white cleats and the Tigers in their road grays with black and orange trim and black shoes.

Oakland had won the wild West, a division akin to the rebellious American Football League or the NHL's rogue Western Division, which featured fists-first clubs like the ferocious Philadelphia Flyers, who were brandishing their knuckles as the up-and-coming Broad Street Bullies.

Just as the NHL filled its Western Division with expansion teams and assigned Original Six royalty—Montreal, Boston, the New York Rangers, Chicago, Detroit, and Toronto—to the East when the league increased in size in 1967, major league baseball followed suit in 1969 when it split the American and National Leagues into two divisions each. In the AL the top five teams from 1968—Detroit, Baltimore, Cleveland, Boston, and the New York Yankees—were placed in the East, and the bottom five—Oakland, Minnesota, California, the Chicago White Sox, and Washington—were placed in the West.

In each of the ALCS's first three years from 1969 to 1971, no Western champion had won so much as a playoff game. Critics called it the "mild, mild West." Still Oakland entered the playoffs favored to beat Detroit. Experts saw the A's as exciting and young. The Tigers were experienced but aging, a team of holdovers from their 1968 title year who some saw as having grown thick in the waist and long in the tooth. Detroit was dubbed the "Over the Hill Gang," a team of thirtysomethings led by "granddaddy" Al Kaline, who was thirty-seven years old; Norm Cash, also thirty-seven; and thirty-two-year-old hurlers Mickey Lolich and Woodie Fryman. The average age of the Tigers was thirty-one; of the A's, twenty-seven. Noting that Detroit had gone 86-70 that season, A's skipper Dick Williams caustically remarked that the latter number—70—approximated the average age of the Tigers' players.

Williams saw the series as one Oakland should win since most of the Tigers' fire came from a guy who would be spending the series on the sideline—Billy Martin. The managers were as different as their teams. Williams was a strict disciplinarian who had to constantly rein in his swaggering troops. Martin, meanwhile, was willing to raise hell if it meant raising a pennant flag over Tiger Stadium. Billy the Kid's tactics didn't find favor with all of the Tigers. Outfielder Jim Northrup said some of the Tigers got sick and tired of reading Martin's quotes in the Detroit newspapers in which he said, according to Northrup, "I manage good and they play bad."

Some Tigers didn't respect Martin, so they ignored what he said and just played ball. The Tigers were not only ignoring their manager, but they were also ignoring their critics. Tired of reading that they were "ageless" and, as Murray Chass wrote in the *New York Times*, "living it up in the old folks' home," the Tigers roared into the playoffs by winning seven of their final ten games. Like another "Over the Hill Gang" that would win an Eastern Division title in 1972—George Allen's Washington Redskins of the NFC—the Tigers were intent on turning back the clock.

Kaline, a man among men in Motown, had injured his wrist, and writers took to describing the Tiger legend as needing bailing wire and adhesive tape to hold his fingers to his wrist bone. Angered at being written off as an old man, the fifteen-time All-Star caught fire in the closing weeks of the heated division race, going 22-for-44 in the final eleven games and lifting his average thirty-five points to .313.

Kaline helped front a team of tough guys. Left-fielder Willie Horton was one of the strongest men in baseball. Horton's cuts at the plate were sometimes so violent that a swing and miss would cause him to nearly spin around in the batter's box. "That's what you call goin' after it," A's announcer Monte Moore observed. Burly Gates Brown, Ike Brown, Bill Freehan, and Frank Howard were Detroit strongmen as well. Martin tried to add Howard, a World Series hero with the Dodgers in 1963, to the post-season roster, but because he hadn't reported to the club until September 1, he wasn't eligible for the ALCS. Hondo served instead as first base coach.

As the A's and Tigers took the sun-streaked field inside the red, white, and blue bunting-bedecked Oakland Coliseum, they were about to embark on one of the most physically demanding and emotionally exhausting playoff series in history. Three of the five games would be decided by a run; two of the five would need extra innings to decide a winner. There would be a bench-clearing brawl, an infamous bat-throwing incident, player suspensions, thinly veiled threats, cursing and snarling from both sides, errors and questionable plays by catchers playing out of position at second base and the outfield, and a superstar's season-ending injury on a daring steal of home.

The teams had a history. The Tigers had temporarily knocked the A's out of first place in August, but Oakland won the season series 8–4. On August 22 the A's had put Lolich's bid to win his twentieth game on hold when outfielder Angel Mangual had returned to the lineup and hit a three-run homer in Tiger Stadium. Mangual was in the on-deck circle in the seventh inning when Campy Campaneris hit the dirt to avoid being hit in the head by a pitch from reliever Bill Slayback. On the first pitch to Mangual, Blue Moon Odom set sail for third on a steal attempt. Considering the A's were five runs ahead at the time, Martin saw the steal as an attempt by the A's to run up the score. From the Detroit dugout Billy the Kid made a gesture to the mound, and Slayback's next pitch flew behind Mangual's neck. Slayback started in toward the plate in case Blue Moon tried to advance two bases. The enraged Mangual met the pitcher halfway and drove his right fist into Slayback's eye.

All hell broke loose. Martin stormed from the dugout and straight for Mangual. Williams cut Martin off and held him back. The Tigers' Willie Horton rumbled in from center field and flattened Epstein with a right hand. In a bizarre scene foreshadowing the Pedro Martinez–Don Zimmer dust-up in the 2003 ALCS, aging A's coach Jerry Adair and Detroit catcher Duke Sims flailed at each other along the third base line. Mangual landed on top of Slayback; Campy, teammate Joe Rudi, and Tigers pitcher Tom Timmerman landed on top of Mangual. Detroit's Ike Brown slugged the A's Dave Duncan from behind; Oakland coach Irv Noren had his eye blackened by a punch. When Darold Knowles reached into a pile to try and pull players out, the immensely strong Horton grabbed the A's reliever and tossed him like a salad.

Detroit also had a history with Williams, dating back to when his Red Sox finished a game ahead of the Tigers in the terrific 1967 pennant race.

The possibility of more fireworks in the playoffs didn't pack the house in Oakland as it had in Pittsburgh. Fewer than thirty thousand were in attendance for Game One in the Coliseum, whose infield still bore the yardlines from the Raiders' hosting of San Diego on October 1. Most northern California fans favored the college football games that day. John McKay's top-ranked USC Trojans—one of the great teams in history—were at Stanford, which had represented the Pacific 8 in the Rose Bowl the two previous seasons and beaten Big 10 champions Ohio State and Michigan, and the University of California was hosting Woody Hayes's rampaging Buckeyes.

As much promise as the NLCS matchup of Gullett and Blass had held, Lolich versus Hunter in the AL promised something better. The two aces had combined for 43 wins in '72, and both were 20-game winners for the second straight season.

Hunter and Lolich began the game in brisk fashion, each retiring the side in order in the first. Cash led off the top of the second, and in an era when teams were allowed to use their own broadcasters in the LCS, Tigers announcers George Kell and Larry Osterman provided the call on WJBK-TV Channel 2 in Detroit:

> **Kell**: *There's a long drive, well-hit, deep to right, way back. . . . It's gone! A home run for Cash! That was a line drive home run. He really laced it into the seats in right and the Tigers have taken a one-nothing lead.*

The homer was Cash's first since August 13, but the A's answered in the third. Campaneris worked a 1-1 walk and sped to third on Matty Alou's single to right. Rudi launched a sacrifice fly to Northrup in center, scoring Campy with the tying run.

Working in and out and up and down, tugging on his oversized cap between pitches and spotting his slider, Hunter retired ten straight from the fourth into the seventh. The hard-throwing Lolich matched the Cat pitch for pitch. Mickey could be overpowering or he could finesse hitters to death. "He's a *pitcher*," Kubek said admiringly, and Gowdy agreed, noting that Lolich's pitches were always swerving, darting, dancing. The lefty's pitches had late life; very rarely did a Mickey Lolich fastball break the same way.

Lolich came from the side with pitches that would dart in against left-handed hitters, and then he came in over the top with offerings that sailed in on the fists of a right-handed hitter. Either way his pitches moved in the strike zone all the time. Facing Baltimore's Brooks Robinson earlier in the season, Lolich had delivered a fastball that looked to be about a foot inside as it darted toward the Orioles' hitter, only to come back and almost into the strike zone. "A live arm," Kubek observed. On top of that, Gowdy called Lolich "a mean competitor on the mound."

Some umpires found it difficult to call a game pitched by Lolich because of the late movement on his pitches. Bill Kinnamon, who umpired American League games from 1960 to 1969, thought that just as soon as he'd made up his mind on the call, the Lolich slider would bust in there. Lolich could also make his pitches ride a bit. Kinnamon knew no one could throw a pitch hard enough to make it jump up—though some hitters swore Sandy Koufax could—but Kinnamon knew there were a few who threw hard enough to make their pitches ride. When a ball is thrown, gravity takes over, and the pitch follows a certain plane. But Lolich's pitches broke from the plane and rode up. The ball looked like it was going down, but it wasn't. If a hitter made up his mind on a Lolich pitch 8–10 feet from home plate, he would probably miss it. The same was true of umpires. Kinnamon eventually could call a Lolich game very well. It was, he thought, a matter of timing.

Emmett Ashford was one umpire who timed Lolich well. An AL ump from 1966 to 1970, Ashford was behind home plate on one occasion when Lolich had a no-hitter heading into the middle innings. Mickey was throwing his roundhouse curve, and Ashford would watch the ball come around sharp and catch the plate right at the outside front corner. Lolich knew the pitch was a strike, and he also knew most umpires didn't call it as such. Emmett, he said at the time, was the first one who did.

By contrast, most umps found it very easy to call a Catfish Hunter–pitched game. Prior to Game Two of the 1977 World Series, home plate umpire Ed Sudol of the National League was worried because it would be the first time he umpired a game the Cat pitched. AL ump Nestor Chylak, a Hall of Fame umpire and veteran of bigger wars than those found on the baseball field—he had been in the Battle of the Bulge and had won the Silver Star and Purple Heart—calmed Sudol's fears. "Ed, you can sit in a rocking chair and call his pitches," said Chylak, who worked the 1972 ALCS. "He has beautiful control."

Lolich and Hunter were aided in Game One by dazzling defense: Reggie's running catch in the outfield; Cash's nifty scoop in the dirt at first base of Aurelio Rodriguez's low throw from third; Ted Kubiak's roaming far to his right to make a diving stop and then throwing from his knees to rob Cash of a hit.

The game was still tied at one in the ninth when Sims, playing for Bill Freehan, doubled to right. With the left-handed Cash coming up, Williams made the move. Vida Blue strode in from the bullpen to relieve Hunter, who had pitched four-hit ball.

Martin ordered Cash to lay down a sacrifice bunt to advance the runner to third. Cash did, and Bando fielded the perfect bunt and fired to first, but the ball was dropped by Kubiak, who was covering the bag. Williams waved in Rollie Fingers to face the right-handed Horton. Martin, his managerial wheels grinding, immediately brought in left-handed hitter Gates Brown. Brown fouled out to Sal Bando, and Martin signaled Northrup to execute a suicide squeeze. Northrup fouled it off, then bounced to Kubiak.

A's announcer Monte Moore called the critical play: *"Count of three-and-one, Fingers throwing. . . . Northrup bounces toward Kubiak, he's got it. . . . Over to Campaneris at second. . . . One. . . . Over to first, double play!"*

Through the ninth and tenth Fingers didn't allow a ball to leave the infield. With one out in the Tigers' eleventh, Kaline stepped to the plate, and Kell provided the call: *"Long fly ball to deep left field. Joe Rudi going back. . . . It's gone! The old pro, Al Kaline, has staked the Tigers to a 2–1 lead!"*

Kaline's homer—his fourth in five games—landed almost directly in front of a banner reading, "Beware the Tigers." Kubek thought Kaline had homered despite a good pitch from Fingers. "One ball, two strikes, [Fingers] threw a perfect pitch, low and outside, a breaking ball, and [Kaline] hit it for a home run," Kubek said.

Lolich headed to the hill in the eleventh to lock it down. He had retired seven straight before Bando, choking up on the bat, pulled a ground single to left and Odom came in to pinch-run for him. Epstein smacked an opposite-field single to left, and Williams sent Mike Hegan in to pinch-run for Epstein. With the right-handed Gene Tenace up, Martin emerged from the Detroit dugout and lifted Lolich for right-handed reliever Chuck Seelbach.

Tenace squared and neatly executed a bunt that was fielded by Rodriguez, who threw to shortstop Ed Brinkman, covering the bag at third, for the force out on Odom. Brinkman's rapid-fire throw to first for the double play pulled Dick McAuliffe—covering for Cash on the play—off the bag. Replays showed McAuliffe tagging Tenace on the back of the right thigh as he crossed the bag. When Chylak, the umpire at first base, signaled Tenace safe, McAuliffe raised his arms in disbelief, and the Tigers roared in protest.

Williams sent lefty Gonzalo Marquez to pinch-hit for second baseman Dal Maxvill. An inning before, Marquez had told Campaneris in Spanish, "I win the game if I get to pinch hit." Marquez's presence in the lineup was ironic since he was with the A's only because Jackson's injury in August had required a left-handed hitting replacement. The twenty-six-year-old native of Venezuela had made his major league debut on August 11 and thus had been in an Oakland uniform just a month and a half. In that time he had hit .381 (8 for 21).

Since Maxvill wasn't much of a hitter—he batted .250 that season—and was a right-handed bat, Williams figured he'd give Gonzo a chance. With the count 1-1, Marquez fouled off the next five pitches.

> **Moore**: *Seelbach ready. . . . Ground to right field, base hit! Here comes Mike Hegan rounding third, he's heading home! Tenace going to third, it's gonna be close. . . . The ball gets away! He's coming in, he scores! The A's win!*

Kaline fielded the ball in right and seeing he had no chance for a play at the plate on Hegan, threw to third to get Tenace. Holding down his bright green batting helmet with his right hand like a commuter holding his hat while trying to catch a train, Tenace tore around the base paths and belly flopped into third. Kaline's peg arrived at the same time, skipped past Rodriguez, and rolled into the seemingly endless environs of foul territory that is one of the Coliseum's trademarks.

Gowdy told viewers Kaline had uncorked a great throw, but it was "one of those tough plays when the ball and the man arrive at third base at the same time."

Tenace took off for home plate, where a waiting Hegan leapt four feet in the air in celebration of the A's dramatic 3–2 win. Kaline was charged with an error on the throw, but as bad as he felt in the aftermath, Eddie Brinkman felt worse. Choking up on his wide-handled bat, he had doubled off Hunter in the eighth. But the Detroit shortstop's feet and legs were numb. He had ruptured a lumbar disk that would require surgery, and he would not play again in '72.

Williams thought it funny in the aftermath that people were looking at his pinch-hitting Marquez and saying, "Oh, that Williams, what a genius!" But Williams knew his decision had nothing to do with genius. He needed a guy who could put the bat on the ball, and Gonzo could do that.

Oakland had seized the series lead with a come-from-behind rally, but the Reds needed no such drama to tie the NLCS the following afternoon in Pittsburgh. Franco Harris, Joe Greene, Terry Bradshaw, and the rest of the Steel Curtain Steelers were in Dallas that Sunday to take on the defending Super Bowl champion Cowboys, and because of a conflict with its NFL schedule, NBC did not televise Game Two of the NLCS. Steel Town fans filled Three Rivers Stadium for a second straight afternoon as a crowd of 50,584 filed into the big ballpark on a splendid sun-lit afternoon.

At 1 p.m. Pirates' 13-game winner Bob Moose fired the first pitch to Rose. The Bucs' right-hander was 0-2 against Cincinnati in the '72 regular season and was roughed up by the Reds in Game Two, failing to record an out while surrendering four runs in the first.

Michaels made the series of calls that all but decided the game in the opening inning:

Three-two [pitch] to Rose is lined into right field for a base hit, that's his third hit in two games. Roberto Clemente gets it back in and the Reds have the leadoff man aboard.

Three-one pitch to Morgan is batted in the hole, right side and through for a base hit. Rose around second, on his way to third, the throw is not in time.

Tolan lines it down the left-field line. . . . It is a fair ball, all the way to the corner! Rose scores, Morgan scores, Tolan has at least a double.

Full count on Bench. . . . The 3-2 pitch is lined into right-center field, Clemente on the run, can't get it. It's up the gap and Roberto cuts it off at the warning track.

Moose with the sign and the 1-2 pitch to Perez is swung on and grounded fair, inside first and down the right field line for extra bases! Tolan scores, Bench scores, Perez has a double and [it's] four-nothing Reds with nobody out in the first inning.

The Bucs battled back and chased Jack Billingham with single runs in the fourth and fifth innings. Continuing his hot hitting, Oliver ignited the comeback when he doubled and scored in the fourth. Clemente followed with an RBI groundout to Morgan in the fifth, and the Pirates cut their deficit to 4–3 when they reached reliever Tom Hall for a run in the sixth on Sanguillen's double and Cash's single.

Pittsburgh would have done more damage had it not been for Hall's superlative performance. Nicknamed "the Blade" because of his 6-foot-1, 150-pound physique, the lanky lefty was a hard thrower who could also break off a good curve. He had playoff experience, having been used as a starter and reliever for Twins' teams that won divisional titles in 1969–70.

Acquired by the Reds for the 1972 season, Hall thrived in Anderson's "Captain Hook" managing style. He had gone 10-1 with eight saves in the regular season and entered Game Two in an unenviable spot—two on, two out and a 2-0 count on Stargell. Hall froze the Pirate slugger with a called third strike and went on to finish the game.

Hall had had 134 strikeouts in 124.1 innings pitched that season and in mid-July had owned the best strikeouts-to-innings pitched ratio in the National League. "Any time you strike out more men than innings pitched," Gowdy remarked, "you've got some stuff."

On an NBC *Game of the Week* that summer Hall told a national audience his strategy upon entering a game: "You're thinking of the situation. You come in and try to get a ground ball, try to get them to hit into a double play if it's that situation. Then, too, if you're not having good stuff in the bullpen it's always going through your mind that you'll have better stuff when you get out there on the mound."

Hall had plenty of good stuff for the Reds in '72, and his contributions to the club continued through the rest of the postseason. He would hurl three innings of one-hit relief in Cincinnati's comeback victory in the pennant-clinching Game Five, save Game Six in the World Series, and overall toss eight and a third scoreless innings of relief against the A's. Anderson always maintained that had he used Hall in late relief in Game Four in Oakland, he was certain the A's comeback would have been blunted and the Reds would have won the Series in six games.

Morgan backed Hall's heroics in Game Two of the NLCS in Pittsburgh by slamming his second homer in as many days. The Pirates were trailing by two in the ninth, and as the Gunner was wont to say, were "a bloop and a blast" from tying the game. Instead Cincinnati won 5–3, Hall working the final four and a third innings to earn the victory. The Reds had accomplished what they wanted: a split in Pittsburgh. Cincinnati took comfort in the fact that the best two out of three for the pennant would take place in Riverfront Stadium.

While Game Two in Pittsburgh had the look of a rout early on, Game Two in Oakland was nothing less than a rumble. Right-hander Blue Moon Odom and lefty Woody Fryman, both of whom had enjoyed comeback seasons in '72, were the starters. Fryman had been 4-10 with the Phillies before being dealt to Detroit, where he went 10-3.

The Tigers, Gowdy said, could not have won their division without Fryman. Fryman had an arthritic left elbow and was pitching with pain. He had been having difficulties early in games and needed time to get in a groove. He had a fastball that rode away from right-handed hitters and a good slider. Fryman and battery mate Duke Sims had opened the season in the National League, Fryman with the Phils and Sims with the Dodgers. When Matty Alou, who had hit .314 with the Cardinals earlier that summer, stepped in as the A's number two hitter, the trio of National Leaguers prompted Gowdy to remark that teams often went to the opposing league to pick up players for the pennant drive.

Just as Fryman helped Detroit, Alou did the same for Oakland. The A's were short one good bat in the outfield to go with Rudi and Jackson, and Alou filled the void in the batting order. Gowdy called Alou a professional hitter. Moore labeled him a magician with the bat.

On a muggy and humid but sun-soaked day in the Bay Area, Blue Moon set the side down in order in the first. Campaneris, outfitted along with his teammates in the "wedding gown" white pullovers the A's wore on Sundays, opened the Oakland half with a single off Fryman. Unlike many base stealers, Campaneris preferred running against southpaws as opposed to right-handers because he could see the ball better. As if to prove his point, Campy swiped second and then third and scored on Rudi's single.

Kubek compared Campaneris to Dodgers great Maury Wills as base runners whose dash and daring put tremendous pressure on the defense. Kubek spoke from experience. As the Yankees shortstop in the 1963 World Series against Los Angeles, Kubek had experienced firsthand the tension and anxieties Wills inflicted on defenses. Campy had the Tigers infielders moving all the time; Dick McAuliffe, his opposite at short with Brinkman sidelined, was sneaking up behind Campaneris to keep him close. But in doing so, McAuliffe was also out of position for a ball hit toward short. Campy's steals of second and third brought the edgy Tiger infield in close to cut off the run. But that allowed Rudi to slap his run-scoring single past Aurelio Rodriguez at third. Had the slick-fielding Rodriguez been playing at his normal depth, he would likely have had time to field Rudi's scorching grounder and throw to first for the out.

Is there another sport, Kubek wondered aloud, where a little man like Campaneris could inflict such damage? Martin knew it. Tigers pitchers were under orders to keep Campy under control. In the fifth, singles by George Hendrick, Campaneris, and Alou made it 2–0 and finished Fryman.

Chris Zachary's wild pitch allowed Campy to race home with another run. Jackson jockeyed the count, and Kubek made the call on Reggie's slashing drive to left-center: *"Base hit, could be extra bases. . . . Here comes Alou. . . . Rudi roaring into third base, he's gonna score. . . . Jackson will be given a double, two RBIs!"*

Armed with a five-run lead, Odom was cruising. He allowed just three hits in going the distance and did not allow a runner from the fifth inning on, retiring 16 straight to close out a 5–0 win. He faced 29 batters, just 2 over the minimum, and did not walk a batter in the course of throwing 101 pitches.

Yet life hadn't always been so good for Johnny Lee Odom.

Gowdy spoke of Odom's comeback from two gunshot wounds in the off-season and from bone chips in his pitching elbow in 1970. Blue Moon had grown up playing baseball in the middle-class African American neighborhood of Macon, Georgia. His father died when Johnny Lee was just five years old, leaving his mother, Florence, to raise two older daughters and her son.

While in grade school, Odom was nicknamed "Blue Moon" by a classmate who thought his round face resembled a moon. By the time Odom was in the ninth grade, he was already pitching for the Ballard Hudson High School varsity. In four years of prep ball Odom went 42-2 with eight no-hitters and numerous one-hitters. He twice led his team to the Georgia state championship and capped his career with an amazing performance: a 19-strikeout no-hitter in the seven-inning state title game. At the time there were twenty major league teams, and eighteen of them sent scouts to Macon.

A's owner Charlie Finley won out after offering a bonus of $75,000 and helping Florence cook a Southern soul meal of fried chicken, black-eyed peas, and greens and then attending Johnny Lee's high school graduation.

San Francisco offered Odom $40,000, and unlike the A's at the time, the Giants were perennial contenders for the pennant. Odom, however, knew the A's needed pitching and figured to get to the majors more quickly.

He figured right. In less than three months the nineteen-year-old Odom made his major league debut for the A's on September 5, 1964. Facing an aging but still scary Yankees lineup of Tony Kubek, Bobby Richardson, Roger Maris, Mickey Mantle, Joe Pepitone, Tom Tresh, Elston Howard, and Clete Boyer, Odom surrendered six runs and was gone after two innings. His next start, on September 11, went much better. He two-hit the Orioles in an 8–0 complete-game win and always considered the game a no-hitter since he said both hits—infield singles—were questionable calls by the official scorer at Memorial Stadium.

Odom spent the next two seasons seeking better control of his sinking fastball and meeting with only mild success. In 1967 he was stunned when A's manager Alvin Dark sent him to the minors. At the time the demotion was the biggest jolt of Odom's career, but it also turned into a blessing. A's minor league pitching coach Bill Posedel changed Odom's windup and delivery.

Kubek, who had been the first hitter Odom faced in the majors, spoke of Blue Moon's transition from a thrower to a hitter: "He's changed his style of pitching since he came up with the A's," Kubek told NBC viewers. "He was a very hard thrower. . . . He has an assortment now of different pitches—a sinkerball; what they call a 'slop curve' that he likes to use a lot; a good slider."

Odom returned to the majors and in 1968 one-hit the Orioles—Davey Johnson had a broken-bat single with two outs in the ninth—and the Senators. Opposing hitters said hitting a Moonball—Odom's heavy, sinking heater—was like trying to hit a sinking shot put. Blue Moon complemented his sinker with a rising temper. By his own admission he was not a nice guy on the mound.

Like many of the A's, he had a history of bad blood with the Tigers. In a 1967 game Detroit's hitters, especially McAuliffe, thought Blue Moon was throwing too many brush-back pitches, and a mass brawl erupted. Odom said he brushed McAuliffe back after he had stolen home with a five-run lead.

The next season Odom had another throwdown with the Tigers. It was said Blue Moon was seen by an umpire running in place on McAuliffe's chest and stomach. Odom shrugged it off. They just met on the field, he said.

They met again on the afternoon of Sunday, October 8, and McAuliffe went 0-for-4 as the Tigers' leadoff hitter. Watching from the dugout, Hunter thought Game Two belonged to Blue Moon. But Odom's outstanding effort was lost in the shadows of Campaneris's at-bat in the seventh.

Leading off against Lerrin LaGrow—the fourth of five pitchers Martin called on that day and a twenty-three-year-old who Williams thought was a young man "with the shakes"—Campy dug in while Moore called what became one of the most bizarre at-bats in baseball history:

> *Here's Campy Campaneris to lead it off for the A's and all the little roadrun-ner has done today is have three hits in three at-bats. . . . Lerrin LaGrow is on the mound and he's winding. Here's the pitch to Campy. . . . Look out! It hit him right in the leg! Campy is mad and he throws the bat at him! . . . Campaneris was hit in the leg by a pitch and he threw his bat at the pitcher. . . . Billy Martin is having to be restrained.*

Kell made the call on the Tigers' television station: *"Excitement aplenty! The umpires are holding Billy Martin, he's trying to get to Campaneris."*

Campaneris had tried to jump out of the way of the pitch, but it hit him on the left ankle. Williams heard the ball bounce off the bone. A review of the video shows the force of the blow spinning Campy around. When he stood up, Campaneris stared out at LaGrow for a second and then reached back and whipped his bat toward the mound. Williams heard someone on the Oakland bench scream, "No!" The bat spun like a helicopter blade, and A's writer Ron Bergman recalled the 6-foot-5 LaGrow prudently shrinking to something closer to 3-foot-5 as the Louisville Slugger sailed past his head.

Nestor Chylak engulfed the 160-pound Campaneris in his left arm and chest protector. (American League umpires at the time wore their chest protectors outside their dark blue blazers; NL umpires wore their chest protectors beneath their blazers.) Chylak initially held Campaneris back from charging the mound but then had to protect the A's shortstop from angry Tigers players climbing over each other to get to Campy.

It was the most deplorable scene in baseball since Giants pitcher Juan Marichal, facing fellow ace Sandy Koufax, suddenly started hitting Dodger catcher John Roseboro in the head with his bat in a 1965 game. Campaneris heaving his bat at LaGrow is a scene that would be repeated in reverse in the 2000 World Series, when Yankees pitcher Roger Clemens picked up Mike Piazza's shattered bat barrel and flung it over the first base line. Piazza was running toward first and believed Clemens had thrown the bat at him.

Clemens claimed he thought the bat shard was the ball, and when he realized it wasn't, he threw it away. Most people didn't see it that way, just as the A's didn't believe LaGrow hadn't thrown his fastball at Campy's ankle on Martin's orders. Williams figured Campaneris was driving Detroit's defense crazy. He looked across the field at Martin and saw his opposite cussing. Williams knew that Martin, like all managers, loved to win in small ball fashion but hated to lose that way. Williams knew Martin wanted to slow Campy down. By getting the A's sparkplug so mad that he might be stopped by suspension, Williams figured Martin had more than accomplished his mission.

Prior to his two-run double Jackson had been decked twice by high heat thrown at his head by southpaw reliever Fred Scherman. The bad blood between the teams had boiled over, and following Campy's flinging of his bat, Martin had to be restrained by both third base umpire Larry Barnett and first base ump John Rice. Detroit infielder Ike Brown found Campaneris's bat, snapped it into pieces, and hurled the offending lumber toward the Oakland dugout. Martin screamed at Campy to come out and fight him and then screamed at the rest of the A's to come out and fight his team. Oakland's players stood on the dugout steps and shook their heads. Epstein thought Martin's challenge was Billy's way of firing up his club, which looked listless against Odom.

Chylak ejected Campaneris and LaGrow, and order was finally restored. Battling Billy, however, was still fuming afterward.

Martin asked for Campaneris to be suspended. He said throwing a bat was as gutless as anything he'd ever seen in baseball. And did you see those A's, he asked reporters. They didn't want to fight. Bando and the A's believed, like Shakespeare's Falstaff, that discretion was the better part of valor. Oakland had nothing to gain and everything to lose by fighting, Bando said.

American League president Joe Cronin told reporters he had not yet reached a decision on whether to suspend Campaneris, but in truth he already had. Williams knew the A's would lose Campy. Cronin was just waiting to inform Campaneris first that he was out for the remainder of the series and would be fined $500.

On the charter plane to Detroit, the star shortstop was subdued. "I no try to hit him with the bat," the thirty-year-old Cuban muttered in broken English. "I can hit him with it if I throw sidearm rather than overhand. I only try to make him scared. I try to let him know not to do it next time."

Forty years later, on October 9, 2012, the A's and Tigers were again battling each other in the playoffs, and Campaneris was back at the Oakland Coliseum throwing—not a bat, but the ceremonial first pitch prior to Game Three.

As the Mustache Gang winged its way to Motown, Williams tried to tune out the Dixieland Band Finley had brought on board the World Airways charter. The A's departure had been delayed an hour due to a bomb threat, and all Williams could think was that despite Oakland's 5–0 win, there was one basic truth about the Mustache Gang: an A's game didn't even have to be close to be full of controversy.

CHAPTER TWELVE

He was a free-swinging, free-spirited player with an ever-present smile.

"Manny being Manny" was popularized by the polarizing Ramirez in the twenty-first century, but in the same summer the future star of the Indians, Red Sox, and Dodgers was born, another Manny was being Manny in Pittsburgh.

Pirates catcher Manny Sanguillen may have labored in the shadows of his more famous teammates and Cincinnati counterpart in 1972, but it was the durable Panamanian who proved to be the difference in Game Three of the National League Championship Series.

Curt Gowdy referred to Sanguillen as the "smiling Panamanian," but Roberto Clemente cautioned observers not to let Sanguillen's syrupy smile fool them. Manny may have been a good-natured needler in the Pirates' riotous clubhouse, but he took the game very seriously. Smiling doesn't always tell everything, Clemente said. Some guys can smile all season and never help the club. Sanguillen had made himself, in Roberto's opinion, the best catcher in baseball in 1972. "He has done it," Clemente added, "by hard work."

Gowdy agreed and lauded Sanguillen for playing aggressive baseball. While the sports world buzzed about Bert Campaneris's bat-throwing incident and the A's and Tigers took a travel day on Monday, October 8, the Pirates and Reds renewed hostilities in Riverfront Stadium. It was the third time in the four-year history of the league championships that the National League had declined a day off for travel. Only in 1971, when the NLCS had opened in San Francisco before shifting to Pittsburgh, had the league scheduled a travel day.

If any player on the Pirates or Reds would be least affected by the lack of time off, it would be Sanguillen. Willie Stargell said if there was one word to describe Sanguillen, it was "durable." Sangy, as his teammates called him, was so strong that he never seemed to tire despite playing the toughest position on the field.

Born and raised in Colon, Panama, Sanguillen was a surprising twenty years old when he began playing baseball. He had grown up playing basketball and soccer and doing some boxing. He had won five of his seven fights and was teaching in a Bible school in Panama when he was asked to play baseball.

Pirates super scout Howie Haak heard of him, and when he saw him, Sanguillen was getting playing time in the outfield, at third base, and at first base. Moments after signing Sanguillen to a contract worth less than $5,000, Haak told him, "You're a catcher."

Manny being Manny, he agreed. "When Howie say I'm a catcher, I say to him, 'Okay, I'm a catcher,'" Sanguillen said.

Eight years passed, and by 1972 Sanguillen had risen to the lofty status as one of the best backstops in the business at a time when guys named Bench, Munson, Freehan, and Fisk were bringing glamour to the gritty position.

Not that the transition came easily to Sanguillen. He couldn't speak English when he began playing at Batavia in the New York–Penn League in 1965. Two years later he joined the Pirates for thirty games, but in 1968 Manny was back in the minors—Columbus in the International League. He was still learning, and the process was impeded at times by the language barrier.

Sanguillen learned with a little help from his friends. When he arrived in Pittsburgh, Manny Mota helped him understand English. Danny Murtaugh helped Manny in the minor leagues; Johnny Pesky helped in Columbus. Clemente, Stargell, Matty Alou, Joe Brown, and others helped Manny make it big in the majors.

By 1972 Pirates manager Bill Virdon could see how Manny had improved in all facets of the game. The biggest change, Virdon opined, was his base running. Sanguillen was not a good base runner when he joined the Bucs.

Because of his inexperience he didn't know how to take advantage of his speed. He routinely ran singles into outs trying for two bases and ran doubles into outs trying for triples.

Sanguillen began catching regularly for the Pirates in 1969, and it was on-the-job training for a guy who wouldn't catch fewer than 128 games in any of his first full seven seasons. He didn't know the tendencies of opposing hitters, didn't know who hit the fastball or who hit the curve. In some cases, he didn't even know the names of the hitters. By '72 he had a mental book on every batter in the National League.

Steve Blass thought Sanguillen deserved all the credit in the world for overcoming as much as he had. The Pirates ace once recalled that when Sanguillen first arrived in the bigs, he'd leave the calling of games up to the pitcher. Bruce Kison recalled that as a young pitcher who didn't yet know opposing hitters, "I was going to rely on Sangy. We shared the game." The only request Manny made of Pirate pitchers was to keep runners close. If they did, Sanguillen felt his arm was strong enough to throw out any man in baseball.

Lou Brock didn't dispute Sanguillen's claim. The St. Louis speedster said Sanguillen was the toughest catcher in the league to run on. Dave Cash recalls Sangy having "some kind of throwing arm. He threw lasers and the ball was on a line. He didn't get a lot of credit because he's Panamanian and didn't speak a lot of English. But we knew how good he was. He was as good as any catcher."

It wasn't just Sanguillen's arm that had the respect of opponents. The Orioles' scouting report for the 1971 World Series warned of the damage Sanguillen could do with his bat. "Every scout who made out a report on the Pirates said the same thing: 'Sanguillen is as tough an out as Clemente,'" Orioles scout Jim Russo said then.

Sanguillen caught every inning of the seven-game Series and battered Baltimore's four 20-game winners and celebrated staff for 11 hits in 29 at-bats, a .379 average. One year later he hit over .300 against the Reds pitching, and it was Game Three where Manny being Manny paid off big for the Bucs.

Cincinnati struck first. Joe Morgan resumed his Red-hot play, reaching Pirates starter Nelson Briles for a run-scoring single to right in the third, then stealing second and scoring on Bobby Tolan's single to center field.

Donning his mustard-gold matte-finished batting helmet—achieved by flocking, a process in which tiny particles of fiber are applied on a surface to create a velvet-smooth texture and mimic the effect of a cloth cap—Sanguillen started Pittsburgh's comeback in the top of the fifth with a leadoff home run against Gary Nolan.

In the seventh, Sanguillen's single to center off reliever Pedro Borbon put Richie Hebner in scoring position, and Rennie Stennett's run-scoring single punched through the right side off Clay Carroll tied the game at 2. Stennett's single was a freak play, the ball taking a high bounce off the Astroturf and over the head of a surprised Perez at first base.

With one out in the eighth and the bases "FOB," in the words of the Gunner, Bob Prince, Sanguillen topped a slow roller and then legged it out while pinch runner Gene Clines scored the eventual winning run.

The blown save was unusual for Carroll, a fireman who was accustomed to putting out fires. To Sparky Anderson, Carroll was "Super Hawk," swooping down on opponents in the late innings with his good sinker and slider. Carroll's approach was a no-nonsense one, as he told an NBC television audience that season: "When I come in with the bases loaded or a couple of guys on base, the tying run or go-ahead run is on base so all I've got on my mind is to get that ball down and try to get them to hit a double-play ball."

Stennett, the Pirates' leadoff hitter, was also one of the heroes in Game Three. Along with his two hits and RBI, Stennett made the defensive play of the game with a perfect peg to the plate that nailed Bench when the Reds catcher was attempting to score on a Cesar Geronimo fly out in the fourth.

Virdon called it the "biggest play of the playoffs" to that point, and it surprised Cincinnati third base coach Alex Grammas. "I honestly didn't think they'd try to make a play on Johnny," he told reporters in the Reds' quiet clubhouse.

Aided by Stennett's startling putout, Briles blanked the Reds through the middle innings with his palm ball, slider, curve, and sinker. Nellie's fall-away delivery occasionally left him face down on the first base side of the mound. "He does that for no reason," Gowdy told viewers during the 1971 World Series. "He can't explain it himself. Sometimes he just collapses out there."

A veteran of postseason play with St. Louis in 1967–68 and Pittsburgh in '71, Briles later attributed his falling off the mound to the lowering of the hill in 1969 from fifteen inches to ten following the "Year of the Pitcher." It was, he said, the product of his having to reach back for more. He wasn't big enough at 5-foot-11, 195 pounds to get a lot of push off the lower mound. He thought the new rule also affected his overhand curve and, minus the leverage of the mound, took a couple of miles off of his 90–92 m.p.h. fastball as well.

Briles worked six innings and left trailing 2–1. Bucs relievers Kison and Dave Giusti protected the eventual 3–2 lead; "a gnat's eyelash," the Gunner called it. Kison, who had a whip for a right arm, got the win, Giusti the save, and Stennett starred in the field. But in the end it was Sanguillen's slashing bad-ball hitting, which resulted in two hits, two RBIs and one run scored, that fueled the furious comeback.

"If that club in Pittsburgh was in New York, everyone would know about Manny Sanguillen," Kison says. "Sangy was a fabulous catcher and hitter."

Gowdy noted that Sanguillen's hits were usually vicious line drives or sharp blows back through the box. Sanguillen would seemingly swing at anything. At the time Manny may have been the best bad-ball hitter since Yogi Berra. Prince called Sanguillen a "scrambling-type hitter." Sometimes Sanguillen's wild swings would, as Prince put it, threaten to "blow the air out of the infield."

Bench was one of the most intelligent catchers when it came to calling a game, and the Reds' plan for Sanguillen was to try and fan him on a bad pitch or get a groundout. But Sanguillen's free-swinging ways made it tough for Bench and the pitchers to work him.

By game's end, Manny being Manny put the Pirates on the brink of a second straight pennant.

The following day in sun-drenched Detroit, Joe Coleman dominated the A's, striking out a then playoff record 14 in a 3–0 win. The result was not wholly unexpected. Coleman, a right-hander who had been rescued from continued toiling for the Washington Senators in the Denny McLain trade in 1970, won 19 games for the Tigers in 1972 and fashioned a 2.80 earned run average that was a career best for a full season.

He was, in fact, no ordinary Joe. Coleman had won 20 games the season before and would win 23 in '73. His success was due in part to his cooling down of a hot temper.

The son of Joe Coleman Sr., who had pitched for the Philadelphia Athletics, Baltimore, and Detroit in the 1940s and '50s, and father of future major league hurler Casey Coleman, Joe Jr. learned from his father that the breaks of the game eventually evened out. Especially, Joe Jr. said, if one was with a good club.

Before being dealt to Detroit, Coleman was with Washington, and by his admission, being with a losing team had a lot to do with his being nicknamed "Boy Blunder" and "Junior" by Senators' teammates for his petulant attitude. Temper tantrums led Coleman to toss his chair around the clubhouse following a loss. What his teammates didn't realize was that because he was a starting pitcher, he would have to sit and stew about a tough loss for five or six days before getting a chance at redemption.

Coleman regretted his tantrums and the reputation they gave him. It was a reputation he didn't want, but he knew it was deserved. Being in the big leagues before he had a right to be had something to do with his attitude. Maybe, he mused, he tried just a little too hard.

Maybe if he had gone to the minor leagues and won nine or ten games in Triple A, he would have had more confidence in himself, he said. He had spent only two seasons in the minors when the Senators called him up in 1967. His minor league record at the time was 9-29, but the Senators' coaching staff had confidence in him, so Coleman tried hard to keep their confidence and it upset him when he didn't. He was put in the starting rotation, and being young and inexperienced, he couldn't adjust to the rapid rise.

He learned a valuable lesson when, after winning four straight late in the season, he was sent back to the minors. The next season his attitude was 100 percent better.

When Coleman was traded to the Tigers, his attitude was as sky-high as the evening charter flight on which the deal was made in October 1970. Senators owner Bob Short was infatuated with big-name players, and he coveted Denny McLain. Detroit general manager Jim Campbell had just finished dinner on the flight from Minnesota to Baltimore in the middle of the ALCS when Short slipped him a note across the aisle. On the piece of paper was Short's latest proposal: Coleman, Eddie Brinkman, Aurelio Rodriguez, and Jim Hannan for McLain, Don Wert, Elliott Maddox, and Norm McRae.

McLain had been suspended for half of the 1970 season and suspended again for dumping water on two writers and carrying a gun. With an opportunity to rid Detroit of baseball's bad boy, the Tigers' GM pulled the trigger on the deal. He spent the rest of the flight feeling as if he were flying a bit higher than the forty thousand feet other passengers were at.

It didn't take long for Coleman to discover the difference between playing in Washington for Ted Williams and playing in Detroit for Billy Martin. Amid miserable weather in a 1970 game, Coleman had thrown a three-hit shutout and afterward recalled being berated by Williams for not throwing more sliders.

The first day of spring training with the Tigers in 1971, Coleman recalled Martin's pulling him aside and telling him he would be his number two pitcher behind Mickey Lolich. Coleman thought Martin's positive attitude, contrasted with Williams's pessimism, was a big reason he won just 8 games his final season with Washington and 20 his first season with Detroit.

The twenty-five-year-old Coleman climbed the hill for Game Three wearing a long-sleeved black undershirt beneath his white home uniform with its trademark "D" in Olde English script on the left breast. Despite the brilliant sunshine bathing ancient Tiger Stadium, fall was in full swing, and players on both sides wore long sleeves and in some cases turtlenecks— those of the A's bright green beneath their gold tops, the Tigers' black—to guard against the dipping daytime temperatures.

It was a glorious October afternoon, and the sights and sounds of the historic old ballpark—the emerald green outfield and contrasting forest green of the outfield walls, the alternating light- and dark-brown dirt of the sunlit infield and shaded area around home plate, the bright white bases and foul lines, the blurring of men in motion on the field, the cheers and chants of the colorfully clad crowd—made the action even more vivid.

Since Tiger Stadium was a hitter's park, that meant more often than not exciting, memorable baseball. The stands were deep in center field but reachable in right, where the distance was very short down the line, and in left. Right-center and left-center were the spots where deep drives usually flew out of the park. The overhang in the right-field corner jutted out about ten feet into fair territory and extended from the second deck over the lower stands. That area was Norm Cash's favorite spot in Tiger Stadium, and in years past former Yankee Roger Maris, another left-handed pull hitter, had also hit many drives off the overhang. Along with the short dimensions in right- and left-center one of the reasons hitters loved to hit in Tiger Stadium was the dark background behind the pitcher. Tony Kubek, who played in Tiger Stadium, said hitters could see the ball perfectly, unlike at some ballparks where there were white shirts in the center-field crowd. The wind inside the stadium could be tricky at times, whipping on occasion from the left-field foul pole to the foul pole in right.

A's announcer Monte Moore made note on the radio of the "beautiful fall day here in Michigan . . . bright sunshine," and it was the latter that led to one other attribute of Tiger Stadium: the sun field in left. In that regard it was like Yankee Stadium, where the glaring sunlight and sweeping shadows made left field a notoriously difficult place to play in October and once prompted Yogi Berra to proclaim, "It gets late early out there."

On this day both Joe Rudi and his Detroit counterpart, Willie Horton, would be staring directly into the bright glare behind the grandstand, but Oakland color analyst Jimmy Piersall, a former center fielder for several American League teams, pointed out that the main difficulty for outfielders in Tiger Stadium was the shadows that descended in late afternoon and early twilight.

Along with Moore and Piersall (whose battles with bipolar disorder led to a book and movie titled *Fear Strikes Out*), the A's broadcast team included the sublime Jim Woods, one of the greatest baseball broadcasters ever. He had broken in with the Yankees in the 1950s and worked for several clubs, teaming with Prince in Pittsburgh, Mel Allen with the Yankees, Russ Hodges with the Giants, Jack Buck in St. Louis, and Ned Martin in Boston. Like Gowdy, Woods owned a low-key, friendly voice. He understood the game and let it unfold naturally but was a great storyteller when the situation called for it. Woods was known as "Possum" or, as Prince often referred to him on the air, "Poss." The nickname came courtesy of former Yankees outfielder Enos Slaughter, who upon first meeting Woods in the clubhouse took note of his short gray hair and slight overbite and announced, "I've seen better heads on a possum."

Woods noted in Game Three that Tiger Stadium had always been known as a hitter's paradise, one favoring a left-handed batter, and taking note of the unpredictable winds, he remarked, "Anything hit up in the air today [there's] no telling what's liable to happen."

With Campy out of the A's lineup, the leadoff spot was assigned to Matty Alou, and the little left-hander pulled Coleman's first pitch down the right-field line for a double. Al Kaline quickly fired the ball in, but Alou beat the throw with a dusty, head-first slide into the bag. It was one of a series-high four doubles for Alou, who would have eight hits overall and bat .381 over the five games, leading all hitters with ten or more at-bats.

Dal Maxvill followed with a walk, and with Joe Rudi, Reggie Jackson, and Mike Epstein set to follow, Coleman was in trouble early. Dropping his right arm down to a sidearm, almost submarine slot, the 6-foot-3 Coleman kept his cool and struck Rudi out looking. Jackson, standing in the shadows of home plate, struck out swinging. Alou stole third but was stranded when Coleman blew a high fastball past a swinging Epstein for the inning-ending strikeout and strode from the mound to raucous cheers.

In the third Alou again led off with a hit, stroking a single that was quickly run down by Kaline near the right-field foul line. Maxvill struck out swinging on an outside pitch before Rudi dipped his bat and dropped a perfectly executed bunt single up the third base line. Amid a whipping wind that stirred up a small dirt storm in front of home plate, Jackson swung violently and ripped a vicious grounder. The ball was hit so hard that it handcuffed Tony Taylor, who dropped it before recovering to toss to Ike Brown at first.

NBC replays showed Reggie crossing the bag before the ball got there, but he was called out by first base umpire Don Denkinger. In 1985 Denkinger would make arguably the most controversial call in World Series history when he ruled Kansas City's Jorge Orta safe at first in Game Six against St. Louis. Denkinger's disputed call set the stage for a two-run rally, and the Royals went on to win the Series in seven games.

Coleman closed out the A's inning by tying up Epstein with an inside pitch, striking him out swinging for the second time.

Oakland put its leadoff runner on board in each of the first three frames and eventually in seven of the nine innings but failed to score. Williams thought his young A's, overanxious for the sweep, were overswinging at the plate. Ken Holtzman, Coleman's opposite, retired eight straight in the early innings. Holtzman was working in and out, shooting for spots. He ran into trouble in the fifth when he issued a one-out walk to Kaline. Catcher Bill Freehan, back from an injury and playing in his first game of the series, caught all of a Holtzman offering over the heart of the plate and doubled past a diving Sal Bando at third. Holtzman loaded the bases when he walked Willie Horton with a pitch that was way outside—Gene Tenace had to reach across his body to snag it.

Brown, glaring out at the mound behind glittering glasses, smashed a grounder that skipped under Holtzman's glove and into center field. George Kell made the call on the Tigers' television network: *"The 1-1 pitch. . . . Ground ball through, a base hit! Here comes Kaline home, he'll score one run! Freehan charging home, run Number Two, and the Tigers lead two-to-nothing!"*

Freehan further celebrated his return when he drove an eighth-inning pitch from Bob Locker into the now shadowy lower left-field seats.

Kell: Here's a long drive, way back, may be. . . . It's gone! Bill Freehan has just pumped one into the lower deck in left field and the Tigers lead three-nothing!

As dugout cameras showed Martin and his coaches applauding in their navy blue nylon jackets, a man in full Bengal Tiger regalia stood among the more than forty-one thousand attendees—"bug-eyed Tiger fans," Woods called them, "who want a victory in the worst way"—and clanged a cow bell as Freehan crossed the plate. The real Tiger, however, was Coleman.

His sidearm action had right-handed hitters flinching throughout the afternoon. Against Jackson and Epstein Coleman was mixing in a three-quarter delivery; Moore said he hadn't seen any right-handed hurler throw as many sidearm pitches to lefty hitters all season. The result was that Coleman's pitches were making little movements backward so that even when the A's did connect, the ball was running in on them and taking away their power. Kell spent the afternoon punctuating his telecast with repeated calls of, "He got him on strikes!" Throwing fastballs at the letters, forkballs and curves on the corners—high heat and breaking balls all delivered from a variety of arm angles—and with his jaw working furiously on a piece of gum, Coleman went the distance to help Detroit avert a sweep. His 14 Ks were the most by an AL pitcher that season not named Nolan Ryan.

In Cincinnati later that day, another tall, mid-twenties right-hander was looking for a similar shut-down performance. Pittsburgh's Dock Ellis took the mound for Game Four opposite fellow free spirit Ross Grimsley, a 15-game winner who had closed the season with victories in each of his final four decisions and posted a 0.63 ERA in September.

Just twenty-six years old, the enigmatic Ellis had already been a controversial figure for a couple of years. He was a California kid who had grown up in Watts hating baseball but became one of the iconic figures of his sport in the early 1970s. He was brash and bold, Charles Barkley before the world knew of Sir Charles. Dock had a sinking fastball, big curve, and big mouth. He was a talker, and his talk made national news.

Oliver found Ellis refreshingly real. In a world where it's often difficult to find someone who is genuine, Dock was genuine. If Ellis had something to say to you, Oliver remarked, Dock would tell it to your face. "If I've got something to say, I'm gonna say it," Ellis said at the time. "Nobody's gonna shut me up."

"Dock kept the clubhouse alive and agitated the hell out of the other team," recalls Cash. "He was always chirping. We used him as a weapon. He was a competitor."

A crusader for African American issues, Ellis had stated the season before that Sparky Anderson, who would be managing the National League All-Stars, would not dare start Ellis opposite "black brother" Vida Blue. Ellis received numerous letters condemning his statement, but among the letters offering encouragement was one he treasured. It was written by Jackie Robinson.

Ellis did start the All-Star Game—he surrendered the historic light-tower homer to Jackson—and went on to a 19-9 record in a season that saw him win thirteen straight. It followed a 1970 campaign in which Ellis no-hit San Diego on June 12, a game he later claimed to have pitched while on LSD.

In 1971 a Pittsburgh newspaper headline proclaimed Ellis "Probably the Most Unpopular Buc of All Time." Ellis was used to negativity. At Gardena High School, a school of largely white students located on the outskirts of Los Angeles, he was called "Watusi" and "spear chucker." In a minor league game in Kinston, North Carolina, Ellis fanned future Indians and Phillies manager Charlie Manuel to end the game and reacted to racial taunts from the crowd by holding his middle finger aloft as he slowly turned in a circle so that everyone could get a full view of his response.

Ellis may have been seen as a bad dude to outsiders, but those who got past his barriers saw something else. Roberto Clemente Jr. considered Dock a surrogate father. Longtime Pirates trainer Tony Bartirome couldn't think of Ellis without thinking of his megawatt smile, his laughter in the locker room.

Ellis and Gene Alley were two of the pranksters in the clubhouse, and shouting and needling were part of the Pirate picture. "It's all in fun," Ellis said then. Sometimes it was misinterpreted by those who weren't around the team all the time. Ellis chided a writer for a piece that accused Dock of "seriously needling" teammate Ronnie Kline.

He was kidding Kline, Ellis said later, but there was no kidding on the mound. Ellis credited former Negro Leaguer Chet Brewer for giving him his first step toward the majors and Kinston manager Bob Clear for providing tips on pitching. But it was former Pirates pitcher and then minor league instructor Harvey Haddix who taught Ellis the elements of his craft, including how to set up a hitter and how to keep the ball off the middle of the plate.

By the time he stared in at Reds leadoff hitter Pete Rose in the bottom of the first inning of Game Four on Tuesday, October 10, Ellis was arguably the hottest pitcher in baseball. The Riverfront crowd of just under forty thousand seemed to realize the same; Bench could sense the tension in the stadium.

The Reds reached Ellis for an unearned run in the first, the Big Red Machine playing small ball. Cincinnati bunched two singles, a sacrifice, a fielder's choice, a stolen base (by Bench), and an error into the grand total of a single run.

Amid brilliant Indian summer weather, Cincinnati scored two more unearned runs in the fourth, and Ellis was lifted for pinch hitter Bill Mazeroski in the sixth. Though he left the game trailing 3–0, Dock hadn't pitched badly. He scattered five hits in five innings but was betrayed by three errors, which led to all the runs against him being unearned.

The Reds blew the game open by blowing up the Bucs' bullpen in the sixth and seventh innings. Pittsburgh's lone counter came on a seventh-inning homer by Clemente. Otherwise Grimsley owned the Pirates.

Bench went into the day hoping Grimsley would be strong but had no idea the twenty-two-year-old would be *that* strong. He had speed and rhythm and was hitting the glove no matter where Bench put it. Grimsley was in just his second season in the bigs, but he had always pitched well against Pittsburgh to that point, and it seemed to Bench that Ross could throw his glove on the mound and beat the Pirates.

Still the Reds didn't expect a complete-game two-hitter. Bench saw Grimsley as an intense, high-strung guy who hated to pitch poorly and hated to lose. That was true, but Grimsley wasn't exactly buttoned up. He had a quirky personality, and though not as well known as early 1970s icons like Ellis, Sparky Lyle, and Bill "Spaceman" Lee, Grimsley was considered something of a flake by Anderson.

"You're crazy," Sparky told him in 1971, when the rookie told reporters stories of his communication with a self-proclaimed witch and indulging in superstition and good-luck charms. Anderson warned that Grimsley would be the "clown of the league" once word got out about his involvement with a witch. Grimsley didn't care what others thought. If he thought it helped him win, why shouldn't he keep in touch with the witch?

It wasn't just witches and good-luck charms that gave Anderson pause. The Reds were a conservative organization, and Ross was radical. The Reds had strict rules about short hair and no facial hair; Grimsley liked to let his dark black locks grow in wavy lengths while sporting a two-day stubble. Along with his sometimes unkempt look, Grimsley was distinctive for large, bulging green eyes that, when fixed on an object, produced a piercing expression. Some found his stare unnerving and called him "crazy eyes."

With his bulging, green-eyed glare, herky-jerky delivery, and overpowering pitching, Grimsley dispatched the Pirates in less than two hours en route to a 7–1 win. He went at them with an assortment of pitches—fastball, curve, a slider on the outside—all the while changing speeds and arm angles, delivering from three-quarters overhand and then over the top. He needed just eighty-four pitches to subdue the Pirates—eighty-four pitches and a good-luck charm, his father, Ross Sr., a former major league hurler.

"That was five times my dad has seen me win," Grimsley said later. "He never has seen me lose."

The Reds succeeded in retying the series, but Cincinnati suffered a setback in the seventh inning when Morgan, running out a ground ball, hit the first base bag hard and severely injured his heel. By the time he got to the clubhouse, he realized he no longer had use of that foot. It was all he could do to leave Riverfront Stadium unassisted, and he spent the night icing his foot, the pain preventing him from sleeping. The next morning, the day of the fifth and final game, Morgan figured the likelihood of his playing was all but nil.

Wednesday, October 11, 1972, marked the day the League Championship Series arrived as an event, a happening. To that point, the three-year-old series had resembled the Super Bowl in its first two years, a sideshow to the main event. In pro football, the down-to-the-wire NFL title games between Green Bay and Dallas in 1966 and '67 were seen by most as the "real" championship, while the Super Bowl with the AFL champion was anticlimactic, a mere formality.

The situation was reversed in baseball. Baltimore had swept each of its first three league championship series in the American League; in the NLCS the New York Mets and Pitsburgh had sandwiched four-game wins around a Cincinnati sweep. Prior to 1972 the LCS was seen as a manufactured playoff lacking any real drama.

The 1972 postseason, primarily the playoff games on October 11, changed that. Watching both games on television, writer Roger Angell was riveted by NBC's coverage that day. He called it an "afternoon of baseball unlike any other in the annals of the sport."

On a cool, cloudy day in Detroit, Catfish Hunter and Mickey Lolich locked up in another mound masterpiece. The Tigers' Tony Taylor doubled to the gap in right-center in the second and advanced to third on Jackson's error. He was stranded when Hunter issued an intentional walk to Aurelio Rodriguez and retired Lolich on a fly out to Reggie. Taylor would also double off Vida Blue in the ninth and combined with Duke Sims to account for the four doubles Detroit would hit in Game Four.

In the third Dick McAuliffe caught hold of a Hunter fastball and drove it deep to right-center field.

Kell: *Way back on the warning track, might be. . . . Home run for McAuliffe! It caught the edge of the second deck, and the Tigers lead!*

With one out in the seventh, Epstein launched a Lolich offering toward the upper deck in right. Woods provided the call on A's radio: *"Lolich delivers. . . . There's a drive by Epstein, way back. . . . Going, going. . . . Tie ball game! Big Mike got a hold of one and this game is even at 1–1!"*

Big Mike, eschewing the long-sleeved gold undershirt some of his teammates were wearing, trotted the bases triumphantly and punctuated his trip with an emphatic hop on home plate. The game raced along because the two aces made it move. While some would get two strikes on a hitter and then waste a pitch, Hunter and Lolich would come right back with a quality third pitch. Over the course of a game it was the difference between throwing 150 pitches or 100 pitches.

Game Four was tied in the tenth when Oakland struck for two runs. Gonzalo Marquez pulled a pitch from reliever Chuck Seelbach and singled past a diving Taylor at second. Alou reached out and roped an opposite-field double off the screen in left. The relay from Jim Northrup to McAuliffe to Freehan had Gonzo out by a good ten feet. But the ball one-hopped Freehan. Marquez and Freehan collided in front of the plate—the collision knocked Freehan's hat off—and as the ball rolled through the batter's box, Gonzo reached out with his right hand and, still prone in the dirt, slapped home plate.

Ted Kubiak's dying quail to short right field dropped in front of an onrushing Kaline and scored Alou for a 3–1 lead. The A's appeared ready to break the game open. Facing lefty reliever John Hiller, Jackson timed a slow curve, but the pitch jammed him. Strong enough to fight it off, Reggie cued it toward third and beat Rodriguez's throw. With runners on the corners, Bando lined Hiller's letter-high pitch right at Northrup for the final out.

Trailing by two and with winter beckoning, the Tigers roared back. Swinging from his open stance, McAuliffe pulled a Locker pitch to right. Kaline followed by getting around on a curve and grounding a single past Bando. Williams walked to the mound and, having already used Blue and Rollie Fingers in relief, waved in right-hander Joe Horlen.

Martin countered by sending lefty Gates Brown in to pinch-hit for Mickey

Stanley. Horlen's wild pitch advanced the runners, and Brown drew a standing ovation from the frenzied faithful when he worked a walk to load the bases.

Freehan followed with a grounder to Bando, who, rather than throw home, threw instead to second base. Tenace, a catcher playing second base for just the third time in four years because Williams had stripped his infield through a series of moves, reached for the throw, which was to the outfield side of the base. Tenace turned and was barreled into by the burly Brown. Williams said later that owner Charlie Finley's orders to rotate second basemen had caused the skipper to run out of guys who could play that position. Williams watched the play at second unfold like someone witnessing an auto accident. The A's second-base experiment effectively ended that afternoon.

With Cash up, Williams brought in rookie southpaw Dave Hamilton. Wearing a batting helmet because he was facing a lefty, Cash walked in the tying run and flung his bat defiantly toward the Tigers dugout. With the stadium lights flaring on the Tigers' navy blue helmets and with thirty-nine thousand rocking old Tiger Stadium, Northrup scraped the steel-gray sky with a deep drive to right over the head of a drawn-in Alou.

> **Kell**: *There she goes! That gets the run home and the Tigers, in a tremendous come-from-behind victory here this afternoon, beat Oakland 4–3! This series is tied!*

The old champs' courageous comeback had the Tigers streaming from their dugout and Detroit fans hopping the outfield fences and rushing the field, their arms thrust skyward in celebration. Those that remained in the stands raised a ruckus to the rusty rafters. Some of the young spectators leaping from the bleachers tore up small sections of turf. The damage wasn't as bad as the destruction following Detroit's clinching of the division title in the regular season's final series. The celebration on this day was pure joy. A half-hour following the final out fans were still in the stadium; they didn't want the moment to end.

In a classic case of "Dewey Defeats Truman," an early edition of a Detroit evening newspaper, certain the Tigers were going to lose Game Four, proclaimed, "Oakland Wins."

Lolich knew better than to count out these Tigers. "You can go all the way back to '68 when we came from behind," he said in a delirious clubhouse. "Today it was the same 'Over-the-Hill-Gang' that brought us back again."

While the Tigers exulted, the A's locker room exploded in anger. Blue, in the bullpen because of an injury to lefty reliever Darold Knowles, and Fingers were screaming at one another and had to be restrained by teammates. Williams shook his head at the ruckus. I'm managing a damn looney bin, he thought.

What was taking place in Cincinnati was scarcely less dramatic. As young guns Don Gullett and Steve Blass prepared to battle for the second time in five days, the enormity of what was about to take place on the turf of Riverfront Stadium was evident to all. No one had to tell any of the players what this game meant. Certainly no one had to tell Morgan, who was taking two shots of Novocain in his heel so that he could play.

With close to forty-two thousand fans in full cry in Riverfront Stadium, Gullett took the mound in the first following a ninety-minute rain delay that only added to the anxiety and expectations.

The world champs knew what to expect from Cincy's super southpaw. Wall-to-wall heat, Stargell thought. What followed over the next two hours and nineteen minutes was one of the great playoff games of all time.

Like most young men, Gullett had a lot of giddy-up, and it showed in his best pitch. One look was all it took for Dodgers manager Walter Alston to compare Gullett's swing-and-miss fastball to that of his former ace southpaw Sandy Koufax.

Gullett had broken in with the Reds as a nineteen-year-old phenom who was less than a year out of McKell High School in South Shore, Kentucky. That first year, he said, made a man out of him real quick. Used primarily as a smoke-throwing reliever, he went 5-2 with a 2.43 ERA as the Reds rolled to the pennant. He saved two of his team's three wins without allowing a run in the playoff victory over the Pirates. In the World Series against the wallbangers of Baltimore, Gullett had a 1.35 ERA in three appearances.

In 1971 Reds pitching coach Larry Shepard suggested that Gullett be taken out of the bullpen and inserted into the starting rotation. By season's end he was 16-6 with a 2.64 ERA and had turned out to be one of the few highlights in Cincy's horrid season. Anderson considered Gullett's breakout campaign a big turning point for the Reds, who could begin to build an adequate staff around their young gun.

Gullett was the bright light in an otherwise forgettable summer, but things turned dark early in the '72 season. By May 2 he was 0-2 in four starts and had yielded 19 runs in fifteen innings. The Reds had Gullett examined by team physician Dr. George Ballou to see if anything was physically wrong. Diagnosed with hepatitis, he missed significant time over the next three months and didn't return to the rotation for good until August 20. He won four straight before losing a pair of one-run games and finished 9-10.

Anderson figured Gullett had missed out on 8–10 wins that season. True to his nature, the quiet, soft-spoken farm boy shrugged and didn't worry about what might have been. What's done, you can't change, he said. Worrying won't help.

By the time he got the sign from Bench to start Game Five, Gullett was older than his twenty-one years. He acknowledged that as a teenaged rookie, all he had tried to do was "throw the ball past the batter." He had learned since that pitching was a science.

Beneath slate-gray skies and threatening clouds Gullett retired Stennett on a fly to right to open the game and struck Oliver out looking. The Cincinnati hordes were howling; one could sense their urgency. Clemente, unmoved, quieted the hostile crowd with a ground single to center. Stargell popped up to Tony Perez at first to end the inning.

Despite the threatening skies Michaels assured his anxious listeners that Game Five would be played without further interruption: *"It is still very overcast here in Cincinnati but those are not rain clouds above us. . . . Broken pattern for the first time today so the forecast says no more rain."*

Gullett knew a Game Five assignment was as much a challenge as an honor, particularly when facing a club full of hard-swinging howitzers. The man most noted for his free-swinging ways, Sanguillen, opened the second with a single and Hebner stepped up. Michaels made the call on Reds radio:

Sanguillen at first base, Gullett at the belt. Hebner hits a line drive and this time it's fair into the right-field corner for a base hit! Geronimo cuts it off, Hebner is digging for two and the throw is not in time. . . . Gets by Chaney and gets by Menke and a run will score! Hebner breaks for third and he's in there. . . .

Cash hits a ground ball up the middle, Hebner scores and it's two-to-nothing Pittsburgh. . . . Johnny Bench going to the mound to talk with Gullett.

Gullett settled down, but when Sanguillen and Hebner opened the fourth with consecutive singles, Gullett's day was done. With Pedro Borbon, Carroll, and Tom Hall ready to go in relief, Sparky wasn't going to stay with his struggling starter.

"Well, Don, you just don't have it today," Anderson told him as he waved in Borbon from the bullpen. "Maybe you'll have it Sunday [for Game Two of the World Series]."

"That gave me a big lift right there," Gullett said, "[Anderson's] telling me that we were going to win the ball game."

Borbon gave up an RBI single to Cash—his second of the game—then slammed the door. The Reds' rally against Blass had begun the inning before, when Rose's routine grounder hit a cutout in the Astroturf and turned into a double that scored Darrel Chaney. Joe Nuxhall called the startling play:

Blass delivers to Rose. . . . Pete swings and bounces it fair, over the head of Stargell and that'll score a run! Rose on his way to second! . . . What looked like a routine ground ball hits the cutout in the sliding pit and bounces over the head of Willie Stargell, Willie getting a glove on it but couldn't control it. . . . A break for the Cincinnati Reds.

The Reds continued to play catch up. In the fifth Cesar Geronimo cut Cincinnati's deficit to a mere run.

> **Michaels**: *Geronimo swings and drills it to deep right. . . . Back goes Clemente. . . . Gone!*

Blass silenced Cincinnati into the eighth and eventually departed having held the Big Red Machine to four hits. Borbon, Hall, and Carroll combined to keep the Bucs off the board. The game was, as the Gunner would say, "close as fuzz on a tick's ear."

The Reds were down to their final three outs when Bench stepped in to lead off the ninth against palm baller Dave Giusti. Lefty reliever Ramon Hernandez had recorded the final two outs in the Reds' eighth, but with three right-handers due to bat in the bottom of the ninth and Giusti ready, Virdon's decision was automatic.

The Bucs knew they were on the verge of knocking off the Reds and advancing to their second straight World Series. Out in center field, Oliver said he was "starting to count my World Series checks," he recalled with a laugh. "We had confidence in our pitchers."

Teammates thought Giusti the best closer in the game. In '71 he had not been scored on in seven postseason appearances. In '72 his 1.93 ERA was the lowest of his career. The Machine needed a spark, but it wasn't coming from Anderson, who went down the dugout steps to get a drink of water and saw batting coach Ted Kluszewski.

"Klu, we've got about five minutes," Anderson said. "If five minutes from now we don't get a run, we'll be on our way home. The way I feel, I suggest we get going."

Bench had a different feeling. From the third inning on he believed he was going to hit one out. In the on-deck circle Bench toyed with the rosin and pine tar. Unlike some hitters, Bench did not wear batting gloves. He wore them in spring training until his hands toughened up, then discarded them. He was not a dirt man; he didn't favor the old-time practice of scooping dirt from the batter's box as Clemente did. Bench favored pine tar and rosin, mixing the two to get his hands sticky. By late in the game, Bench's hands would almost be black from the pine tar, but he would have a good feel for the bat.

Bench watched Giusti throw his warmup pitches. No one had to tell the Reds' slugger what the stocky Pirates' right-hander would throw. Every hitter dreaded Giusti's palm ball, which was a sinker pitch away from the plate.

Bench noticed the big crowd had grown quiet. Giusti, he thought, had a way of depressing opposing optimists. As he walked to the batter's box, he heard people calling his name. He paid no attention; then he heard someone say, "It's your mother!" He turned around, and there was Katy Bench, standing in an aisle and leaning over the railing. She gave her son a smile, then offered some motherly advice: "Hit me a home run!"

Bench bombed the first pitch deep but foul. He heard someone shout, "He's up! He's up!" meaning Giusti was high in the strike zone with his pitches. In the Reds broadcast booth Tom Hedrick and Waite Hoyt were drinking in the drama. Bench in '72 had been amazing, Hedrick recalled. He had torn up the league. "Bench is a tough guy," Hedrick said, "and he's a smart guy."

Bench was also a guy who could block out the crowd, even the frenzied fans in Riverfront. What he did when hitting well was barely put his hands on the bat handle. If Bench relaxed his hands, Hedrick said, he could hit to right field. If he squeezed too hard, he would pop up.

"Bench is gonna pop it up," Hoyt told Hedrick. The former right-handed ace of the famed "Murderers' Row" Yankees of 1927–28, Hoyt was the Yankees' winning pitcher in the 1920s. He told Hedrick in Game Five, "The Pirates are just a little bit better than the Reds, my friend."

Giusti worked the count to 1-2, then wound and threw his specialty: the palm ball.

> **Michaels**: *The pitch to Bench. . . . Hit in the air to deep right field, back goes Clemente, at the fence. . . . She's gone! . . . The game is tied!*

"Bench comes up and hits the ball to right field," Oliver remembered. "I'm going to back up Roberto, and I'm halfway there when I see the ball going out."

Bench knew he had hit it well. He watched the ball rise toward Clemente and keep carrying. Then he heard the roar of the delirious crowd. As he circled the bases, Bench couldn't be certain he was even touching the ground. People who had left the ballpark heard the noise and came rushing back in. Players on both sides thought the emotion inside the stadium unbelievable. Fans were on their feet the entire inning. The Reds felt like little kids. Bench always believed that while growing old was mandatory, growing up was optional. The Reds were kids and played the game like kids.

"When Bench hit that home run, it's the greatest feeling I ever got in my life and it's the most excited I ever got," Rose told Nuxhall after the game.

Driving the ball to the opposite field was the act of a disciplined hitter, and it showed how far the Reds' catcher/slugger had come since his sub-par '71 season. Gowdy told Bench in July of '72 that '71 might have been the best thing that ever happened to him. "He found out," Gowdy said, "that the game wasn't that easy."

Kubek thought that along with Bench's adjustment in attitude there was an adjustment in his approach to hitting. Kubek noted that Johnny crouched more at the plate, hitting to right field more while keeping his head down and his eyes on the ball. Bench was hitting more to the opposite field, and the home runs were coming. "He's getting the pitch away and he's going that way," Kubek said.

Perez singled to center and was pinch-run for by George Foster. When Denis Menke singled to left, Virdon brought in Bob Moose. It was unusual to see Giusti removed in the ninth with the game on the line, but Virdon, believing his relief ace was rattled, made the move. In came Moose, who had made thirty starts during the season and just one relief appearance, though it had resulted in a save.

Riverfront fans were in a frenzy. Most of the players had never heard sounds like those before. People downtown could hear the noise from the stadium. Working as carefully as a man diffusing a ticking time bomb, Moose got Geronimo to fly to Clemente in deep right, a drive that allowed Foster to race to third. Chaney popped to Gene Alley at short, and the pennant had come down to pinch reliever Moose and pinch hitter Hal McRae. Moose issued two pitches and then gripped the seams for a slider.

> **Michaels**: *The 1-1 pitch to McRae. . . . In the dirt, it's a wild pitch! Here comes Foster, the Reds win the pennant! Bob Moose throws a wild pitch and the Reds have won the National League pennant! Four-to-three Cincinnati!*

The Reds stormed the field in celebration. Sparky grabbed Foster in a hug. Across the field the Bucs were disappointed, but the indomitable Clemente, whom Gowdy called the "unsinkable Pirate," would have none of it. "Get your f—— heads up!" Roberto shouted upon entering the clubhouse. "We had a great year!"

Oliver said the Pirates still believed they were the best team in baseball. It was tough to lose on a wild pitch, but he didn't think Pittsburgh had played to its potential. "We knew we had done the best we could," Oliver recalled. "We didn't have excuses. It just wasn't meant to be."

Bench felt empathy for Sanguillen. The only way Manny could have reached that ball was to backhand it, but the pitch was far outside and it bounced straight up. No catcher could have shifted that far to make the play, Bench thought.

The Big Red Machine was a great team, but to this day its members believe the '72 Pirates have never received the credit they deserved, and it was because they lost that NLCS. Up in the broadcast booth, a smiling Hoyt turned to Hedrick. "Isn't it interesting," said Hoyt, who had predicted a Pirates victory, "how wrong the experts can be?"

Bench had never seen a team so happy, never seen a town so happy. Now the question was whether the Reds come down off this emotional high and get their heads back into it in time for the World Series.

The Big Red Machine's opponent would be decided the following day in Detroit. Thursday, October 12, brought more somber weather suited to the winner-take-all showdown in Motown.

Moore set the stage for the decisive fifth game: *"The championship game of the 1972 American League season. . . . The nation is watching and listening to this one today."*

Moore mentioned in his broadcast that hundreds of telegrams had been sent to the A's from around the nation. One of them came from Raiders quarterback Daryle Lamonica, who sent a telegram to Bando wishing his fellow rebels from Oakland well in their postseason run.

Blue Moon Odom and Woodie Fryman met in a rematch of Game Two, and with a crowd of 50,276 cramming Tiger Stadium on a cold and blustery day, Detroit did more in its first at-bat than it had in its nine previous innings against Odom. The scrappy McAuliffe, who had blasted two A's infielders trying to tag him out in this series and had drawn a hard tag from Bando in return, opened with a ground single to right to an enormous roar.

"Unbelievable enthusiasm from this city," Moore told his radio audience. "The A's are not only battling the nine Tigers [on the field], they're battling over 50,000 Tiger fans. . . . Boy, these fans are already going like it's the 10th inning instead of the first."

"The Corner" had become the Cardiac Corner. Detroit had drawn nearly 1.9 million fans to Tiger Stadium in 1972, and the Tigers' total attendance led the American League and ranked second in the majors behind the Mets. The fans were fully engaged from the first pitch of Game Five, and the radio broadcast reveals a loud roar when McAuliffe moved to second after Duke Sims drew a walk. Sims, who started the first two games at catcher for Freehan, was moved to left field to give Detroit another left-handed bat in the lineup. One of the few players in major league baseball in 1972 to wear glasses, Sims stood so close to home plate that Moore remarked only half jokingly that Duke could "be hit with a strike."

With Freehan up, Odom uncorked a low, inside pitch that got away from Tenace and rolled to the backstop. The passed ball advanced both runners, and Freehan topped a grounder to Maxvill at short.

Amid a backdrop of a raucous crowd Kell provided the call on the Tigers' TV network: *"Here's a grounder to short, he's going to go to first with it, and Mac will score!"*

An early mistake cost the A's a run since Freehan's ground ball was tailor-made for a double play. Tigers fans took their good luck with glee and took aim on the playing field.

> **Moore**: *Tiger fans are already throwing debris from the center field bleachers out onto the field. . . . Everything you can think of is going out of the center field bleachers.*

The A's responded in the second inning when Jackson drew a leadoff walk and stole second as Freehan's peg sailed far left of the bag. Bando connected on a deep drive to right, and Kaline made the catch, then spun and fired toward third. The throw was cut off as Jackson did a dramatic head-first dive into the bag. Fryman, looking a bit wild as Odom had in the top of the first, threw high and tight on a 1–2 count to back Epstein off the plate and hit the A's first baseman. Big Mike dropped his bat and clutched the fingers of his left hand, now throbbing from pain and the cold weather.

League rules dictated a pitcher be limited to eight warmup deliveries between innings. But because of the cold weather home plate umpire Nestor Chylak told Odom and Fryman they could take a little extra time to try and get warm. Moore noted the many fans who had spent the night prior to Game Five in sleeping bags outside the stadium. He hoped for their sake they were lined sleeping bags, Moore said, because the overnight temperature had dipped to freezing in Detroit.

Already soaring were the emotions of both sides. The normally unruffled Rudi was furious over a strike three call in the first; Fryman was visibly upset over a called ball in the second. Fryman fanned Tenace for the second out, and with runners at the corners and light-hitting Dick Green at the plate, Williams made the most daring decision of the postseason and dialed up one of the most exciting plays in baseball: a delayed double steal. Moore made the call on one of the more memorable plays in playoff history:

Here goes the runner from first, the pitch is taken, throw down to second, he's safe! Here comes Jackson toward the plate, here comes the throw. . . . He is safe! Reggie Jackson steals home but he may be out of it! He crashed into Bill Freehan and he is hurt on the field! A fantastic collision between Jackson, running like a runaway train, and the great big fireplug Bill Freeehan. What a collision that was!

One of the critical plays of the season was filled with moving parts. Replays showed a charging Taylor taking Freehan's peg well in front of the bag—he cut off the throw after seeing Reggie breaking from third—and firing the ball over the head of a ducking Fryman. Freehan, a fullback in catcher's gear, was standing directly in front of home plate when the heavily muscled Jackson slid in cleats first. Reggie's left knee buckled as it collided with the bulky black-and-orange shin protector on Freehan's left leg. The force of the collision was such that Freehan's shin protector was knocked free from his leg. Jackson's face contorted in pain. Rolling over onto his stomach, Reggie reached for his left hamstring. Freehan, face down in the dirt but still clutching the ball, looked up to see Chylak spreading his arms wide in a safe sign. Martin argued vehemently, but NBC's replays showed Chylak's call to be correct.

His left hamstring torn, Jackson was lost for the rest of the season. He had initially felt the tear when he was still some thirty feet from home plate. When he crashed into Freehan, Jackson said he felt "everything tear loose." Reggie, who would be called Mr. October for his clutch play in future Fall Classics, slid so hard that something popped. He ruptured his hamstring, pulling it away from the bone while stretching the ligaments in his knee.

Williams thought Reggie's determination to score illustrated a truism about the A's: they knew how to play this game. Tenace agreed. He thought it a "beautiful double steal," capped by Jackson's "terrific slide." Small ball had paid off big for the A's but had also come at a big price. Fighting for their playoff lives in a hostile atmosphere, Oakland was now without Jackson, Campy Campaneris, and lefty relief ace Darold Knowles.

More dash and daring—and a disputed call involving first base ump

John Rice—led to a 2–1 A's lead in the fourth. Hendrick, who replaced the injured Jackson, opened the inning by bouncing a low inside pitch to deep short. McAuliffe took three mincing steps to his right, gloved the chest-high hopper, and gunned it to first. The throw was low, and Cash, knowing Hendrick had good speed, leaned forward to snare it. His back foot left the bag just as Hendrick's white cleat crossed it. When Rice called Hendrick safe, Cash spun in disbelief and kicked the dirt in frustration. Rice responded by raising his hands and holding them a foot or so apart, illustrating, in his opinion, how far Cash's foot had been off the bag. Frank Howard protested so loudly and so long that he was ejected.

NBC's camerawork indicated Cash had been toeing the bag as Hendrick's left foot landed on it. The *Detroit News*' front-page photo the next days showed as much. Kell, the Tigers Hall of Fame third baseman and longtime broadcaster, said plays like that happened dozens of times during the season. "This time," Kell said, "the umpire decided to call it."

It wasn't the only call Rice made that chill afternoon that the Tigers had trouble with. Sims said he smacked a ball down the right-field line that Rice ruled foul but that Sims believed was fair. Sims said when he told Rice the ball was fair, Rice responded with a comment that Sims said was something less than should be published.

Benefiting from the blown call, Bando sacrificed Hendrick to second. Woods called the decisive play of the series:

> *Here's the pitch to Tenace, line drive into left field, it's gonna be tough to score on. . . . Here's Hendrick around third. Here's the throw coming on into the plate. . . . He's safe! The ball was dropped by Freehan and Oakland moves into the lead, 2–1, on Gene Tenace's first hit of the playoffs!*

The play was similar to one that would occur two years later in the A's World Series against the Dodgers. With Bando on third in Game Two, Jackson lofted a high fly to right field. Joe Ferguson, a catcher playing the outfield, charged the ball and fired a perfect peg home. With Bando bearing down on him, catcher Steve Yeager applied the tag and amid a hard collision held onto the ball.

Sims, like Ferguson a catcher playing the outfield, fielded Tenace's liner on one hop and rifled a frozen rope that reached Freehan just as Hendrick was arriving. Freehan made the tag and in the collision with the sliding Hendrick dropped the ball. The drop wasn't costly since Chylak had already signaled Hendrick safe.

For the Tiger faithful, the two crucial plays at the plate could have been replays of Cardinals roadrunner Lou Brock's dash home in Game Five of the 1968 World Series. Freehan had blocked the plate, and Brock, rather than slide, tried to step around the Detroit catcher and was tagged out. The pivotal play helped lead to a Tigers' victory in their eventual seven-game upset of St. Louis. In the 1972 postseason, however, Jackson and Hendrick scored where Brock hadn't four years before.

Northrup, never a fan of Martin's managing, thought Billy cost the Tigers Game Five. He believed Martin's decision to keep Freehan behind the plate despite his injury and to keep Sims in left field weakened the team at two positions and cost the Tigers two critical runs. If they had had Sims behind the plate and Horton in left field, Northrup said, Detroit would have won Game Five.

Northrup called Martin the worst manager he had ever played for. When someone said Martin's penchant for self-destruction made Billy his own worst enemy, Northrup snapped, "Not as long as I'm alive."

Odom held the Tigers hitless from the third through fifth innings. Tenace, back behind the plate, thought Moon was in total control. The way Odom was pitching, Tenace figured the A's wouldn't need many runs. But at the end of the fifth inning Blue Moon headed for the tunnel rather than the bench. He bent over and began hyperventilating. "Skip, I can't go anymore," he told Williams. The rowdy A's collapsed in laughter. "Those weren't the dry heaves," one player yelled. "They were the dry chokes!"

Blue Moon broke down, Tenace recalled. The pressure got to him. Williams got Blue to warm up in the bullpen along the right-field line. Making his third relief appearance in as many days, Vida battled the Tigers the rest of the way. It was an intriguing matchup—baseball's best pitcher in '71 against the veterans of baseball's best team in '68.

Vida retired the side in order in the sixth and struck out the side in the seventh. He gave up a leadoff pinch-hit single to Horton in the eighth, then fielded McAuliffe's grounder and got the force out at second. Kaline and Sims popped out, and from the sixth through the ninth Detroit would hit just three balls out of the infield. It was a clear indication that the Tigers, professional hitters all, weren't able to get their bats around quickly enough.

In the ninth Blue got Freehan to pop out to lead the inning. Cash singled to right, and Motown fans hoped for another miracle. In '68 they had watched their Tigers rally to win in their final at-bat twenty-eight times. Martin sent one of the heroes of '68, Mickey Stanley, in to pinch-hit for Northrup. The move stung Northrup. He had two of the Tigers' five hits, including a single off Blue in the seventh. Still Martin pinch-hit for him. "Who knows," Northrup later asked, "why Martin did what he did?" Blue induced a ground out that erased pinch runner Joe Niekro.

The huge crowd was restless. Shivering in the shadows of the late-afternoon gloaming, Detroit fans were stung by the cold, stung by the idea of the season ending, stung by the knowledge that a Michigan winter was setting in, and stung by the sight of the A's in their California gold jerseys. The image of California was pretty low in Michigan. California was home to the anti–Vietnam War movement. Bill Walton, head of the "Walton Gang" that had led UCLA to another national championship in April '72, was among those arrested on Wilshire Boulevard for protesting the mining of harbors in northern Vietnam. Oakland, a rebel city housing rebellious teams in the A's and the NFL's Raiders, was also associated with the Black Panthers and the hippie culture.

From the standpoint of some Tigers fans there was a lot to hate about the A's. Holtzman had a smoke bomb thrown at him while warming up in the eighth; Hendrick was hit in the head by a bottle, hit in the back by a sock-covered rock, hit in the jaw by an ice cube, and hit in the glove by a can spurting beer. Fans in the outfield sectors bombarded the field with rolls of toilet paper and firecrackers. Play was halted several times to clean up the debris. Police issued 114 tickets to people in and around Tiger Stadium.

For some the mayhem was a reminder of the rowdy lawlessness of the Detroit riots of 1967, which had affected the entire city, including the southern area around Tiger Stadium. The frustrated Tiger faithful had known from the start of this series that their team was up against it. The A's future was in front of them; Detroit fans saw its squad as over the hill. Yet this series was going down to its final pitch, and the doggedness of this Detroit team is why memories of the '72 Tigers are cherished by many in Michigan.

With the Tigers down to their last out and Taylor at the plate, Moore made the final call of the ALCS: *"The count is two balls and two strikes.... Vida gets set, he kicks high, he throws.... There's a drive into center field, back goes George Hendrick.... He is under it.... The Swingin' A's have won the American League championship!"*

As Hendrick made the series-clinching catch, a beer can careened into his back; another one whistled past his ear just as Taylor's drive landed in his glove. Williams recalled so many beer cans being thrown in Hendrick's direction that his young center fielder was forced to make a mad dash for the dugout. Tenace said the angry mob and barrage of beer can missiles had the A's so scared that they barely celebrated on the field. "We just ran right into the clubhouse," he remembered.

"This was our greatest victory and it followed our worst loss," Williams announced in the lathery locker room. "It shows what kind of club we are."

Vida's performance—four shutout innings, nine infield outs—in Game Five is on par with Pedro Martinez's six innings of relief against Cleveland in the fifth and final game of the 1999 division series. Williams's waving Blue in from the bullpen—he pitched in four of the five LCS games and would throw in four of the seven World Series games—foreshadowed a future Bay Area skipper, Bruce Bochy, bringing his former ace, Tim Lincecum, on in relief in key situations in the 2012 postseason.

The '72 playoffs were the first to go the full five games and the only time in history both were decided by a single run. They foreshadowed five-game encounters between the Mets and Reds and A's and Orioles the following October, the Yankees and Royals in '76–77, the Phillies and

Astros in '80, the Dodgers and Expos in '81, the Brewers and Angels in '82, and the Padres and Cubs in '84.

The '72 postseason prompted Jerome Holtzman to write in *The Sporting News*: "So many of those people who have been insisting that baseball is dead, or dying, etc. suddenly have changed their tune. The best of five playoffs, in both leagues, woke them up and now they have returned to jump with joy, and are saying baseball still is and always will be the nation's No. 1 sport."

Rose fired the first salvo for the Fall Classic: "We're going to the World Series this year healthy," he said, "and we're gonna win it."

Pete didn't pull any punches, and neither did the A's. True to their manager's words, the Mustache Gang couldn't even celebrate a series-clinching win without some controversy. In Oakland's clubhouse following Game Five, Blue walked past Odom's locker. "How come you starters can't finish what you begin?" Vida shouted. "I know why."

Blue lifted his right hand to his throat to simulate choking. "Gaaaaag," he yelled mockingly. Blue Moon blew up. He rushed at Vida but was restrained by teammates. It was almost assuredly the first fight in a champion's clubhouse in history. We've got to get to the World Series, Williams thought, before we kill ourselves.

Three years after *Peyton Place* had run its course on ABC, "Hatin' Place," starring the Swingin' A's, was airing live on NBC. Fighting opponents, fighting their owner, and fighting themselves, the Mustache Gang was ready to go to war with the Big Red Machine in the Fall Classic.

CHAPTER THIRTEEN

Fans, players, and media found October baseball in the fall of '72 intoxicating. The dramatic late-afternoon shadows; the red, white, and blue bunting in banner-bedecked stadiums; the howling, hopeful zealots; and the incredibly intense brand of ball all combined to make for must-see TV. The soothing soundtrack of summer had been replaced by the furious rush of fall—kids running home from school in the afternoon and adults rushing home from the office to catch postseason games on NBC.

For more than a decade, the Peacock Network's broadcasting team of Hall of Fame announcer Curt Gowdy and former Yankees shortstop Tony Kubek served as the sound of the season when it came to the baseball playoffs and World Series on television. A veteran and versatile play-by-play announcer, Gowdy was NBC's lead announcer for a wide range of sports. A native of Wyoming, he was called "Cowboy" but was also nicknamed the "Broadcaster of Everything" for his numerous network assignments—the World Series, the Rose Bowl, NCAA men's basketball, Super Bowls, and American Football Conference games.

Gowdy's voice was instantly recognizable to millions of fans. Author John Updike thought Gowdy's warm, informal broadcasting style made him sound "like everybody's brother-in-law." Unlike many of his peers and those who would follow, Gowdy never relied on catchphrases, preferring instead to describe the action in an easy, straightforward manner. His illustrious peers in 1972 included Chris Schenkel of ABC and Ray Scott of CBS, but to columnist Joe Falls of *The Sporting News*, Gowdy was television's premier sports announcer, the successor to radio's Red Barber.

The reason he chose Gowdy, Falls wrote in the fall of 1972, was that he "wears so well." This despite getting the most important assignments, which meant Gowdy was on TV almost all the time. The danger of being overexposed was critical. Nothing is worse for an announcer, Falls stated, than someone turning on the TV and saying, "Oh, him again."

That didn't happen with Gowdy. His approach was smooth and knowledgeable. He didn't excite viewers with a flamboyant phrase, but he didn't bore them either. The Cowboy may not have ups, said Falls, but he didn't have many downs. That Gowdy liked his job and knew what it was about transcended his telecasts and was picked up on by viewers. He wasn't perfect; he made errors but was quick to correct them.

Gowdy battled network executives on how best to broadcast games. The Cowboy would listen quietly as Madison Avenue suits went on and on in meetings about how to present periphery events—pregame, halftime, and postgame shows. Finally an exasperated Gowdy would raise his hand.

"What is it, Gowdy?"
"Fellas, we're broadcasting a game. A *game*."

The Cowboy's cool professionalism fused nicely with Kubek's boyish, eager approach, which many found refreshing. Falls thought it a pleasant departure from the "rehearsed . . . handsome-face style that is so irritating on TV." Kubek got away with his lack of TV polish because the former All-Star knew the game so well. Falls favorably compared Kubek to ABC's college football color analyst Bud Wilkinson as broadcasters who could provide astonishingly accurate predictions of upcoming plays. Gowdy had that knack as well. He noted during a national telecast of a Cubs game that summer that Chicago's Jim Hickman averaged a home run every seventeen times at bat. It was a pretty good ratio, the Cowboy declared, and as if on cue, Hickman homered moments later.

Gowdy and Kubek had their critics. Earlier that summer a *TV Guide* editorial had criticized announcers for talking too much during sporting events. Gowdy and Kubek were among the parties cited. Writer Jack Craig of *The Sporting News* thought *TV Guide*'s criticism odd since he had recently sat through a one-sided Pirates-Dodgers telecast and the only thing that had prevented him from switching stations was the "sparkling verbalizing" of Gowdy and Kubek. Their commentary, which he noted was usually directed at fans but sometimes to each other, was not the product of an impromptu approach. It was, Craig wrote, the product of much pregame hustling by Gowdy and Kubek.

Craig recalled a Saturday telecast at Fenway Park when he had arranged to interview Kubek prior to the first pitch. It was difficult to do, Craig discovered, because Tony spent almost all of the pregame talking with players and gathering information for use in the broadcast. Kubek's file of material was so large that he used only a portion of it that day in Boston, but it was timely enough that he was able to incorporate it into Red Sox telecasts later in the season.

Craig considered the between-pitches remarks by Gowdy and Kubek a difficult task made to look easy by their professionalism. They had to get in and out with a complete thought without preempting the report on the next pitch. Kubek had to master that task in his role as color analyst and did it well enough that he rarely got caught in the overflow.

"Kubek had the proper training and it made a difference," Gowdy said, referring to Tony's working the backup game on NBC before moving up to the national telecast.

Gowdy shrugged off *TV Guide*'s criticism that he and Kubek were too talkative. "You're damned if you do and damned if you don't," he said. Gowdy remarked that since the audience for NBC's Monday night baseball games may include more casual fans than the Saturday telecasts, he and Kubek would explain something they knew sounded routine to longtime followers of the sport. On those occasions Gowdy would preface his remarks with an apology of sorts to veteran fans. As far as Craig was concerned, Gowdy and Kubek had little to apologize for. A baseball fan for more than thirty years and someone who knew the game and its subtleties, Craig found Gowdy and Kubek's comments and remarks "invariably informative, sometimes even provocative."

NBC's camerawork in the 1972 postseason also drew praise. Future Hall of Fame writer Roger Angell thought NBC's work alert, subtle, and up to every occasion. It was television at its best, Angell wrote, and it had almost conquered the obstacles and difficulties of covering a spacious, three-dimensional sport in a two-dimensional medium. NBC's multiple cameras captured vivid close-ups—Rollie Fingers and his waxed mustache, Bobby Tolan and his Lady Liberty stance—and provided viewers with details sometimes missed by fans in the stands. Falls watched some of the postseason games on television and said he saw more than he would have had he been at the ball park. To Falls, NBC's work in the 1972 postseason was "as masterful as any network could do on any sports event."

There would be plenty for NBC to cover as the Fall Classic opened at Riverfront Stadium on Saturday, October 14. Game One of the World Series is like Opening Day of the major league season in that it as much spectacle as it is sport. The stadium banners and bunting, ceremonial first pitch, and inevitable first clash of armor combine to make the game an event. Game One through the years had delivered some of sport's most iconic performances—Sandy Koufax striking out 15 Yankees in 1963, Bob Gibson fanning 17 Tigers in '68.

NBC's TV broadcast began with its classic theme song followed by panning cameras and Gowdy's voice-over promoting the World Series matchup and the network's sponsors: Gillette and Chrysler. As Reds general manager Bob Howsam, resplendent in a red blazer, took up residence in the lower-level blue seats by the Cincinnati dugout and looked across the field at Finley and his extravagantly attired A's in their gaudy gold jerseys, a record crowd of 52,918 filed along the concrete concourse and into the stadium, filling the levels of green, yellow, and red seats that circled the field. Some unfurled banners aimed at the A's daily green-and-gold fashion show and their long locks:

The A's Have Weird Uniforms
Women's Lib Will Destroy the Family

The Series opener would be played under overcast skies, rain having left huge carpet stains on the synthetic surface, which would itself be a topic of conversation. No one doubted or denied that the advent of Astroturf had altered the way baseball was being played. The ball bounced higher than on natural grass and traveled faster, forcing infielders to play farther back than they normally would in order to have enough time to react. Because the playing surface was as hard and fast as a billiards table, ground balls that would have been slowed on grass scooted through the infield.

Because of artificial grass, speed rather than power was becoming the name of the game in the National League. The success of 1960s teams like Maury Wills's Dodgers and Lou Brock's Cardinals had the league trending back to the era of quickness on the bases, and that trend accelerated in the 1970s. Riverfront's carpeted confines, however, posed a potential problem for the A's, who played primarily on grass fields in the American League. In 1972 Comiskey Park was the lone AL stadium to sport artificial surface, and that was only in the infield and adjacent foul territory.

Synthetic surfaces were a staple of baseball at that time, like Pete Rose's Prince Valiant haircut and afternoon World Series games. It didn't require God's sunlight to thrive, and maintenance was limited to regular vacuuming. Cincinnati was one of six National League stadiums to sport synthetic surface in the 1970s, Houston, Pittsburgh, Philadelphia, San Francisco, and St. Louis being the others. It was enough, Dodgers longtime manager Walter Alston said at the time, to alter the concept of the game in numerous ways. Since more runs were going to be scored, managers were going to have to be more patient with their pitchers. If only one or two fields had artificial surface, skippers could manage those games as they would on natural grass. Now that half of the twelve-team National League had synthetic surface, managers had come to accept more scoring and wouldn't be pulling pitchers the way they used to.

Baseball was entering a new era, one that harkened back to the quick, daring brand of ball Alston had experienced, albeit briefly, as a twenty-four-year-old rookie infielder with the Gashouse Gang Cardinals late in the summer of 1936. With the modern game opening up, teams would be less likely to play for one run in the early innings the way they had a decade earlier. That meant fewer bunting situations, and many wondered whether the bunt was still a viable strategy on artificial surfaces. The slick turf made it difficult to deaden the ball; it rolled so fast that defenses had an excellent chance at a force play.

Infielders played so deep, they appeared to be playing shallow outfield positions. Reds second baseman Joe Morgan played his position 12–15 feet deeper on the Riverfront rug than he did on grass. Infielders could play better defense, but at bat their hits had to be solid; there were few bad-hop singles on Cincinnati's carpet. Helping defenders but handicapping singles hitters, the Riverfront rug gaveth and tooketh away.

Former Orioles veteran Frank Robinson returned to the NL in '72 to play for Alston's Dodgers and found the ball did indeed move faster on artificial turf. He found that the ball also bounced higher, and the combination of speed and height was something veteran fielders had to adjust to. Players knew for the most part what a certain type of hit would do on natural grass; Robinson said they weren't so sure on synthetic surface, and that made for some uncertain fielding.

Additional pregame conjecture centered on the caliber of ball played in the American and National Leagues. Cincinnati skipper Sparky Anderson, who liked to shoot from the lip, spoke openly about the differences between the leagues: "I'm not saying Oakland can't beat us," he told reporters. "But I'm saying that you can't compare our league to theirs. Our league is tougher from top to bottom. The National League playoffs between Cincinnati and Pittsburgh brought together the two best teams in baseball."

Anderson added that if he said the American League was as good as the National League, he'd be lying. Oakland could play in the National League and be competitive, as could maybe Boston too. But they were the only ones, he stated. Privately he told his coaches the Reds would win in four straight.

Rose didn't back away from comparing leagues either. The real World Series, he told reporters, had been between the Reds and Pirates. He said people asked every year if he would get two hundred hits. Now how many people get that question in the American League, he asked. Still the man who would become baseball's all-time hits leader admitted to being impressed by the A's pitching arms: "I looked at those ERAs," he said, "and

I don't care if you're pitching for the Rhode Island Reds in the Chicken League, a good ERA is a good ERA."

The 1972 World Series would be the first since 1968 that did not include Robinson. As someone who had starred in both leagues, he was in a unique position to compare the AL and NL, and he did so in an article for *Sport* magazine. Robinson believed the National League was better and that most ballplayers in the NL shared that belief. The basic difference was personnel. The AL had good players, but the NL had more.

Robinson pointed to the NL's readiness to sign black players and the AL's reluctance to do the same. NL teams were willing to sign any promising prospect regardless of color, he said. The AL was only interested in can't-miss black prospects. By not signing raw talent that would develop in a few years, the AL missed out on outstanding players. The NL was more willing to employ subs and second-line players who were black. Robinson referred to it as "selective discrimination." Because of it, the NL got the reputation among blacks as a black player's league, and since blacks preferred signing with NL teams, that added to the imbalance between the leagues.

Robinson thought the NL was weighted one way, the AL another way. The recent Yankees dynasty that ended in 1964 had only a few black play-ers. The Red Sox and Senators, he said, had for years only a few "token" blacks. He compared those clubs to the Dodgers, who he said became a dominant team because they had more black players than other teams. The Dodgers also had Koufax and Drysdale, arguably the greatest pitching combo in history, at the top of their rotation. Robinson pointed to the Birds' conquerors in '71, the Pirates. They were the first major league team to start an all-black lineup in a game, and they won the World Series. He pointed out that there were black stars and white stars in both leagues but noted that the NL's stars were mostly black (Willie Mays, Hank Aaron, Roberto Clemente, Willie Stargell, Willie McCovey, Orlando Cepeda) and the AL's stars largely white (Harmon Killebrew, Boog Powell, Brooks Robinson, Carl Yastrzemski, Rico Petrocelli, Frank Howard). The same was true, he said, when it came to pitching. Many of the NL's best pitchers (Bob Gibson, Juan Marichal, Ferguson Jenkins, Al Downing) were men of color, while most of the AL's top pitchers (Jim Palmer, Catfish Hunter, Mickey Lolich, Wilbur Wood) were white. Sure, he said, there were outstanding white players (Pete Rose, Johnny Bench, Tom Seaver, Joe Torre) in the NL and equally outstanding black stars (Reggie Jackson, Vida Blue, Tony Oliva, Rod Carew) in the AL, but the balance was bad.

The racial makeup of the leagues dictated strategy, Robinson asserted. NL managers played a more exciting, wide-open game because they had more to work with: more speed, more power. The NL had power hitters (Mays, Clemente, Aaron) who could run the bases. The AL's power hitters (Powell, Killebrew, Howard) were bigger, heavier types who didn't run as well. Thus AL managers didn't call for the steal or the hit-and-run as much; they were more conservative than their NL counterparts. A case in point was Oakland's opponents in the postseason. The Reds stole 140 bases; the Tigers, 17.

If there was one AL team that could match up with the NL's best, Robinson said, it was Oakland. And it was because the A's had tremendous black talent (Jackson, Blue, Campaneris) to go with their white stars (Hunter, Holtzman, Fingers, Rudi, Bando).

Neither Jackson, balancing himself on crutches, nor Blue toed the company line when it came to league comparisons. The A's injured slugger said the National League had more depth, better personnel overall, and more good young black players than the American League. Blue told reporters he didn't believe Oakland had the best club in baseball: "I'd rate Cincinnati and Pittsburgh better," he declared.

Their boss, Dick Williams, didn't agree with the assessment that the AL was inferior. "I've seen some pretty bad National League teams on television," he told the media. "Which team is best remains to be seen."

Williams knew he had a good ball club. Not great but good—damn good, he told *Sport* magazine writer Al Hirshberg in the visiting manager's office the morning of Game One. As he spoke, Williams lit another cigarette; he was well on his way to his three-packs-a-day average. "I don't know if we'll win this thing," Williams told Hirshberg. "All I want is to win today. That's all I ever want—win today."

Shortly thereafter Williams emerged from the runway between the locker room and dugout and walked toward a swarm of media, officials, promoters, and privileged visitors. An avalanche of questions followed: "Is your pitching rotation set? . . . What about Vida Blue? . . . Does Finley tell you what to do? . . . How will you pitch Bench? . . . How will you stop Tolan and Morgan?"

Williams didn't mind the media horde. He knew it beat the alternative—sitting home and watching the World Series on TV. A baseball official approached and whispered something. "Damn right I want to see him," Williams replied. "He's my buddy."

With writers on his heels Williams walked across the field and embraced a grinning Anderson. Teammates at Fort Worth in 1950 and longtime admirers of one another, they were two of the friendliest rivals in the long history of the Fall Classic.

Williams and Anderson had been down the Series road before. Williams's experience in 1967 had been kind of a drag, as the Buckinghams sang that year, Williams and the Red Sox falling to the St. Louis Cardinals in seven games. Anderson had been to the Fall Classic in 1970, the Reds bowing to the Orioles in five games.

This time around, the Reds were looser, more confident. Tony Perez told team announcer Joe Nuxhall following the win over Pittsburgh that the Big Red Machine was "gonna have a picnic" in the World Series. During a Reds workout on the field Rose spotted A's shortstop Bert Campaneris, who had been suspended in the ALCS for his bat-throwing incident but reinstated by Commissioner Bowie Kuhn for the Fall Classic.

"Hey Campy!" Rose shouted. "I just want you to know that bats don't carry too well in this ball park."

Before Game One, Hunter, Bando, and Tenace were at a Cincinnati restaurant when they spotted Johnny Bench surrounded by what Hunter called an "entourage." The Catfish thought the star catcher was carrying himself like a god and talking big about how the A's had better not pitch him this way or that way.

Hunter said he walked over to where Bench was sitting. "I'll throw it right under your nose if I want to," the Cat told him. Bench, he said, just stared at him, as though you weren't supposed to talk to a superstar like that.

Bench didn't know what to think of Charlie Finley's Oakland A's, with their mustaches and mule. He watched the deciding game of the ALCS on television, and what he saw of the A's impressed him; they knew how to execute.

Prior to the Series opener Bench met Jackson for dinner at Scarlata's, a favorite dining place for Bench. The two talked baseball before Bench dropped Jackson off at the A's motel. As they walked past the players' rooms, Bench said he smelled the unmistakable aroma of marijuana. The A's, he thought, were smoking dope as they got ready for the World Series. Bench was shaken and wondered how could they be doing this.

Bench knew that flower children were alive and well and that the Reds represented the establishment and the A's, the California kids. Their players landed in Cincinnati wearing mustaches, beards, long hair, and sideburns of every variety—Martin Van Buren–like muttonchops, Mexican-style mustaches, Fu Manchus, and a Snidely Whiplash look. Writer Pete Hamill referred to them as the "mustached bravos." Columnist Jim Murray of the *Los Angeles Times* said the A's were "really the Oakland Hair-o's, a bunch of guys so hirsute you half-expected them to take off their clothes and start dancing at any minute." He called the A's starters "eight guys wearing costumes right out of Flo Ziegfeld."

Baseball writer Joe Trimble of the New York *Daily News* labeled the A's "bad guys, the ones with the mustaches and beards." The Reds were "good guys, the clean-shaven Cincys."

Even the team nicknames—Swingin' A's, the Mustache Gang, the Big Red Machine—conjured up images of Berkeley students taking on the military-industrial complex. This wasn't going to be a World Series, Bench thought. It was going to be a war between the Bikers and the Boy Scouts, the new and old orders, liberals versus conservatives, the hairs versus the squares.

Bando agreed with Bench that the "Mustaches versus the Machine" angle was the focal point of the media. Captain Sal called it a contrast of different styles. Maverick owner Charlie Finley and his A's flaunted rules and were cast as casual Californians, but Bando believed the A's themselves didn't fully buy into the concept that the Reds represented Middle America while the A's were anti-establishment. He did believe that young people were likely leaning toward the A's while older people were rooting for the Reds. One wasn't going to find hordes of hippies, for instance, in Cincy's Fountain Square.

On some level, the sixty-ninth World Series was baseball's equivalent to the 1969 Super Bowl, with the A's as the shaggy New York Jets of the upstart American Football League and the Senior Circuit Reds cast in the role of the clean-cut Baltimore Colts of the older NFL.

Much was made of what the A's looked like and supposedly stood for, and a lot of people were forgetting that the Mustache Gang could, as Bench stated, "play the game pretty well." The A's had downed Detroit, a team Bench saw as tough but tired and old. With Jackson out for the series, there was really no way the A's were expected to beat the Big Red Machine. That notion comforted the conservative Cincinnati fans, whose slogan was "Paint the Town Reds" and who felt that when the Fall Classic was finished, their Reds would make the baseball world safe from mustaches, mules, and Charles O. Finley.

Rarely has a World Series featured such a startling contrast in championship clubs. It was a David and Goliath matchup, and while Oakland owned an eclectic combination of personalities and characters with whom people around the country identified, experts favored Goliath. Along with Jackson, the A's had also lost to injury reliever Darold Knowles, a hard-throwing lefty who owned a 1.37 ERA that season.

Perez's prophecy that the Big Red Machine would have a "picnic" in the World Series wouldn't come true, but one made by Knowles would. On the A's bus ride to Riverfront Stadium for the opener, Knowles announced he had dreamed the night before that Tenace or George Hendrick would be Series MVP.

"I hope you're right," Tenace said. "Because if one of us wins the MVP, it means we won the Series."

Tenace had been given a vote of confidence by Williams following the win over Detroit and was so relaxed for the showdown with the Reds that he almost felt as if the World Series games were spring training exhibitions.

With game-time temperatures in the mid-60s, Reds right-hander Gary Nolan fired the first pitch to Campaneris—"a strike at the knees," NBC radio announcer Jim Simpson told listeners. Amid the sound and fury inside Riverfront Stadium the sixty-ninth World Series was under way. Riverfront's flaring lights brightened somber skies overhead. Campy eventually singled, but Nolan, who had a team-high 15 wins that season and a 1.99 ERA, retired Joe Rudi on a fly to Cesar Geronimo in center and got Matty Alou, hitting as usual from deep in the box and far off the plate, to ground to Morgan for a double play.

In Nolan, A's hitters were facing a man who owned one of the best change-ups and one of the most deceptive pitching motions in the majors. One of the reasons for the success of Nolan's change-up was that he threw it off the same motion as his fastball. Nolan lifted his leg high, then drove it forward as he drove his right arm down.

"He throws every pitch in the same way—the left leg kick and the right arm coming through," Gowdy said. "He's had that rhythm all year. That's why his change-up is so effective because the change-up is thrown with the same leg drive and arm drive as his fastball. It deceives the batter."

Simpson told his listeners that since Nolan didn't have the flaring fastball he used to due to arm problems in 1968–69, he had to make good pitches, had to have good control. "If he does not make good pitches, does not have good control," Simpson stated, "Gary Nolan is in trouble."

Ken Holtzman, making his first mound appearance in Riverfront Stadium since no-hitting the Reds the previous June 3 while with the Cubs, faced Rose, Morgan, and Tolan in the bottom of the first. Sporting an 11-5 lifetime record against the Reds going into Game One, Holtzman didn't allow a ball to leave the lime green infield. This first collision between Cincinnati's celebrated table setters and the A's stylish pitching was significant.

"Look at the first three men in this Cincinnati lineup," Kubek said during the season, "and I don't think there's any other team in baseball that can put three men up who have as good eyes or are as good hitters or run as well as Morgan, Rose and Tolan."

"It's an impressive front three," Gowdy responded. "They can get in there and set the table for Bench and Perez."

The pressure Morgan, Rose, and Tolan put on a defense, Kubek stated, was significant: "They're hit-and-run threats, they're base-stealing threats, you've got to be moving around [defensively], leaving your position . . . a lot of pressure. You've got to play more shallow, especially on the artificial surface. [The ball] can scoot by you."

Viewers settled in for a clash that extended even to the umpires. The A's and Reds knew balls and strikes were called differently in the two leagues. AL umps gave the high strike; NL umps, the low strike. AL hitters hacking away at high strikes produced more pop-ups; NL hitters golfing for low strikes produced more grounders. The result was often low-average hitters with higher home run totals in the AL and more high-average hitters in the NL since some of those ground balls were going to get through the infield on artificial turf. The differences extended to how the league umpires dressed (NL umpires in black jackets and pants; AL umps, in navy blue blazers and gray slacks), how they stood behind home plate, and where they stood to cover second base.

AL umpire Jim Honochick worked the 1972 Fall Classic, and he knew there would always be differences among umps in style and technique. The rule book stated that the strike zone extends from a batter's armpits to his knees, but Honochick knew every umpire had a different interpretation. Early Wynn, a major league pitcher from 1939 to 1963, complained that the strike zone had shrunk "like a cheap suit." Wynn's complaint, umpire Ron Luciano wrote, was lodged at a time when the strike zone was "a bit larger than Australia." The strike zone varied in part because of the size differences of the players and the umpires. A smaller hitter would have a smaller strike zone; so too would a smaller umpire. The 6-foot-4, 300-pound Luciano couldn't bend as low behind home plate as the 5-foot-9, 175-pound Rich Garcia, so the top of Luciano's strike zone was higher than Garcia's. Ed Runge, an American League umpire from 1954 to 1970, was said to have a strike zone that stretched from dugout to dugout; he wanted the hitters to swing the bat. Runge was the home plate ump in the 1967 All-Star Game when a record 29 batters struck out.

Differences also extended to the wearing of chest protectors. Some umps wore them inside; others, outside. Honochick liked the latter style for health reasons. Unless an ump was foolish or careless enough to stick his arms out, Honochick believed there was no way he could be injured while wearing the outside protector. The same couldn't be said for inside protectors. Lou Jorda, whom Honochick considered a fine umpire, was working a game at the Polo Grounds and was hit over the heart while wearing an inside protector. His heart was damaged, and Jorda was done umpiring.

Honochick understood all the differences, but he didn't think AL and NL umpires should work independently of each other during the season. Major league umpires, he thought, should have uniformity in the way they worked.

Game One had a National League umpire, Chris Pelekoudas, behind home plate. It was the second Fall Classic for the Chicago native, and if the A's were looking for positive omens, they might have found one in the fact that in Pelekoudas's previous World Series, in 1966, a similar AL underdog—the Orioles—had upset the NL favorite, the Dodgers. One other omen for fans who couldn't get enough of October baseball involved Honochick, who was working first base in the opener. This was his sixth and final World Series, and each of the previous five had gone the full seven games.

Pelekoudas's road to serving as crew chief in the 1972 World Series was an interesting one. He had failed a tryout with the 1934 Cardinals and began umpiring while serving in World War II as an Army Special Services officer. He worked in the minors from 1948 to 1959, then got his first big major league assignment in 1961 when he was named to the crew for the second All-Star Game that summer. He worked the 1967 and '75 All-Star Games, as well and the NLCS in 1969 and '73. On August 18, 1965, Pelekoudas ordered an apparent Aaron home run nullified because Aaron had stepped out of the batter's box when he made contact. Pelekoudas was also the first ump to eject Gaylord Perry for using an illegal greasy substance on the ball. He was a witness to history on several occasions: Willie Mays's four home runs in 1961; six no-hitters, including Koufax's in 1963 and Sandy's perfect game in 1965; the first game at Shea Stadium in 1964.

In October '72, Pelekoudas's crew included Mel Steiner and Bob Engle of the NL and Honochick, Frank Umont, and Bill Haller of the AL. Umont was a former NFL player, a tackle for the New York Giants from 1943 to 1945. Haller was the older brother of Tigers catcher Tom Haller, who had just made his final appearance as a player on October 4. The Hallers had made major league history on July 14, 1972, when they became the first brothers to appear in the same game as home plate umpire and catcher. Bill Haller also appeared in an El Producto cigar commercial that summer. He was one of the last umpires to wear an outside chest protector and in 1980 was involved in a now legendary confrontation with feisty Orioles skipper Earl Weaver. Honochick gained national fame when he appeared in one of the many sports-celebrity commercials sponsored by Miller Lite beer. After putting on glasses, Honochick finally recognized his fellow Miller Lite pitchman. "Hey! You're Boog Powell!"

High-profile umpires like Honochick and Luciano were a bridge to colorful showboats in blue from the past like John "Beans" Reardon and those in the future—namely, "Dutch" Rennert and "Cowboy" Joe West.

Nolan sailed through the first two outs in the top of the second. Just twenty-four years old, he had a history of neck and shoulder problems, but on this day he was strong. He looked like the pitcher who had led the league with a .750 winning percentage, and he and Bench were working well together. Hendrick drew a two-out walk, and Tenace stood in. Nolan was moving the ball around, not trying to overpower the hitters. But he veered from his breaking pitches and tried to slip a fastball past Tenace. Gowdy made the call: *"There's a long blast to deep left. . . . That one is going and it is . . . gone! A home run for Gene Tenace! And the A's grab the lead in the top of the second inning with a two-out, two-run homer by Gene Tenace, who hit only five homers all year."*

Bench was startled. Nolan had left a fastball over the plate, and veteran *Game of the Week* viewers remembered a meeting with the Cubs in

Riverfront that summer when Nolan had tried to slip a fastball past Jim Hickman only to see it go sailing over the same left-field wall. But Hickman had 17 homers that season; nobody had said anything about Tenace having power. It was surprising since Ray Shore had scouted the A's for a month, and "Snacks," as Shore was called by Anderson and others, could have taught Sherlock Holmes about super sleuthing.

As far as Sparky was concerned, Shore was baseball's answer to the CIA and the FBI. He had every Oakland player pinpointed—what he hit, what he didn't hit, where to play him, how to play him. The Reds' reports on Oakland's offense told Cincinnati pitchers it was key to keep Campaneris off base and to limit the damage done by Alou, Rudi, Bando, and Epstein. Shore told the Big Red Machine's bombers—Rose, Morgan, Bench, Perez, et al.—that while he wouldn't say Oakland had the best pitching in baseball, the A's were good. To give Reds hitters a barometer with which they were familiar, Cincinnati's super scout compared Hunter to Rick Wise and Blue to Steve Carlton.

Anderson thought Shore's report accurate, but it wasn't when it came to Tenace. His 1-for-17 in the ALCS included some hard outs, and his lone hit was the series winner. Because Tenace had been stinging the ball and didn't strike out as much as the A's other catcher, Dave Duncan, Williams had played an educated hunch when filling out his lineup.

Seen by reporters as one of the lesser lights on a colorful club considered a big underdog, Tenace was largely ignored by the hundreds of media members milling around as the A's took batting practice. Anonymity aided Tenace on this occasion. While scribes conducted interviews with Bando, Campy, et al., Tenace was left alone to take additional cuts in the cage. Hunter compared Tenace's short, compact swing to that of Minnesota Twins Hall of Famer Harmon Killebrew. His teammates knew Tenace would eat fastballs for lunch. Fortunately for the A's, Hunter said, the Reds never did figure out how to pitch Gino.

A report on the A's filled out in the summer of '72 by Steve Vrablik, a scout of more than forty years for the Chicago White Sox and then the Seattle Mariners, shows that Tenace was rated as a "3" in power, which was considered good and just below the "3.5" given to Mike Epstein and the maximum of "4" to Jackson.

Williams stated later that the sudden emergence of a balding reserve was "a great story." In the space of eight days in October, twenty-six-year-old Gene Tenace would become so famous that he would be the target of an assassin's threat. Jokes about his name—"Tenace, anyone?" and "Tenace the Menace"—became commonplace around the country.

Tenace had become a part of baseball mythology, but he was a better ballplayer than many thought. In limited action he had hit .305 in 1970 and .274 in '71, and his slugging percentage those two seasons was .562 and .430 respectively. As a starter from 1973 to 1976 he hit 22 or more homers four consecutive seasons with a high of 29 in '75. His 91 homers over that span ranked third on the A's behind Jackson and Bando. Two things about Tenace: he never moved from the batter's box once he stepped in, keeping his feet firmly planted in the same spot, and he had an exceptionally trained eye for a power hitter. He had six seasons of more than 100 walks and twice led the league in bases on balls. Among catchers, Tenace would retire tied for third with Bench and Joe Torre in OPS, trailing Roy Campanella and Yogi Berra.

Tenace paved his path to the bigs by batting .319 with 20 homers in 1969 with Binghamton in the Southern Association. The previous summer he had rapped 21 homers for Peninsula in the Carolina League. Tenace played for Valley High in Lucasville, Ohio, some one hundred miles from Cincinnati, and had been scouted by Reds bird dog Gene Bennett.

Tenace had a stubborn self-belief stemming at least in part from a paternal grandfather who had emigrated from Italy and settled in the steel-tough Pittsburgh area. Tenace was born in Russellton, a coal-mining town in western Pennsylvania. The Yankees operated a farm club in nearby Butler, and Gino grew up a fan of a team that boasted a bevy of Italian American stars: Berra, Tony Lazzeri, Joe DiMaggio, Frankie Crosetti, Phil Rizzuto, Vic Raschi, et al. Tenace's father, Fiore, was a semipro baseball player—"A pretty good one," Gene remembered—and he pushed his son to be a good athlete as well. "He drove me to be a big leaguer," Tenace said, "and when I say 'drove,' I'm not kidding. He was on me all the time, telling me to do better."

Tenace, whose name was Anglicized to Fury Gene Tenace, developed an ulcer at age thirteen. He was also called "Steamboat" because some considered him clumsy. Despite the physical and emotional problems that developed at least in part from his father's prodding, Tenace helped Valley High win a state championship. The Reds and Yankees scouted him but passed on signing him. The Yankees' rejection proved particularly disappointing. They were his favorite team, but when Tenace approached one of their scouts, he was told there was no way he would make it to the big leagues. Danny Carnevale, a scout for the then Kansas City Athletics, didn't agree, and Tenace was selected in the twentieth round of the 1965 draft. He debuted for the A's on May 29, 1969, going 0 for 4 as Hunter lost to Denny McLain and Detroit in the Oakland Coliseum.

Tenace spent the 1969 and '70 seasons as Oakland's third-string catcher before becoming Duncan's backup in '71. One year later he was shocking the Reds in the Fall Classic. He was an overnight sensation, and it had taken him only several years to become one.

The Reds trailed 2–0, but Bench believed the Big Red Machine would get to Holtzman. He made sure of it by being a catalyst in both of the Reds' rallies. He started the bottom of the second with a single to left and took second base on a single by Perez. A walk to Denis Menke loaded the bases and brought up Cesar Geronimo. Williams walked to the mound, pulled a sheet of paper out of his pocket to read to Holtzman, then retreated to the dugout. The paper provided details on how to pitch Geronimo. Holtzman induced a pop-out before Dave Concepcion, the stadium lights flaring on his bright red helmet, grounded the ball to his opposite, Campaneris.

Jim Simpson provided the call on NBC Radio: *"Ground ball. . . . High hop to Campaneris, flips to Green, Green back to first base. . . . Safe! It's 2–1 as Bench scores from third!"*

Holtzman struck out Nolan to end the uprising. A pattern had been established that would last throughout this Series. Tenace's power would plague Reds pitchers; Bench would come to bat fifteen times over the seven games with the bases empty; and Williams, making the first of his staggering forty-two trips, would wear a path to the pitcher's mound.

Batting leadoff again in the fourth, Bench walked and took third on Perez's single to right-center. Menke's grounder scored Bench, and the Reds tied the game at 2.

Bench was excelling on defense as well. Tenace watched the Reds' workouts and witnessed Bench's whistling throws to second base. "That isn't an arm," Tenace told bystanders. "That's a rifle." Gowdy called Bench the "human shotgun." From 1970 to 1976 the Reds played in forty-two postseason games, and opponents stole just two bases off Bench.

Observers looked forward to the confrontation between Bench and the A's roadrunner, Campaneris. The Oakland Express was the American League's premier base stealer from 1965 to 1972, leading the league in steals six times and twice reaching his career-high of 62. He led again in '72, pirating 54 bases.

In the third inning Campaneris stroked a one-out single to left and took his lead off first base. Campy had speed to spare, but Bench had thrown out 60 percent of attempting base stealers that season. It's likely many leaned forward in anticipation of the early showdown between Bench's cannon-like arm and Campy's fleet feet. Bench could get rid of the ball very quickly, but Campaneris was known to simply outrun the ball to the bag.

As Nolan cut loose with a 1-1 curve to Joe Rudi, Campy scorched the soggy synthetic surface with his speed. Gowdy, Kubek, and Reds radio voice Al Michaels—NBC at that time invited the announcers of the participating teams to join the national TV broadcast for their clubs' home games—analyzed what followed:

Gowdy: *There goes Campaneris, the throw by Bench and he's out at second base!*

Michaels: *Campaneris [had] a pretty good jump. . . . Johnny Bench can throw out anybody if he throws a strike and that's what he threw to Joe Morgan!*

Kubek: *Campy had a good lead off first base but that rifle arm of Johnny Bench. . . . What more can you say?*

Campaneris had plenty to say to second base umpire Mel Steiner, and replays show Campy was correct to dispute the call. He had beaten Bench's throw, his right foot hitting the bag in a cloud of dirt in the sliding pit as Morgan applied the tag on Campaneris's calf.

Oakland got a run back in the fifth, as Simpson told listeners: *"Here's Tenace. . . . Nolan throws him a curve and he lines it down the line, very deep, inside the flag pole and it is a home run! Gene Tenace, who went 0-for-15 and then won the playoff game against Detroit, hit a home run in the second inning off a fastball, hit a hanging Gary Nolan curve and has lined his second home run in two times at bat."*

The Reds had pitched him more carefully, but still Tenace tagged one. There was fury in Fury Gene's bat as he became the first player in World Series history to homer in his first two trips to the plate. Nolan thought his pitch "hung like a feather." Holtzman made the lead stand up by successfully stalling the Big Red Machine. He got Tolan with a slick pickoff move in the third.

The A's had agreed that any time any of the Reds' first three batters got on base, the pitcher would make several throws over to keep the runner close. "Tolan broke when I raised my arms," Holtzman said, "and we got him."

Bench, batting leadoff for the third straight time, doubled to right to start the sixth. Williams, wanting a "fresh arm," waved in reliever Rollie Fingers. A's announcer Monte Moore made the calls as the "Cucamonga Kid"—as teammates called Fingers—stranded Bench on second, courtesy of some hard, biting pitches: *"Fingers kicks that white shoe in the air, throws a curve and strikes out Perez! That ball really broke! Fingers at the belt, here's the pitch. . . . Swinging strike three! He left Menke up there."*

In the seventh the Reds rallied behind a leadoff single from Concepcion. Testing Tenace's arm, Concepcion broke for second on a steal attempt. Tenace, figuring the Reds might run in this instance, had called a pitchout and pegged a strong throw to second. Believing Campaneris had tagged

Concepcion high on the shoulder, Steiner called him out. It was the Reds' turn to argue, and the Series film backs them up, Concepcion sliding under Campy's tag.

"The umpire said he tagged me on the shoulder, but I didn't feel it," Concepcion said.

"The replay showed that Campaneris did not tag him," snorted Anderson. "It was the turning point of the game." Rose followed by working Fingers for a walk, and Vida Blue was brought in to face Morgan. A wild pitch sent Rose to second, and after walking Morgan, Blue got out of the jam by retiring Tolan on a foulout to Tenace.

The Big Red Machine had one more chance against Vida in the ninth. In a situation strikingly similar to Game Five of the National League Championship Series, pinch runner George Foster was on third. With Rose at bat and two outs, Williams headed to the hill again. Bando moved closer to the plate from his position at third base. Rose tried a two-out squeeze and fouled off a bunt. Blue stared in for the sign as Moore made the climactic call of Game One: *"Vida Blue winds, here's the pitch. . . . High, bouncing ball on the infield, they're gonna have to hurry. . . . Kubiak has got it, throws to first. He's got him! And the Oakland A's have won the first game of the 1972 World Series! The final score of an exciting ball game: Oakland 3, Cincinnati 2!"*

"If Kubiak plays me right," Rose snapped in the postmortem, "then he never gets me. I'm not impressed with the A's. Outside of Gene Tenace they didn't do much. They only got four hits so I'm not impressed with their offense. They had a couple shots at double plays and they didn't make them so I'm not impressed with their defense. Johnny Bench threw out the only two guys who tried to steal so I'm not impressed with their base running. And Holtzman didn't throw as hard as when he was with the Cubs."

Rose's frustration would last throughout much of the Series. Over the previous decade he had been baseball's most consistent hitter, hitting over .300 eight straight seasons and collecting more than two hundred hits five times. But he didn't get a hit in Game One and didn't reach base. It was another trend taking shape that would slow the Big Red Machine in its drive to win a world championship.

Oakland's win was a tribute to the detailed scouting reports provided by Al Hollingsworth and Sherm Lollar. Known as "Boots" during his major league career, Hollingsworth had pitched for the Reds and four other teams from 1935 to 1946. Lollar had been an All-Star catcher in the 1950s with the St. Louis Browns and Chicago White Sox and had also played for the Cleveland Indians and New York Yankees.

Hollingsworth followed the Big Red Machine for their final thirty-two games of the season and provided a report that was among the most extensive Williams had ever seen. It detailed how to pitch to the Reds, where to play them in the field, how the Reds played hitters, and how they pitched. The reports were instrumental in pitching to Geronimo (a .275 hitter that season, he would bat just .158 against the A's) in the second inning and also informed the A's that Rose liked to bunt in situations similar to the one in the ninth. Williams relayed the info to Blue, and Vida responded by throwing fastballs rather than the off-speed pitches that Rose would have preferred.

"I was hoping for a curve that I could bunt," Rose admitted. "But he fed me fastballs."

Blue's pitch selection was a credit to Hollingsworth and Lollar, the A's answers to Shore. The advance work of these super scouts would prove as instrumental in determining the World Series winner as anything that happened between the white lines. Kubiak thought the reports provided by Hollingsworth and Lollar picked up on even the most obscure tendencies of the Big Red Machine.

Prior to the Series the A's went over the reports on the Reds so thoroughly that by the time they took the field at Riverfront Stadium, they felt as if they had been playing Cincinnati all season. Kubiak retired Rose for the final out of Game One on a grounder that was anything but routine on the rain-stained rug; the ball was hit over the mound and to the right of second base. A startled Rose asked reporters afterward, "How the hell could [Kubiak] be in that spot?"

Kubiak said it was the combination of the A's detailed scouting reports and the fact that he had played with Pete in the minors that led him to know what Rose would do in certain situations. That's what intelligence does, Kubiak said. "It helps you out."

Hollingsworth helped A's hurlers by advising them not to let Bench beat them with his bat. One way to do that was to not throw Bench any fastballs or curves, just a steady stream of sliders. Another way was to turn Cincinnati's cleanup hitter into a leadoff batter, which the A's accomplished in Game One.

In Game Two, played on a sun-drenched Sunday afternoon with Jackie Robinson looking on from the commissioner's box, the Reds' slugger found himself in the same situation when facing Hunter.

There's an adage in postseason baseball that your momentum is your next day's starting pitcher. The A's, armed with a one-game lead, looked to build on their momentum by sending their ace to the mound. A control pitcher with outstanding off-speed stuff and a moving fastball, Hunter on this splendid afternoon was a Cat toying with his prey—always putting his off-speed stuff out there and then taking it away. The crafty Catfish threw his entire repertoire at the Reds: fastballs, sliders, and change-ups, going up and in on one pitch, nicking the corner with the next.

Cincy's sluggers were familiar with Holtzman from his years with the Cubs, but Hunter was an unknown. Their only knowledge of the Cat came from the occasional All-Star at-bat and Cincinnati's scouts. But Morgan and his mates knew that while you could scout a pitcher and read all the reports, until a hitter stood in the batter's box and saw how fast the pitches were coming and how much movement they had, the arm speed and the arm motion, the hitter really didn't have a feel for what he was facing.

Before another Riverfront record crowd of 53,224 and amid what Simpson referred to as a "brilliant, sunshiny afternoon," Hunter helped his own cause in the second inning. The Catfish followed singles by Bando and Dick Green off Ross Grimsley with a two-out single to left to score Hendrick with the game's first run.

In the bottom of the inning, Bench, wearing a cherry red turtleneck and long sleeves beneath his bright white jersey, led off with a ground single. Perez walked. The Reds would eventually load the bases, but the Catfish clamped down:

> **Moore**: *Menke dug in at home plate for Hunter's pitch. . . . It's a swinging strike three! Hunter threw the high, hard one right by him. . . . Geronimo. . . . Swinging strike three! [Hunter] got another one! So Ross Grimsley will have it on his shoulders. . . . Here's the 1-2 pitch. . . . [Hunter] struck out the side! Catfish Hunter, displaying fantastic courage with a runner at third and nobody down, strikes out Menke, Geronimo and Grimsley!*

Cincinnati's struggles with the Cat continued. The Big Red Machine was finding out what American League hitters already knew. The Catfish, Bobby Murcer said, didn't overpower hitters with his stuff; he beat them by being one of the savviest pitchers to ever take the mound. Bench believed it. Hunter, he said later, was tough.

In the third, Rudi turned on Grimsley's thigh-high fastball on the inside part of the plate and drove it toward the left-field bleachers.

> **Moore**: *Pitch to Rudi is hit up into the air in deep left field. . . . That baby has really got a charge in it and it is going and theerrrrree she goes! A home run for Joe Rudi!*

Rudi would make the play of the Series—one of the great plays in World Series history—in the ninth. Hunter, his long hair flowing almost to the shoulders of his kelly green jersey, hurled eight shutout innings, then surrendered a leadoff single to Perez in the ninth. The Cat was tiring, and he had hoped to get Menke on inside pitches. Instead Hunter's first pitch was a mistake: a fastball down the middle. Menke was a line-drive hitter who Gowdy noted didn't hit the ball well to right but could pull it to left. That is precisely what Menke did, lifting the ball into the menacing sun field.

> **Gowdy**: *There's a long drive to deep left. . . .*

"I thought it was out," Menke said. So did Hunter. Rudi thought the same, and so did the A's watching from the dugout. Three Octobers prior to Carlton Fisk's performing the most memorable bit of body language in baseball history, members of the Mustache Gang were using body language to will the ball to stay on the A's side of the wall.

Gowdy: *That ball is going, going. . . .*

As he flipped his sunglasses down and began tracking the ball, Rudi saw that this was exactly the kind of play he'd worked on with legendary Yankees outfielder Joe DiMaggio—a drive almost straight over his head. This one was a little to Rudi's left, and as he broke back on the ball, he put his right hand out to feel for the twelve-foot wall. When Rudi spotted the ball through his shades, it was on the edge of the sun; there was no sky between the sun and the ball. If it had been hit a few more inches to his left, Rudi knew there was no way he would have caught it.

Staring up into the sharp glare, Rudi positioned himself on the edge of the warning track, then poised for an instant. With a sudden leap he turned and pinned himself chest-first against the wall, reached up with his glove hand, and pulled in Menke's drive. Williams thought Rudi's left arm looked at least eight feet long as he stretched to make the catch.

Gowdy: *It is caught by Rudi! Joe Rudi robs him of extra bases against the wall! What a grab by Joe Rudi!*

Simpson sounded just as stunned in making the call on NBC Radio: *"The pitch. . . . Lined to left field. . . . Back goes Rudi, looking up. . . . He's got it! Against the wall! . . . Hendrick is all the way over in left field slapping Rudi on the back."*

Williams called the catch "unbelievable." Rudi's spectacular grab ranks among the best in World Series history: Willie Mays's in 1954, Sandy Amoros's in '55, Ron Swoboda's and Tommie Agee's in '69, and Al Gionfriddo's in '47 against Rudi's mentor, DiMaggio.

Simpson called it the fielding gem of the Series. Hunter thought it might have been the best play in the history of the World Series. The Reds had watched the play from the top step of their dugout. A double for sure, Bench thought, maybe even a homer. As Rudi literally laid out against the wall, the Reds at first thought he had trapped the ball. But when Rudi caught it, he turned his glove so the ball wouldn't pop free when he hit the wall. The ball was showing white through the webbing of his glove, and Rudi retrieved it with his right hand, then held it up for all to see, and then fired it back to the infield to try and double up Perez. Rudi pulled his glove away fast because if it had hit the wall, the ball probably would have popped out.

"It was not my greatest catch," said Rudi, who would make a running, tumbling grab at Shea Stadium in Oakland's 1973 World Series victory over the New York Mets. "But it certainly was the most important one I ever made."

Williams cried, "No! No!" when he saw Rudi displaying the ball for the umpires. Williams believed it gave Perez the chance to avoid the double play and cost the A's when Perez later scored. When you get this close to the mountain top, Williams thought, you can't let the little things kill you.

Rudi would build an All-Star career out of doing the little things right. He was a thinking man's player. Jackson compared him to NBA great Bill Bradley, who played for a New York Knicks squad that was a contemporary of the A's and was in the midst of its own championship season, playing the same kind of smart defense as the A's.

Anderson knew now that the Reds had seriously underestimated the A's. Oakland's left fielder showed in Game Two that the Big Red Machine was in for a Rudi awakening. It seemed perfectly fitting that Rudi hailed from Modesto, California. The name of the town where he grew up and married his high school sweetheart contains a most apt description of the A's quiet star: Modest. Reggie thought Rudi the nicest guy in the league, an underrated, underpaid, self-made star.

Robinson compared Rudi's "total reliability" as a player and teammate to that of Al Kaline. Rudi could do it all—hit for average (he batted a team-best .305 in 1972), hit for power (19 home runs, .486 slugging percentage), bunt, and field.

The only thing Rudi didn't do despite being featured on the cover of

The Sporting News that summer was generate a lot of publicity. He was baseball's quiet man, its Mr. Nice Guy, and he got more ink from not getting ink than anything he did on the field.

His style, Rudi said, was to keep his mouth shut, do his job, and keep out of people's way. His style on the field was more pronounced. When he dug in in the batter's box, he displayed a closed stance—left foot planted at the plate, right foot in the back of the box—and semi-crouch. His bat was on his shoulder, a cardinal sin among hitting coaches. But his quick swing equaled a quick and nimble mind. In Game Five of the '74 World Series, Rudi rightly believed during a disturbance in the outfield that Dodgers reliever Mike Marshall, who had neglected to throw warmup pitches during the delay, would go with his fastball. Dodgers pitchers had successfully jammed Rudi with inside fastballs the game before, and the astute A's star figured Marshall would try to do the same. Marshall did, and Rudi deposited the pitch over the left-field wall for the final run of the Series.

Rudi was an excellent all-around player but not a naturally gifted one. He played baseball and football in high school, but his father, Oden, a product of Norway, never saw him play. Where Tenace's father had pushed his son to play ball, Rudi's father prodded his son *not* to play. Rudi remembered it as a "constant battle" between him and his father, who was from the old country, where baseball and football weren't part of the culture. Oden thought his son should be doing more constructive things—homework, for instance. He didn't understand Joe's need to practice and would tell him to stop the foolishness and concentrate on preparing himself for a real career. Oden reminded his son that in Norway young men worked hard learning to be shipbuilders, fishermen, or engineers. They didn't waste time fooling with bats and balls.

Rudi enrolled at Downey High in Modesto as a sophomore and despite being big for the position—he was 6-foot-2, 215 pounds—played shortstop on the baseball team. He was also a heavyweight wrestler and played split end and cornerback. Rudi loved defense and thought seriously about playing college football rather than baseball. But when he saw that there would be players weighing up to one hundred pounds more than he, he decided to stick with baseball.

Hit on the left hand by a pitch from future major leaguer Pat Jacquez—Rudi would stay in the game and hit a two-run homer—Joe's baseball career was in jeopardy. Oden believed the injury—a broken bone in the hand—was a sign that sports was ruining his son. The four or five scouts following him believed it ruined Rudi's hopes of a big league career. One scout stuck by him. Don "Ducky" Pries of the Athletics called Rudi to check on him, drove him to the doctor's office, and told him that because some of the players on the Athletics were older, Rudi would have a better chance of making it to the majors with the A's.

Rudi signed and in 1966 was assigned to Modesto, one of the top teams in the California League. He hit .297 with 24 homers and 85 RBIs and, more important, Oden began attending his games. Another benefit of playing in his hometown was that Rudi was able to marry Sharon Nickerson six months sooner than he had planned.

Rudi's sweeping swing had been good enough for minor league ball, but he struggled when called up to the majors in 1969. His turnaround came in the spring of 1970, when he began working with A's hitting guru Charlie Lau. Rudi credited Lau for changing his whole batting style.

Rudi had been using an open stance at the plate, but Lau instructed him to put the bat on his shoulder and move his left foot in closer. Lau also taught him the mental aspects of hitting. Rudi thought Lau's instructions enlightening and likened the experience to going from the boonies to the big city and finding the metropolitan library.

Rudi spent the '71 season splitting time between major league baseball and the Marine Reserves. By '72 he was lining hits to all fields and ranked either first or second in the league in batting average, hits, doubles, and triples. It wasn't just his hitting that improved. DiMaggio, an A's outfield coach in 1968–69, had taught Rudi how to go back on drives hit over his head. Bob Kennedy, the A's first manager when they moved to Oakland in 1968, was also instrumental in Rudi's development defensively. Kennedy had been a strong-armed outfielder in a major league career that ran from 1939 to 1957, and he helped make Rudi a much better defensive player.

The A's awesome display of defense wasn't over. Geronimo followed with a low liner that seemed destined to be a double to right. Mike Hegan, playing first base for Epstein in Oakland's late-innings defensive platoon, dove to his right. Smothering the ball on the turf, he turned and scrambled—lobster-like—and beat the speedy Geronimo to the bag.

Williams said Hegan blocked everyone's view of Geronimo's pretty hit with a prettier dive to stop it. Hegan had been playing the baseline to prevent an extra-base hit down the line. While the outfield was still soaked in sunlight, late-afternoon shadows covered the infield. It was difficult to see the ball in those conditions, and when Geronimo pulled Hunter's pitch, Hegan reacted by diving to his right and reaching for the ball. Following Rudi's gem, Hegan's rob-job was another game saver.

Rudi's kangaroo catch is more famous, but some believe Hegan's stop just as impressive. Williams praised his defense-minded first baseman in the locker room, telling reporters Hegan was the best left-handed fielding first baseman in baseball. "And," Williams added, "that includes Mr. [Wes] Parker."

The statement angered some National League observers since Parker, a slick fielder for the Dodgers, was considered by many the best defensive first baseman in the game. Williams, who had played first base in his major league career, considered Hegan the finest fielding first baseman he had coached in his twenty-one years as manager. That included Steve Garvey, whom Williams had managed in San Diego and who he claimed broke Hegan's 178-game errorless record through a fluke.

Pinch hitter Hal McRae followed with a single to left that plated Perez. Hunter was fatigued but still fighting for the final out. Williams headed to the hill.

"I don't want to come out," Hunter said. "I'm still throwing good. I'm not missing by much."

Moments earlier the Catfish had been badgered by Bando. "You're not even trying!" Bando yelled from his position at third base. Hunter knew it was the captain's way of encouraging his pitcher in tough spots, trying to get the Cat so mad that he would work his way out of the jam.

Williams, however, was thinking about the great plays made by Rudi and Hegan, particularly the latter. Geronimo had smoked the ball, and his drive sounded to Williams like a sure double. He had left Hunter in two hitters too long, Williams thought. Rudi and Hegan had taken their skipper off the hook, but in Williams's mind they shouldn't have had to.

Williams signaled for Fingers. Anderson answered with pinch hitter Julian Javier, a Series-seasoned veteran of the Cardinals' title teams of the 1960s. Oakland's lead had been trimmed to 2–1, and Cincinnati had the tying run on base in the person of pinch runner Concepcion. With the roaring of a sold-out stadium serving as a backdrop, Simpson called the final pitch of Game Two: *"Big curve ball, it is popped up, in play. . . . Hegan comes off first base, has it! Oakland goes home leading two games to none!"*

Williams was ecstatic. "We'd have been thankful for a split," he said.

The Big Red Machine, a team so heavily favored that it was predicted by some pundits to win the best-of-seven series in *three* games, had dropped the first two in its own stadium. Was it possible, Bench wondered, the Reds were down two games to *Oakland*?

It suddenly seemed as if all the leaves were brown and the sky was gray in Cincinnati.

The A's, meanwhile, were California dreamin' as they prepared to wing westward.

CHAPTER FOURTEEN

The team flights from Cincinnati to Oakland provided a startling study in contrasts. Trailing 2–0 in the World Series and facing the fact that no team had ever lost the first two Series games at home and come back to win it all (the 1985 Kansas City Royals would become the first team to do it), the Reds were singing and dancing in the aisles.

What had been billed as a breezy coronation for the Big Red Machine had become a brutal battle, but there was Johnny Bench leading the Reds in a rousing rendition of "The whole town's batty / About Cincinnati."

The Swinging A's, true to their combative nature, were set to start swinging at each other. Benched catcher Dave Duncan screamed in the face of owner Charlie Finley, and manager Dick Williams and hulking first baseman Mike Epstein nearly came to blows.

Williams said Epstein had cursed his way into the dugout in the sixth inning of Game Two after drawing a walk from Pedro Borbon and then being replaced by pinch runner Allan Lewis. Williams said he had been planning on substituting defensive specialist Mike Hegan for Epstein regardless and felt Hegan's stunning play at first on Cesar Geronimo's liner in the ninth justified his move. Epstein acknowledged that Hegan's play was "a beauty" but believed he could have done the same. Both men were left-handed, meaning it was to their benefit to not have to suddenly turn and make a backhanded stab, which they would have had to do had they been right-handers. Epstein, however, had committed 12 errors in '72 and had a .990 fielding percentage. Hegan, albeit playing just over one-tenth of Epstein's 1,101 innings that season, fielded his 175 chances flawlessly.

But Big Mike was a proud man. A product of the Baltimore Orioles farm system, Epstein drew a Star of David on his glove while playing for Class AAA Rochester. He got his nickname, "Super Jew," in the minors when he launched a homer over the light tower in right-center and third base coach Rocky Bridges told him, "You launched that one in the night, you Super Jew." A clubhouse kid picking up bats nearby heard it, and when Epstein arrived at the ballpark the next day, "Super Jew" was written on his locker and his equipment. The nickname stuck, and though Epstein didn't like the phrase, he took it as a compliment.

Epstein believes his "Jewish side" gave him tenacity and perseverance and allowed him to overcome his doubts and survive in the majors. In '72 the bull-like Epstein—he had played fullback at the University of California at Berkeley for future NFL head coach Marv Levy—ranked third in the AL in homers (26), fifth in slugging percentage (.490) and OPS (.866), and sixth in on-base percentage (.376).

Big Mike thought Williams's taking him out of the game made him look like a goat. Williams thought Epstein selfish. On the flight home, the A's were imbibing while getting hit in the butt by the trombones of Finley's roving Dixieland band members. Williams, Scotch in his hand, found himself confronted by an angry Epstein.

"I feel you don't appreciate me," Epstein said, and Williams thought Big Mike was slurring his words. "I've been busting my ass all season and you take me out of a World Series game and I don't appreciate it. I don't want it to happen again."

Williams could take everything but that last line. Epstein didn't want it to happen again? To the surprise of all who thought they were in the midst of a party, Williams began screaming back at Big Mike: "You get your ass to the ballpark tomorrow and be ready to play! I'm the manager and I'll do whatever I want!"

Williams wanted to slug Epstein, and he knew Epstein wanted to slug him. "We nearly went fist city," Williams recalled in his autobiography.

Here were the A's, two wins from a world championship, and the skipper wanted to beat up his first baseman and vice versa. Even the A's, Williams thought, weren't *that* crazy.

Oakland's fans, however, were going crazy. Despite repeating as Western Division champions, the A's ranked fifth in the twelve-team American League in attendance. Yet some eight thousand fans had crowded the airport when the A's plane brought them back from a five-game postseason road trip. Accustomed to lukewarm loyalty from fans, the A's were shocked by the reception when they returned from Cincinnati. "Where Is the Love?" was a 1972 hit song by Roberta Flack and Donny Hathaway, and the A's often wondered the same when it came to fan support.

"I can't believe we're in Oakland," a startled Sal Bando said upon seeing the throng.

After their 707 jet, bearing a huge picture of Finley, his mule Charlie O., and the words "Good Luck Swinging A's" on its nose, taxied to a stop, some players and their wives were mauled by the delirious mob. A few of the A's bolted for the team buses rather than the terminals. Finley exploded. Any player too scared to go to the terminal and show appreciation to the fans, he shouted, was someone he didn't want on his team. He ordered Jimmy Piersall to "round up these cowards and bring them in here."

One player unafraid of the Oakland crowd was Bert Campaneris. The A's scrappy shortstop had been booed loudly on each of his plate appearances in Cincinnati. Oakland fans at the airport greeted him with thunderous approval. They were aware that without their speedy sparkplug for the final three games of the American League Championship Series against Detroit the A's had lost twice before prevailing. With Campy back in the lineup Oakland had beaten Cincinnati two straight.

Campaneris was the first A's player to speak to the roaring crowd, and it reacted as if he was a rock-and-roll idol. Teenaged girls swooned, and people of all ages reached out to touch him. Homemade signs were held high showing their support for the roadrunner.

The fans' outpouring of affection was a bit surprising, considering that it was offered at the time that everyone knew Campy Campaneris but few knew Dagoberto Campaneris. Born in 1942 in Pueblo Nuevo, Cuba, he began playing ball as a young boy. He loved the game so much that he worked as a groundskeeper just so that he could be close to the playing fields. Campaneris tells people he never worked while in Cuba; all he did was play baseball.

Campaneris's father played as well, and because he was a catcher, his son started out as a catcher. Signed in 1962 by scout Felix Delgado, it was apparent that Dagoberto, weighing all of 142 pounds, wasn't going to be a catcher any longer. The transition to shortstop was a painful one since Campaneris lacked the gifted hands of a natural fielder.

What he did have was speed and quickness. He pilfered 27 bases his first year in the minors in 1962, another 25 two years later. Yet when he made his major league debut with the Kansas City Athletics on July 23, 1964, it was his surprising power that gained notoriety. He hit the first big league pitch thrown to him—a delivery made by Minnesota's Jim Kaat—for a home run, then homered again. At the time, he was just the second man in major league history to have two home runs in his first game.

One year later Campaneris led the league in triples and steals and snapped Luis Aparicio's run of nine straight stolen base titles. In a thirteen-inning game against California on September 8, 1965, Campaneris became the first man to play every position in a single game. When he took the mound for an inning in the eighth, he pitched ambidextrously, throwing right-handed to righty batters and southpaw to left-handers.

To improve his fielding he took hours of infield practice. Still he struggled. He made 40 errors in '65, 30 at shortstop alone. Two years later he tied for the league lead with another 30 errors and committed 34 in '68. By 1970 continued hard work helped him dramatically reduce his miscues, and then A's manager John McNamara was calling Campy "one of the finest defensive shortstops in the league."

Teammate and fellow Cuban reliever Diego Segui said Campaneris was always thinking and talking about baseball. Campy made a science of running the bases and stealing. He studied pitchers and catchers and developed multiple ways of sliding into the bag. One of his favorites was to keep his left leg stiff, thus giving the fielder covering the base little more than the tip of Campy's white cleat to tag.

By 1972 Campaneris had established himself as the AL's premier base pirate over the previous decade. What kept him from becoming more well known was a language barrier. Quiet and contemplative, he struggled with his English. He believed the language gap caused reporters to avoid him. It cost Campy interviews, and some believed it would cost him even more—the 1973 World Series MVP award that went to Reggie Jackson.

There was no shortage of love for Campaneris on the A's return trip to Oakland. Nor did Campy feel anything but genuine regard for the synthetic surface in Cincinnati's Riverfront Stadium. Oakland infielder Dal Maxvill thought it didn't take long for the A's to acclimate themselves to the Astro-turf. Maxvill said Campaneris and Bando liked the artificial surface because of the true bounces and because the ball got to them quicker.

There was nothing artificial about the angry words surfacing between the two teams. Like the hit song that year from the group America, the heady A's felt as if they were cruising California's Ventura Highway in the sunshine, the free wind blowing through their hair.

"We're handling Cincinnati easier than we did the Texas Rangers," Vida Blue crowed.

"Before the Series is over we'll thank Vida Blue," Sparky Anderson shot back. "I've always heard that when you've got an athlete down, you let him sleep. Don't wake him."

The Reds were seizing on every slight, perceived or real, as motivation. In the A's clubhouse following Game Two, Catfish Hunter told reporters he thought the Big Red Machine might have underestimated the speed of his fastballs. The Cat's comment caused Pete Rose to explode in anger. "He's a good pitcher but I'm not gonna make him out to be a super pitcher because he's not," the Reds' captain spat. "If they don't get those two plays in the ninth, he's just a super loser."

Rose compared Hunter to lesser known National League pitchers Rick Wise of the Cardinals and Jim McAndrews of the Mets. "That's about how hard he throws," Rose said. "He certainly is no Tom Seaver or Bob Gibson."

Now it was Hunter's turn to be angry. The Cat said he might deck Rose the next time he pitched against him. The Catfish Hunter–Charlie Hustle imbroglio was part of what was becoming a white-hot war of words between the two teams. At the same time, Rose coldly analyzed the Big Red Machine's lack of offense over the first two games.

The Reds had rolled over opponents that summer with a strategy that was wonderfully simple: table-setters Rose, Morgan, and Tolan got on base, and big guns Bench and Perez brought them home. During the regular season Morgan reached base 282 times, Rose 278, and Tolan 221. They combined to score 317 runs, steal 111 bases, and reach base at least once in 153 of the Reds' 154 games that season.

But as *Sporting News* writer Lowell Reidenbaugh noted at the time, the Big Red Machine had not been facing the A's armada of arms in the regular season.

Rose scoffed. "Don't tell me their pitching is that much better than Pittsburgh's," he snapped. But he acknowledged the A's had kept him, Morgan, and Tolan from hitting.

"I don't want to make any excuses, but it's just that we put so much into that series with Pittsburgh," said Rose, overlooking the fact that Oakland had overcome Detroit in an equally emotional five-game series.

On the rare occasions the Big Red Machine stalled, one of the chief mechanics proved to be Perez. The Reds were a club loaded with stars, and Morgan recognized Rose and Bench as the team's twin peaks. But he thought Perez as important a star as the Reds had. He was among baseball's best, a future Hall of Famer, but Perez was also among the game's most overlooked players.

Perez would play twenty-three years in the majors and be an integral part of six division champions, five pennant winners, and two world champions. He hit 379 homers and plated 1,652 runs and ranks alongside Rogers Hornsby, Joe DiMaggio, Mickey Mantle, Ernie Banks, Mike Schmidt, and Willie Stargell as a run producer. Numbers alone never did Perez justice, however. Morgan thought they didn't begin to tell who Perez was and what he meant to the Reds.

Like Campaneris, Perez was a native Cuban, born in 1942 in Camaguey to Jose and Teodora Perez. He grew up in a two-bedroom house owned by the sugar mill that employed the Perez family. Tony had an ability to play ball—he was a shortstop for the sugar mill's team, Central Violeta—and was signed to a pro contract at age seventeen by Tony Pacheco, a Cuban scout for the Reds. Perez was assigned to the Havana Sugar Kings. His bonus cost the Reds $2.50 for an exit visa and plane ticket from Havana to Tampa.

Perez's family loved him enough to allow him to pursue his career, even though it meant never seeing him. His early years in the United States were a struggle. He had little money and no guarantees he could make a career in baseball. Playing for the Reds' Class D affiliate in Geneva, New York, in 1960, Perez was a teammate of both a nineteen-year-old Pete Rose and Martin Dihigo Jr., son of the Hall of Fame Cuban and Negro League star.

Perez debuted for the Reds on July 26, 1964, drawing a walk in his first at-bat and then going a combined 0-for-6 in a doubleheader split with Pittsburgh in Crosley Field. In 1967 he earned the first of seven All-Star selections and was named the game's MVP after his home run off Hunter gave the National League the victory in a fifteen-inning classic that was the longest All-Star Game in major league history to that point.

Perez had driven in 102 runs that summer, the first of seven seasons he would drive in 100 or more. By 1970 Perez was the Big Dog, hammering 40 home runs and driving in 129 and hitting .317 for a Reds squad that steamrolled its way to the World Series.

In '72 Perez had plated 90 runs for the resurgent Red Machine, and Anderson marveled that the Big Dog could drive in that many while batting behind Bench, who was in the midst of an MVP campaign. Perez figured he would have had more RBIs had he not injured his hand checking his swing earlier in the season. The injury caused him to refrain from pulling the ball with power to left field as was his wont. Because his hand was sore, Perez said, he was hitting a lot to right and right-center.

At the beginning of the '72 season Rose and Morgan were playing well and would horse around in the clubhouse, saying how well they were hitting. Perez, in broken English, boomed out, "You two guys, you think you so great or something?"

Perez was hitting .220, Rose and Morgan .350. As Perez pointed out, the Reds were in fourth place. "When the Big Dog starts hitting," Perez said, "we will go to the top." Two weeks later Perez strolled by Rose and Morgan in the clubhouse. "Hey, what place are we in?" Perez asked.

"First place," Morgan said. Perez beamed in triumph. "The Dog is hitting .280, and look where we are!"

Bench thought Perez's positive attitude integral to Cincinnati's success. Doggie was always up, always had a sense of humor, and had a passion for winning. Because he struggled with the English language, Perez stayed in the background and let others get the credit. Rose called him the silent superstar. Perez didn't say much, Bench noted, but you were aware of him because of his bat. What Doggie did best, Morgan believed, was win. He was a great clutch hitter, and the Reds never doubted his ability when the game was on the line.

Cincinnati's season was on the line as the Series switched to the Oakland Coliseum for Game Three. A sudden squall, complete with heavy rain and hail, forced a postponement from Tuesday to Wednesday. The Reds could see the Coliseum from the freeway in their approach. The stadium sat near the Oakland Airport and San Francisco Bay, and the smell of salt air was refreshing as the Reds disembarked from their bus.

The Coliseum's size was impressive, but it was a drab, gray structure. Nancy Finley, whose father Carl had served as Charlie Finley's right-hand man from the A's years in Kansas City up to Charlie O.'s sale of the team in 1980, was grateful for the A's bright uniforms. The vibrant green, gold, and white, she thought, made up for the lack of color in the Coliseum. To some, it looked like an outbuilding of nearby Alcatraz. Writer Furman Bisher thought the Coliseum had all the festive atmosphere of a quarry.

A's players called the Coliseum "the Mausoleum." When the Reds arrived at the stadium, Anderson was not impressed. It was raining, and the field was a mess. "It's ugly," Anderson muttered. "I thought Charlie O. had more class than this."

Anderson didn't know he was being taped by the media and was surprised to hear his comments played back on television that night. The comments prompted Bay Area columnist Glenn Dickey to write, "A team of boors, the Cincinnati Reds are in our midst this week.... The boorishness starts with Manager Spark Anderson ... a short-hair freak."

Dickey's characterization of Anderson and the Reds was likely shared by many in the Bay Area. Oakland in the 1960s and 1970s was home to fringe elements ranging from the rebellious Raiders football squad to the funk music scene that produced Sly and the Family Stone, from the Black Panthers to the Hells Angels. Gang-controlled drug crimes pushed Oakland's homicide rate in the '70s to double the figures in New York or San Francisco. One murder grabbed the nation's headlines. In November 1973 two members of the Symbionese Liberation Army assassinated Oakland superintendent of schools Dr. Marcus Foster and wounded his deputy, Robert Blackburn.

There was also a heightened racial tension between the poverty-stricken black community and predominantly white police force. In response to police brutality Merritt College students Huey Newton and Bobby Seale formed the Black Panther Party. In a 1972 televised interview Angela Davis, a former assistant professor in the philosophy department at UCLA and counterculture activist, declared that the "Black Panthers are extremely active in the Oakland community."

A growing antiwar movement led to rebellious chants of "Hell no, we won't go!" at college campuses across the country as opposition to the war in Vietnam reached a historic high. In 1972 students at UCLA protested by tearing up draft cards at Meyerhoff Park. The protestors, UCLA All-America basketball great Bill Walton among them, marched through Westwood, staged sit-ins in buildings and streets, and walked out of classes. An editorial in the student-published campus newspaper, *Daily Bruin*, told students, "Ending the war starts with you, not the next guy. Keep marching, keep it shut down, until the war ends. It's the only way, people, ... the only way."

One day after the freak hailstorm, the sun was bright and the skies blue as Blue Moon Odom, accompanied by the roar of more than forty-nine thousand fans, delivered the first pitch of Game Three to Rose. Odom continued the starvation of the Reds' top three hitters, striking out Rose and Morgan and getting Tolan to ground out.

Odom's opposite, Jack Billingham, responded in kind, sandwiching strikeouts of Campaneris and Rudi around a Matty Alou groundout.

The starting time of the game—5:30 on the West Coast—was arranged to accommodate prime-time viewing back east. The field, still lined with white yardage stripes and hash marks from the Raiders' victory over visiting Buffalo the previous Sunday, was wet and heavy and the air misty, and the players saw extended shadows everywhere they looked.

Williams blamed the twilight start on his boss. Finley insisted on playing a World Series game at night, and the A's skipper was fine with that as long as the game *started* at night. He figured Finley forgot that when it was prime time on the East Coast, the sun was still shining low on the West Coast—Low enough, Williams knew, to cast long shadows and screw up hitters. Thanks to Charlie, Williams thought, it was his own team, his million-dollar baby, that was the first to get fouled up by the twilight start.

Due in part to the shadowy setting, Game Three was dominated by the right arms of Blue Moon and Cactus Jack. Odom would fan 11—3 more than his season high—in seven innings; Billingham, 7 in eight-plus innings.

For all of the feisty words leading up to it, Game Three was a quiet affair. In the third inning Rose reached on a walk, stole second, and pressured catcher Gene Tenace into a throwing error that allowed Pete to hustle to third. He was stranded when second baseman Dick Green roamed far to his right and some ten feet onto the soggy outfield grass, making a diving stop of Morgan's apparent hit for the final out.

The Reds threatened in the fifth, but with runners on second and third Rose was called out looking. Pete protested violently, screaming at home plate umpire Mel Steiner and slamming his bat into the dirt at home plate. A's fans, seeing Rose in person for the first time, littered left field with eggs and assorted produce. Reds rooters responded by unfurling a "Rose Garden" banner behind where Pete positioned himself in left field. It was all reminiscent of the 1934 World Series, when Cardinals left fielder Joe "Ducky" Medwick was the target of apples, oranges, and grapefruits tossed by irate Tigers fans.

Billingham was in serious trouble just once, when Oakland loaded the bases with one out in the sixth. But Cactus Jack got Bando to ground to Morgan for the inning-ending double play. Other than that rally, Williams thought his offense was sleepwalking through Game Three.

Bench believed there was another reason for Oakland's lack of offense. After seeing the A's attack in the first two games, he wished Cactus Jack could have started Game One. Bench believed that of all the Reds' pitchers Billingham was the one whose style was most suited to beating the Mustache Gang. Cactus Jack pitched to corners and had a sinker and big slider, and Bench believed that was the best way to get the A's out.

The game's lone run came in the seventh and was provided by Perez. The Big Dog began the inning with just the second hit of the game for Cincinnati, a ground single to left.

Denis Menke sacrificed Perez to second, and Geronimo lofted a soft single to shallow center. The A's home field betrayed them. The ball came to a sudden stop on the sodden turf, and as center fielder George Hendrick slogged in to retrieve it and then returned the ball to the infield with a surprisingly casual underhand throw, Perez raced home.

Curt Gowdy would call what happened next "the most surprising play of the Series." As he rounded third, Perez slipped on the slick grass near the coaching box. Bando's shouts of "Home! Home!" were drowned out by the big crowd. Perez got up and ran as Campaneris, his back to the infield, held the ball. The throw had gone to Campy rather than to the proper cutoff man, Green.

Perez thought the A's might get him when he went down, but since he had been waved home, he got up and kept going. Maybe Oakland could have got Perez, Tenace said, but Campy had his back to the infield, and there was no way for him to hear Bando above the crowd noise.

Leading for the first time in this Fall Classic, the Reds sought an insurance run in the ninth against Blue, who had replaced Odom an inning earlier. Blue Moon wanted to stay in. "It was," he said, "one of the best games I ever pitched."

Williams announced following Game Two that rather than start Game Four, Vida would be used out of the bullpen. Williams later said he made a mistake in not telling Blue of his plans. Vida shrugged it off. "I'll do anything they want," he told *Sport* magazine's Al Hirshberg on the flight to Oakland. "If being there [in the bullpen] helps the team win, that's where I go."

Rose thought it a brilliant move by the A's skipper. The Reds, he said, would look at that left-hander warming up and know what they were going to have to face if they knocked the starter from the game.

Vida retired Rose on a lineout to second but then walked Morgan and surrendered a single to Tolan. Williams headed to the hill and brought in Fingers to face Bench. Rollie ran the count to 3-2, then was joined by Williams and Tenace in a mound conference. Prior to heading to the hill, Williams told pitching coach Bill Posedel that he was going to go the mound and act like he was giving Fingers hell because he shouldn't be giving Bench anything to hit with first base open. Williams was going to wave his arms and act like he was calling for an intentional ball four. At the same time he was going to tell Fingers to throw the ball over the plate for strike three.

"Bench will never know what hit him," Williams said. He had tried the ploy a few times in the minors, but it had never worked. This would be the first time he tried it in a major league game. Posedel was stunned Williams would try such a Little League stunt in the World Series. He looked at his skipper and asked, "What the hell are you talking about?"

Bench saw Fingers raise his hand as if objecting to something William was telling him. Despite the pantomime Williams was telling Fingers to be sure he threw a breaking ball because if he threw a fastball and Bench realized what the A's were trying to pull, he would hit the hell out of the ball.

Fingers said Williams was "pointing everywhere, and all the while he's telling Tenace and me how Gino is going to stick his arm out and then hop back behind the plate."

Tenace extended his right hand to indicate an intentional walk. Watching from the dugout, Williams wasn't confident the A's could pull it off. Morgan, leading off third, figured it out and yelled to Bench, "Be alive! They're going to pitch to you!"

Fingers was playing it cool, acting nonchalant, but when he looked over to third and heard Morgan yelling, he got rid of the ball—quickly. "I don't know whether Bench heard him or not," Fingers said. "He looked about half-ready."

Tenace jumped back behind the plate. Bench was ours, Williams thought. Bench stood frozen as the pitch sliced over the outside part of the plate. Williams called it a "nasty slider." Fingers thought it the "best slider I've ever thrown." Williams figured he had just grabbed his fifteen minutes of fame by fooling Johnny Bench on national TV. The Coliseum crowd hooted and shrieked as sixty million people watching on national television gawked at the sight of the A's faking an intentional pass and figuratively pulling down the pants of the greatest catcher in the game.

Bench heard Morgan yell at him to be alive. He could have swung at the ball if it had been down the middle. But since it was down and away he had no chance.

Fingers thought Bench looked like he couldn't tell if it was going to be a ball or strike and thus figured he might be better off taking it. Fingers thought the pitch couldn't have been in a better place, and Williams agreed. He said the play wouldn't work unless the ball broke sharply, adding, "Fingers threw it perfectly."

Critics screamed that the unconventional A's would do anything to win. All the proud Bench knew was that the A's had made him look, in his words, "like an ass." When a teammate told Bench, "[You] couldn't have hit that pitch anyway," it was small comfort. "Everybody Plays the Fool" was a hit song that year by the Main Ingredient, and Bench could relate. "I felt like an idiot," he said.

On Joe Garagiola's "World Series Report," which opened NBC-TV's Game Four coverage, Bench told the nation the Reds were now aware of the type of ball the A's played.

The bigger story was Billingham. The twenty-nine-year-old's 12-12 record that season was deceiving. After dropping his first five decisions, he rebounded to become the Reds' most reliable pitcher, fronting the Cincinnati staff in innings pitched and strikeouts.

Billingham's heavy lifting in the latter part of the season belied the fact that in the Reds' clubhouse Cactus Jack was also Sleepy Jack and responded to calls of "Rip." His teammates figured anyone who required 12–14 hours of sleep must be kin to Rip Van Winkle, who, legend had it, stole away to take a twenty-year snooze in the Catskills.

Billingham was anything but sleepy in his first outing in Oakland. If he could make the A's beat the ball into the ground, Billingham believed he would be all right. But he would have to keep the ball low. He was a sinker ball pitcher and knew he would run into trouble if his pitches were up in the zone. Cactus Jack followed his plan perfectly. The A's three hits off him were of the infield variety, and two of them were bunts. Oakland hit just three balls to the outfield against Billingham.

Clay Carroll closed out Game Three, and Cincinnati went into Game Four seeking to tie the series. NBC viewers were greeted with the network's opening—the instrumental theme music, Joe Garagiola's "World Series Report," and then a camera-panning shot of a cloud-shrouded Coliseum and the classic Gowdy voice-over: *"Temperature in the mid-50s. . . . Misting, overcast in the Bay Area. Welcome to Game Four of the 1972 World Series."*

It was a misty, chill night, the weather as crisp and tart as apple cider. Garagiola advised batters to hit the ball in the middle of the bat; anything at the top or near the handle would sting the hands "like a swarm of bees." The fourth consecutive sellout crowd saw a mound matchup that brought together two of the top left-handed hurlers of the 1970s—Ken Holtzman and Don Gullett. They were key contributors to six consecutive World Series champions from 1972 to 1977, and they dueled deep into the night in Game Four.

Bench was looking forward to the showdown between the fire-balling Gullett and the A's hitters. "Gullett's gonna overpower them," Bench told Garagiola in the pregame. "I think he can beat this club."

Gowdy opened NBC's Game Four coverage by asking, "When are the hitters going to start hitting?" The Reds were confident they would reach Holtzman for a couple of runs and even take the Series. They put two runners on in the top of the first before Holtzman put down the uprising by fanning Perez. Gullett blew away the A's for the first three frames.

The early innings were marked by web gems from Menke at third and Dave Concepcion at short and by the hard slides into Green at second by Bench and Hal McRae. In the top of the fifth Rose sent Alou to the wall in right for the final out. In the Oakland half, Tenace stepped in with one out. Jim Simpson made the call on NBC Radio over the excited roar of 49,410: *"Tenace hits this one a long way to left field, down the line. . . . It is gone!"*

Holtzman protected the slim lead into the eighth. Concepcion stroked a leadoff single and eventually reached third with two outs. Blue came on for his third relief appearance and after walking Morgan gave up a two-run double to Tolan down the right-field line.

Trailing 2–1 and down to the final two outs of the game, Williams was clutching at straws when he had Gonzalo Marquez pinch-hit for Hendrick. Marquez was a left-handed hitter, Hendrick a righty, and Williams thought Marquez had a better chance than Hendrick of making contact against right-handed reliever Pedro Borbon.

Ray "Snacks" Shore's scouting report reminded the Reds that Marquez had been successful as a pinch hitter and that when the rookie first baseman from Venezuela hit the ball in the air, it was usually to left-center and when he hit it on the ground, it was up the middle.

"Let's have our infielders play him to pull the ball," Snacks said, "and the outfield shade him a little toward left."

Concepcion objected. "No, no, he is Venezuelan like me. I play against Gonzalo many times in winter ball. I see him hit everything to left field."

Shore said Concepcion was wrong. Snacks had seen the A's for the last month and insisted the Reds should play him to pull. Anderson cast the deciding vote: "Okay, Snacks, we're going your way."

Concepcion, according to Anderson, decided to do it his way. Moments later Marquez hit a high chopper over Borbon's head and through the middle. Sparky was bitterly self-reproachful. He should have called time, he thought, and ordered Concepcion to move. Had Davey been playing where he was supposed to, Marquez would have been out. Instead Marquez got the A's started.

Williams sent Lewis to first base to pinch-run. Anderson trotted to the mound to talk with Borbon.

"Nobody hurt," Anderson told his pitcher. "Only one thing you got to do is you got to make [Lewis] stop over there. You don't have to throw over there [to first base]. I don't want you throwing over there. Just make him stop."

Borbon nodded but became flustered and tried a pickoff move. When he fell behind 2-1 to Tenace, a visibly angry Anderson headed back to the hill.

"All right, Petey, I'm gonna bring in the Hawk," Anderson told Borbon as he signaled for Carroll. When Borbon departed the mound, Anderson told Bench that Borbon had "lost his concentration. . . . That won't happen to Hawk."

Carroll, trying to nail down the Series-tying win, surrendered a ground single to left by Tenace. The managerial machinations in full swing, Williams sent Don Mincher to hit for Green. Anderson had southpaw Tom Hall ready in the bullpen to face the left-hand hitting Mincher but elected to stay with the right-handed Carroll. Mincher smoked the ball to right-center to score Lewis with the tying run. It would be the last hit of Mincher's career and remains the most vivid in his memory. Amid a sea of green and gold pennants waving wildly in the Coliseum, Odom entered the game to run for Mincher. Williams figured Blue Moon's speed could break up a double play.

Rollie was due up, and Williams, whom Gowdy called a "mustachioed marvel," made one final move, sending in pinch hitter Angel Mangual. Three pinch hitters in the same inning was a World Series record. With runners on the corners, the A's needed somebody who could make contact. Mangual could do that better than Fingers. Get a good pitch to hit, Williams told Mangual as he headed to the plate, and hit it safely.

Simpson: *Mangual steps in. . . . A ground ball. . . . Oakland wins!*

Mangual made just enough contact to send a bleeder through the right side between a desperately straining Morgan and Perez. To a riotous celebration of cheers and noisemakers, Tenace danced across home plate to complete a shocking 3–2 comeback.

The Reds couldn't believe it. Mangual's game-winning hit had come off his bat handle. It skittered just to the left of Morgan, who was playing in to cut down Tenace at home. It was just out of Morgan's reach and rolled slowly into shallow right. National League boosters couldn't believe it either. One NL skipper grumped in the postmortem that Williams kept making mistakes but kept getting lucky.

The A's literally had an Angel on their shoulders as they carried Mangual off the field in triumph. Angel had put Oakland one win away from a world championship, but there was trouble in paradise. While Finley stood from his box seat and cheered as fireworks exploded in the night air, Mangual brooded because he had not been Williams's choice to replace Jackson in the outfield.

"The things people do to you here," he told reporters in a voice tinged with sadness. Williams shrugged off the comments. These being the Swingin' A's, the manager was happy Mangual wasn't slugging somebody.

Oakland's rally gave Fingers his second Series win in relief, and his one inning of work marked his fourth appearance in as many games. A national television audience was being introduced to Roland Glen Fingers, and what was gaining their attention wasn't just the handlebar mustache with the waxed tips. It was the nasty sliders he was dealing.

It was a pitch Fingers perfected when he went to the Dominican Republic following the 1970 season. He worked on the pitch, he said, until he could throw it where he wanted to nine times out of ten—the outside part of the plate.

On May 15, 1971, Fingers made his final major league start. He was 1-4, and Williams, noting that Fingers tended to fret between starts, figured Rollie might be better suited to the bullpen, where he could make more frequent appearances. Fingers didn't complain. He wasn't doing the job as a starter, he thought, so he might as well try the bullpen.

Fingers did the job well enough to finish the season with 17 saves and a 3.00 ERA. In '72, his first season as a full-time reliever, Fingers had 21 saves, an 11-9 record, and a 2.51 ERA, and he fanned 113 in 111 innings. He had benefited tremendously from knowing from the moment he arrived at the A's spring training site what his position would be.

That certainty was a nice switch for Fingers, whose life and career had survived some close calls. In 1966 Fingers and Jackson were teammates on the California League team in Modesto. Fingers was supposed to pick up Jackson and Stan Jones on the way to the ballpark, but Rollie was pitching that day and was thinking so much about the game that he and car mate Steve Kokor forgot about Jackson and Stone. Another driver ran a red light and smashed the left rear of Fingers's car, causing it to flip over. If Jackson or Jones had been in the car that day, they would have been sitting on the left side, which was crushed in the accident. "They would have been dead," Fingers said.

Fingers and Kokor climbed out of the window of the wreck with bruises, bumps, and scratches. A year later Fingers was chosen by Birmingham manager John McNamara to pitch the season opener against Evansville. Rollie worked three scoreless innings but in the fourth threw a change-up that Fred Kovner ripped on a line back to the mound.

Fingers instinctively threw his arms up for protection, but the ball was hit so hard that it crashed through and hit Rollie in the face. Fingers fell face down in the dirt. Teammates rushed to the mound and rolled him over. McNamara saw blood flowing from Fingers's right eye and thought Fingers was dead.

Rollie's high school sweetheart and newlywed wife, Jill, sat frozen in the stands. She didn't know if her husband was dead or alive; he was motionless on the field. Finally she saw Rollie raise his leg and knew he was alive.

Fingers was rushed to the hospital, where his jaw was wired shut. For three days he vomited through his teeth; he was allergic to a drug doctors were giving him. Finley called Rollie and Jill and told them to go anywhere they wanted in Florida for a delayed honeymoon; he would pay their expenses. Fingers spent six and one-half weeks on the disabled list as the right side of his face was reconstructed with metal wiring.

It was one more twist to a tale that had begun in Jack Benny's favorite town, Cucamonga, California. Fingers's father, George, had moved west from Ohio to work in a nearby steel mill. George Fingers had been a pitcher as well, spending four years in the Cardinals' minor league system.

Rollie was a pitcher and left fielder for Upland High's baseball team and a center for the school's basketball squad. Upon graduation Fingers didn't find himself swamped by baseball scouts, so he and Jill enrolled at Chaffey Junior College. In 1964 Fingers helped lead Upland American Legion Post 73 to the national title. He threw a three-hitter in the title game, and his .450 batting average led all teams. Named American Legion Player of the Year, he was given an offer by the Dodgers. Fingers looked at the pitching-rich organization, saw Sandy Koufax and Don Drysdale at the peak of their powers, and signed with the Athletics.

The A's initially didn't know whether to use Fingers as a pitcher or a hitter. But in his first spring playing pro ball the organization decided Fingers's future was in pitching. In 1971 his role was further defined as relief pitcher. It was perfect for a guy whose idol wasn't Walter Johnson but W. C. Fields. Larger-than-life posters of the wise-cracking comedian covered the walls of Fingers's suburban Oakland home in Newark, California. Jill gave her husband a two-foot-high statue of Fields for his 26th birthday in August 1972.

Some considered the "Cucamonga Kid" a flake, a daydreamer, but when Fingers did daydream, it was about baseball. His relief work had helped tame the Tigers in the ALCS, and now he was doing the same to the Big Red Machine. Oakland's 3–1 Series lead was thought by some to be insurmountable. The Reds thought otherwise.

Morgan believed the Big Red Machine's mood was anything but despondent. The Mustache Gang was earning all A's for their play, but the Reds still thought they were the better team. They believed that if they played ball the way they had all summer, they would win. All they had to do was stay focused.

The Reds' resolve was evident from the first pitch of Game Five. Catching all of a Hunter fastball, Rose homered over the 375-foot sign in right-center. Rose's blast wasn't surprising since the Catfish was known as a home run pitcher; his good control meant his pitches were always around the plate. What was surprising was that it was Rose who took Hunter deep. Pete was sturdily built, but he had hit just 6 homers in 731 plate appearances that season.

Rose's drive was the first salvo in a gritty Game Five, a back-and-forth affair played out amid the soft sunshine of a Friday afternoon. It was Oakland's last chance to win the World Series in front of its home crowd, which packed the Coliseum for the fifth straight sellout. It was Cincinnati's last chance, period.

The A's answered the Reds' run in the second. Epstein walked, Hendrick singled, and Tenace pulled a Jim McGlothlin pitch to deep left for a 3–1 lead. The homer was Tenace's fourth of the Series, and the Coliseum scoreboard lit up with an announcement that Fury Gene had tied a record held by Babe Ruth, Lou Gehrig, Duke Snider, and Hank Bauer. Tenace saw the announcement and thought, I don't belong with those guys.

McGlothlin was familiar with the A's and the Coliseum. The right-hander had debuted with the California Angels in 1965, and his final American League game had come in 1969 in the Coliseum. He went 14-10 for the pennant-winning Reds in 1970 and 9-8 in '72. McGlothlin was 3-5 against the A's lifetime, but as Monte Moore observed in the NBC pregame, McGlothlin was the kind of pitcher who could rise to the occasion. The former AL All-Star had won five games over the final two months of the season.

Game Five's mound matchup between Hunter and McGlothlin favored Oakland, and the A's armed their ace with a 3–1 lead. It was all up to him, Hunter thought. But the Cat was struggling. In the Cincinnati fourth Menke found balm for his Game Two pain by driving a Hunter delivery well beyond the reach of Rudi in left. Like Rose's, Menke's homer was just his second hit of the Series.

Bando's leadoff walk in the fourth prompted Anderson to bring in Borbon, but Oakland increased its lead when Marquez, batting for Green, worked more pinch-hit magic with an RBI single to center to score Bando.

Trailing 4–2, the Reds refused to die. Morgan worked Hunter for a two-out walk in the fifth, and Tolan followed with an RBI single to right. Morgan had gotten such a good jump, he was almost at second base when the ball was hit. Knowing he had no chance to get back to first if the ball was caught, Morgan motored to third. Third-base coach Alex Grammas waved him home, and Morgan scored on what was essentially a routine single to right. Fingers came on and prevented any further damage, but the Reds' dugout had come back to life. Go-Go Joe's spectacular sprint around the bases had electrified the team.

The Big Red Machine's comeback continued in the eighth. Morgan, who had been criticized in the papers following Game Two for not being a clutch player, drew another walk and stole second. Tolan again came through, stroking a single to right-center that scored Morgan with the tying run.

The season was running out, and tempers were running short. In the Cincinnati seventh Rose took offense when Tenace, thinking Pete had struck out looking, started to throw the ball to third. If you want to umpire, Rose snapped at Tenace, why don't you get an indicator? Shut up and swing the bat, Tenace replied. Rose and Carroll gave first base umpire Bill Haller the choke sign. Haller later ejected Carroll, an inning after the Reds reliever left the game. Commissioner Bowie Kuhn fined Carroll for abusive language.

Umpire Jim Honochick continued to have his problems with the A's. They had started in Game One, when Honochick had to make close calls on several bang-bang plays. The veteran AL ump had been umpiring World Series games since 1952 and didn't like it that Williams kept coming out and putting on a show, kicking dirt, etc. Honochick believed Williams had no use for him and that at their manager's instigation the A's had it in for him. To Honochick it was obvious Oakland was going to give him a going-over on every close call that didn't go the A's way.

An example was the run-in Honochick had with Bando in Game Five. Tolan stole third in the eighth inning, and though Tenace's throw was in time, Bando didn't get the tag down quickly enough. Bando jumped around in vigorous protest, and Williams hurried out and wanted to know how the hell Honochick could make a call like that. When the A's learned later that the instant replay confirmed the call was correct, Bando sought out Honochick to apologize. The embattled ump told the A's captain where he and his skipper could stick their apologies.

The A's also had issues with Rose, mainly because of his belittling comments about the Catfish, and didn't like the liberties the Reds were taking with Green at second base. A day earlier, McRae hadn't even bothered to slide while attempting to break up a double play, preferring instead to lower his shoulder into Green and knocking the second baseman some ten feet behind the base. Bench also barreled into Green on what some observers thought a vicious play. Green insisted he didn't mind. Actually, he said, he liked hard play.

The Reds rallied to take the lead in the ninth. Geronimo opened by bouncing a single to right and was sacrificed to second. Concepcion reached on an error, and Rose redirected a Fingers pitch to center. Cincinnati led 5–4, but the Swingin' A's would go down swinging. Tenace walked to lead off the Oakland half. Ross Grimsley retired Ted Kubiak on a bunt pop fly to first and was replaced by Billingham. Williams, looking to repeat the miracle from the night before, sent Odom in to pinch-run for Tenace. Williams hated to risk possible injury to his starting pitcher, but he had already used his top pinch runner, Lewis. When you're going for all the marbles, Williams said, you have to take chances.

Duncan, his long blonde locks flowing under his helmet, continued the A's amazing pinch-hitting success with a single down the left-field line that sent Odom to third. It was Game Four all over again, Williams thought. His charmed lineup card was working. No Bay Area team had ever won a major world title, and Williams believed the A's were not only going to win the title, but they would also do so in front of their fans.

With two outs and the tying run at third Campaneris stepped in against Cactus Jack. Bench eyed Campy warily. He's another, Bench thought, who swings at everything. Campy lifted a high foul down the right-field line.

Perez and Morgan converged on the ball, but Morgan didn't like the way Perez was positioning himself and called him off.

The A's report on Morgan was that he had a weak arm and should be tested. Morgan knew Blue Moon was going to tag and break for home. So did Bench, and he positioned himself to block the plate. Because of the recent rain and because the tarp hadn't covered that part of the field, the foul territory was slick. As Morgan stabbed at the ball, his feet slipped on the wet grass. Third base coach Irv Noren, knowing the scouting report and field conditions, sent Odom on a daring dash for home. Putting his hands out so he could bounce back up off the turf, Morgan threw home. It was a perfect peg, and Bench knew there was no way Blue Moon was going to score. Amid a cloud of dirt Bench swiped at the ball with his mitt hand and made a sweeping tag.

Home plate umpire Bob Engel got down on one knee to make the call and pumped his right fist in the air to signify an out call. Odom erupted. He climbed from the dirt and bumped Engel, who was still in a low crouch. Reds general manager Bob Howsam wondered what Kuhn would do about *that*. The commissioner decided against suspending Odom, hitting him instead with a $500 fine.

Williams didn't dispute the call. Morgan had made the perfect throw, and Odom was out on the back end of a double play, no question about it, he said. Odom had taken a calculated risk and nearly gotten away with it. Williams was happy to see the game end on a fighting note, with Blue Moon blowing up at Engel.

Bench cared little for Odom's tantrum. He flipped the ball on the field. We'll win it now, he thought.

CHAPTER FIFTEEN

The A's four-hour return flight to Cincinnati was miserable. To accommodate Charlie Finley's numerous guests—"his whole damn entourage," one Oakland player spat—the team plane was jammed to its full capacity of 163 passengers. Overflowing with people and cramped with so much luggage that the latter was stuffed into restrooms so as to render them unusable, the plane finally touched down in Cincinnati at 1:30 a.m. on Saturday, October 21, the morning of Game Six.

The big news emanating from the A's flight, however, didn't involve Charlie O.'s ever-growing entourage or his band. It involved another near brawl at a cruising altitude of thirty-five thousand feet. A New York *Daily News* story reported that Finley had thrown a punch at an unnamed Chicago sportswriter. According to the report, it was Finley's way of exacting revenge for a story about him that the A's boss felt was unflattering.

The crowded flight and near fight were just the beginning of what would become a day to forget for the Mustache Gang. Oakland World Series hero Gene Tenace was informed that a threat had been made against his life. A woman waiting in line at Riverfront Stadium to purchase standing-room tickets for the game that day overheard a man state that if Tenace hit another home run, "he won't walk out of this ballpark." The woman contacted stadium authorities, who alerted the A's.

Finley and Dick Williams decided not to tell Tenace but did ask Major League Baseball to provide additional security. Cincinnati police afforded extra protection to Finley and his wife Shirley. Three uniformed officers stood near the Finleys as they took their seats behind the Oakland dugout. Acting on the woman's information, police arrested a man carrying a loaded pistol.

The Reds barely needed a plane to fly home from Oakland. Joe Morgan thought the entire team was excited because winning Game Five meant they would return to Riverfront Stadium for the final two games of the World Series. Even though the A's led 3–2, the Big Red Machine believed it had the Mustache Gang right where it wanted it.

Pete Rose, happy he was finally hitting, told reporters, "I know we can take these guys. Don't forget, this is the kind of situation we like best—coming from behind."

Tuesday's rainout the previous week meant there was no travel day between Game Five in Oakland on Friday and Game Six in Cincinnati on Saturday.

Game Six had set the stage for more than one World Series memory: Babe Ruth caught stealing to end the 1926 Fall Classic, Jackie Robinson and Clem Labine keeping the Boys of Summer alive in '56, Frank Robinson sliding home to extend the Series in '71. Game Six of the 1972 Series didn't match the magic provided by some of its predecessors or successors. Its distinction is that it was the lone game not decided by a single run.

October 21 was still a magical afternoon for the Reds and their fans because it finally showed the nation the brand of ball that had been played by the Big Red Machine all summer. More than that, Game Six was glorious for Bobby Tolan, Cincinnati's splendid outfielder whose courageous comeback from a potentially devastating injury proved inspirational. For Tolan, a native Californian who had grown up in Los Angeles, his comeback was something straight out of a Hollywood script.

Tolan was a key to the Reds' resurgence in Games Five and Six, collecting 4 hits, 4 RBIs, 4 steals, and 2 runs scored. Curt Gowdy thought Tolan's speed and power reminiscent of another recent hero of the Fall Classic—Lou Brock. Tolan's performance capped an incredible comeback for a man who had fought to recover from a ripped Achilles tendon suffered in January 1971.

The Achilles tendon stretches from the bones of the heel to the calf muscles. The tendon allows a person to point the toes and extend the foot. The list of professional athletes who have suffered torn Achilles tendons is long and star-studded: John Unitas, Kobe Bryant, Ryan Howard, Dominique Wilkins, David Beckham, and Adrian Peterson, among others. One-third of professional athletes who injure their Achilles tendons never return to competition. Many who do compete again find their performance severely affected.

Tolan's game was speed—his cousin was the late U.S. Olympic sprinter Eddie Tolan, a Gold Medal champion in the 100- and 200-meter dashes in the 1932 Olympics—and prior to his injury Bobby led the majors in stolen bases in 1970 with 57. What a torn Achilles tendon would do to the slender speedster depressed a Reds squad that had raced to the pennant in '70. Tolan's workouts in Florida in the spring of '71 were interrupted when he tore the tendon a second time. His absence from the top of the Reds' order was one reason Cincinnati had suffered a sub-par season. It had also spurred GM Bob Howsam to trade for Morgan and restore speed to the Reds.

When Tolan returned to the Reds in the spring of '72, his progress was followed intently not only by the Reds, but by athletes and coaches in other sports as well. If Tolan could come back, there was cause to believe other athletes could as well.

"What a comeback he's made," Gowdy said at the time. "Anytime you tear an Achilles tendon there's danger you won't play sports again. I think two dramatic recoveries from an Achilles tendon [injury] are Tolan, who's running with abandon again and his old speed, and maybe even more remarkable, 38-year old John Unitas."

Tolan said in '72 that Unitas was an inspiration to him. "I'm a young man, and Unitas coming back in football with that pass rush against him, that was something."

Tolan's return was also spectacular. He drove in 20 runs in his first nineteen games and hit over .400 the first three months of the summer. By season's end Tolan had hit .283 with 82 RBIs and 42 stolen bases. Tony Kubek took note of Tolan's unusual stance, which saw him standing very erect with his bat held high. Kubek noted the hitch Tolan had in his swing in bringing his bat from very high to down low but said in Tolan's case the hitch was a good thing. Indeed. Bobby's performance played a pivotal role in the Reds' pushing the series to Game Seven.

When some criticized Tenace for Tolan's brazen piracy on the base paths, Tolan took the A's catcher off the hook. "No catcher is going to throw me out if I get a big enough lead," he said, and his statement sounded like a veiled indictment of the inability of Oakland's pitchers to prevent Tolan from taking sizable leads off base.

Tolan stole five bases in the first six games, and his fifth steal, coming in the seventh inning, when the Reds were romping, raised eyebrows among some of the game's purists, who thought Tolan might have been trying to embarrass the A's. Tolan denied it.

A big part of his game was running, stealing bases, and scoring runs, he said. Why take away from his game because the Reds were winning? Williams put the issue to rest when he agreed with Tolan. Any runs you can get, get them, Williams said. Under the circumstances Williams said he would do the same thing.

Where Tolan's Game Six story was glorious, Gary Nolan's was gritty. In the Reds' regular rotation Nolan would have started Game Five, but because he had had trouble loosening up the day before, he was replaced by Jim McGlothlin. Sparky Anderson had, in fact, scratched Nolan from further appearances due to an ailing shoulder.

With the Reds facing their second straight "must-win" game, Cincinnati's skipper sought out his right-hander in the hope he could give a tired staff some needed relief. Anderson asked Nolan to give him the best he could for as long as he could. "Just four good innings," Anderson told Nolan.

Nolan nodded. This was a guy used to having to battle to succeed. Just twenty-four, he was already the dean of the Cincinnati mound corps. He was mature for his age, but you grow up quickly when you're eighteen, married, and the father of a one-and-a-half-year-old son.

Nolan arrived in the majors in 1967, an eighteen-year-old less than a year out of Oroville High in California. He had signed with Cincinnati the previous June for a reported $40,000 after being the Reds' top pick in the 1966 amateur draft. Assigned to Sioux Falls, South Dakota, in the Northern

League, the 6-foot-3, 190-pound Nolan had an impressive first season in pro ball, going 7-3 with a 1.82 ERA and riding a dominant fastball and impeccable control to 163 strikeouts and 30 walks in 104 innings.

In his first major league outing on April 15, 1967, Nolan struck out the side in the first inning en route to a 7–3 win over Houston. One of his more memorable outings came June 7 against the Giants at Crosley Field. Nolan fanned Willie Mays four consecutive times in a 15-strikeout performance. The Reds lost 4–3 on Tom Haller's single in the ninth, and someone in the Cincinnati clubhouse said it was enough to make a grown man cry.

"I did cry," Nolan responded.

By season's end Nolan had set modern records for a pitcher who had begun the season eighteen years old or younger by going 14-8 with a 2.58 ERA and 206 strikeouts in 227 innings. The Reds had seemingly struck gold with their signing of the right-hander from Oroville, an old gold rush town. But Birdie Tebbets, the Reds' manager in Nolan's rookie season, tempered the team's enthusiasm with words of caution. Pitching in the major leagues just isn't that easy, Tebbets said. Sooner or later, everyone has to pay his initiation dues.

Nolan's dues came due sooner rather than later. The following spring he sat on a trainer's table in the clubhouse following his first Grapefruit League start. It was a cold, windy day, and Nolan had suffered an apparent shoulder strain. He figured he had thrown too hard too early but was shocked when he heard Howsam announce that the club may send him to the minors to "get in shape." Nolan resented the implication that he was out of shape, resented that no mention was made of his shoulder injury.

When he read in the sports pages that the Reds had acquired pitcher George Culver from Cleveland, Nolan told his wife Carol, "I guess this means I'll be pitching at Indianapolis this year."

"I guess that means more pork and beans and cornbread for us," Carol replied.

It was the beginning of arm troubles that plagued Nolan the next two years. He bounced between the majors and minors in 1968 and again in

'69, worrying that every pitch could be his last. Reds pitching coach Larry Shepard sympathized. It was a frightening experience, he said, when a young pitcher like Nolan encountered his first arm trouble.

To complement his fastball and take strain off his throwing arm Nolan developed a change-up during his time at Indianapolis in 1969. In 1970 he went 18-7. He highlighted his season with a 3–2 win over the Astros on September 19 that clinched a tie for the division title and opened the NLCS with nine innings of scoreless ball against the Pirates.

Nolan's roller-coaster career continued with a disappointing 12-15 campaign in '71. In '72 he had 13 wins before the All-Star break but painful neck and shoulder pain caused him to be put on the disabled list. When he returned, Nolan went 15-5, led the league with a .750 winning percentage, and owned a 1.99 ERA that was just slightly behind the 1.97 posted by the Phillies' Steve Carlton.

"I'm a pitcher now, not a thrower," Nolan announced at the time. Going into Game Six, he was being asked to pitch one of the biggest games of his young life.

Amid steel gray skies and game-time temperatures in the 50s, the ailing Nolan and arm-weary Vida Blue matched scoreless innings in matching gritty performances. It was Blue's fourth appearance in the Series and his eighth overall in the '72 postseason, and it was also his long-awaited first start.

Cincinnati struck in the fourth. Bench, aching to see a fastball after being fed so many off-speed pitches by the A's, got a Blue darter from Vida and lifted it into the left-field seats to a standing ovation from the standing-room only crowd of 52,737.

Sal Bando, whose struggles at the plate caused Williams to drop him from fourth to fifth in the batting order, singled to left-center to start the fifth. Two outs later Dick Green doubled to deep right-center, scoring Bando from first and tying the game. Oakland might have had more, but both Rose and Tolan made sterling catches at the wall, Pete bouncing into the left-field wall to pull down Angel Mangual's drive.

Anderson had asked Nolan for four good innings and received four and two-thirds. Ross Grimsley was called in, and after walking Blue, he retired Bert Campaneris on a pop to Morgan to end the threat.

The Reds reclaimed the lead in their half of the inning. Hal McRae led off with a double high off the wall in left, took third on Denis Menke's ground out, and scored when Dave Concepcion, whom Gowdy noted had good power to right-center field, delivered the tie-breaking run on a sacrifice fly to deep center. The Big Red Machine motored to a two-run lead in the sixth. Tolan ended Blue's afternoon by chopping a two-out single to center. With the scoreboard flashing "GO . . . GO" Tolan swiped second against reliever Bob Locker. Bench was given an intentional walk, and Tony Perez stepped in.

Jim Simpson called the play on NBC Radio: *"One ball, one strike. . . . Perez ready. . . . There go the runners and the ball is hit up the middle! . . . Tolan will score . . . 3–1!"*

Anderson, pushing buttons like a Manhattan switchboard operator, played his Captain Hook role to the hilt. He replaced Nolan with Grimsley in the fifth and one inning later brought in Pedro Borbon for Grimsley. In the seventh Anderson called on Tom Hall to relieve Borbon and face pinch hitter Dave Duncan.

"Tommy, you know Duncan," Anderson said on the mound. "Low fastball hitter." Hall, heeding Anderson's words, fanned Duncan with a high fastball.

The Reds broke the game open in the seventh against relievers Dave Hamilton and Joe Horlen. Hitting, running, and stealing almost at will, the Reds scored five runs to take an 8–1 lead. Concepcion got the rally started with a single and stolen base. Rose walked, and Morgan, who had snapped his Series hitless streak with a double off Blue in the first inning, slashed the ball to the opposite field in left.

With the crowd nearly drowning out his delivery, Simpson made the call: *"Hamilton throws. . . . Down the left field line. . . . It is in there! Concepcion will score! Rudi is over to pick it up. . . . Here's the throw to third base and going in safe is Pete Rose. . . . Down to second goes Joe Morgan!"*

Rose, having raced from first to third, emerged from his dusty slide, wiped dirt from the front of his uniform, and pumped his fist toward

Morgan. Morgan had headed to second when Rudi threw to Bando at third to try and erase Rose.

Game Six was an inspiring performance by Morgan, who was nursing not only a tender right heel, but also a pulled muscle behind his left knee, the latter occurring when he had slipped on the slick grass of the Oakland Coliseum on his game-saving throw to end Game Five.

Tolan stepped in and stepped up yet again.

> **Simpson**: *There's a line drive, this should score two! Tolan was able to lace it into right field.... For the third game in a row Tolan has driven in two runs!*

Cincinnati's surge made Game Six less a sporting event than an upheaval of nature. To A's announcer Monte Moore, the Red were on a hitting and running rampage. Glowering from the A's owner's box was a glum Finley; Good Time Charlie had the blues.

Bench drew another intentional walk, and following a wild pitch by Horlen, Geronimo brought in Tolan and Bench by slapping a single to the opposite field in left. Finally, Bench thought, the Reds were doing what they had done all season. Facing Ted Kubiak in the ninth, Hall finished with a flourish.

> **Simpson**: *Hall throws and there's a ground ball to third base.... Menke will step on third.... Ball game is over, the Reds have evened the Series! Tomorrow afternoon at 12:45 Eastern time we'll begin the game that will decide the 1972 World Series.*

Almost overlooked in the Big Red Machine's breakout was the brilliant defensive play of Menke. Williams was moved to say after the game that he didn't know Sparky had imported Brooks Robinson for the Series. Anderson, meanwhile, felt less pressure in Game Six than in Game Five. "It wasn't like yesterday when I needed a dozen pills for my ulcer," he told reporters. "I needed only one."

In the wake of Cincinnati's first World Series victory at home since 1940 the Reds' clubhouse was happy and confident. Held down by A's pitchers the first four games, the top of the Big Red Machine's batting order—Rose, Morgan, and Tolan—was on a roll. In Games Five and Six they had combined for 9 hits, 7 runs, 5 steals, and 4 walks.

Tolan, Rose, and Morgan caught fire when the Reds needed it most. Now it all came down to one game, the entire season encapsulated in a single game. The A's, despite having lost two straight, were ready. Asked if he could work an inning or two in Game Seven, Blue replied, "If it means money, I'll even pitch right-handed."

The Mustache Gang broke the tension with a bit of gallows humor. "If you got to go, Gino," Jackson said, referring to the threat on Tenace's life, "at least it will be on national television."

Tenace admitted the death threat had shaken him. It scared him, he said, but he was still going to play. He wasn't going to let it affect him even though it wasn't something he could shove aside. What could he do? he asked. Tell the manager not to play him?

Tenace laughed when a writer asked if he thought he would win the car *Sport* magazine awards to the Series MVP. "What the hell. Even if I do the Reds will steal it from me."

Williams, talkative and affable in the postmortem, praised the Big Red Machine. "They got to our second-line pitching and we just got the devil kicked out of us," he said. "But we'll be ready to go Sunday. We've got to be."

"Game Seven." These are the two most magical words in sport. A certain amount of stardust is sprinkled on a Game Seven of the World Series; it is the ultimate contest, the "stuff of dreams," Williams called it.

The 1972 World Series marked the twenty-sixth Game Seven in history but the twenty-fourth that was decisive. Prior to the adoption of the best-of-seven format with the famous Pittsburgh vs. Detroit, Honus Wagner vs. Ty Cobb Classic in 1909, the Series had been a best-of-nine affair. October '72 was the second of three straight World Series to go to Game Seven and one of five in the fiercely competitive seventies. Only the psychedelic sixties had more (1960, '62, '64, '65, '67, '68).

As the A's arrived at sold-out Riverfront Stadium on Sunday, all Williams could think was that this would be a time to work his tail off. For him and

Anderson, it would be a day to pay attention to detail like never before, every tiny detail. Nothing could be left to chance, no allowing for excuses that could haunt a manager the rest of his days.

Williams had walked to the mound twenty-six times in the previous six games. Game Seven saw him make the trip another sixteen times. He wanted a face-to-face with his hurlers prior to every critical pitch, every crucial situation. The current rule that a manager must remove his pitcher if he makes two trips to the mound in the same inning should be called the Dick Williams Rule. The current rule was adopted, Williams believed, by league officials sick of seeing him stroll from the dugout to the mound.

Williams had been in a Game Seven before. Five years earlier his Red Sox had pushed their Series against St. Louis to its limit. Williams had 22-game winner Jim Lonborg going in the decisive game at Fenway Park, and despite the fact his ace was throwing on two days' rest and facing Bob Gibson, Williams boldly predicted a Boston victory. "Lonborg and champagne," Williams declared after his Sox won Game Six. The *Boston Globe* put his giddy guarantee at the top of their sports section.

Working on fumes, Lonborg lost, and as Williams entered the Cardinal locker room to offer congratulations, he heard St. Louis celebrating with a chant. "Lonborg and champagne! Lonborg and champagne!"

Leaden skies and light rain threatened Game Seven in Cincinnati. Pre-game workouts were halted at noon as the grounds crew covered the infield with tarpaulin. A capacity crowd of 56,040 filled Riverfront Stadium; 5,000 standing-room-only tickets had been sold for this historic game. Gowdy noted that the closest World Series in history was also the most-watched World Series in history to that point

The decisive encounter promised the best of both worlds. The Reds had regained their tee-it-high-let-it-fly approach at the plate, but the A's arsenal of arms was available. Something had to give.

Although the A's would be starting right-hander Blue Moon Odom, Anderson elected to use Concepcion, a right-handed hitter, rather than switch hitter Darrel Chaney. Chaney had started each of the previous three games against Oakland right-handers but was struggling. He would go hit-less while Concepcion batted .308. Anderson said that when Concepcion was concentrating, he could be the best shortstop in baseball. "He's ready for this game," he told reporters.

Williams was shaking up his lineup as well. Looking to tighten his defense and add punch to his offense, Williams benched Mike Epstein and moved Tenace to first base and Duncan behind the plate. Williams also altered his batting order, moving the hot-hitting Tenace from seventh to fourth. Angel Mangual would start in center and hit second; right fielder Matty Alou, who had had one hit in the first six games, was dropped to sixth.

As Simpson described for listeners the Reds taking their defensive positions to start the game, his broadcast partner for the games in Cincinnati, Oakland's Monte Moore, related that A's players were saying the morning of Game Seven that they would be returning to the West Coast drenched in champagne or tears.

Moments later Moore called the opening pitch of Game Seven: *"Campy Campaneris leads it off for the Oakland A's in a vastly changed lineup for this, the last game of 1972.... The first pitch, swung on, popped out into short right field where Cesar Geronimo is under it. He's got it! One pitch means one out."*

Williams's lineup changes paid big dividends early. Billingham, a low-ball pitcher, was up high, and Campaneris had aggressively jumped on the first pitch and flied out. Mangual, one of the A's heroes in Game Four, stepped in. Moore made the call:

> There's a curveball lined [to] right-center field, coming on [is] Tolan, he leaps, it goes off his glove to the wall! Mangual goes to first, heads to second, he's rounding second on his way to third! The throw comes in and he makes it standing up! ... It's an error on Bobby Tolan and the A's get the first break of the game!

"The ball just took off suddenly," explained Tolan, who saw it glance off the top webbing of his glove. "I wasn't set to leap. If I had been, I could have caught it."

In a nationally televised game at Riverfront that summer a ball had nearly bounced over Tolan's head, and Gowdy had remarked that outfielders on artificial surface had to guard against the high bounce. Billingham got Joe Rudi on a pop to Rose in left field, bringing Tenace to the plate. From the dugout Anderson motioned to Menke to move back a step.

> **Moore**: *Tenace bounces it to the third baseman. . . . Hard bounce off his glove into left field! Here comes Mangual in to score and the A's lead one-to-nothing!*

Tenace torched the turf, and cameras caught the ball hitting a seam of the Astroturf on its second hop and careening over the head of a startled Menke. A motorbike fanatic who knew all about sudden bounces, Menke said he sensed a bad hop coming but couldn't do a thing about it.

Riverfront's synthetic turf was supposed to give Cincinnati a huge home field advantage over Oakland. But in the first inning of Game Seven it had betrayed the Big Red Machine not once but twice.

Billingham struck out Sal Bando to end the A's half of the first, and the Reds responded in their first at-bat. Rose beat out a leadoff single to enormous cheers from the crowd. Williams ran out to protest to first base umpire Jim Honochick. "I know I'm no first baseman," Tenace told Williams. "But, Skip, we had him." After the A's lost another close call at first in the third inning, Williams would go out to coach first base—just to see at close range, he explained later, what was going on.

Blue Moon quieted the masses in the Reds' first by getting Morgan to ground to Campy for a double play and ended the inning with another ground ball, this one fielded by Tenace, who flipped to Odom for the final out.

Over the first four innings Odom faced just thirteen batters—one over the minimum. In the fourth Rose lined to deep center for the first out, and Morgan followed with a walk. Odom, gifted with a good move to first, had announced the night before that no Reds runner would steal on him. With the big crowd chanting, "Go! Go!" Morgan took his lead.

That summer Morgan had explained to Kubek and a national television audience his approach to base stealing: "I think about getting as big a lead as possible because you can get thrown out at second base by half a step just like you can running from home to first. So I think about getting as big a lead as possible and figuring out the pitcher's moves. His first movement toward home plate is when I make my dash toward second."

Odom, eyeing the Reds' roadrunner warily, threw over three times before firing home. From his vantage point at first base Honochick figured Odom's strategy of chasing Morgan back to first with repeated throws was to tire the Cincinnati speedster so that he couldn't steal. But Honochick took issue with what he saw as another A's ploy: Tenace deliberately sitting on Morgan to tire him even more. Honochick called Tenace on it and told him he knew what the A's first baseman was doing.

Tenace professed innocence. "He tripped me."

Honochick would have none of it. "Who the hell are you kidding? I'm standing here looking at you and he hasn't come close to tripping you."

The A's antics might have had an effect. Morgan broke with the next pitch, but Duncan's peg to Campaneris was on time and on target, and Go-Go Joe was caught stealing for the first time in the Series.

Just as the bright sun broke through the clouds, the Big Red Machine broke through in the fifth. Perez lined a leadoff double just inside the left field line for his tenth hit of the Series. Odom steadied and struck out Menke, but a walk to Geronimo and a 2-1 count on Concepcion brought Catfish Hunter from the bullpen.

Before the game Hunter had soaked up the surroundings: Game Seven, more than fifty-six thousand fans packing the big stadium. This is baseball as it ought to be, he thought.

Facing Concepcion, the Cat fired two off-target pitches to finish the walk and load the bases. Billingham was due up, and had the score been tied, Anderson said he would have allowed Cactus Jack to bat. But Sparky knew the Reds needed a run, so he sent McRae up to pinch-hit.

Hunter knew McRae well, knew that he sprayed the ball to all fields. Since McRae liked to go to the opposite field, the Cat would try to jam him so that he couldn't get his arms extended enough to punch the ball with power. It was sound strategy, but McRae got around on Hunter's first offering and drove it deep to center field. Anderson thought the ball was gone, and all Hunter could think was that he hoped he hadn't just served up a grand slam in the World Series.

> **Simpson**: *It is hit high and deep to center field.... Mangual is back near the wall and has it in front of the wall! Tagging from third with the tying run is Perez.... It's one-to-one!*

The Cat stepped off the slab to regroup as Rose dug in. Pete pounded a deep drive; another NASA shot, Hunter thought. The ball headed to right-center field, but Mangual, on his horse again, hauled it in to end the inning.

Campaneris and the A's countered immediately against Borbon, who was making his sixth appearance in the Series. Campy opened the sixth with a single and took his lead as Mangual dipped his bat for a sacrifice bunt.

> **Simpson**: *For the first time since the first game the leadoff man, Campy Campaneris, who makes the offense go, is on at first.... A breaking pitch, bunted up the line, Perez will have to go to first base.... Morgan covering, the sacrifice bunt is complete.*

Rudi's ground out to Morgan moved Campaneris to third and brought Tenace to the plate. Borbon, his Reds hat tilted back on his head, stared in for the sign.

> **Simpson**: *Strike one to Tenace, who never moves from that batter's box, he keeps those feet planted and just stays in there until Borbon gets the new ball.... There's an off-speed pitch, lined into left field away from Rose, it's 2–1! Around first base, on his way to second is Tenace.... He's in with a double and his ninth RBI!*

Tenace, who had set a slugging mark for a seven-game Series, was taken out for pinch runner Allan Lewis. On his way to the dugout an unhappy Tenace yelled at Williams, who yelled back. Williams's unconventional managing again paid immediate dividends. Bando, who had led the A's in game-winning hits during the season, did it again.

Simpson: There's a ball hit to straightaway center field, Tolan goes back, near the warning track, reaches up and it'll be off the wall! It is now 3–1! The ball gets away from Tolan, into second base goes Bando with a double!

NBC cameras showed Tolan streaking toward the warning track and then suddenly reaching back and clutching his left leg. His hamstring had cramped, causing Tolan to crumple to the ground. Tolan had jumped for the ball and suddenly felt pain. He finished the inning but was unable to continue playing and was replaced by George Foster.

Morgan thought the Reds, now down two runs and unable to reach Hunter, were deep in the hole. Catfish surrendered hard outs but held Cincinnati scoreless in the sixth and seventh. With six outs left in the season, Morgan tried to rally the Reds in the eighth.

"This is the inning, now is the time to do it!" he shouted to teammates on the bench. Rose led off with a single to center, prompting Williams to make another trip to the mound.

"I know you're getting guys out, Cat, but you're damn near scaring me to death," Williams told Hunter. "I gotta make a change."

With Morgan up, Williams brought in Holtzman. Because Morgan had not hit well in the Series, the A's were no longer playing him to pull. They were instead shading their defense to the left side of the field. Morgan also noticed Oakland was not holding Rose at first. Morgan figured the A's had to be thinking that Pete wasn't a threat to steal and that since Cincinnati was down 3–1, his run wouldn't beat them.

Despite the fact that he could be hitting for the final time this season, Morgan felt calm in the batter's box. He thought Holtzman's first two pitches seemed to slow down as they approached the plate. Morgan knew he was seeing the ball perfectly, and when the next pitch arrived—a 1-1 fastball—he was ready. His left arm flapping furiously—"The more critical the situation the faster it goes," Kubek noted—Morgan pulled Holtzman's pitch inside the first base line and into the right-field corner.

The ball was hit so sharply that Rose had to hold up to avoid being hit. He then had to leap over A's first baseman Mike Hegan, who was sprawled in the dirt after a diving attempt at a catch. The small fraction of time Pete lost proved pivotal and was one more bit of bad luck that descended on Cincinnati. Rose raced into third, but as he rounded the bag, third base coach Alex Grammas threw up his arms to halt him there. Rose jammed on the brakes so suddenly that his red batting helmet flew off and he belly flopped back into the bag. When he regained his feet, Rose kicked the bag in frustration.

Morgan had hit the brakes as well between second and third and was as startled and frustrated as Rose. From the moment he hit the ball, Morgan was thinking triple. He had seen Alou shifted toward center, saw the acre of open space between Alou and the ball, and saw the ball kicking around down the line. Morgan was certain he would end up at third and Rose would score. Morgan knew the Reds didn't want to run themselves out of a big inning, but what bothered him was believing Rose could have scored since the A's were not concerned with Pete's run; they were worried about Morgan's game-tying run.

Williams headed back to the hill. He motioned for Fingers. Rollie was worried. Perhaps worn down at last by the long season, his bullpen session had been less than scintillating. His breaking pitches weren't breaking, and his fastball wasn't taking off.

When he took the mound, Fingers found his pitches "falling into place." He got pinch hitter Joe Hague to pop to Campaneris and was told by Williams to walk Bench intentionally. Fingers didn't agree, but unlike some of his teammates he wasn't about to argue with his manager, even though Bench represented the potential winning run. Williams could hear groans from A's fans behind the Oakland dugout mixing with cheers from Reds' supporters.

Williams knew he was putting the go-ahead run on base, knew he was breaking unwritten rules by walking Bench and pitching to the hot-hitting Perez. But he remembered A's super scout Al Hollingsworth's warning him before the Series not to let Bench beat them with his bat. Even if it meant going against the percentages, Williams was going to stick with what A's scouts told him.

Perez stepped in, and Bench believed if anybody could come through in the clutch, Doggie Perez could.

> **Simpson**: *Fingers.... Another curveball.... Laced out to right field, Alou says he has it. Tagging at third base is Rose.... Alou has it. Rose comes home to score the second run, Morgan goes to third.... The tying run is at third base with two out in a 3–2 ball game.*

Perez got good wood on the ball, but it wasn't enough. His fly to right scored Rose and would have scored Morgan had he been at third as he believed he should have been. Instead Morgan was stranded when Menke lifted a soft fly to Rudi in left.

Hall retired the A's without issue in the ninth. The 1972 World Series would come down to Fingers versus the Big Red Machine one final time.

Rollie retired Geronimo on a pop to Campaneris and got Concepcion to ground to Green. Down to their final out, the Reds received new life when Chaney was hit on the ankle by a slider. Williams, intent on bringing in Blue to face Rose, walked briskly to the mound. Williams considered the switch-hitting Rose a dangerous hitter swinging either way but would rather have him swinging right-handed.

Duncan had other ideas. "Don't take him out," the A's catcher barked at Williams. "He's got great stuff. He's throwing the hell out of the ball."

Fingers pleaded his case as well. "Dick, I can get him."

Williams retreated to the dugout. The A's were clinging to a 3–2 lead, but the Reds had the tying run on first and winning run at bat.

The 1972 season had come down to this: two teams, two dreams. Above the din of a standing-room-only crowd, Simpson called the climactic play of the World Series: *"Even with two outs in the last of the ninth the wheels continue to turn.... This Series isn't over yet. Rose steps in. He is two-for-four today and has made great contact all four times. The other two were driven deep to the center-field wall."*

Fingers stared in for the sign. The Reds captain glared out at the A's relief ace from behind an upraised right shoulder. Rollie kicked his white cleat toward the graying skies and delivered. Rose, uncoiling from his crouch, connected.

Simpson: *Fly ball, deep left field, Rudi goes back, near the warning track.*

EPILOGUE

In the moment one might have heard, as Simon and Garfunkel sang, the sound of silence.

> **Simpson**: *Fly ball, deep left field, Rudi goes back, near the warning track, is there. . . . The World Series is over! Rose is out and the underdog Oakland Athletics win their first championship!*

As Jim Simpson made his excited call on NBC Radio, a standing-room-only crowd in Riverfront Stadium fell into eerie silence. The only sounds one could hear were the clapping and hollering from the small contingent of A's players and their fans. Out in left field Joe Rudi pumped both arms toward the steel-colored skies, and the Mustache Gang cavorted briefly in time-honored tradition on the Riverfront rug before crowding into the visitors' clubhouse.

Photographers snapped their shutters as Epstein, Duncan, Rudi, and Bando—all proudly displaying their long locks, mustaches, and in some cases shaggy beards—gathered in a group with arms around each other's shoulders and whooped and hollered as they drenched themselves in champagne. Their celebration would later appear on a TV commercial hawking hair spray.

The Bikers had beaten the Boy Scouts, and while the rest of the baseball world may have been stunned, the least surprised group was the A's themselves.

"They said this Series was between the long hairs and the short hairs, the liberals against the conservatives," a bearded Duncan told reporters in Oakland's lathery locker room. "I think we proved it's not how a person looks like [on the] outside that counts but what he's got inside. We had it inside, heart and guts."

A writer poured champagne on the thinning white hair of Oakland owner Charles O. Finley. "This is the greatest day in my life!" Finley gushed. "None of you can appreciate what this means to me."

A writer asked A's manager Dick Williams to compare the '72 Mustache Gang to the '67 Red Sox squad he skippered.

"This is a much better club than we had in '67," Williams announced without hesitation. One big reason, he stated, was Oakland's superior depth. Williams went on to compare the Swingin' A's to the "Boys of Summer" Brooklyn Dodgers clubs of which he had been a member. "This club," he opined, "is even better than the Dodgers of the Fifties."

Back in Oakland the forecast called for bright skies with passing showers of confetti. But one member of the A's who wasn't in a celebratory mood was Reggie Jackson. Because of his crutches, Oakland's injured star couldn't get on the field to celebrate with teammates or even shake their hands. Jackson was so disassociated from the triumph that he felt at the time it was the worst day he had ever experienced as an athlete.

When Cincinnati second baseman Joe Morgan appeared in the A's clubhouse to offer congratulations, Williams told him, "Great Series! I'm gonna see if Charlie can get you!"

Reds manager Sparky Anderson visited the A's as well. On his way out of the locker room, he bumped into Epstein.

"I hope we see you guys here next year," Big Mike said smiling.

Anderson returned the smile. "So do I. If we can just get past those doggone Pirates!"

The Reds had come to respect the A's; Anderson called reliever Rollie Fingers "as good as anyone we've got in the National League" and said Cincinnati scouts had told him prior to the Series that of all the American League teams, Oakland came closest to playing National League–style ball.

Johnny Bench, who had dinner with Jackson prior to Game Seven, sought out Reggie after the game, congratulated him, spotted Finley dancing in the aisles, and trudged toward the Reds' dugout. Bench's mood would be brightened when the lesion he had removed from his lung weeks later turned out to be benign.

Cincinnati's locker room was morgue-quiet. Center fielder Bobby Tolan, who had misjudged a fly ball in the first inning and was victimized by an injury in the sixth, murmured apologies to teammates. Morgan thought there was no need for recriminations. The season was over, and in the course of the long campaign things happened.

Yet more than forty years have passed since the final out of the 1972 World Series, and Morgan has said he's still sickened when he thinks of what might have been. He won four pennants and two World Series, but on a personal basis no postseason ever promised more joy and delivered more pain for the Hall of Famer than 1972.

Anderson felt his players' frustration. "Look how many times we had men on second and third and couldn't score," he told reporters. "We're a better hitting team than that. We got the best pitching we've gotten all year and we got beat four times by one run."

The Reds' skipper was bitterly reproachful in the postmortem. He told reporters he second-guessed himself about his decisions late in Game Four.

"I stayed with Clay Carroll against [Don] Mincher," he said. "I guess I should have brought in [Tom] Hall, as I look back and see how Hall pitched all Series."

The Series was over, but in Sparky's mind he was still managing. He knew Carroll was 0-1 with a 1.59 ERA in five appearances in the Series and knew Hall had not been scored upon in eight and a third innings.

"Of course," Anderson added, "if I bring in Hall they come with [Angel] Mangual for Mincher and it's tough to double up Mangual, where if Mincher hits the ball on the ground there's no way you can't double him."

Anderson said once that there was no future in living in the past. Yet when he thought of the 1972 World Series, he said he should have been charged with two critical errors. He called it a psychological error to downgrade the A's prior to the Series, to state that the NLCS had brought together the "two best teams in baseball." It was, he said, "foolish . . . stupid . . . idiotic" to make such a statement, even if he felt that way. He backed up his belief by pointing to Dick Allen:

> You certainly wouldn't rate Allen at the top when he was in our league—there'd be maybe a half-dozen guys you'd rate above him, fellows like Roberto Clemente, Willie Stargell, Billy Williams, Hank Aaron, Tony Perez and others. But he gets over in the American League and all of a sudden he's a superstar, just tearing that league apart. We handled him in this league but in that league he was on a plateau all alone. That's the kind of thing that makes me suspect the overall strength of the other league.

Anderson applied the same argument to Gaylord Perry and Sam McDowell. Perry, he pointed out, went to the American League and won 24 games. McDowell went to the National League and won 10 games. What Sparky didn't mention and what writers at the time failed to report was that Perry had won 23 games just two years prior while pitching for San Francisco and had won 21 in '66. McDowell, a flame thrower who led the AL in strikeouts five times, including 304 in 305 innings in his 20-win season with Cleveland in 1970, was in the process of flaming out. Persistent back and neck pain would precipitate a physical decline that forced Sudden Sam from major league baseball on June 26, 1975.

Sparky said the second error he made in the '72 Series was a tactical one. It involved his decision to not call time in the ninth inning of Game Four and order shortstop Dave Concepcion to adhere to Reds' scout Ray Shore's report on how to defend against Oakland pinch hitter Gonzalo Marquez.

Anderson was set to order Concepcion to stick with the Reds' scouting report but didn't. Aw, hell, he thought in the heat of battle, David should know. Moments later, Marquez bounced a ground ball back toward the middle. Had Concepcion been playing where Shore advised, Anderson believed it would have been an out.

"That got the A's started," Anderson recalled, and Oakland rallied in its final at-bat to win 3–2 and push the Big Red Machine to the brink. Had he ordered Concepcion to shade Marquez toward the middle of the field,

Anderson felt the Reds would have won Game Four and tied the Series at two. Cincinnati would go on to claim Games Five and Six. "We would have won the Series," Anderson reasoned, "four games to two."

Anderson continued with his mental gymnastics concerning the '72 World Series for years. Rose, as direct as the line drives he ripped to the outfield, remained firmly on the rails when it came to recalling the loss. For one week, Rose said, Gene Tenace had become Babe Ruth. "He beat our brains out."

Morgan agreed. Tenace won the Series for them—he and their pitching staff, he said. None of the other seven guys in their lineup hurt the Reds with their bats. Morgan said no one could take credit away from Tenace. But he was disappointed Cincinnati's pitchers let him do all that damage. One guy, he said, shouldn't hurt you as much as he did.

Tenace reached Reds pitchers for 4 homers and 9 RBIs; none of his teammates had more than 1 RBI, and Rudi was the only other Oakland player to homer. The A's scored 16 runs and didn't score more than 3 in any of their four victories. Through 2013 Oakland's .209 team batting average ranked as the tenth all-time lowest for a World Series champion. The combined .209 batting average of the A's and Reds broke the seven-game Series low of .213 set by the Yankees and Giants ten years earlier.

True to form, the A's teased their Series hero in the aftermath. He had surrendered 11 steals in 15 attempts over the first six games. When it was announced that Tenace was the Series MVP and had won a car that went with the award, someone in the Oakland locker room shouted, "Hey, Gino, don't let anybody steal the car, too!"

Some observers felt as if underdog Oakland had stolen the Series from Cincinnati. *Baseball Digest* called the A's triumph the most unexpected surprise of the season. "The A's, man-for-man, were a much inferior team to the Reds—or for that matter, to the Pittsburgh Pirates," George Vass wrote. "What made the A's victory even more surprising was their loss before the World Series of their best player, Reggie Jackson. . . . Yet without Jackson the A's beat the Reds. . . . They did it with superb pitching and exceptional hitting by one man who shouldn't have hit, Gene Tenace."

Vass and others considered Tenace's slugging outburst a fluke. But given a chance to start and play regularly, Tenace proved he could hit, hammering 24 homers the following season, 26 in '74, a career-high 29 in '75, and 22 in '76. The truth is that Tenace was more of an unknown than a fluke in '72.

As subsequent seasons would show, the same could be said for the A's, whose victory over the Reds really wasn't much of an upset given the benefit of hindsight. Oakland went on to win world championships in 1973 and '74—the first post-1960s "three-peat"—and the A's stand with the Yankees of 1936–39, 1949–53, and 1998–2000 as the only teams to win three straight World Series. In the '73 and '74 Fall Classics the A's conquered the Reds' conquerors those seasons, the Mets and Dodgers respectively.

Many believe that if the A's had not been broken up by Hunter's free agency in '74 and subsequent trades, Oakland might have won four or five straight World Series. By the time the Mustache Gang wiped out the Dodgers in five games in '74, the average age of the A's starters was just twenty-eight, the average age of their superb pitching staff just twenty-seven. The A's, as Curt Gowdy noted during NBC's Game One coverage in '74, were just approaching their prime years.

Beyond their stars Oakland had quality depth. Outfielder Claudell Washington was a nineteen-year-old star in the making; he earned All-Star status the following season. Young infielders Phil Garner and Manny Trillo would become key starters for World Series–winning teams in Pittsburgh and Philadelphia respectively.

Jackson, Hunter, and Fingers were future Hall of Famers. Hunter helped key the Yankees' return to glory in the mid-seventies; he won 23 games in '75 and was the staff ace in '76, when New York ended a twelve-year postseason drought and returned to the World Series. The Yanks were overmatched by the Big Red Machine, who swept them in four straight to repeat as world champions, and the only game New York came close to winning was Hunter's complete-game outing in Game Two.

Jackson arrived in the Bronx the following season and put the exclamation point on a turbulent season with his legendary three-homer night in Game Six against the Dodgers. New York beat Los Angeles again in '78, the

Catfish pitching the clinching Game Six, a victory punctuated by Reggie's rocketing a drive to the bullpen in Dodger Stadium to seal the deal.

Fingers took his Snidely Whiplash mustache and sharp slider to Milwaukee and won the Cy Young award in 1981. In '86 Fingers was approached by Rose, then the manager of the Reds, and offered a contract to play for Cincinnati. The club still had its clean-shaven policy, so Fingers, displaying some of the old A's irreverence, told Reds general manager Bill Bergesch, "You tell [owner] Marge Schott to shave her Saint Bernard and I'll shave my mustache."

Adversaries in the 1972 postseason became allies in future years. Detroit manager Billy Martin joined Hunter and Ken Holtzman on the '76 Yankees, and Battling Billy finally got his chance to take on the Big Red Machine in that year's Fall Classic after missing out in '72. In '77 Jackson joined the Yanks, along with former Cincinnati ace Don Gullett. In a sign of things coming full circle, Bert Campaneris came out of retirement in 1983 to play for the Yankees. His manager was Martin.

Some adversaries stayed as such. Williams won another World Series with Oakland in '73 and fed up with Finley, bolted Oakland before the champagne stains were even dry. He eventually landed in San Diego and in 1984 rematched with Anderson, then managing Detroit, in the Fall Classic. Sparky and the Tigers won in five games.

The end of the A's dynasty in '75 coincided with the Big Red Machine's rise. Cincinnati succeeded Oakland as World Series champions, edging Boston's heroes of '72—Luis Tiant, Carl Yastrzemski, Carlton Fisk—in a classic seven-game Series in '75 and sweeping the Yanks in '76.

Just as the Mustache Gang was brought down by free agency and trades, so too was the Big Red Machine. Gullett's departure for the Yankees via free agency crippled Cincinnati's mound corps, and the trading of Perez to Montreal to make room for Dan Driessan proved disastrous, particularly from the standpoint of team chemistry and locker room leadership.

By '79 Rose was gone as well, signing a free agent deal with Philadelphia, and Anderson was fired following a second-straight second-place finish in '78. The '79 season saw the remnants of the '72 Big Red Machine—Bench,

Morgan, Concepcion, Foster, Geronimo, Borbon—put together one final bravura performance.

The Reds ended the Dodgers' two-year reign as Western Division champions but were swept by their playoff adversaries from '72—Willie Stargell and the Pittsburgh Pirates—in three games in the NLCS. It was the fourth and final postseason meeting of the decade between the Reds and Pirates. Like Ahab and the white whale, the two ancient adversaries spent the seventies locked in a continuous and contentious struggle.

The A's, Reds, Pirates, and Yankees dominated the decade, each franchise winning at least two world championships. As a foursome they combined to win nine of the 10 World Series in the '70s, 20 division titles, and 12 pennants. The '75–76 Reds are on everybody's short list of baseball's greatest teams, and the Big Red Machine deserves its lofty status. Cincinnati's blend of speed, power, and defense; its combination of four Hall of Fame–caliber talents—Rose (the all-time hits leader), Bench (recognized by many as the greatest catcher ever), Morgan (arguably baseball's best little big man and one of the top second basemen in history), and the productive and consistent Perez—along with a Hall of Fame manager in Anderson makes the '75–76 Reds one of history's premier teams.

How good were the Reds? *Sports Illustrated* posed that question in its October '76 cover story after Cincinnati became the first National League team since the 1921–22 New York Giants to win back-to-back World Series. Managed by John "Mugsy" McGraw, the Giants played in four straight World Series and beat the Babe Ruth–led Yankees in '21 and '22, the latter a four-game sweep. The 1921–24 Giants rank with the 1931–34 St. Louis Cardinals, 1942–44 Cardinals, 1963–66 Dodgers, 1964–68 Cardinals, 1975–76 Reds, and 2010–14 Giants as the only NL teams since 1920 to win multiple World Series. There have been other senior circuit squads who have enjoyed sustained periods of excellence, notably the 1949–56 "Boys of Summer" Brooklyn Dodgers, 1991–99 Atlanta Braves, and 2008–11 Philadelphia Phillies, each of whom won one World Series and at least two NL pennants.

Of these only the Boys of Summer fielded an everyday lineup comparable to Cincinnati's "Great Eight." Both featured four Hall of Famers, and the position-by-position analysis of the '76 Reds and '55 Dodgers shows the strong similarities:

Catcher—Johnny Bench and Roy Campanella;
First base—Tony Perez and Gil Hodges;
Second base—Joe Morgan and Junior Gilliam;
Shortstop—Dave Concepcion and Pee Wee Reese;
Third base—Pete Rose and Jackie Robinson;
Left field—George Foster and Sandy Amoros;
Center field—Cesar Geronimo and Duke Snider;
Right field—Ken Griffey and Carl Furillo

Baseball historians question the validity of comparing teams and players across eras. Joe DiMaggio believed the game changes every fifteen years, and a timeline shows that to be mostly accurate: late '40s—integration; early '60s—westward expansion and the expanding strike zone; early-to-mid '70s—Astroturf, the designated hitter, and free agency; late '80s—drugs and expanded LCS; mid-90s—additional playoff rounds, interleague play, and steroids.

Some, like filmmaker Ken Burns, believe you can compare eras in baseball. Others, like longtime baseball writer Peter Gammons, disagree. The differences across decades are many, as noted above—integration, expansion, equipment, training, night games, strike zones, stadiums, playing surfaces, schedules, regular season and postseason, etc.—but fans love to compare. It's why they debate Lombardi's Packers versus Pittsburgh's Steel Curtain; Michael Jordan's Bulls against King James and the Heat; Gretzky, Messier, and the Oilers versus the Broad Street Bullies; Ali against Tyson; Tiger versus Hogan.

Don Zimmer, a member of Brooklyn's Boys of Summer, managed against the Reds in 1972 and was a bench coach for the Derek Jeter–Mariano Rivera–Andy Pettitte–Jorge Posada Yankee dynasty that won five World Series and seven pennants from 1996 to 2009. Zimmer said he ranked the Big Red Machine with the '50s Dodgers and '90s Yankees as the best he'd seen. Zimmer's benchmate on the dynastic Yankees, skipper Joe Torre, played against the Big Red Machine. He thought the 1998 Yankees' lineup comparable to the '76 Reds and New York's pitching to be superior.

Often left out of the debate is the 1936 Negro National League champion Pittsburgh Crawfords, who listed five future Hall of Famers among their great eight: catcher Josh Gibson, first baseman Oscar Charleston, third baseman Judy Johnson, infielder Jud "Boojum" Wilson, and center fielder James "Cool Papa" Bell.

Gibson is considered the greatest hitting catcher in history, better than Bench, Yogi Berra, and Mike Piazza, though not the equal of Bench, Ivan Rodriguez, or Yadier Molina defensively. The multi-talented Charleston is recognized by many baseball historians to be the best player in Negro League history; Johnson is said to have been a third baseman superior defensively to Brooks Robinson, Mike Schmidt, or Pie Traynor.

Gibson called the fiery Wilson the best hitter in the Negro Leagues, and Satchel Paige opined that Bell was faster than Jesse Owens. Owens himself thought Bell "just about the fastest ballplayer I've ever seen." Bell had incredible speed and was an excellent leadoff hitter and a superb outfielder. For all-time comparisons, think Ty Cobb, Lou Brock, and Rickey Henderson. Flanking Bell were Jimmie Crutchfield and Sam Bankhead, giving the Craws what is recognized as the swiftest outfield in history.

Add Hall of Fame pitchers Paige, Bill Foster, and an aging Smoky Joe Williams, along with lefty ace Leroy Matlock and fellow southpaw Sam Streeter, and the 1932–36 Crawfords rank with the greatest clubs ever.

Beyond the National League, the Reds' Great Eight has been favorably compared with the 1927 Yankees, '30 Philadelphia Athletics, '36 Yankees, '61 Yankees, and '70 Orioles. Each of those powerhouses featured at least two Hall of Famers in their great eight—the '27 and '36 Yankees had the most with four (Babe Ruth, Lou Gehrig, Tony Lazzeri, and Earle Combs in '27; Gehrig, Lazzeri, Joe DiMaggio, and Bill Dickey in '36); the Athletics had three (Jimmie Foxx, Al Simmons, and Mickey Cochrane); and the '61 Yankees and '70 Orioles had two each (Mickey Mantle and Yogi Berra for the former, and Brooks Robinson and Frank Robinson for the latter).

The startling fact about the Cincinnati Great Eight is that it played only eighty-eight games together over the '75–76 seasons. However, as Reds writer John Erardi and team historian Greg Rhodes note, the Great Eight's combined career total of 19,230 games is some 5,000 more than any other great eight lineup. In their eighty-eight games the Great Eight went 69-19, a .784 winning percentage. In '76 seven of the Great Eight made the NL All-Star team. The eighth member—Geronimo—batted .307 and won his third straight Gold Glove.

The Great Eight played its final game together on an arctic night in Yankee Stadium. It was fitting in hindsight since in the more than three decades since only one team—the 1996–2001 Yankees—has drawn serious comparison to the Big Red Machine. The dynasty debate between Anderson's Reds and Torre's Yankees escalated following the Yankees' historic 125-win season in 1998.

While the Reds had the Great Eight, the A's flashed the Big Four in their pitchers: Hunter, Fingers, Blue, and Holtzman. Just as the Big Red Machine showed that for them the swing was the thing, as far as the Mustache Gang was concerned, it was more a matter of "You ain't got a thing if you ain't got that fling."

Hunter was widely considered the best big game pitcher of his era. The Catfish fronted a starting staff that, while together for only three seasons, won its division, the LCS, and the World Series each of those years. That's a level of clutch pitching unmatched in the modern era. The 1998–2000 Yankees three-peat staff came close, but the only two mainstays were Andy Pettitte and Orlando "El Duque" Hernandez. By 2000 David Cone had effectively been replaced by Roger Clemens, who had come to the Bronx the year before in the David Wells deal.

Hunter, Fingers, and Vida Blue each won a Cy Young in their respective careers, the Cat pitched a perfect game, and Holtzman had two no-hitters. Blue and Fingers combined with Glenn Abbott and Paul Lindblad on a no-hitter. There had been ace relievers before Fingers—the much-traveled Hoyt Wilhelm, Luis Arroyo with the '61 Yankees, Barney Schultz with the '64 Cardinals, Ron Perranoski with the '65 Dodgers—but it was Fingers, along with contemporaries Dave Giusti, Sparky Lyle, Tug McGraw, Mike

Marshall, and Goose Gossage, who popularized the modern role of the ace reliever. They set the stage for decades of dominant closers: Bruce Sutter, Dennis Eckersley, and Mariano Rivera preeminent among them.

The role of the relief ace has become more refined over the decades. Fingers was brought in to "close" as early as the fifth inning, Gossage and McGraw in the seventh. Both scenarios would have been unimaginable to Rivera, Brad Lidge, or Sergio Romo.

Hunter, Holtzman, and Blue each won 20 games in 1973 and through 2014 remain the last major league trio to accomplish that feat. Since 1900 only 14 AL staffs and 8 NL rotations have boasted three 20-game winners in the same season.

In an era when 20-win seasons have diminished, the '73 A's pitching staff's place in history won't be threatened any time soon. Hunter and Blue gained added fame as the subjects of songs. Bob Dylan rhapsodized about the Catfish in 1975, Hunter's first year with the Yankees. The bluesy classic was later covered by Joe Cocker. Blue's tribute song was some tight funk done by Detroit soul singer Albert Jones.

Catfish and Vida comprised one-half of an A's Fearsome Foursome that, like the Reds' Great Eight, can be compared to baseball's all-time best. The team that comes closest to matching the Mustache Gang in recent years is another world champion from the Bay Area, the 2010 and '12 San Francisco Giants. The 2010 Giants featured a Big Four of starters Tim Lincecum, Matt Cain, Jonathan Sanchez, and closer Brian Wilson; the 2012 group was even deeper, with Lincecum, Cain, Madison Bumgarner, Barry Zito, Ryan Vogelsong, and relief ace Sergio Romo. The 2012 Giants paralleled the '72 A's in that both featured a former ace (Lincecum, Blue) in the role of a bullpen stopper.

Along with that of the Giants, the A's armada of arms compares favorably with the great Series-winning staffs of the past half-century: the 1998 Yankees (Wells, Cone, Pettitte, and Rivera); the '95 Braves (Greg Maddux, Tom Glavine, John Smoltz, and Mark Wohlers); the '89 A's (Dave Stewart, Storm Davis, Mike Moore, Bob Welch, and Eckersley); the '70 Orioles (Jim

Palmer, Dave McNally, Mike Cuellar, and Pete Richert); the '65 Dodgers (Sandy Koufax, Don Drysdale, Claude Osteen, and Ron Perranoski); and the '61 Yankees (Whitey Ford, Ralph Terry, Bill Stafford, and Luis Arroyo).

It is not just Oakland's pitching that leads many observers to rank the 1972–74 squads as among the best ever. The A's were a well-rounded outfit. Jackson, who went on to become "Mr. October," is one of the game's all-time great sluggers and clutch hitters. Campaneris was the AL's premier base stealer of his era; Rudi, baseball's best left fielder in the early '70s. Williams is a Hall of Fame skipper and was one of the game's top strategists; Dick Green, one of the best defensive second basemen of his generation; and Captain Sal, one of the most respected leaders in sports during the decade of the '70s.

The '72 A's brought the first major sports championship to the Bay Area, but fans' hopes that they would host two title teams as Baltimore had done in 1970 with the Orioles and Colts were sadly disappointed on Saturday, December 23, 1972. Franco Harris's "Immaculate Reception" in the final seconds at Three Rivers Stadium paced the Pittsburgh Steelers past the stunned Oakland Raiders. The Pirates and A's had just missed colliding in the postseason two months prior, but that December 23 marked the start of a Pittsburgh-Oakland NFL rivalry that would run from 1972 to 1976 and rank as one of the most fiercely fought in history.

Bay Area fans barely had time to recover from the Raiders' last-second loss when the San Francisco 49ers were stunned by the Dallas Cowboys in similarly shocking fashion that same day. West Coast fans referred to the season-ending defeats as "Black Saturday."

While the A's and Reds made their respective marks in the 1970s, so did other teams and players. In 2012 the 1972 Chicago White Sox were honored with induction to the Chicago Baseball Museum as "the team that saved the Sox."

"The 1972 team stands out in franchise history," Sox senior vice president of marketing Brooks Boyer said. "Personalities and stars like Dick Allen, Goose Gossage, Bill Melton and many others changed this franchise and deserve to be recognized."

Allen played two more seasons with the White Sox before being traded back to Philadelphia. He ended his career in '77 with the A's, the club that had edged Allen and the White Sox in the wild West race in '72.

Nolan Ryan dominated the American League the remainder of the decade. His Ryan Express fastball, fired from a compact and powerful delivery, led the AL in strikeouts in seven of the eight seasons from '72 to '79 and blazed a path for him to Cooperstown.

The trade for Willie Mays didn't produce a postseason trip for the Mets in '72, but they would upset the Reds in the '73 NLCS and force the A's to rally to win the World Series in seven games.

Pittsburgh's run of division titles ended at three straight following the '72 season, but the Bucs returned to the top of the East in '74 and repeated in '75.

The building toward the future that began for the Dodgers and Phillies in '72 continued in earnest. Los Angeles reached the World Series in '74; Philadelphia won the East in '76. In '77–78 the Dodgers and Phils collided in the playoffs, the former taking both best-of-five series in four games. Two years later the Phillies, anchored by their Sesame Street Gang from '72—Schmidt, Greg Luzinski, Larry Bowa, Bob Boone, and Steve Carlton—captured their first world championship.

Los Angeles followed suit in '81. The infield of former Baby Dodger Blues Steve Garvey, Dave Lopez, Bill Russell, and Ron Cey made its final appearance together that October and went out in style by celebrating an elusive World Series title.

Those who made the '72 season one of the more memorable in history have gone their separate ways. Some, like Hunter, Williams, Anderson, and McGraw were taken too early. Hunter's passing was particularly moving. Following an injury-ridden 9-9 season in 1977, he was diagnosed with diabetes in the spring of '78. He retired following the '79 season and spent his retirement years as a gentleman farmer.

In 1999 Hunter was diagnosed with amyotrophic lateral sclerosis (ALS), a progressive and ultimately fatal disease that had claimed another famous but humble Yankee, Lou Gehrig. The disease left Hunter, a superb all-around athlete and pitcher, unable to grip a baseball or move his arms. There were days, he said at the time, when he and his wife Helen would just sit together and cry. On August 8, 1999, he fell, and robbed of the ability to extend his arms to brace himself, hit his head on concrete steps at his home. He was unconscious for several days in the hospital and died one month later on September 9.

Hunter's combative adversary from '72, Pete Rose, was banned from the sport for life by then commissioner Bart Giamatti on August 24, 1989, for gambling on baseball. At the time, baseball's all-time hits king held nineteen major league records. In 2004 Rose publicly admitted to betting on games as the Reds' manager.

While Rose had problems with gambling, Vida Blue battled drug addiction. Years later he acknowledged that drug use had contributed to his sub-par 1972 season. The problem prevented him from becoming one of baseball's all-time great pitchers—as it did Mets superstar Dwight Gooden, "Dr. K," who arrived in the majors a decade after Vida.

Whatever their life paths, the personalities of '72 left their imprint. Blue, speaking of the Mustache Gang but in a very real sense speaking of his contemporaries, was proud of the imprint they left on the game and on their times. They were fun, they were different, and they were good, he said.

Perhaps never more so than in the tumultuous summer of '72.

BIBLIOGRAPHY

Addie, Bob. "Relief Pitching in Series: A Clue to Baseball's Future?" *Baseball Digest*, January 1973.

Albers, Bucky. "Everything You Wanted to Know about Johnny Bench." *Popular Sports Baseball*, 1973.

Allen, Maury. "A's versus Tigers: Baseball's Hottest Feud Will Get Hotter." *Baseball Sports Stars of 1973*.

———. "For Pete Rose: A World Series to Forget." *Sport Magazine*, October 1973.

———. "Ralph Houk Faces His Biggest Challenge." *Sport World*. New York: Hammond Media Corporation, 1973.

Alfano, Pete. "Wilbur Wood: No Knock on Wood." *Baseball Extra*, 1973.

Anderson, Sparky, and Si Burick. *The Main Spark: Sparky Anderson and the Cincinnati Reds*. New York: Doubleday, 1978.

Andre, Lee. "Can Pete Rose Make the Reds Forget?: *Sport World*. New York: Hammond Media Corporation, 1973.

Bench, Johnny, and William Brashler. *Catch You Later: The Autobiography of Johnny Bench*. New York: Harper and Row, 1979.

Bergman, Ron. "A's Big 3 Like a Brotherhood Week Poster." *The Sporting News*, October 20, 1973.

———. "Blue Moon Rises, Pulls A's Up Too." *The Sporting News*, June 14, 1969.

———. *Mustache Gang: The Swaggering Saga of Oakland's A's*. New York: Dell, 1973.

———. "New Swat Style Working Wonders for Rudi." *The Sporting News*, July 22, 1972.

———. "Quiet Campy Stealing Thunder . . . and Bases." *The Sporting News*, April 25, 1970.

———. "Rollie's Follies Real Oakland Thigh-Slapper." *The Sporting News*, March 3, 1973.

———. "Will Dissension Wreck the Oakland A's?" *Popular Sports Baseball*, 1973.

Bilovsky, Frank. "Steve Carlton's Power of Positive Pitching." *Popular Sports Baseball*, 1973.

Blass, Steve, with Erik Sherman. *Steve Blass: A Pirate for Life*. Chicago: Triumph Books, 2012.

Bobrow, Norm. "Cesar Cedeno: Super Baby." In *Baseball Stars of 1974*. New York: Pyramid Books, 1974.

———. "Harmon Killebrew: Once Every 12 ½ Times." In *Baseball Stars of 1971*. New York: Pyramid Books, 1972.

Bortstein, Larry. "Catfish Hunter: The Automatic." In *Baseball Stars of 1974*. New York: Pyramid Books, 1974.

———. "Cesar Cedeno: Hungry Hitter." In *Baseball Stars of 1973*. New York: Pyramid Books, 1973.

———. "Johnny Bench: Facing Up to Pressure." In *Baseball Stars of 1974*. New York: Pyramid Books, 1974.

———. "Nate Colbert: The "Wild" Day." In *Baseball Stars of 1973*. New York: Pyramid Books, 1973.

———. "Roberto Clemente: The Best of All." In *Baseball Stars of 1972*. New York: Pyramid Books, 1972.

———. "Tony Oliva: The Swinger." *Baseball Stars of 1972*. New York: Pyramid Books, 1972.

———. "Willie McCovey: Big Mc Still Giant Terror." *Baseball Extra*, 1973.

Burick, Si. "Williams Gambled and Got Away with It." *Baseball Digest*, January 1973.

Chass, Murray. "Dick Allen: What It Takes to Keep Him Happy—And Why He's Worth It." *Dell Baseball*, 1973.

Claassen, Harold W. "Billy Williams in Depth." *Sports Quarterly Presents Baseball*, 1973.

———. "Colbert Socks It to 'Em." *Baseball Extra*, 1973.

Clark, Tom. *Champagne and Baloney*. New York: Harper and Row, 1975.

Coleman, Bill. "Tony Oliva: An Overlooked Star." *Baseball Digest*, June 1971.

Condon, Dave. "Charlie O.: Amazing Sports Maverick." *The Sporting News*, January 6, 1973.

Dark, Alvin, and John Underwood. *When in Doubt, Fire the Manager: My Life and Times in Baseball*. New York: E. P. Dutton, 1980.

Deindorfer, Robert G. "Sparky Lyle: Late-Inning Magic." In *Baseball Stars of 1973*. New York: Pyramid Books, 1973.

Devaney, John. "Boog Powell: The Triggerman and the Sea." *Sport Magazine*, June 1971.

Dickey, Glenn. "Ken Holtzman Has a Problem: He Likes Living in Oakland." *Sport Magazine*, October 1973.

Donnelly, Joe. "A Reporter's Notebook on Bobby Murcer." *Popular Sports Baseball*, 1973.

Durocher, Leo, with Ed Linn. *Nice Guys Finish Last*. New York: Simon and Schuster, 1975.

Durslag, Mel. "Artificial Turf Is Changing the Game." *Baseball Digest*, June 1971.

Elderkin, Phil. "Reggie Jackson: He Dared the A's to Win." *Baseball Digest*, January 1973.

Ellison, James Whitfield. "Willie Mays: Still Doing His Thing." In *Baseball Stars of 1971*. New York: Pyramid Books, 1972.

Feeney, Charley. "Likable Manny Draws Buc Needles." *The Sporting News*, July 15, 1972.

——— . "Pirates and Reds Engage in Swap of Opportunities." *The Sporting News*, October 21, 1972.

——— . "Pitching or Talking, Dock Rings Bell." *The Sporting News*, August 21, 1971.

——— . "Supremely Confident—Buc Belter Al Oliver." *The Sporting News*, September 30, 1972.

Fitzgerald, Ray. "Carlton Fisk's Plan to Beat the Sophomore Jinx." *Dell Super Sports*, July 1973.

Ford, Whitey, with Phil Pepe. *Slick: My Life in and around Baseball*. New York: Dell, 1987.

Frizzell, Pat. "Giants Flatten Foes with Mule's Kick." *The Sporting News*, June 26, 1971.

Furlong, William Barry. "Billy Williams: Swinger in the Windy City." In *Baseball Stars of 1973*. New York: Pyramid Books, 1973.

——— . "Dick Allen: Chisox Colossus." In *Baseball Stars of 1973*. New York: Pyramid Books, 1973.

——— . "Dick Allen: Money Guy in Chi." In *Baseball Stars of 1974*. New York: Pyramid Books, 1974.

——— . "Ferguson Jenkins, Anonymous Ace." In *Baseball Stars of 1972*. New York: Pyramid Books, 1972.

——— . "Johnny Bench: Cincy's Cinch Hall of Famer." In *Baseball Stars of 1971*. New York: Pyramid Books, 1972.

——— . "Wilbur Wood: All in the Knuckles." In *Baseball Stars of 1973*. New York: Pyramid Books, 1973.

——— . "Wilbur Wood: Iron Knuckles." In *Baseball Stars of 1972*. New York: Pyramid Books, 1972.

Gergen, Joe. "Here Come the Fat Pitchers." *Popular Sports Baseball*, 1973.

Gershman, Michael. *Diamonds: The Evolution of the Ballpark*. New York: Houghton Mifflin, 1993.

Gibson, Bob, and Reggie Jackson, with Lonnie Wheeler. *Sixty Feet, Six Inches*. New York: Doubleday, 2009.

Gluck, Herb. "It Doesn't Pay to Get Steve Carlton Angry!" *Baseball Sports Stars of 1973*.

Goldaper, Sam. "Closeup: Steve Carlton." *Sports Quarterly Presents Baseball*, 1973.

Golenbock, Peter. *Dynasty: The New York Yankees 1949–64*. New York: Berkley Books, 1975.

Green, G. Michael, and Roger D. Launius. *Charlie Finley: The Outrageous Story of Baseball's Super Showman*. New York: Walker, 2010.

Gutman, Bill. "Bobby Murcer's Magic Ingredient." *Team Magazine*, July 1973.

Hano, Arnold. "Billy Williams: "Invisible" Iron Man." In *Baseball Stars of 1971*. New York: Pyramid Books, 1972.

———. "Bobby Bonds: Out of the Shadow." In *Baseball Stars of 1974*. New York: Pyramid Books, 1974.

———. "Lee May: The Man behind the Astros' Surge." *Sport Magazine*, August 1972.

———. "Mike Epstein: Vulnerable Guy." In *Baseball Stars of 1973*. New York: Pyramid Books, 1973.

———. "Nolan Ryan: Stri-k-k-k-e in the Night." In *Baseball Stars of 1974*. New York: Pyramid Books, 1974.

———. "Nolan Ryan: The Untouchable." In *Baseball Stars of 1973*. New York: Pyramid Books, 1973.

———. "Willie Stargell: Some Man!" In *Baseball Stars of 1972*. New York: Pyramid Books, 1972.

Harmon, Pat. "Johnny Bench: Baseball's Winner." *Baseball Illustrated*, 1973.

Harrelson, Bud. "The Real Tom Seaver." *Sport Magazine*, August 1972.

Hawkins, Jim. "Coleman Cools Temper and Heats Up Pitches." *The Sporting News*, June 16, 1973.

———. "Rudi's Catch Rates with the Greatest." *Baseball Digest*, January 1973.

Helyar, John. *Lords of the Realm: The Real History of Baseball*. New York: Villard Books, 1994.

Hillyer, John. "Everybody Loves Dick Allen Now." *Baseball Illustrated*, 1973.

Hines, Maury. "Analyzing the New Breed of Hitters." *Sport World*. New York: Hammond Media Corporation, 1973.

Hirshberg, Al. "Carl Yastrzemski: Missing by a Whisker." In *Baseball Stars of 1975*. New York: Pyramid Books, 1975.

———. "Carlton (Pudge) Fisk: Take-Charge Backstop." In *Baseball Stars of 1973*. New York: Pyramid Books, 1973.

———. "Dick Williams' Second World Series: This Time the Heroes Wore Mustaches." *Sport Magazine*, October 1973.

———. "Henry Aaron: On the Babe's Trail." In *Baseball Stars of 1972*. New York: Pyramid Books, 1972.

———. "Luis Tiant: Fu Manchu's Comeback." In *Baseball Stars of 1973*. New York: Pyramid Books, 1973.

———. "The Smallest Cog Powers the Big Red Machine." *Sport Magazine*, August 1973.

———. "Wilbur Wood and the Art of the Knuckleball." *Sport Magazine*, August 1972.

Hirshey, Dave. "Close-up: Steve Blass." *Baseball Extra*, 1973.

Holtzman, Jerome. "Cub Belter Williams Earns Player of the Year Crown." *The Sporting News*, October 21, 1972.

———. "Cubs Deny A's Got Edge in Holtzman-Monday Deal." *The Sporting News*, October 21, 1972.

Hunter, Bob. "No 20-Win Button in Sutton's Goal." *The Sporting News*, May 13, 1972.

Hunter, Jim "Catfish," and Armen Keteyian. *Catfish: My Life in Baseball*. New York: McGraw-Hill, 1988.

Jablow, Paul. "Mike Schmidt: Not-So-Futile-Philly." In *Baseball Stars of 1971*. New York: Pyramid Books, 1972.

Joyce, Dick. "Bench No. 1 Catcher of All-Time?" *Baseball Extra*, 1973.

Koppett, Leonard. *The New Thinking Fan's Guide to Baseball*. New York: Simon and Schuster, 1991.

Kuhn, Bowie. *Hardball: The Education of a Baseball Commissioner*. New York: McGraw-Hill, 1986.

Lang, Jack. "Mets Were Major Mystery—How Did They Ever Win 83?" *The Sporting News*, October 21, 1972.

Langford, George. "Chicago's Swingers: Allen & Williams." *Popular Sports Baseball*, 1973.

Lawson, Earl. "Grimsley Moves Year Ahead in Reds' Standout Schedule." *The Sporting News*, October 28, 1972.

———. "Hard Luck Brings Out Best in Nolan." *The Sporting News*, June 17, 1972.

———. "Sparky Calls Gullett Best Lefty in N.L." *The Sporting News*, April 17, 1976.

———. Tolan Typifies Reds' All-Around Great Season, *The Sporting News*, October 21, 1972.

———. "Wild Pitch Sets Off Reds' N.L. Pennant Party." *The Sporting News*, October 28, 1972.

Leggett, William. "Pinstripes Are Back in Style." *Sports Illustrated*, July 2, 1973.

———. "A Riot Act Changes the Scene." *Sports Illustrated*, May 3, 1971.

Lewis, Allen. "Steve Carlton's Rare Pitching Achievement." *Baseball Digest*, January 1973.

Libby, Bill. *Charlie O. & the Angry A's*. New York: Doubleday, 1975.

———. "Frank Robinson Sounds Off! Why the National League Is Different—Better." *Sport Magazine*, September 1972.

———. "The Great Catcher Controversy. Bench or Sanguillen—Who's the Best?" *Baseball Sports Stars of 1973*.

Lindblom, John. "Reggie Jackson: A Tale of a Soulful Man." *Baseball Illustrated*, 1973.

Linn, Ed. "Billy Martin: A Foreign Body in the Tigers' System." *Sport Magazine*, June 1971.

Litsky, Frank. "All Hail, Cesar." *Sports Quarterly Presents Baseball*, 1973.

———"Ryan Express Becomes a Blur." *Baseball Extra*, 1973.

Luciano, Ron, and David Fisher. *Remembrance of Swings Past*. New York: Bantam Books, 1988.

McClure, Bill. "Pete Rose—Enos Slaughter with Talent." *Countrywide Sports*, August 1970.

McLain, Denny, with Dave Diles. *Nobody's Perfect*. New York: Dial Press, 1975.

Meagher, Michael. "Rating The Pitchers." *Sport World*. New York: Hammond Media Corporation, 1973.

Michelson, Herb. *Charlie O*. Indianapolis: Bobbs-Merrill, 1975.

Miller, Ira. "'Baseball Owners Are Stupid!' Charlie Finley." *Dell Super Sports*, July 1973.

Miller, Marvin. *A Whole Different Ball Game: The Inside Story of the Baseball Revolution*. Chicago: Ivan R. Dee, 2004.

Morey, Charles. "Dick Allen's Coming Drive for Diamond Immortality." *Sport World*. New York: Hammond Media Corporation, 1973.

Morgan, Bruce. *Steve Carlton and the 1972 Phillies*. Jefferson NC: McFarland, 2012.

Morgan, Joe, and David Falkner. *Joe Morgan: A Life in Baseball*. New York: W. W. Norton.

Munves, Jim. "Tom Seaver: Mainly With Heart." In *Baseball Stars of 1974*. New York: Pyramid Books, 1974.

Munzel, Edgar. "Top A.L. Pitcher of Year? 'Wood!' Chisox Claim." *The Sporting News*, October 28, 1972.

Murray, Jim. "How the A's Curbed the Big Red Machine." *Baseball Digest*, January 1973.

Newhan, Ross. "Nolan Ryan: The New Strikeout King." *Popular Sports Baseball*, 1973.

Newhouse, Dave. "In Depth with the Catfish." *Baseball Extra*, 1973.

———. "An Oakland Dynasty?" *Sports Quarterly Presents Baseball*, 1973.

Ogle, Jim. "Late Collapse Accents Yanks' Need for Changes." *The Sporting News*, October 21, 1972.

Oppenheimer, Joel. *The Wrong Season*. New York: Bobbs-Merrill, 1973.

Peck, Ira. "Bob Gibson." In *Baseball Stars of 1971*. New York: Pyramid Books, 1972.

Post, Greg. "Stories You Never Heard about Reggie Jackson." *Team Magazine*, 1973.

Ray, Ralph. "Blue Puts A's Colors on A.L. Pennant." *The Sporting News*, October 28, 1972.

———. "Swinging A's Put Tigers Down for Two Count." *The Sporting News*, October 21, 1972.

Reidenbaugh, Lowell. "Amazin' A's Reign as World Champs." *The Sporting News*, November 4, 1972.

———. "A's Open with Fury in Tenace's Bat." *The Sporting News*, October 28, 1972.

———. "Rudi's Bat and Glove Help Hunter to Shoot Down Reds." *The Sporting News*, October 28, 1972.

Robinson, Ray. "Bobby Murcer: Tradition, Tradition." In *Baseball Stars of 1972*. New York: Pyramid Books, 1972.

———. "Gene Tenace: Assassin's Target," In *Baseball Stars of 1973*. New York: Pyramid Books, 1973.

———. "Johnny Bench: Oak behind the Plate." In *Baseball Stars of 1973*. New York: Pyramid Books, 1973.

———. "Mickey Lolich: Invisible Man." In *Baseball Stars of 1972*. New York: Pyramid Books, 1972.

———. "Reggie Jackson: The Spirit of Oakland." In *Baseball Stars of 1974*. New York: Pyramid Books, 1974.

———. "Roberto Clemente: Mayor or Manager." In *Baseball Stars of 1971*. New York: Pyramid Books, 1972.

———. "Roberto Clemente: 'Nobody Does Anything Better.'" In *Baseball Stars of 1973*. New York: Pyramid Books, 1973.

———. "Steve Carlton: Super Southpaw." In *Baseball Stars of 1973*. New York: Pyramid Books, 1973.

———. "Tom Seaver: Education of a Pitcher." In *Baseball Stars of 1972*. New York: Pyramid Books, 1972.

———. "Vida Blue: 'I Think I'm For Real.'" In *Baseball Stars of 1972*. New York: Pyramid Books, 1972.

———. "Wilbur Wood: Easy Does It." In *Baseball Stars of 1974*. New York: Pyramid Books, 1974.

———. "Willie Mays: Twilight Time." In *Baseball Stars of 1972*. New York: Pyramid Books, 1972.

Rogers, Tony. "Hodges' Secret Plan For Seaver & Koosman." *Countrywide Sports*. August 1970.

Rose, Pete, and Roger Kahn. *Pete Rose: My Story*. New York: Macmillan, 1989.

Rosenthal, Bert. "Rating the Top Relief Pitchers." *Baseball Sports Stars of 1973*.

Russo, Neal. "Card Specialty—Stranding Runners." *The Sporting News*, October 21, 1972.

Schaap, Dick. "Bobby Murcer: Lost on a $100,000 Turf." *Sport Magazine*, August 1973.

Schlossberg, Dan. "Hank Aaron: 41 to Go." In *Baseball Stars of 1973*. New York: Pyramid Books, 1973.

———. "Pete Rose: The Hustlin' Man." In *Baseball Stars of 1973*. New York: Pyramid Books, 1973.

————. "Reggie Jackson: Much More than a Mouth." In *Baseball Stars of 1975*. New York: Pyramid Books, 1975.

————. "Rod Carew: Franchise from Panama." In *Baseball Stars of 1974*. New York: Pyramid Books, 1974.

————. "Willie Stargell: In Roberto's Footsteps." In *Baseball Stars of 1974*. New York: Pyramid Books, 1974.

Silverman, Al. "Pete Rose: Captain Hustle." In *Baseball Stars of 1971*. New York: Pyramid Books, 1972.

————. "Reggie Jackson: He Cares." In *Baseball Stars of 1972*. New York: Pyramid Books, 1972.

Smith, Norman Lewis. "Mayberry Ought to Be a Chauffeur, He Drives So Many Men Home." *Sport Magazine*, October 1973.

Spoelstra, Watson. "'Old Pro' Kaline Climaxes Tigers' Smashing Season." *The Sporting News*, October 21, 1972.

————. "Only One Tie Possible in Torrid A.L. East Race." *The Sporting News*, September 30, 1972.

————. "30-Win Forecasts Annoy Tigers' Ace Lolich." *The Sporting News*, June 10, 1972.

————. "Tigers' Coleman Makes Critics Eat Words." *The Sporting News*, October 28, 1972.

Stellino, Vito, ed. *Sports All-Stars 1973: Baseball*. New York: Maco, 1972.

Taubman, Philip. "Baseball's Super Showman: Oakland's Charlie Finley." *Time Magazine*, August 18, 1975.

Tuite, James. "The Quality of Murcer." *Sports Quarterly Presents Baseball*, 1973.

Twombly, Wells. "Folk Legend in Ho-Hum Era—That's Speier." *The Sporting News*, April 28, 1973.

————. "Nobody Can Turn 'Em On like Mays." *The Sporting News*, July 17, 1971.

Weber, Bruce. *All-Pro Baseball Stars*. New York: Scholastic, 1977.

Wilson, John. "Cesar Cedeno Is Turning the Clock Back for Leo Durocher." *Dell Sports Scene*, July 1973.

————. "Rollie Fingers: The Man Who Shut the Door." *Baseball Digest*, January 1973.

Williams, Dick, with Bill Plaschke. *No More Mr. Nice Guy*. Orlando FL: Harcourt Brace Jovanovich, 1990.

Zimmer, Don, with Bill Madden. *A Baseball Life*. Chicago: Contemporary Books, 2001.